Shojo Beat

kimi ni todoke
From Me to You

Vol. 3

Story & Art by
Karuho Shiina

Volume 3

Contents

Episode 8: Saturday Night ------------------------ 3

Episode 9: Practicing on My Own ------------- 47

Episode 10: A New Friend ------------------------ 91

Episode 11: Support ---------------------------- 137

Story Thus Far

Sawako Kuronuma has always been a loner. Though not by choice, this optimistic 15-year-old can't seem to make any friends. Stuck with the unfortunate nickname "Sadako" after the haunting movie character, rumors about her summoning spirits have been greatly exaggerated. With her shy personality and scary looks, most of her classmates barely talk to her, much less look into her eyes for more than three seconds lest they be cursed. Except for Shota Kazehaya. Kazehaya's the most popular boy in class, and his friendly attitude toward Sawako bewilders their classmates. But this unlikely friendship has changed Sawako's life. Drawn out of her shell by Kazehaya, Sawako is slowly becoming more outgoing. But her budding friendship with Yoshida and Yano goes down the tubes when nasty rumors spread that Yoshida was in juvi and Yano is a slut. Sawako starts avoiding them, thinking it's all her fault. But when she confronts some gossiping girls, they accuse *her* of being behind the rumors! Finally expressing her own feelings and clearing up the misunderstanding, Sawako has made some friends for the first time in her life.

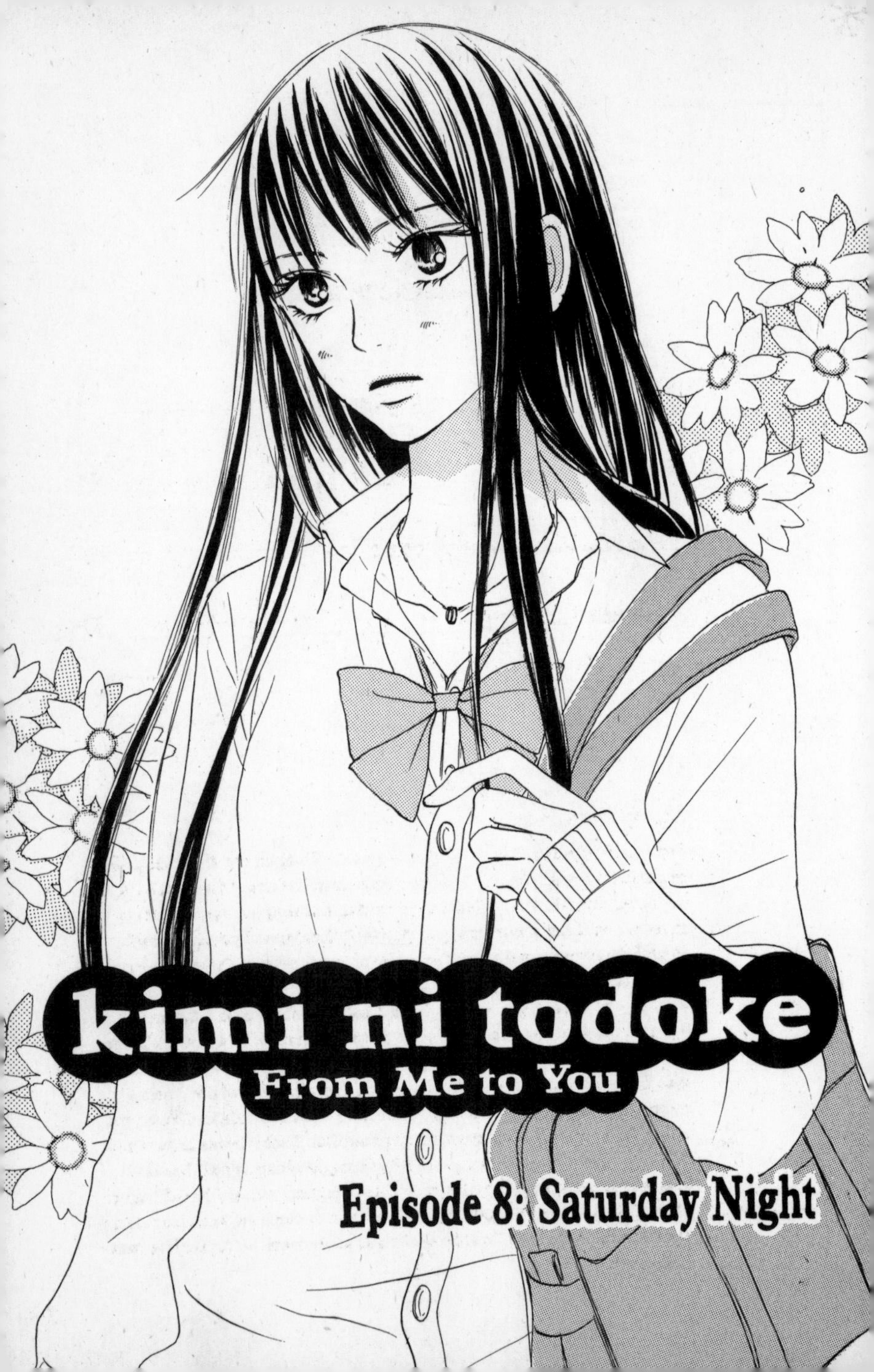
kimi ni todoke
From Me to You
Episode 8: Saturday Night

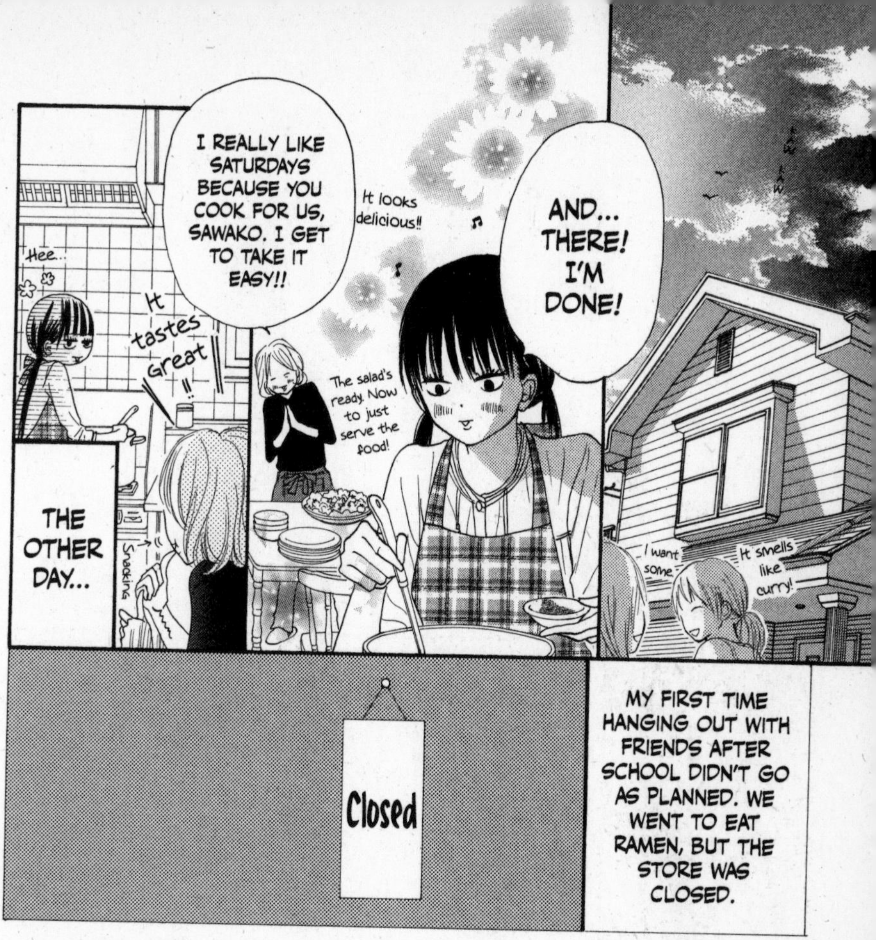
KAW KAW
It smells like curry!
I want some
AND... THERE! I'M DONE!
It looks delicious!!
The salad's ready. Now to just serve the food!
I REALLY LIKE SATURDAYS BECAUSE YOU COOK FOR US, SAWAKO. I GET TO TAKE IT EASY!!
Hee...
It tastes Great!!
Snacking
THE OTHER DAY...
MY FIRST TIME HANGING OUT WITH FRIENDS AFTER SCHOOL DIDN'T GO AS PLANNED. WE WENT TO EAT RAMEN, BUT THE STORE WAS CLOSED.
Closed

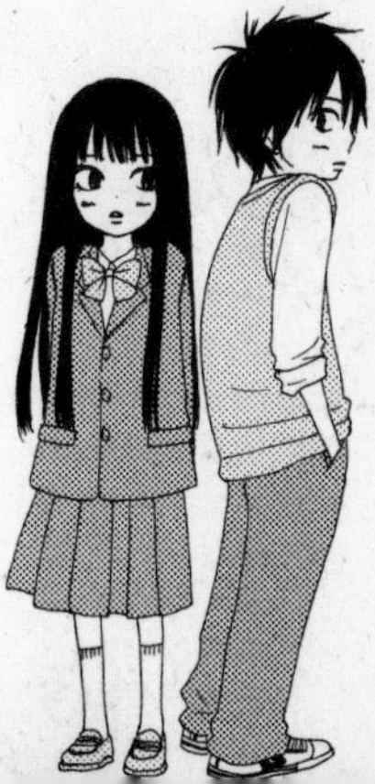

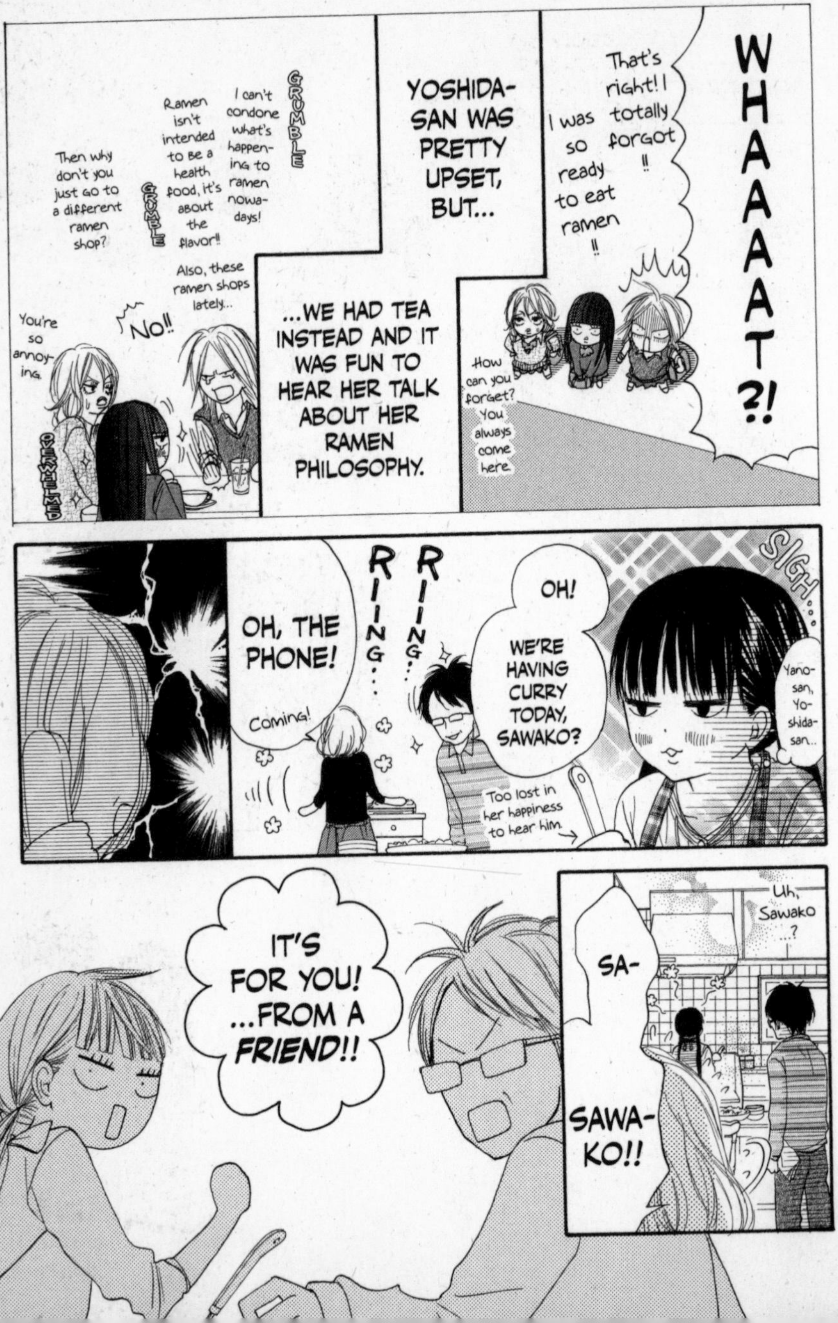
WHAAAAT?!
That's right!! I totally forgot!!
I was so ready to eat ramen!!
How can you forget? You always come here.
YOSHIDA-SAN WAS PRETTY UPSET, BUT...
...WE HAD TEA INSTEAD AND IT WAS FUN TO HEAR HER TALK ABOUT HER RAMEN PHILOSOPHY.
GRUMBLE
I can't condone what's happening to ramen nowadays!
Ramen isn't intended to be a health food, it's about the flavor!!
GRUMBLE
Then why don't you just go to a different ramen shop?
Also, these ramen shops lately...
No!!
You're so annoying.
OVERWHELMED
SIGH...
Yano-san, Yoshida-san...
OH!
WE'RE HAVING CURRY TODAY, SAWAKO?
Too lost in her happiness to hear him.
RIIING...
RIIING...
OH, THE PHONE!
Coming!
Uh, Sawako...?
SA-
SAWAKO!!
IT'S FOR YOU! ...FROM A FRIEND!!

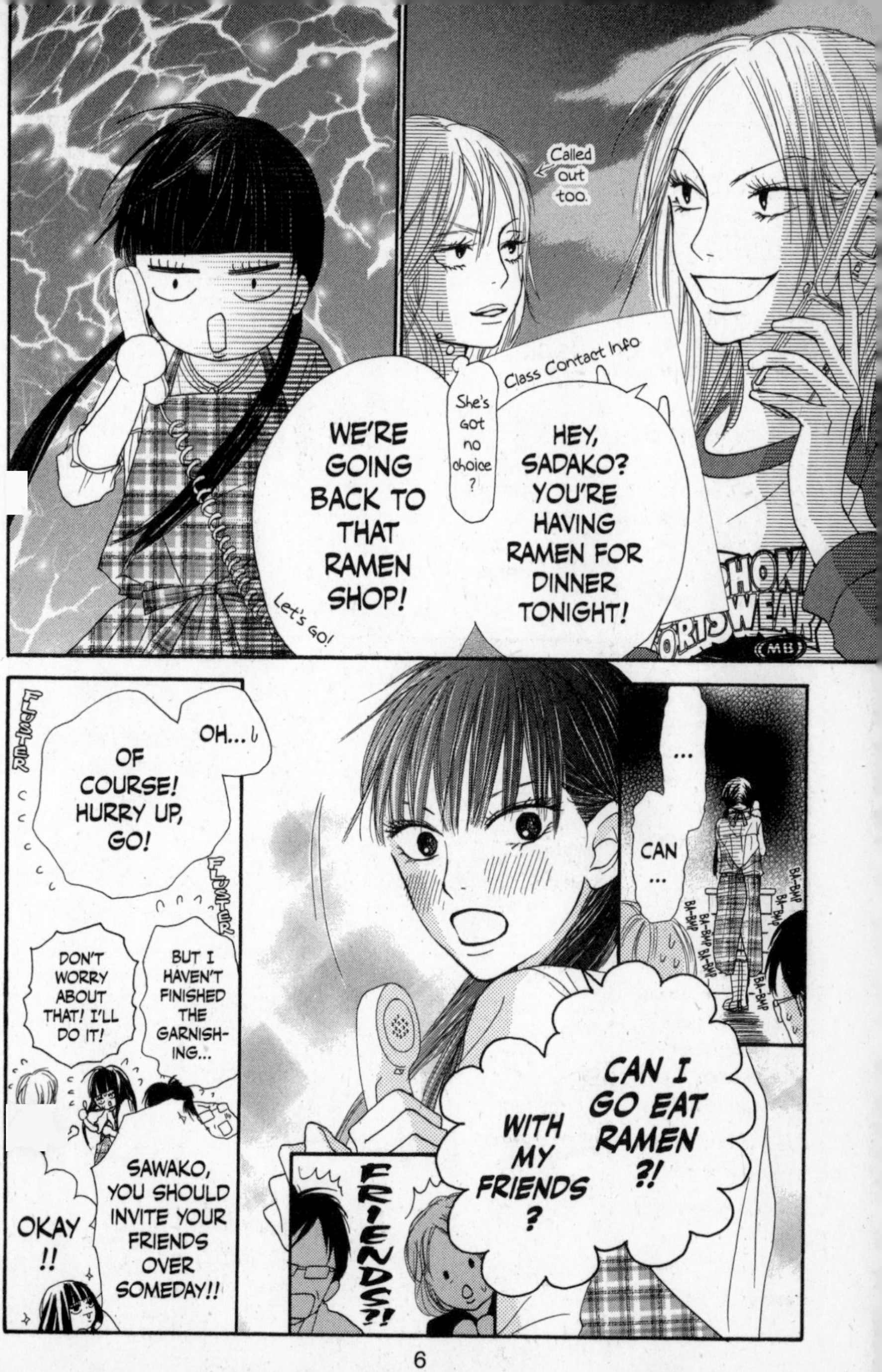
Called out too.
Class Contact Info
HEY, SADAKO? YOU'RE HAVING RAMEN FOR DINNER TONIGHT!
She's got no choice?
WE'RE GOING BACK TO THAT RAMEN SHOP!
Let's go!
...
CAN ...
BA-BMP BA-BMP BA-BMP BA-BMP BA-BMP
CAN I GO EAT RAMEN
WITH MY FRIENDS?
FRIENDS?!
FLUSTER
OH...
OF COURSE! HURRY UP, GO!
FLUSTER
BUT I HAVEN'T FINISHED THE GARNISHING...
DON'T WORRY ABOUT THAT! I'LL DO IT!
SAWAKO, YOU SHOULD INVITE YOUR FRIENDS OVER SOMEDAY!!
OKAY!!

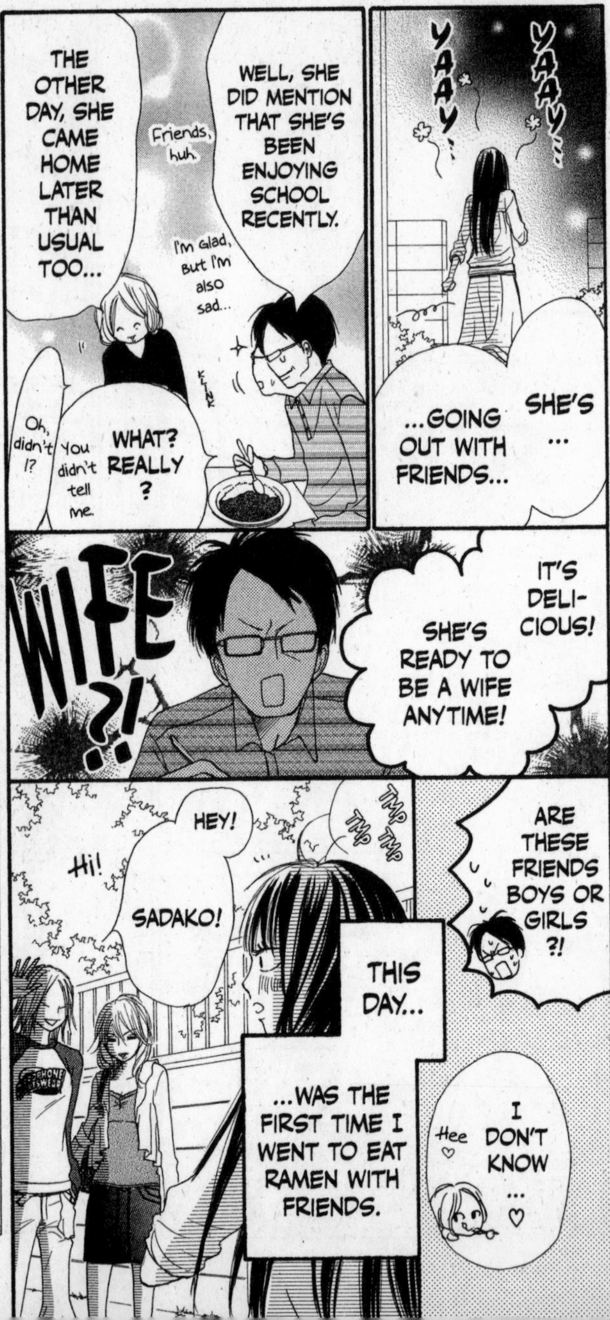
YAAAY...
YAAAY...
SHE'S ...
...GOING OUT WITH FRIENDS...
WELL, SHE DID MENTION THAT SHE'S BEEN ENJOYING SCHOOL RECENTLY.
I'm Glad, But I'm also sad...
Friends, huh.
THE OTHER DAY, SHE CAME HOME LATER THAN USUAL TOO...
KLINK
WHAT? REALLY?
You didn't tell me.
Oh, didn't I?
IT'S DELI-CIOUS!
SHE'S READY TO BE A WIFE ANYTIME!
WIFE?!
ARE THESE FRIENDS BOYS OR GIRLS?!
I DON'T KNOW... ♡
Hee ♡
TMP TMP TMP
HEY!
SADAKO!
Hi!
THIS DAY...
...WAS THE FIRST TIME I WENT TO EAT RAMEN WITH FRIENDS.

KARUPIN on JAPAN 1

Hello! How are you doing? My name is Shiina. Nice to meet you.

Maybe it's because I'm getting older and am starting to sag, but recently when I apply makeup, I look unnatural and kind of weird. Also, because it's just before the deadline when I'm haggard...

I'm about to go meet my editor so I'm wearing makeup today. I usually don't wear any. Because it's such a hassle!

Well, not that any of that matters to you...

I featured "little men" in the previous bonus manga pages and got a lot of responses from my readers about their experiences.

Thank you for sending me all your stories!

I enjoyed it very much!

Yaaay! To be gontinued. ← Whoops, I made a typo.

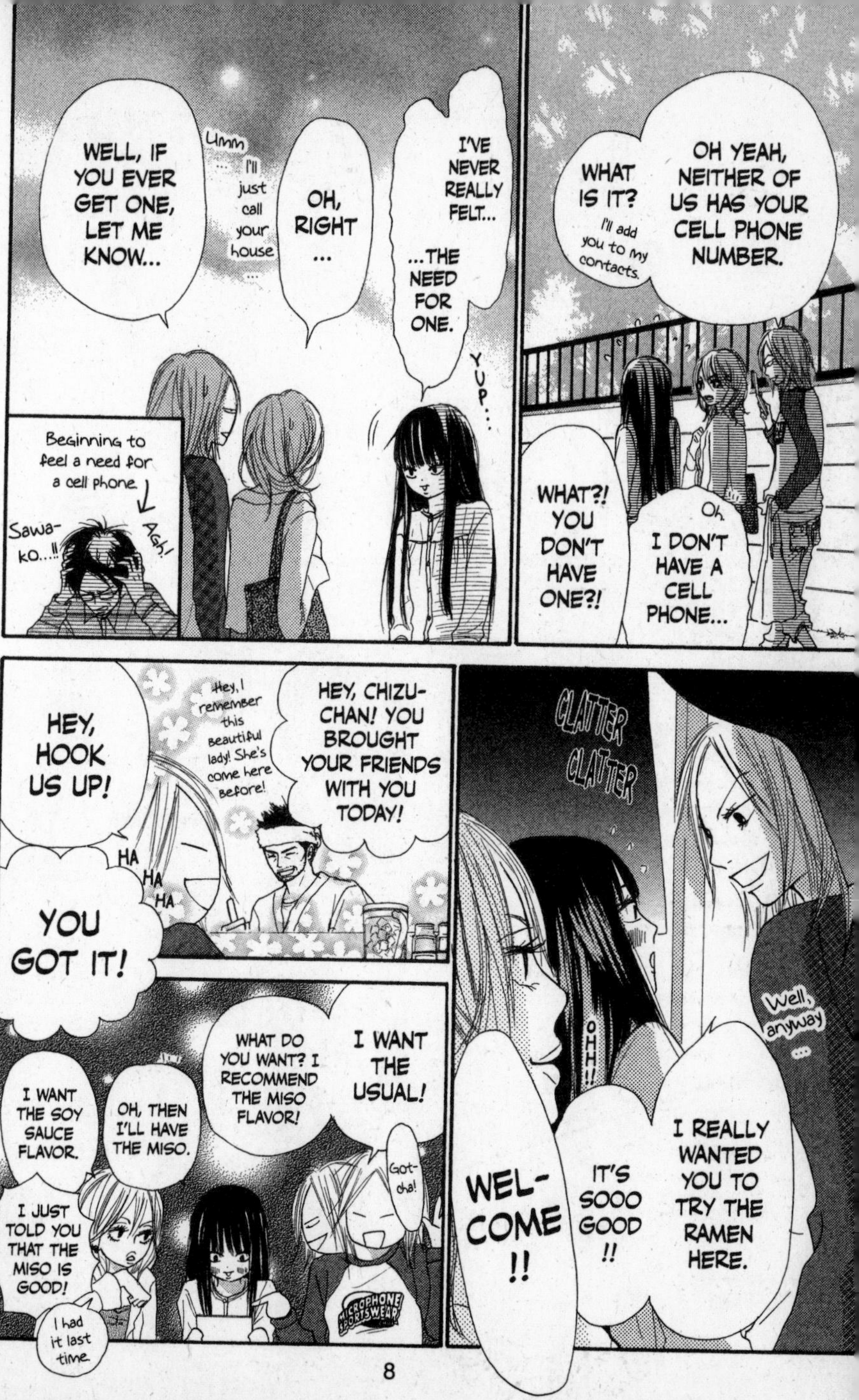
OH YEAH, NEITHER OF US HAS YOUR CELL PHONE NUMBER.
WHAT IS IT?
I'll add you to my contacts.
Oh.
I DON'T HAVE A CELL PHONE...
WHAT?! YOU DON'T HAVE ONE?!
I'VE NEVER REALLY FELT...
...THE NEED FOR ONE.
YUP...
OH, RIGHT...
Umm... I'll just call your house...
WELL, IF YOU EVER GET ONE, LET ME KNOW...
Beginning to feel a need for a cell phone
Agh!
Sawa-ko...!!
CLATTER
CLATTER
Well, anyway...
I REALLY WANTED YOU TO TRY THE RAMEN HERE.
IT'S SOOO GOOD!!
OHH!!
WEL-COME!!
HEY, CHIZU-CHAN! YOU BROUGHT YOUR FRIENDS WITH YOU TODAY!
Hey, I remember this beautiful lady! She's come here before!
HEY, HOOK US UP!
HA HA HA
YOU GOT IT!
I WANT THE USUAL!
Got-cha!
WHAT DO YOU WANT? I RECOMMEND THE MISO FLAVOR!
OH, THEN I'LL HAVE THE MISO.
I WANT THE SOY SAUCE FLAVOR.
I JUST TOLD YOU THAT THE MISO IS GOOD!
I had it last time.
MICROPHONE SPORTSWEAR

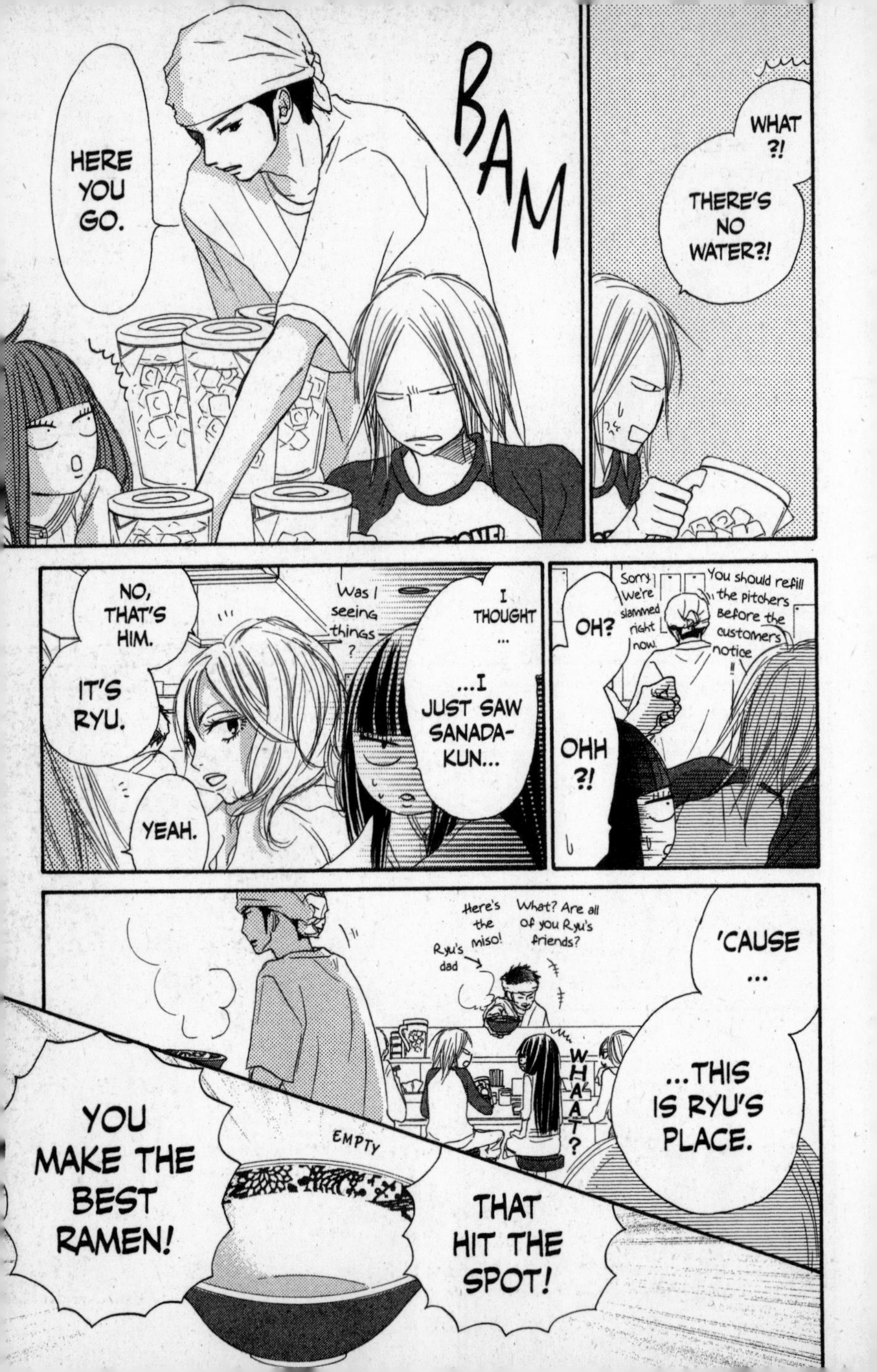
WHAT?! THERE'S NO WATER?!
BAM
HERE YOU GO.
OH?
You should refill the pitchers before the customers notice!!
Sorry. We're slammed right now.
OHH?!
I THOUGHT...
...I JUST SAW SANADA-KUN...
Was I seeing things?
NO, THAT'S HIM.
IT'S RYU.
YEAH.
'CAUSE...
...THIS IS RYU'S PLACE.
What? Are all of you Ryu's friends?
Here's the miso!
Ryu's dad
WHAAT?
THAT HIT THE SPOT!
EMPTY
YOU MAKE THE BEST RAMEN!

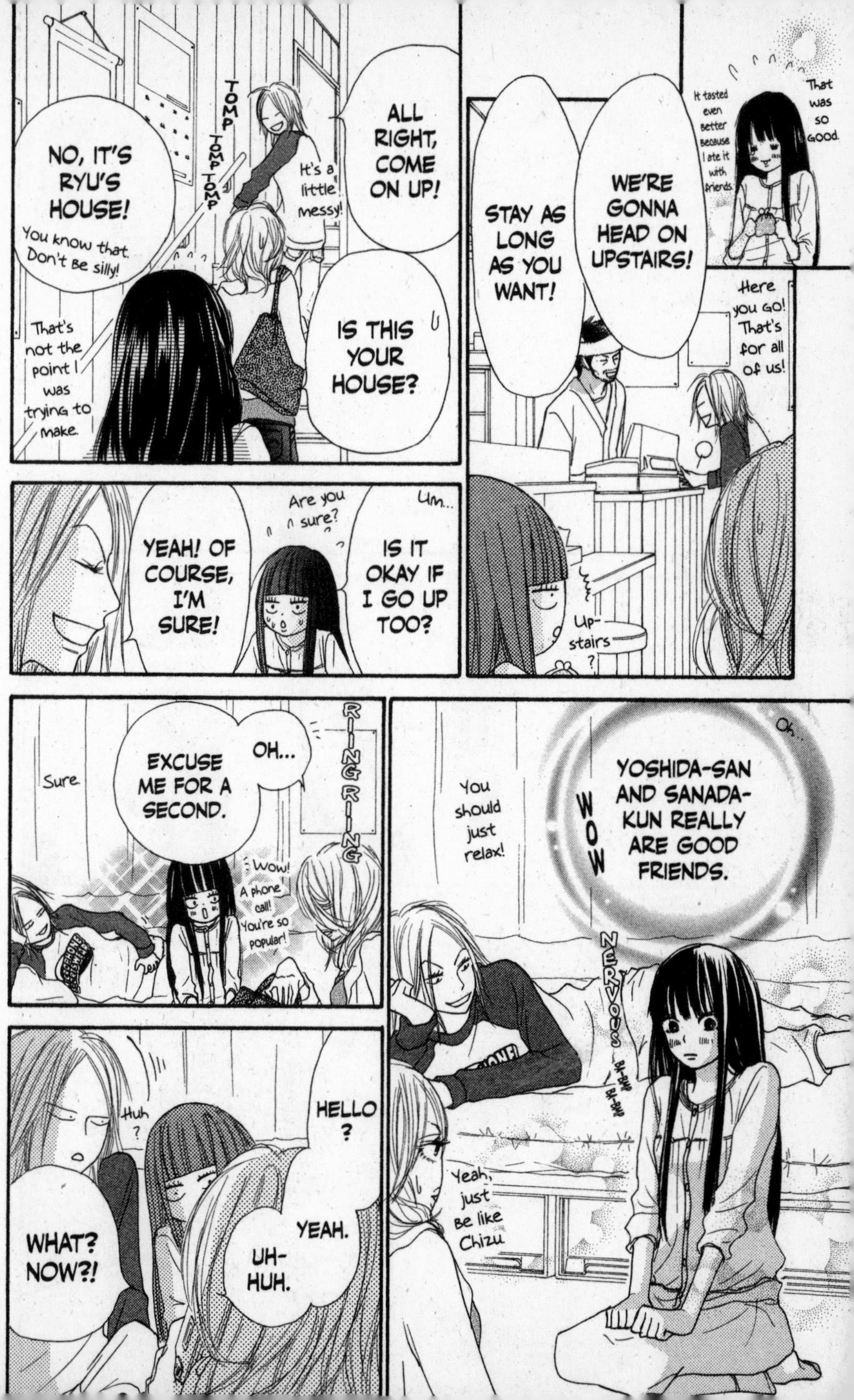
That was so good.
It tasted even better because I ate it with friends.
Here you go! That's for all of us!
WE'RE GONNA HEAD ON UPSTAIRS!
STAY AS LONG AS YOU WANT!
Up-stairs?
ALL RIGHT, COME ON UP!
It's a little messy!
IS THIS YOUR HOUSE?
TOMP TOMP TOMP TOMP
NO, IT'S RYU'S HOUSE!
You know that. Don't be silly!
That's not the point I was trying to make.
Um...
IS IT OKAY IF I GO UP TOO?
Are you sure?
YEAH! OF COURSE, I'M SURE!
Oh...
YOSHIDA-SAN AND SANADA-KUN REALLY ARE GOOD FRIENDS.
WOW
You should just relax!
NERVOUS
BA-BMP BA-BMP
Yeah, just be like Chizu.
RING RING
OH...
EXCUSE ME FOR A SECOND.
Sure.
Wow! A phone call! You're so popular!
HELLO?
Huh?
YEAH.
UH-HUH.
WHAT? NOW?!

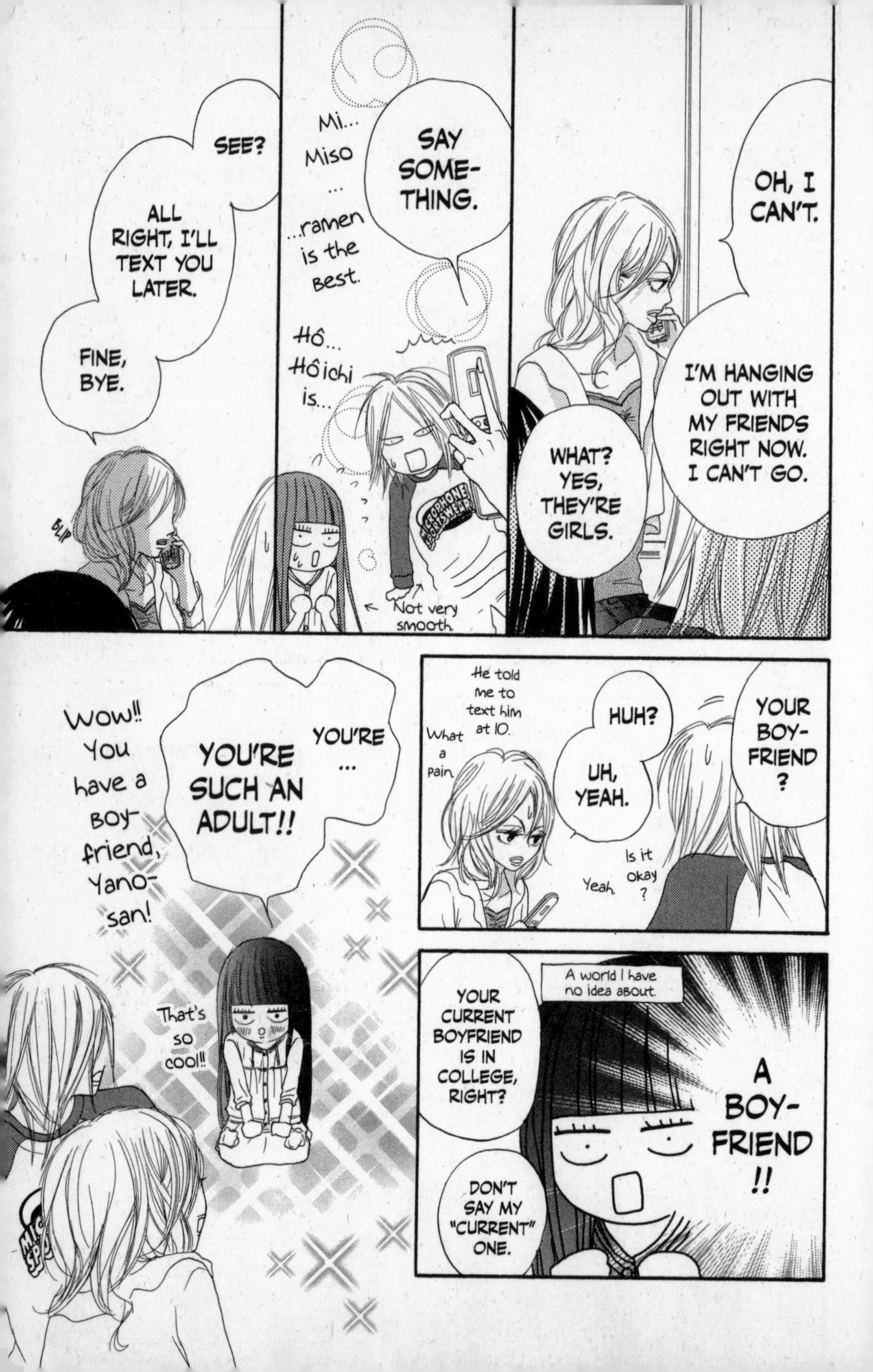
OH, I CAN'T.
I'M HANGING OUT WITH MY FRIENDS RIGHT NOW. I CAN'T GO.
WHAT? YES, THEY'RE GIRLS.
SAY SOME-THING.
Mi... Miso ... ...ramen is the best.
Hô... Hôichi is...
Not very smooth.
SEE?
ALL RIGHT, I'LL TEXT YOU LATER.
FINE, BYE.
BLIP
YOUR BOY-FRIEND?
HUH?
UH, YEAH.
Is it okay?
Yeah.
He told me to text him at 10.
What a pain.
A BOY-FRIEND!!
A world I have no idea about.
YOUR CURRENT BOYFRIEND IS IN COLLEGE, RIGHT?
DON'T SAY MY "CURRENT" ONE.
YOU'RE ...
YOU'RE SUCH AN ADULT!!
Wow!! You have a boy-friend, Yano-san!
That's so cool!!

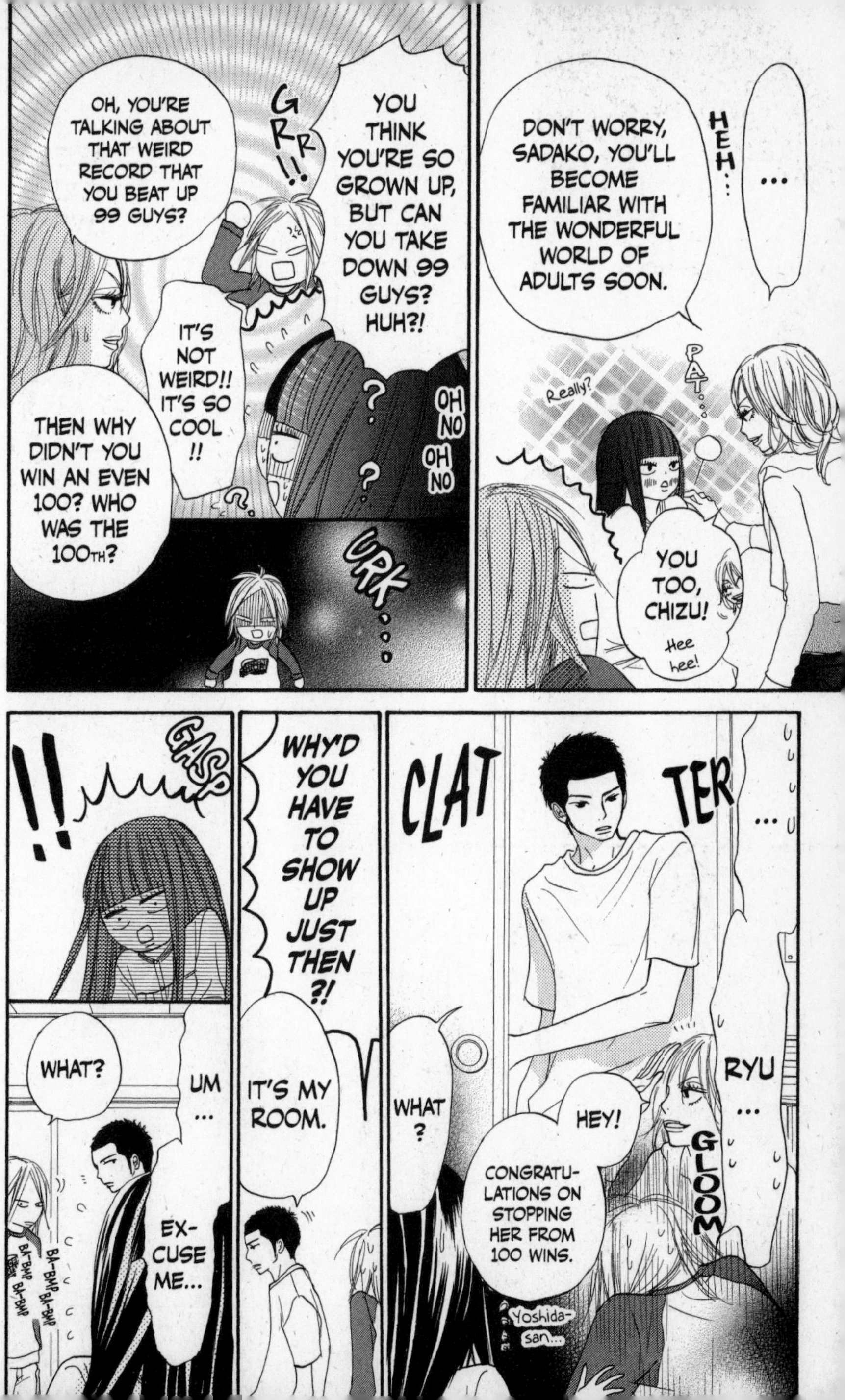
...
HEH...
DON'T WORRY, SADAKO, YOU'LL BECOME FAMILIAR WITH THE WONDERFUL WORLD OF ADULTS SOON.
PAT...
Really?
YOU TOO, CHIZU!
Hee hee!
YOU THINK YOU'RE SO GROWN UP, BUT CAN YOU TAKE DOWN 99 GUYS? HUH?!
GRR!!
OH, YOU'RE TALKING ABOUT THAT WEIRD RECORD THAT YOU BEAT UP 99 GUYS?
IT'S NOT WEIRD!! IT'S SO COOL!!
OH NO OH NO
THEN WHY DIDN'T YOU WIN AN EVEN 100? WHO WAS THE 100TH?
URK...
CLATTER
...
RYU...
HEY!
CONGRATULATIONS ON STOPPING HER FROM 100 WINS.
GLOOM
WHAT?
Yoshida-san...
WHY'D YOU HAVE TO SHOW UP JUST THEN?!
IT'S MY ROOM.
GASP
!!
WHAT?
UM...
EXCUSE ME...
BA-BMP BA-BMP BA-BMP BA-BMP

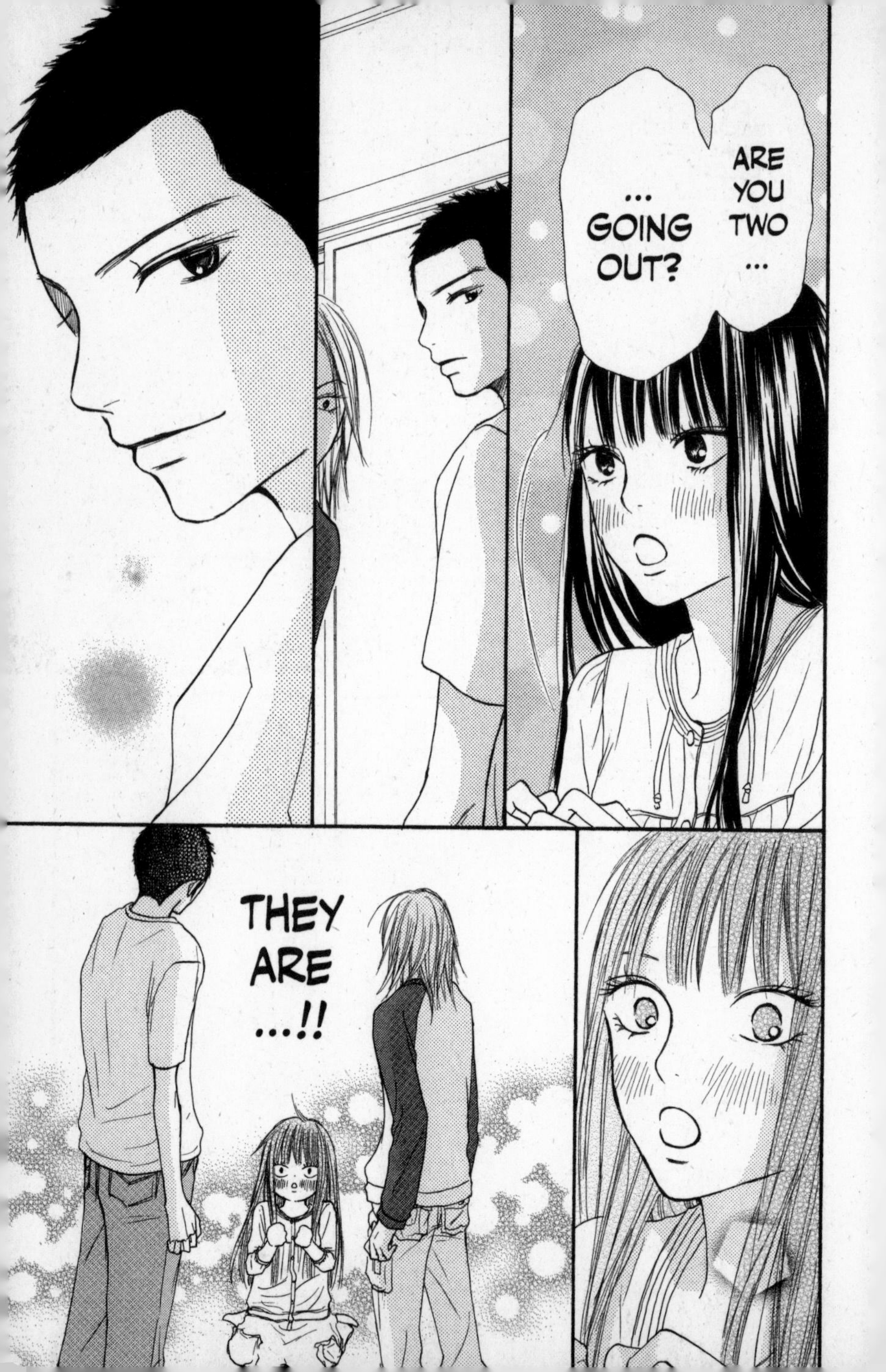
ARE YOU TWO ... ... GOING OUT?
THEY ARE ...!!

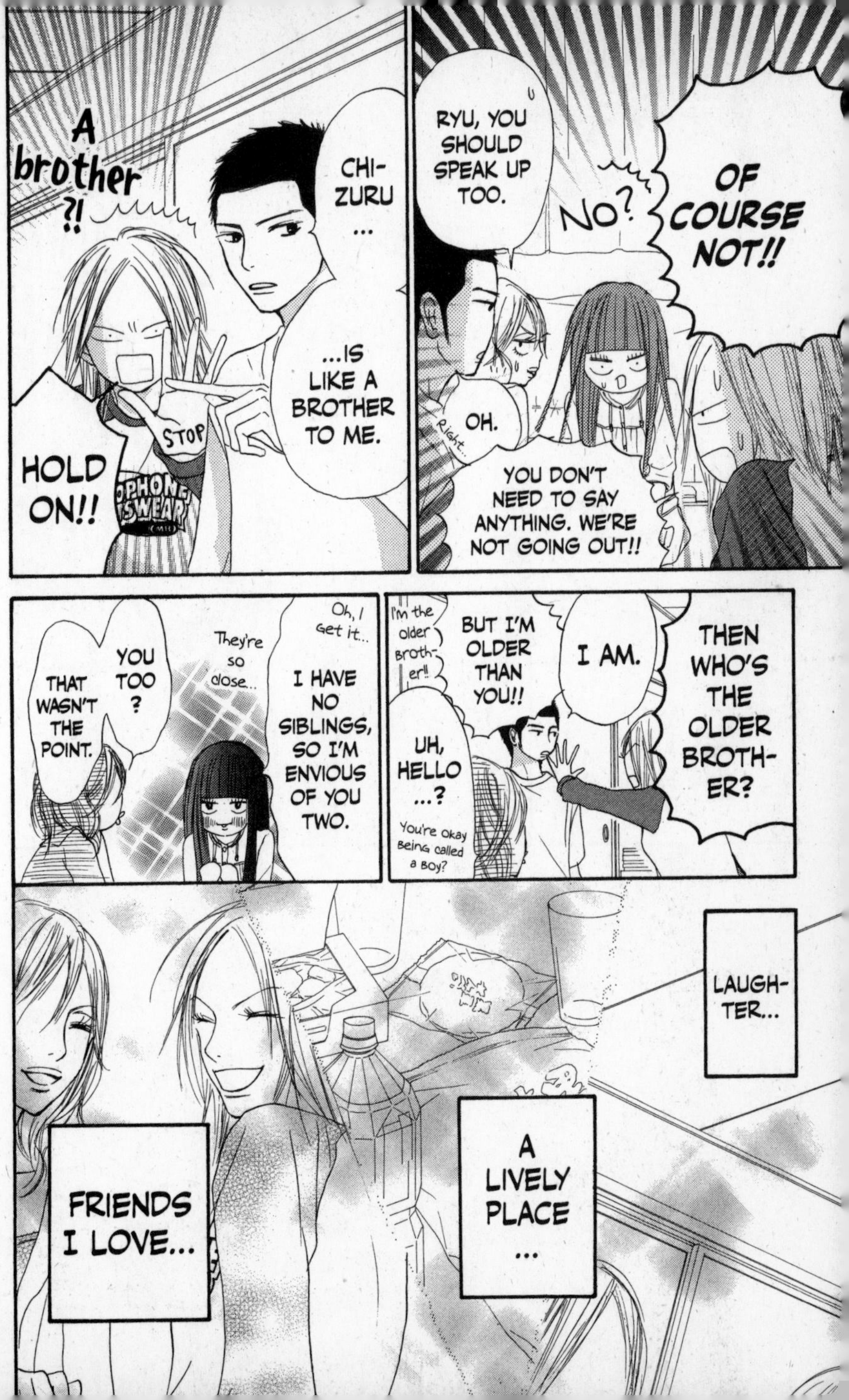
OF COURSE NOT!!
No?
RYU, YOU SHOULD SPEAK UP TOO.
OH.
Right...
YOU DON'T NEED TO SAY ANYTHING. WE'RE NOT GOING OUT!!
CHI-ZURU ...
...IS LIKE A BROTHER TO ME.
A brother ?!
HOLD ON!!
STOP
THEN WHO'S THE OLDER BROTH-ER?
I AM.
BUT I'M OLDER THAN YOU!!
I'm the older broth-er!!
UH, HELLO ...?
You're okay being called a boy?
Oh, I get it...
I HAVE NO SIBLINGS, SO I'M ENVIOUS OF YOU TWO.
They're so close...
YOU TOO ?
THAT WASN'T THE POINT.
LAUGH-TER...
A LIVELY PLACE ...
FRIENDS I LOVE...

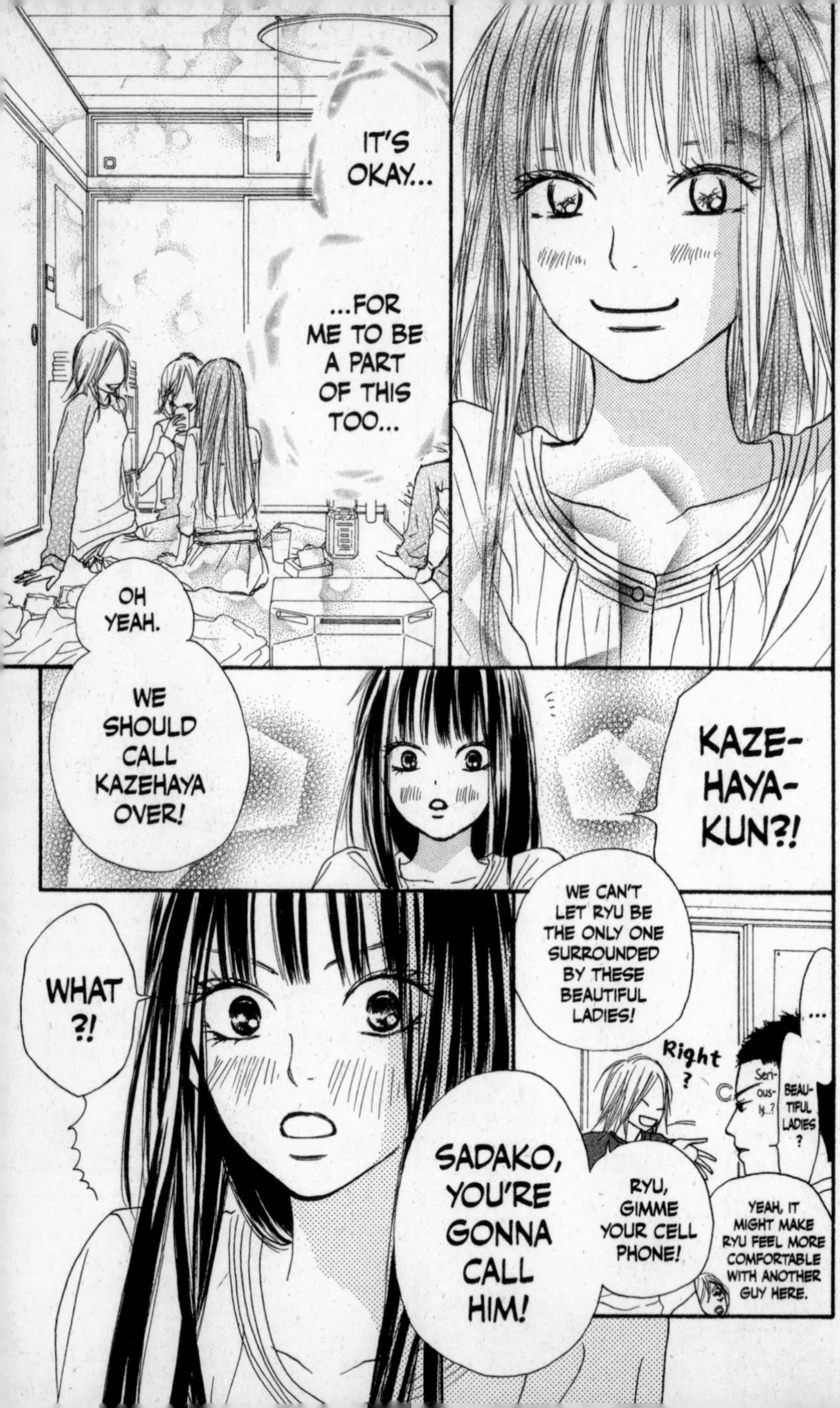
IT'S OKAY...
...FOR ME TO BE A PART OF THIS TOO...
OH YEAH.
WE SHOULD CALL KAZEHAYA OVER!
KAZE-HAYA-KUN?!
WE CAN'T LET RYU BE THE ONLY ONE SURROUNDED BY THESE BEAUTIFUL LADIES!
Right?
...
Seri-ous-ly...?
BEAU-TIFUL LADIES?
YEAH, IT MIGHT MAKE RYU FEEL MORE COMFORTABLE WITH ANOTHER GUY HERE.
RYU, GIMME YOUR CELL PHONE!
SADAKO, YOU'RE GONNA CALL HIM!
WHAT?!

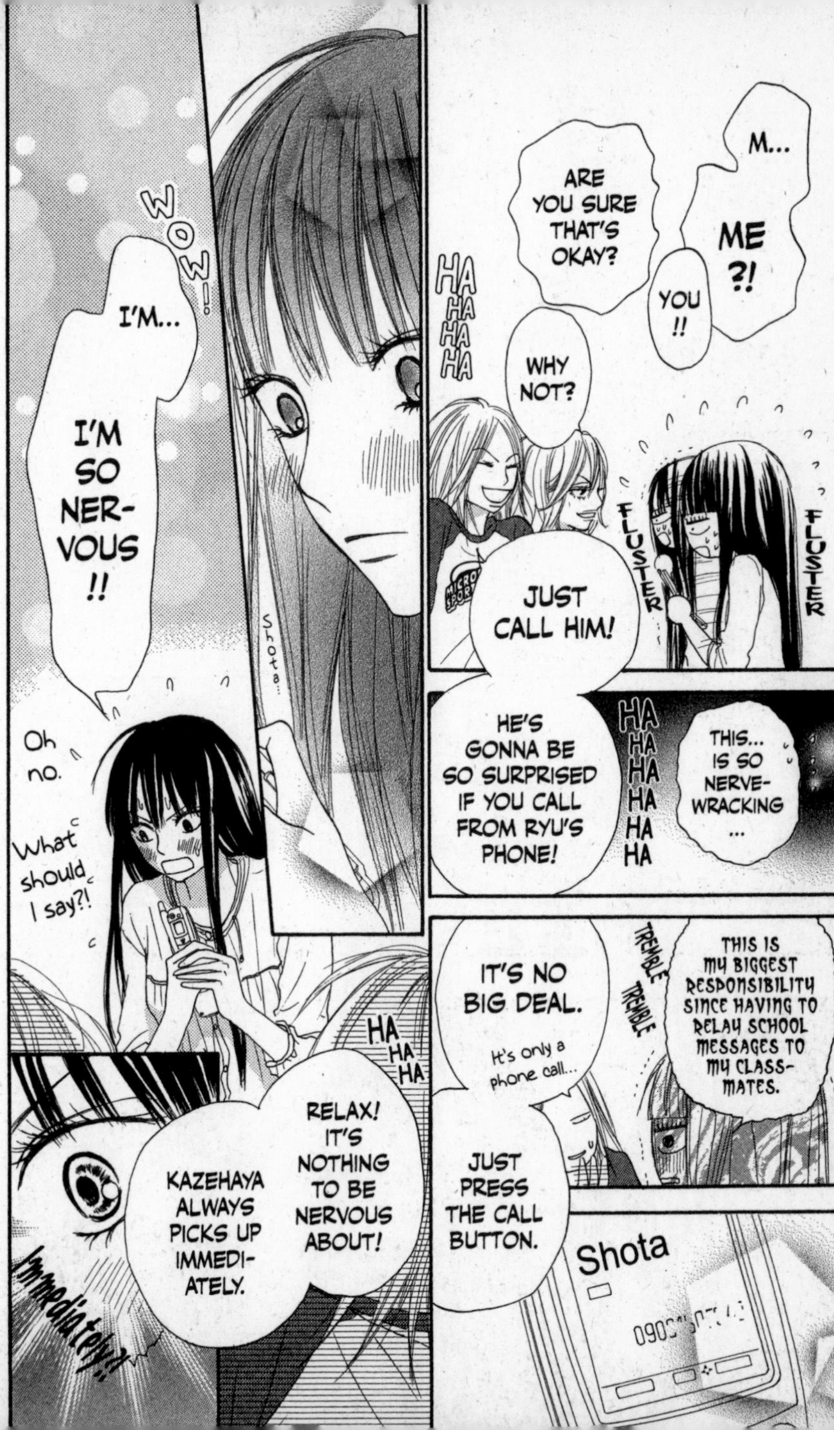
M...
ME ?!
YOU !!
ARE YOU SURE THAT'S OKAY?
HA HA HA HA
WHY NOT?
FLUSTER
FLUSTER
JUST CALL HIM!
THIS... IS SO NERVE-WRACKING ...
HA HA HA HA HA HA HA
HE'S GONNA BE SO SURPRISED IF YOU CALL FROM RYU'S PHONE!
THIS IS MY BIGGEST RESPONSIBILITY SINCE HAVING TO RELAY SCHOOL MESSAGES TO MY CLASS-MATES.
TREMBLE TREMBLE
IT'S NO BIG DEAL.
It's only a phone call...
JUST PRESS THE CALL BUTTON.
Shota
Shota...
WOW!
I'M...
I'M SO NER-VOUS !!
Oh no.
What should I say?!
HA HA HA
RELAX! IT'S NOTHING TO BE NERVOUS ABOUT!
KAZEHAYA ALWAYS PICKS UP IMMEDI-ATELY.
Immediately?!

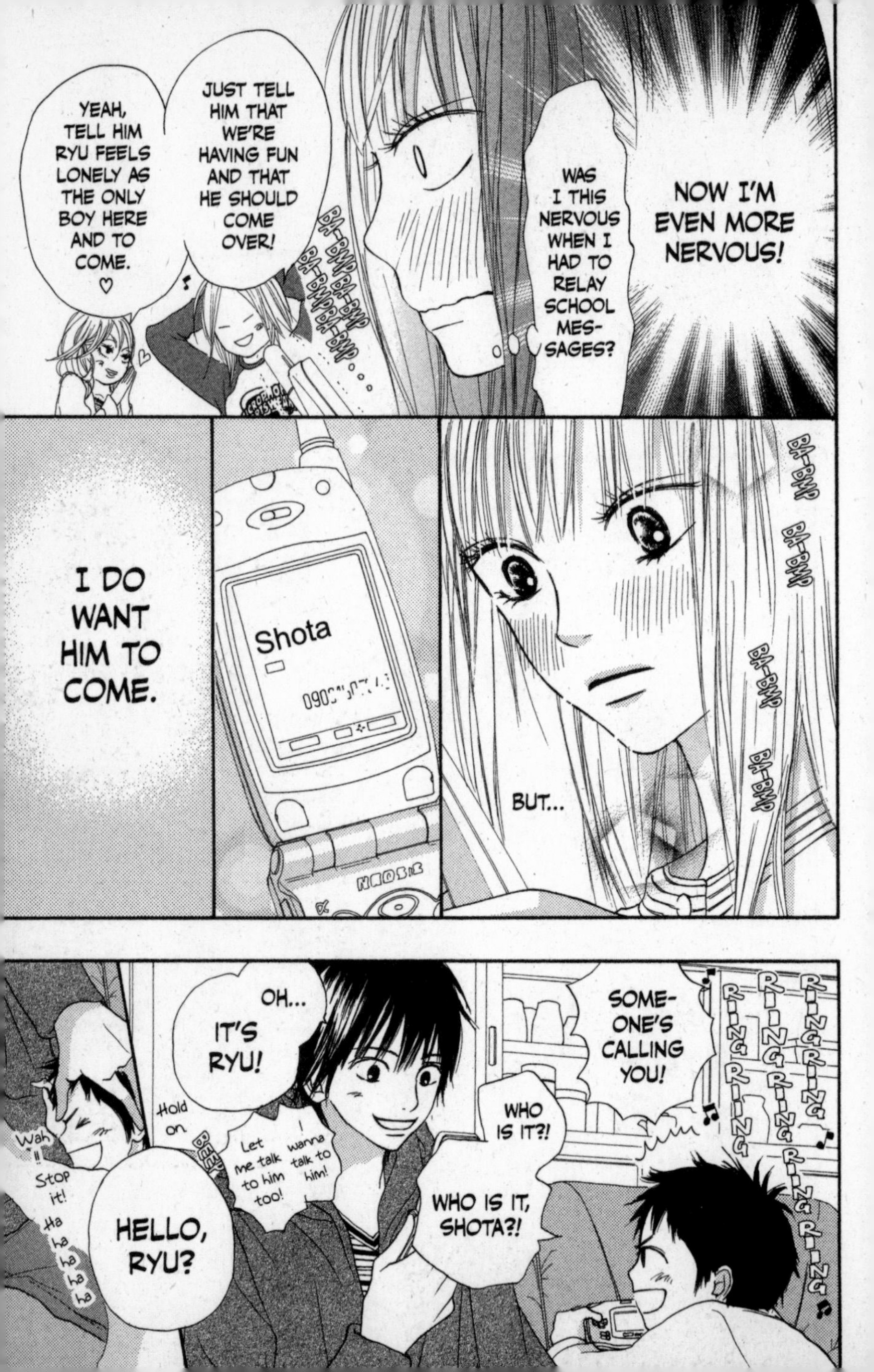
NOW I'M EVEN MORE NERVOUS!
WAS I THIS NERVOUS WHEN I HAD TO RELAY SCHOOL MES-SAGES?
BA-BMP BA-BMP BA-BMP BA-BMP BA-BMP
JUST TELL HIM THAT WE'RE HAVING FUN AND THAT HE SHOULD COME OVER!
YEAH, TELL HIM RYU FEELS LONELY AS THE ONLY BOY HERE AND TO COME. ♡
BA-BMP BA-BMP BA-BMP BA-BMP
BUT...
Shota
I DO WANT HIM TO COME.
RING RING RING RING RING RING RING RING RING RING
SOME-ONE'S CALLING YOU!
WHO IS IT?!
WHO IS IT, SHOTA?!
OH... IT'S RYU!
I wanna talk to him!
Let me talk to him too!
Hold on.
BEEP
HELLO, RYU?
Wah!! Stop it!
Ha ha ha ha ha

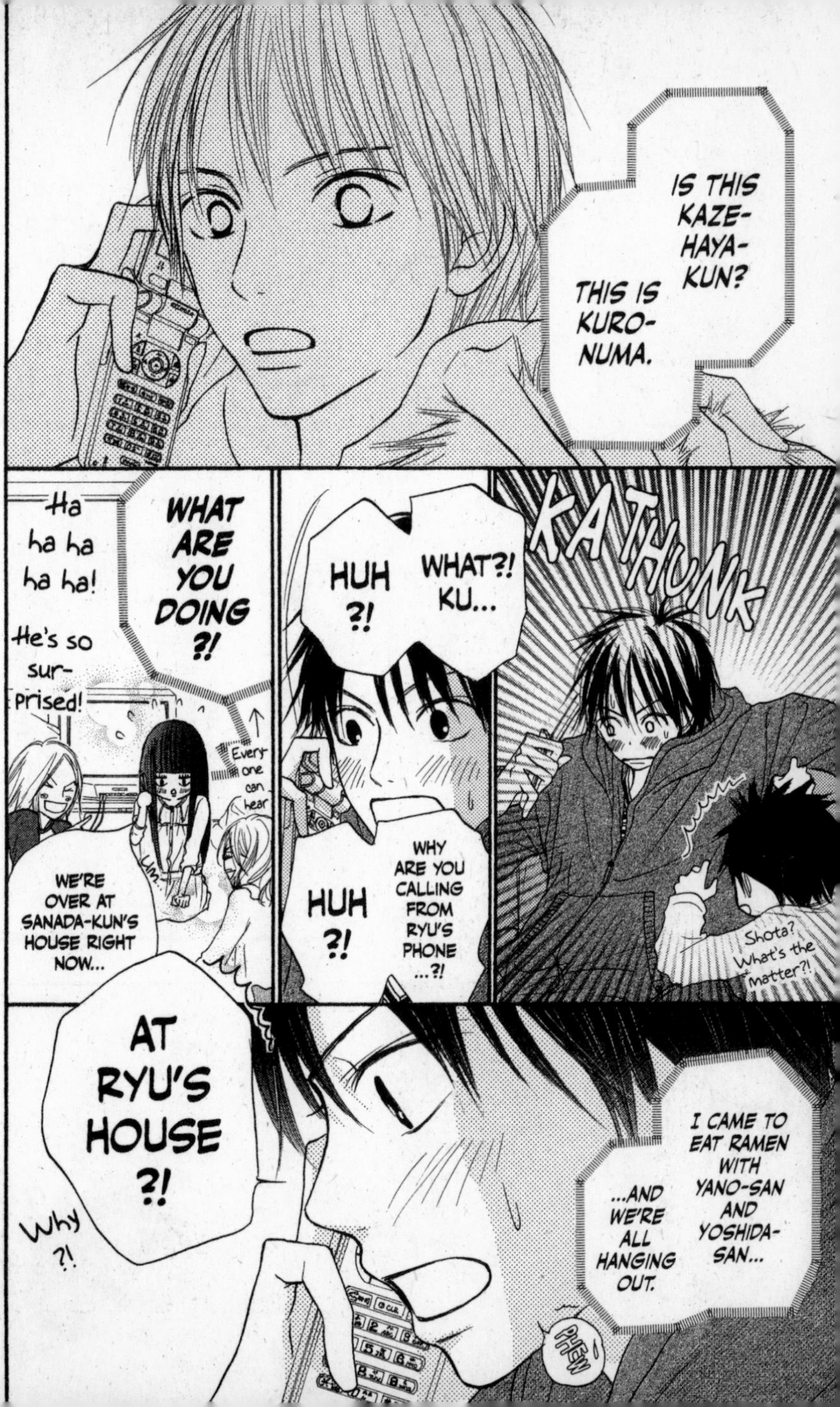
IS THIS KAZE-HAYA-KUN?
THIS IS KURO-NUMA.
KA THUNK
Shota? What's the matter?!
WHAT?! KU...
HUH ?!
WHY ARE YOU CALLING FROM RYU'S PHONE ...?!
HUH ?!
WHAT ARE YOU DOING ?!
Ha ha ha ha ha!
He's so sur-prised!
Every one can hear
Um...
WE'RE OVER AT SANADA-KUN'S HOUSE RIGHT NOW...
I CAME TO EAT RAMEN WITH YANO-SAN AND YOSHIDA-SAN...
...AND WE'RE ALL HANGING OUT.
PHEW
AT RYU'S HOUSE ?!
Why ?!

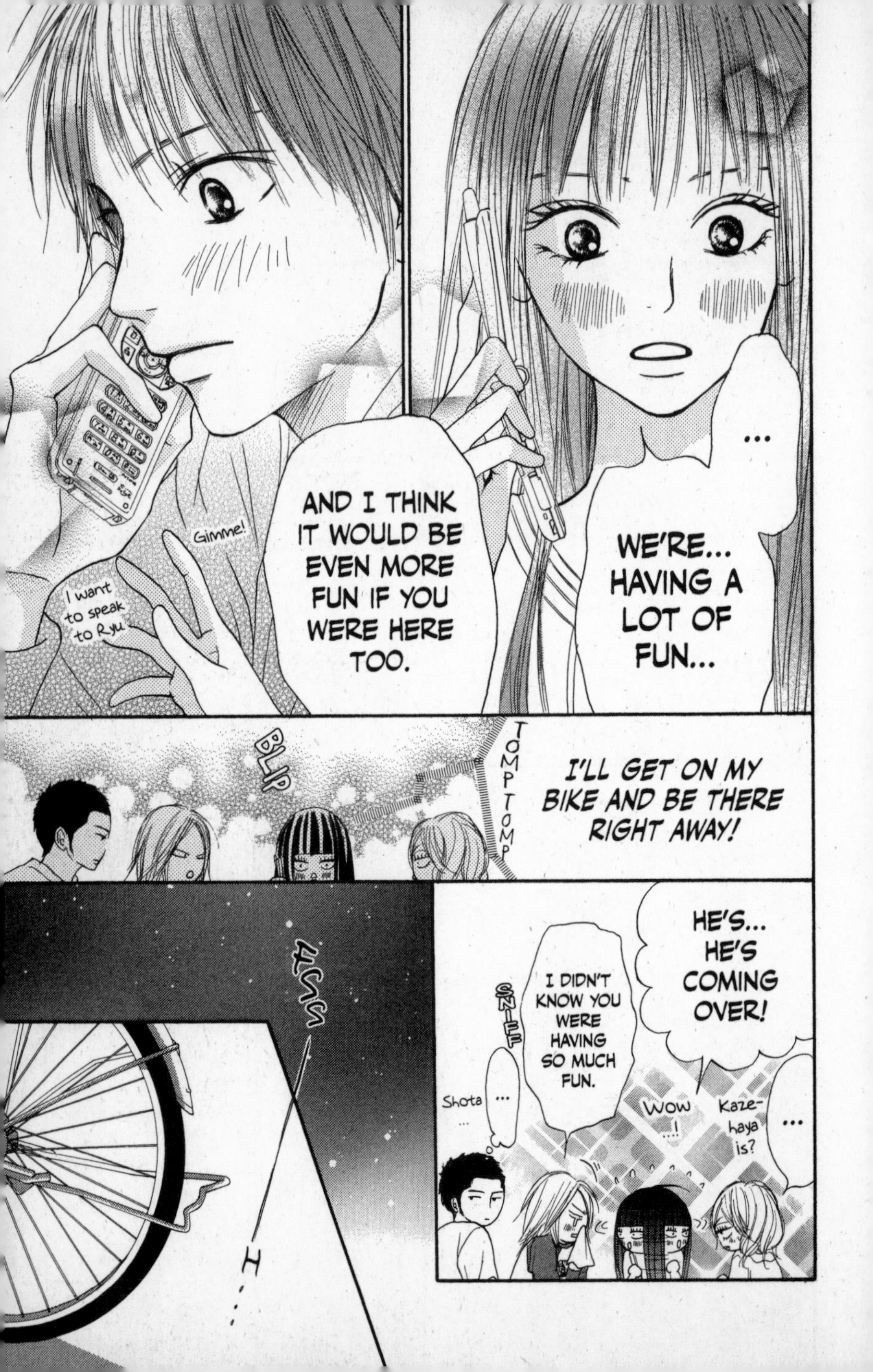
...
WE'RE... HAVING A LOT OF FUN...
AND I THINK IT WOULD BE EVEN MORE FUN IF YOU WERE HERE TOO.
Gimme!
I want to speak to Ryu
I'LL GET ON MY BIKE AND BE THERE RIGHT AWAY!
TOMP TOMP
BLIP
HE'S... HE'S COMING OVER!
...
Kaze-haya is?
Wow...!
I DIDN'T KNOW YOU WERE HAVING SO MUCH FUN.
SNIFF
...
Shota ...
FSSS
H...

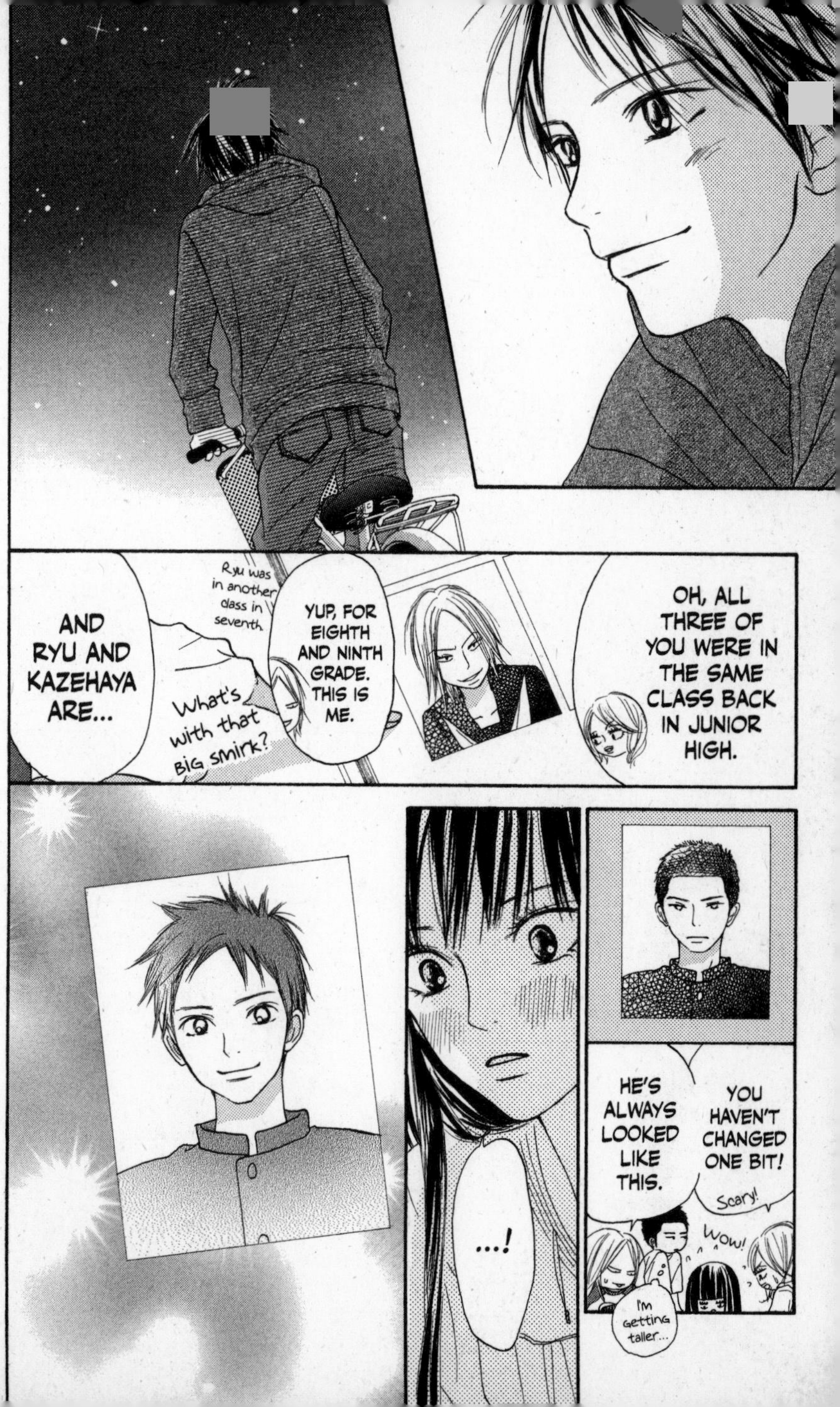
OH, ALL THREE OF YOU WERE IN THE SAME CLASS BACK IN JUNIOR HIGH.
YUP, FOR EIGHTH AND NINTH GRADE. THIS IS ME.
Ryu was in another class in seventh.
What's with that big smirk?
AND RYU AND KAZEHAYA ARE...
YOU HAVEN'T CHANGED ONE BIT!
HE'S ALWAYS LOOKED LIKE THIS.
Scary!
Wow!
I'm getting taller...
...!

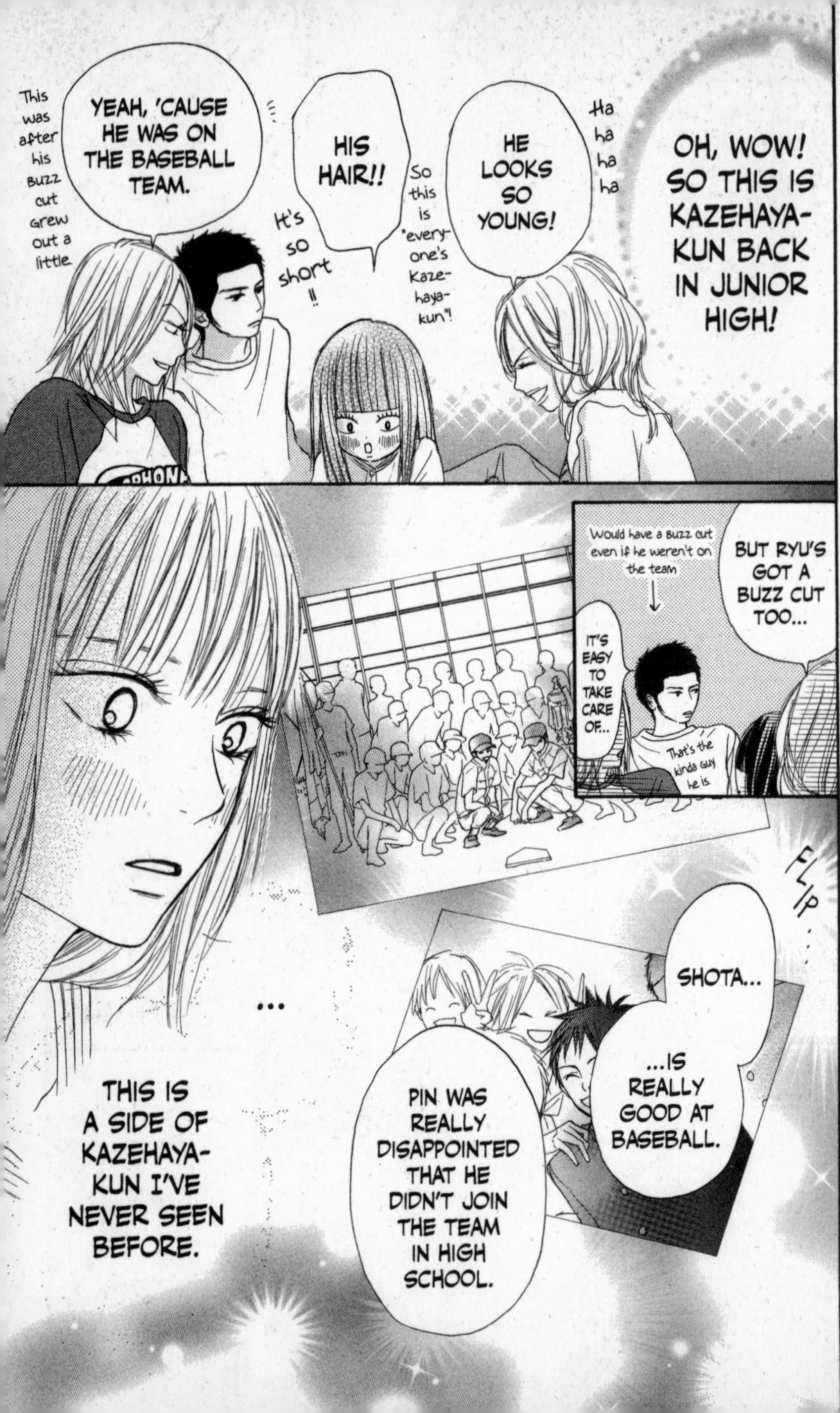
OH, WOW! SO THIS IS KAZEHAYA-KUN BACK IN JUNIOR HIGH!
Ha ha ha ha
HE LOOKS SO YOUNG!
So this is "everyone's Kazehaya-kun"!
HIS HAIR!!
It's so short!!
YEAH, 'CAUSE HE WAS ON THE BASEBALL TEAM.
This was after his buzz cut grew out a little
BUT RYU'S GOT A BUZZ CUT TOO...
Would have a buzz cut even if he weren't on the team
IT'S EASY TO TAKE CARE OF...
That's the kinda guy he is.
FLIP...
SHOTA...
...IS REALLY GOOD AT BASEBALL.
PIN WAS REALLY DISAPPOINTED THAT HE DIDN'T JOIN THE TEAM IN HIGH SCHOOL.
...
THIS IS A SIDE OF KAZEHAYA-KUN I'VE NEVER SEEN BEFORE.

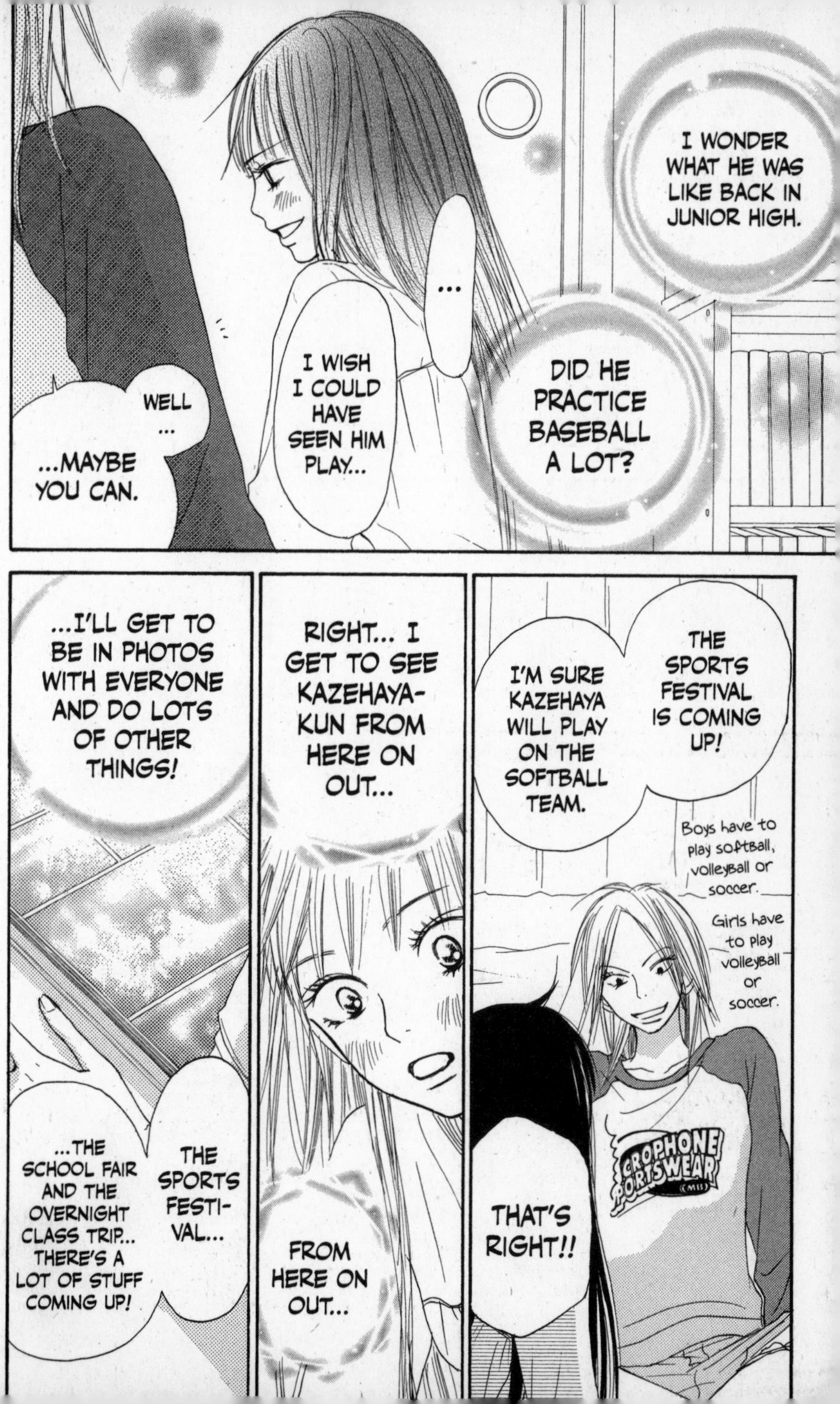
I WONDER WHAT HE WAS LIKE BACK IN JUNIOR HIGH.
DID HE PRACTICE BASEBALL A LOT?
...
I WISH I COULD HAVE SEEN HIM PLAY...
WELL ...
...MAYBE YOU CAN.
THE SPORTS FESTIVAL IS COMING UP!
I'M SURE KAZEHAYA WILL PLAY ON THE SOFTBALL TEAM.
Boys have to play softball, volleyball or soccer.
Girls have to play volleyball or soccer.
CROPHONE PORTSWEAR
THAT'S RIGHT!!
RIGHT... I GET TO SEE KAZEHAYA-KUN FROM HERE ON OUT...
FROM HERE ON OUT...
THE SPORTS FESTI-VAL...
...THE SCHOOL FAIR AND THE OVERNIGHT CLASS TRIP... THERE'S A LOT OF STUFF COMING UP!
...I'LL GET TO BE IN PHOTOS WITH EVERYONE AND DO LOTS OF OTHER THINGS!

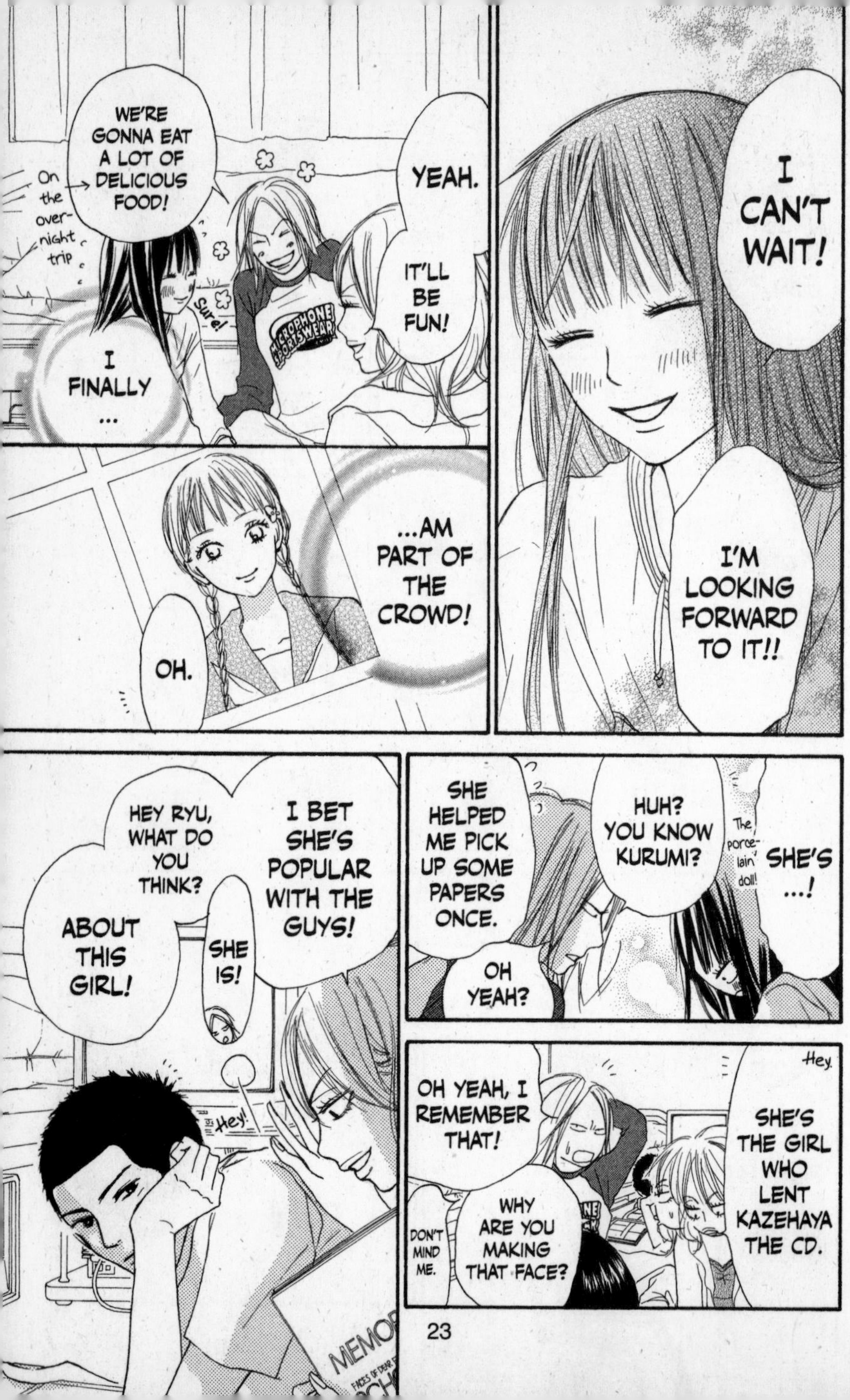
I CAN'T WAIT!
I'M LOOKING FORWARD TO IT!!
YEAH.
IT'LL BE FUN!
WE'RE GONNA EAT A LOT OF DELICIOUS FOOD!
On the over-night trip
Sure!
MICROPHONE SPORTSWEAR
I FINALLY...
...AM PART OF THE CROWD!
OH.
HUH? YOU KNOW KURUMI?
The porce-lain doll!
SHE'S...!
SHE HELPED ME PICK UP SOME PAPERS ONCE.
OH YEAH?
Hey.
SHE'S THE GIRL WHO LENT KAZEHAYA THE CD.
OH YEAH, I REMEMBER THAT!
WHY ARE YOU MAKING THAT FACE?
DON'T MIND ME.
I BET SHE'S POPULAR WITH THE GUYS!
HEY RYU, WHAT DO YOU THINK?
ABOUT THIS GIRL!
SHE IS!
Hey!

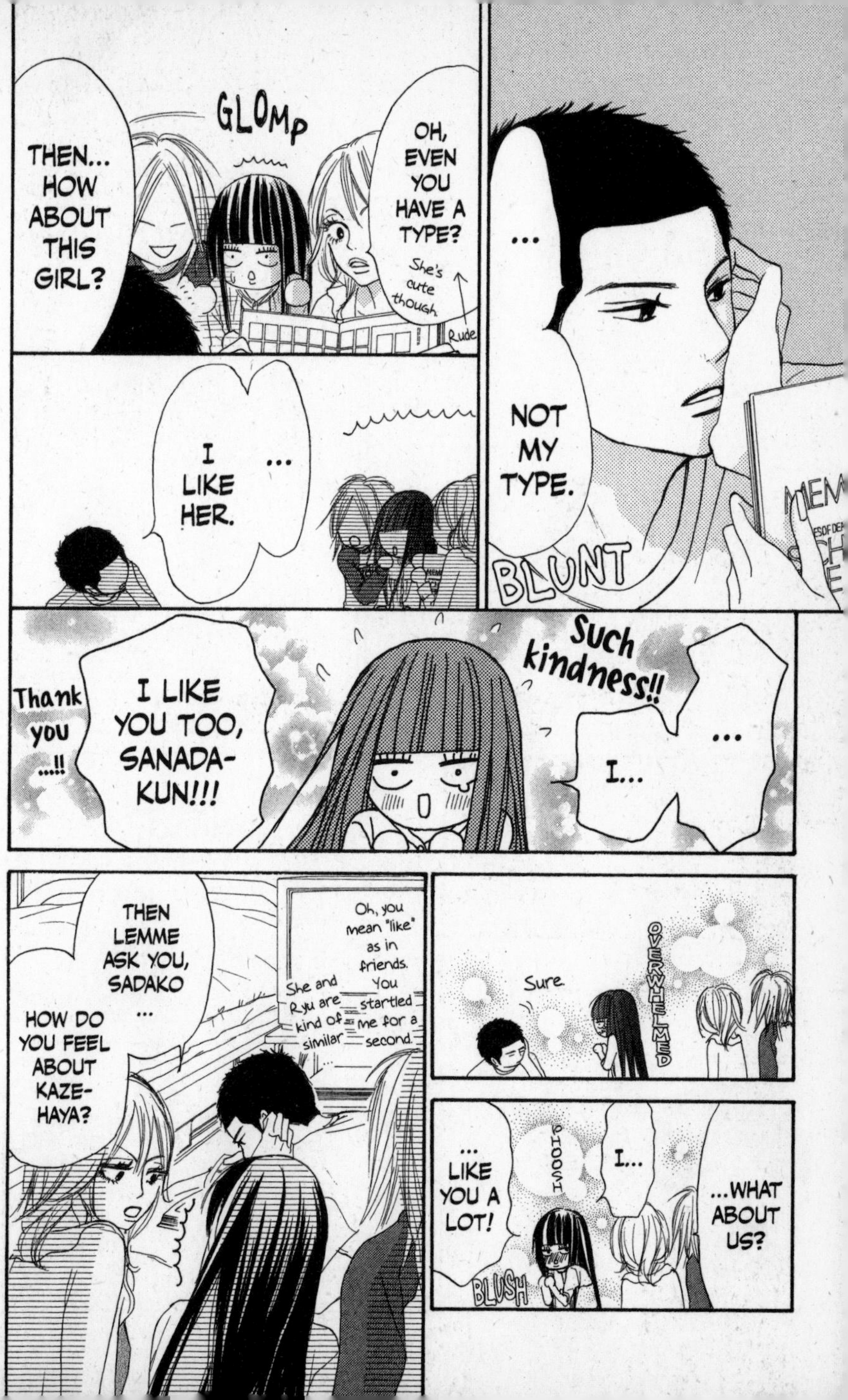
...
NOT MY TYPE.
BLUNT
OH, EVEN YOU HAVE A TYPE?
She's cute though.
Rude
GLOMP
THEN... HOW ABOUT THIS GIRL?
...
I LIKE HER.
... I...
Such kindness!!
I LIKE YOU TOO, SANADA-KUN!!!
Thank you ....!!
Sure.
OVERWHELMED
...WHAT ABOUT US?
I...
PHOOSH
... LIKE YOU A LOT!
BLUSH
Oh, you mean "like" as in friends. You startled me for a second.
She and Ryu are kind of similar...
THEN LEMME ASK YOU, SADAKO ...
HOW DO YOU FEEL ABOUT KAZE-HAYA?

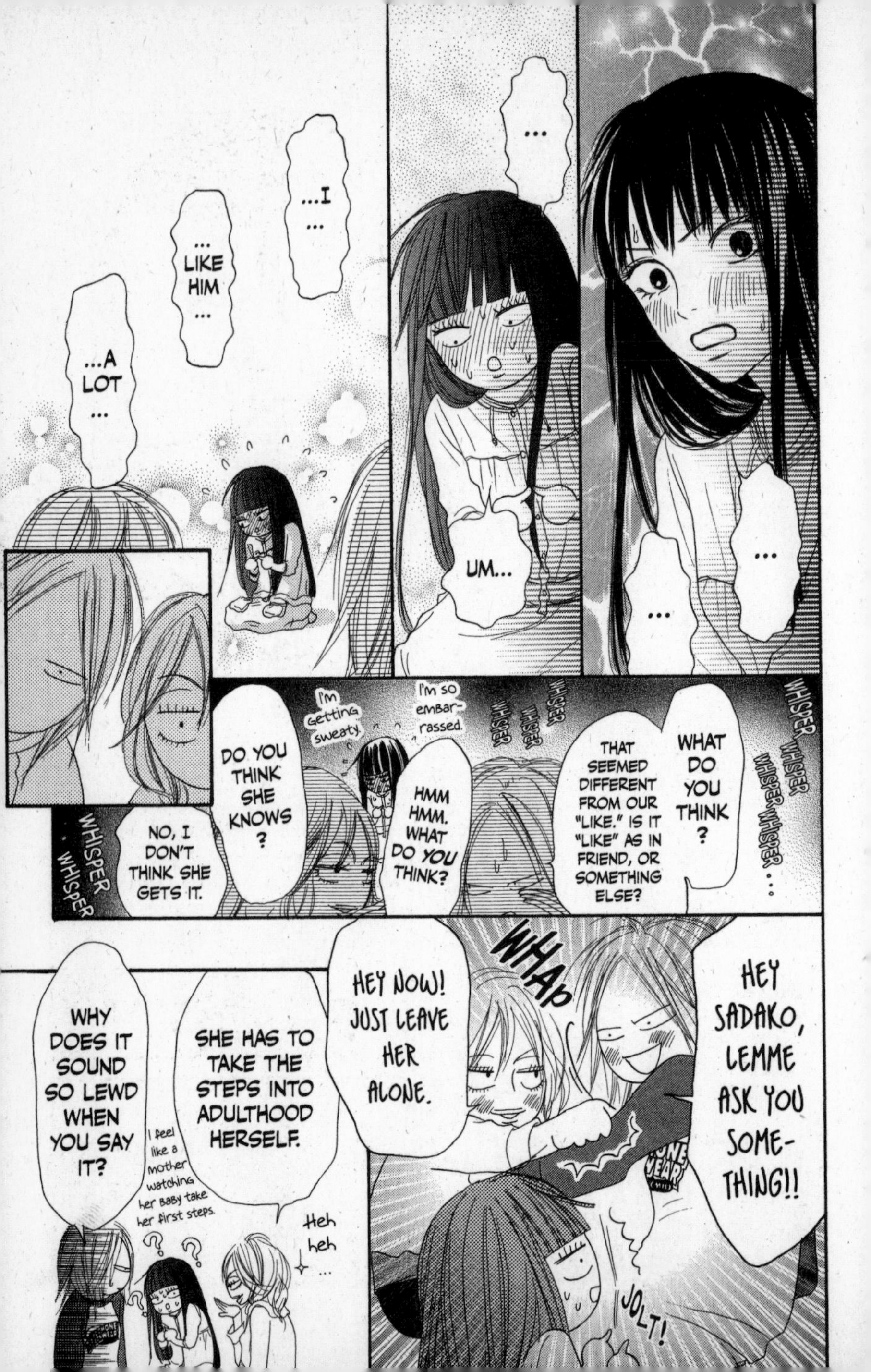
...
...
...
UM...
...I ...
... LIKE HIM ...
...A LOT ...
WHISPER WHISPER WHISPER WHISPER...
WHAT DO YOU THINK ?
THAT SEEMED DIFFERENT FROM OUR "LIKE." IS IT "LIKE" AS IN FRIEND, OR SOMETHING ELSE?
WHISPER WHISPER WHISPER
HMM HMM. WHAT DO *YOU* THINK?
I'm so embar-rassed.
I'm getting sweaty.
DO YOU THINK SHE KNOWS ?
NO, I DON'T THINK SHE GETS IT.
WHISPER WHISPER
HEY SADAKO, LEMME ASK YOU SOME-THING!!
WHAP
HEY NOW! JUST LEAVE HER ALONE.
JOLT!
SHE HAS TO TAKE THE STEPS INTO ADULTHOOD HERSELF.
Heh heh ...
I feel like a mother watching her baby take her first steps.
WHY DOES IT SOUND SO LEWD WHEN YOU SAY IT?

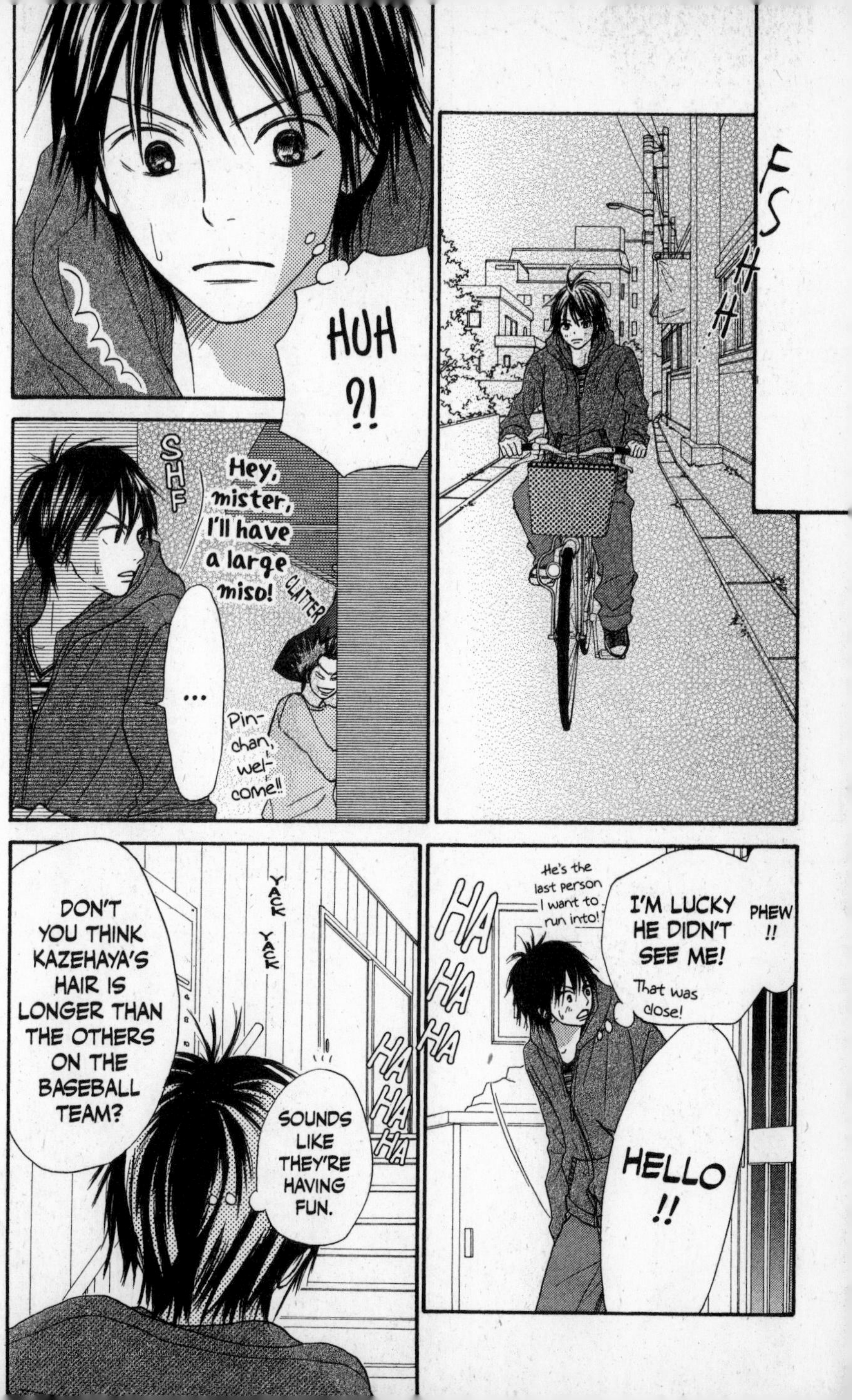
FSHHH
HUH ?!
SHF
Hey, mister, I'll have a large miso!
CLATTER
...
Pin-chan, wel-come!!
PHEW !!
I'M LUCKY HE DIDN'T SEE ME!
That was close!
He's the last person I want to run into!
HA HA HA HA
HA HA HA HA
HELLO !!
DON'T YOU THINK KAZEHAYA'S HAIR IS LONGER THAN THE OTHERS ON THE BASEBALL TEAM?
YACK YACK
SOUNDS LIKE THEY'RE HAVING FUN.

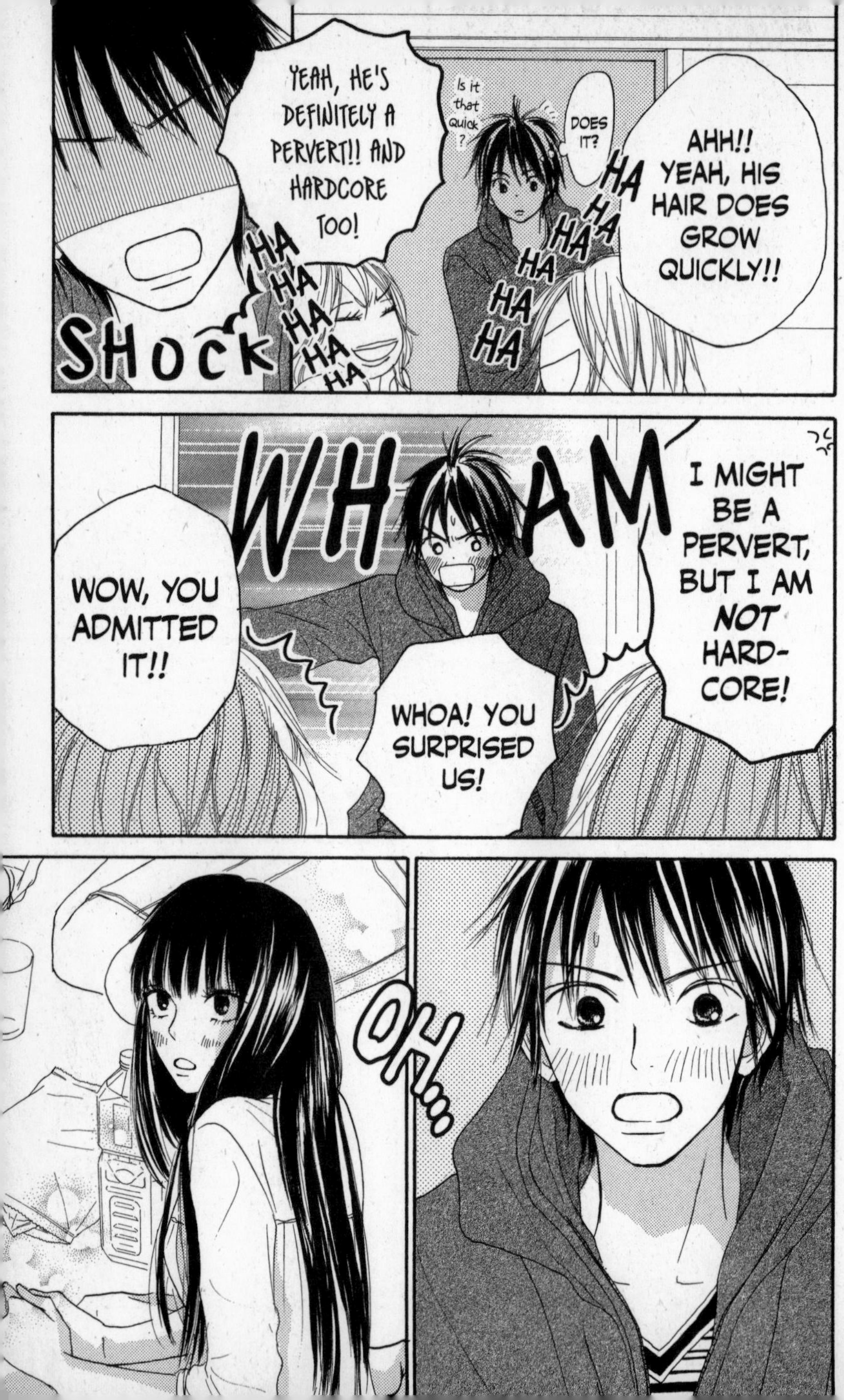
AHH!! YEAH, HIS HAIR DOES GROW QUICKLY!!
HA HA HA HA HA HA
DOES IT?
Is it that quick?
YEAH, HE'S DEFINITELY A PERVERT!! AND HARDCORE TOO!
HA HA HA HA HA HA
SHOCK
WHAM
I MIGHT BE A PERVERT, BUT I AM *NOT* HARD-CORE!
WHOA! YOU SURPRISED US!
WOW, YOU ADMITTED IT!!
OH...

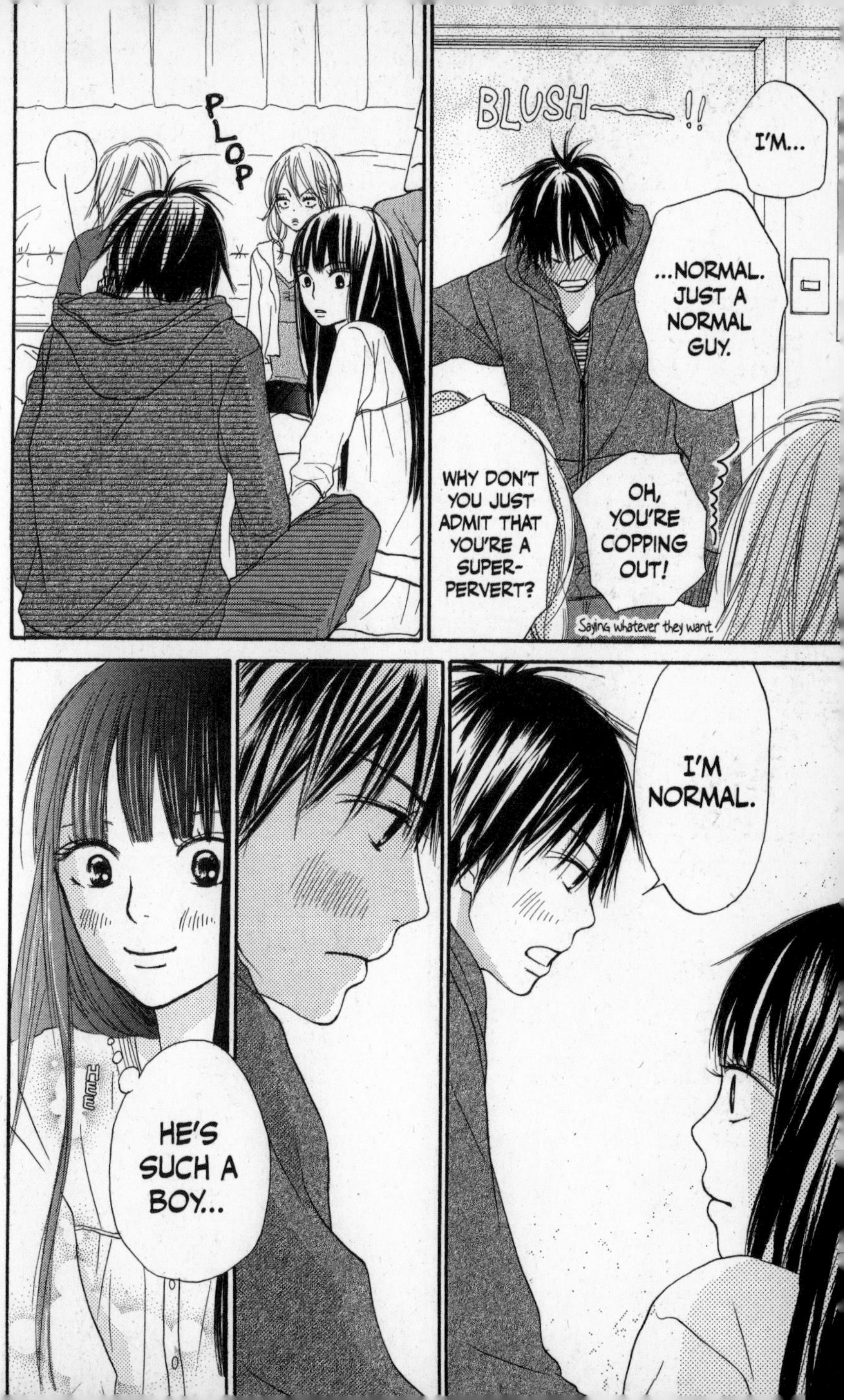
BLUSH——!!
I'M...
...NORMAL. JUST A NORMAL GUY.
OH, YOU'RE COPPING OUT!
WHY DON'T YOU JUST ADMIT THAT YOU'RE A SUPER-PERVERT?
Saying whatever they want.
PLOP
I'M NORMAL.
HEE
HE'S SUCH A BOY...

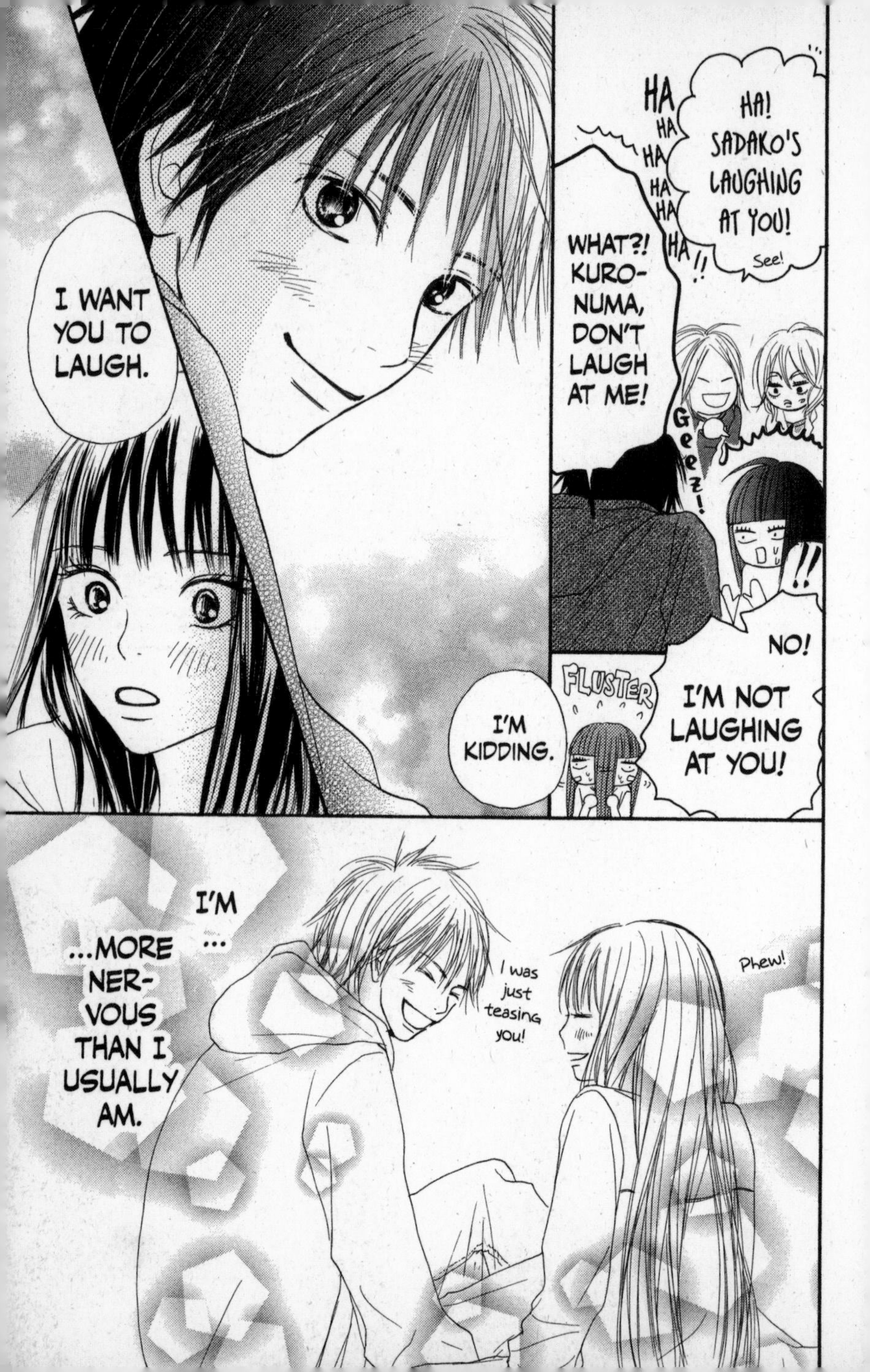
HA! SADAKO'S LAUGHING AT YOU!
See!
HA HA HA HA HA HA!!
WHAT?! KURO-NUMA, DON'T LAUGH AT ME!
Geez!
NO!
I'M NOT LAUGHING AT YOU!
FLUSTER
I'M KIDDING.
I WANT YOU TO LAUGH.
Phew!
I was just teasing you!
I'M ...
...MORE NER-VOUS THAN I USUALLY AM.

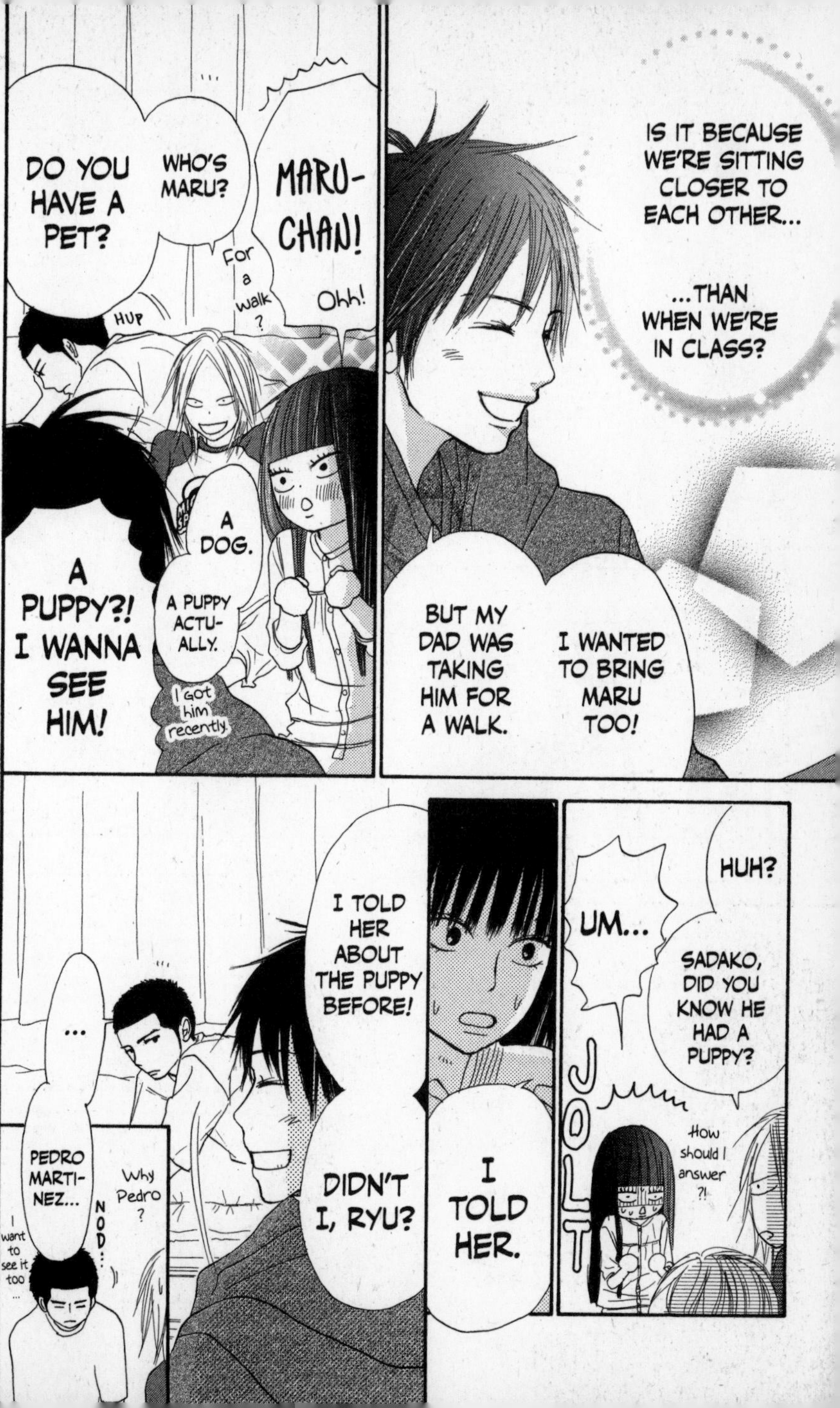
IS IT BECAUSE WE'RE SITTING CLOSER TO EACH OTHER...
...THAN WHEN WE'RE IN CLASS?
I WANTED TO BRING MARU TOO!
BUT MY DAD WAS TAKING HIM FOR A WALK.
MARU-CHAN!
Ohh!
WHO'S MARU?
For a walk?
...
DO YOU HAVE A PET?
HUP
A DOG.
A PUPPY ACTUALLY.
I got him recently.
A PUPPY?! I WANNA SEE HIM!
HUH?
SADAKO, DID YOU KNOW HE HAD A PUPPY?
UM...
JOLT
How should I answer?!
I TOLD HER ABOUT THE PUPPY BEFORE!
I TOLD HER.
DIDN'T I, RYU?
...
...
PEDRO MARTINEZ...
Why Pedro?
NOD...
I want to see it too...

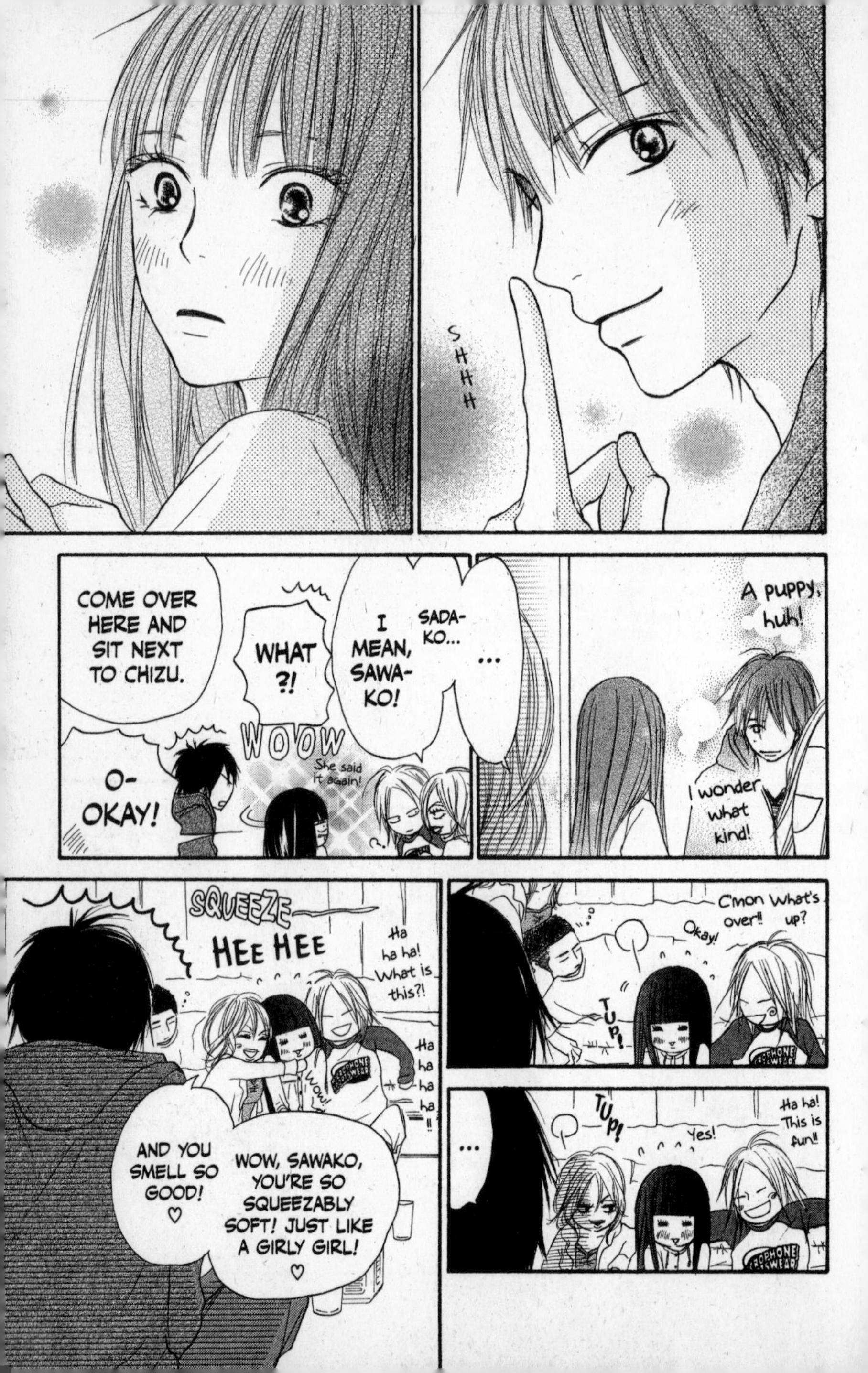
SHHH
A puppy, huh!
I wonder what kind!
...
SADA-KO... I MEAN, SAWA-KO!
WHAT?!
COME OVER HERE AND SIT NEXT TO CHIZU.
WOOW
She said it again!
O-OKAY!
What's up?
C'mon over!!
Okay!
TUP!
Ha ha! This is fun!!
Yes!
TUP!
...
Ha ha ha! What is this?!
Ha ha ha ha!!
HEE HEE
SQUEEZE
WOW, SAWAKO, YOU'RE SO SQUEEZABLY SOFT! JUST LIKE A GIRLY GIRL! ♡
AND YOU SMELL SO GOOD! ♡
Wow!

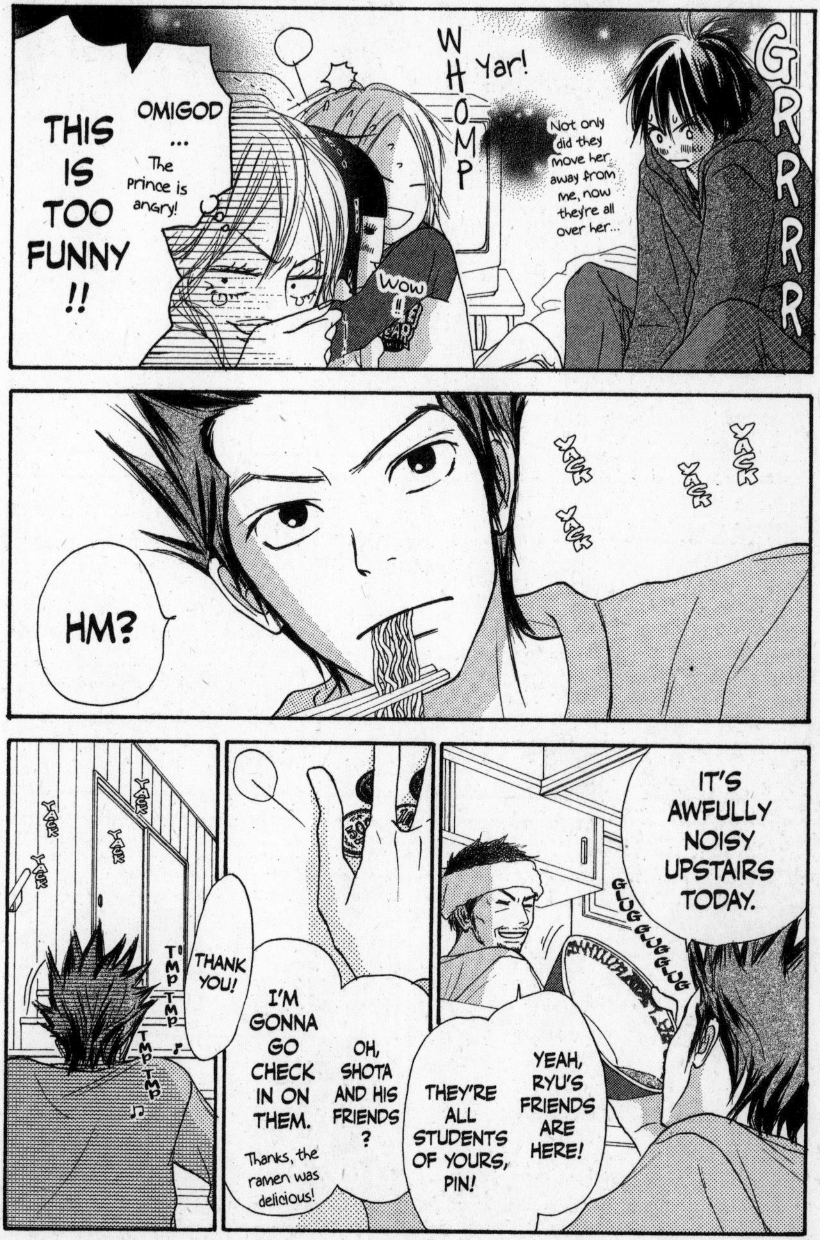
GRRRR
Not only did they move her away from me, now they're all over her...
WHOMP
Yar!
WOW!!
OMIGOD... The prince is angry!
THIS IS TOO FUNNY!!
YACK
YACK
YACK
HM?
IT'S AWFULLY NOISY UPSTAIRS TODAY.
GLUG GLUG GLUG GLUG
YEAH, RYU'S FRIENDS ARE HERE!
THEY'RE ALL STUDENTS OF YOURS, PIN!
OH, SHOTA AND HIS FRIENDS?
I'M GONNA GO CHECK IN ON THEM.
Thanks, the ramen was delicious!
THANK YOU!
YACK
YACK
YACK
TMP TMP TMP TMP

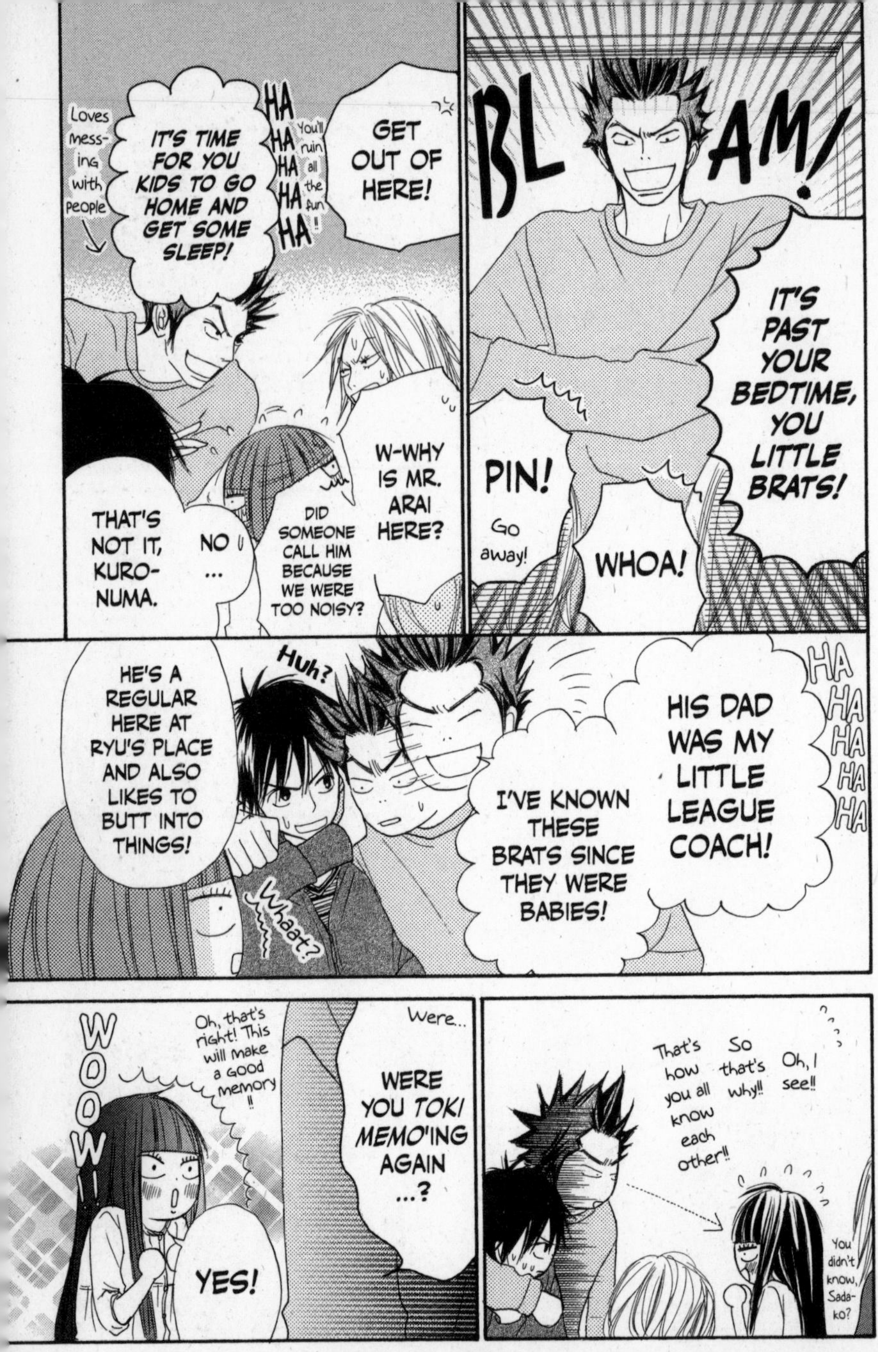
BLAM!
IT'S PAST YOUR BEDTIME, YOU LITTLE BRATS!
PIN!
Go away!
WHOA!
GET OUT OF HERE!
You'll ruin all the fun!!
HA HA HA HA HA
IT'S TIME FOR YOU KIDS TO GO HOME AND GET SOME SLEEP!
Loves messing with people
W-WHY IS MR. ARAI HERE?
DID SOMEONE CALL HIM BECAUSE WE WERE TOO NOISY?
NO...
THAT'S NOT IT, KURONUMA.
HA HA HA HA HA
HIS DAD WAS MY LITTLE LEAGUE COACH!
I'VE KNOWN THESE BRATS SINCE THEY WERE BABIES!
Huh?
HE'S A REGULAR HERE AT RYU'S PLACE AND ALSO LIKES TO BUTT INTO THINGS!
Whaat?
Oh, I see!!
So that's why!!
That's how you all know each other!!
You didn't know, Sadako?
Were...
WERE YOU TOKI MEMO'ING AGAIN...?
Oh, that's right! This will make a good memory!!
WOOOW!
YES!

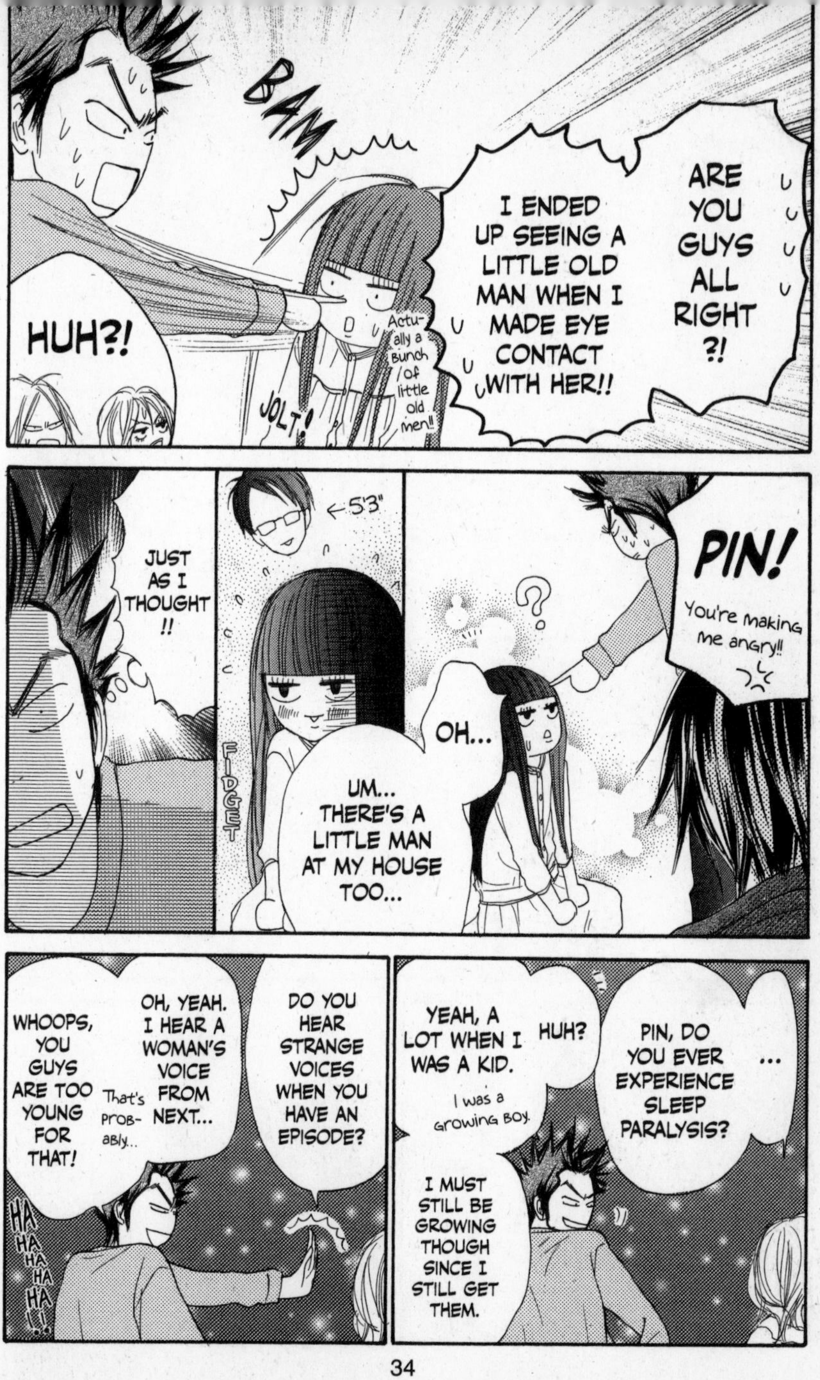
ARE YOU GUYS ALL RIGHT?!
I ENDED UP SEEING A LITTLE OLD MAN WHEN I MADE EYE CONTACT WITH HER!!
Actually a bunch of little old men!!
BAM
JOLT!
HUH?!
PIN!
You're making me angry!!
OH...
← 5'3"
UM... THERE'S A LITTLE MAN AT MY HOUSE TOO...
FIDGET
JUST AS I THOUGHT!!
...
PIN, DO YOU EVER EXPERIENCE SLEEP PARALYSIS?
HUH?
YEAH, A LOT WHEN I WAS A KID.
I was a growing boy.
I MUST STILL BE GROWING THOUGH SINCE I STILL GET THEM.
DO YOU HEAR STRANGE VOICES WHEN YOU HAVE AN EPISODE?
OH, YEAH. I HEAR A WOMAN'S VOICE FROM NEXT...
That's probably...
WHOOPS, YOU GUYS ARE TOO YOUNG FOR THAT!
HAHAHAHAHA!!

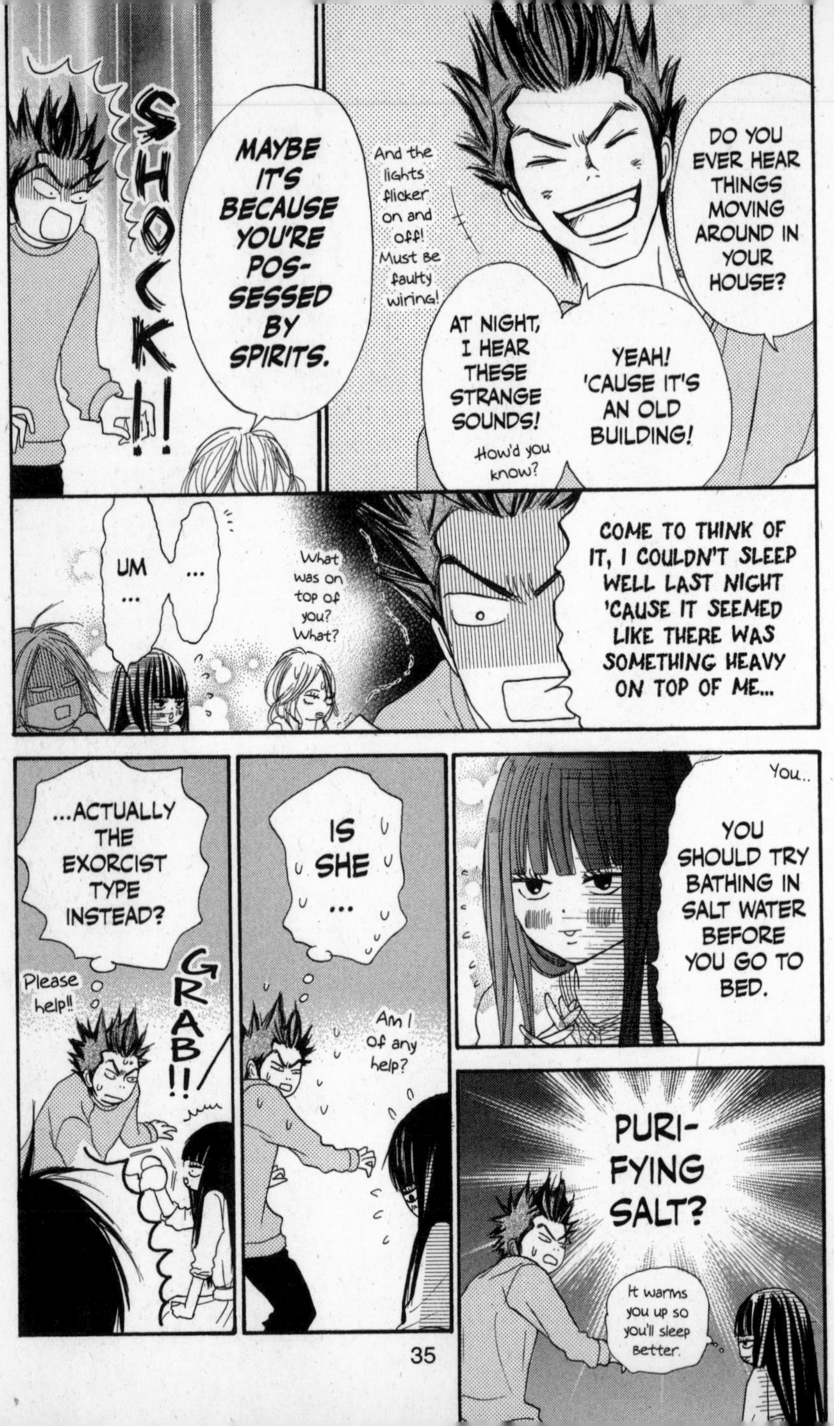
DO YOU EVER HEAR THINGS MOVING AROUND IN YOUR HOUSE?
YEAH! 'CAUSE IT'S AN OLD BUILDING!
AT NIGHT, I HEAR THESE STRANGE SOUNDS!
How'd you know?
And the lights flicker on and off! Must be faulty wiring!
MAYBE IT'S BECAUSE YOU'RE POS-SESSED BY SPIRITS.
SHOCK!!
COME TO THINK OF IT, I COULDN'T SLEEP WELL LAST NIGHT 'CAUSE IT SEEMED LIKE THERE WAS SOMETHING HEAVY ON TOP OF ME...
What was on top of you? What?
UM... ...
You...
YOU SHOULD TRY BATHING IN SALT WATER BEFORE YOU GO TO BED.
PURI-FYING SALT?
It warms you up so you'll sleep better.
IS SHE...
Am I of any help?
...ACTUALLY THE EXORCIST TYPE INSTEAD?
GRAB!!
Please help!!

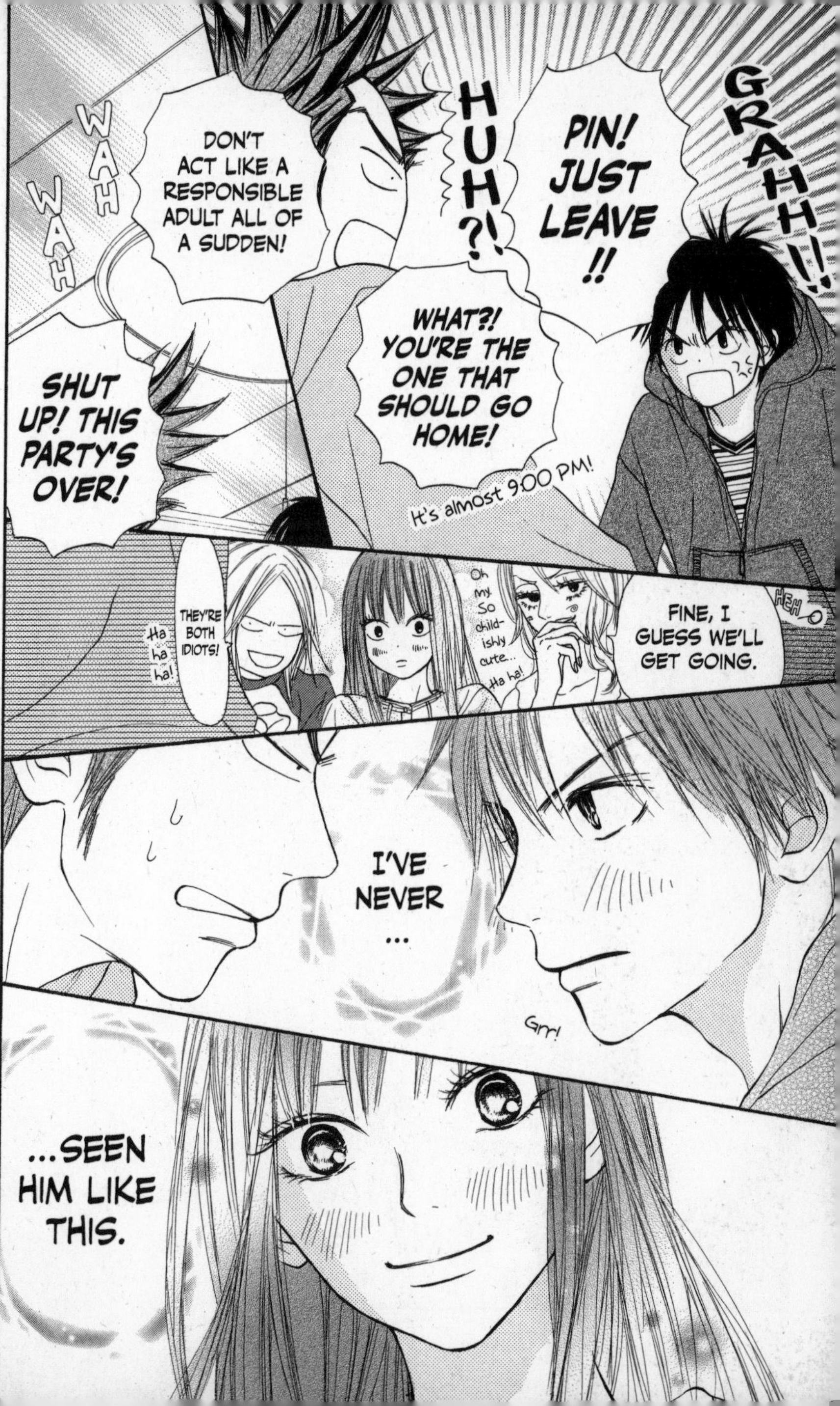
GRAHH!!
PIN! JUST LEAVE!!
HUH?!
DON'T ACT LIKE A RESPONSIBLE ADULT ALL OF A SUDDEN!
WAH WAH
WHAT?! YOU'RE THE ONE THAT SHOULD GO HOME!
It's almost 9:00 PM!
SHUT UP! THIS PARTY'S OVER!
HEH
FINE, I GUESS WE'LL GET GOING.
Oh my. So childishly cute... Ha ha!
THEY'RE BOTH IDIOTS!
Ha ha ha!
I'VE NEVER ...
Grr!
...SEEN HIM LIKE THIS.

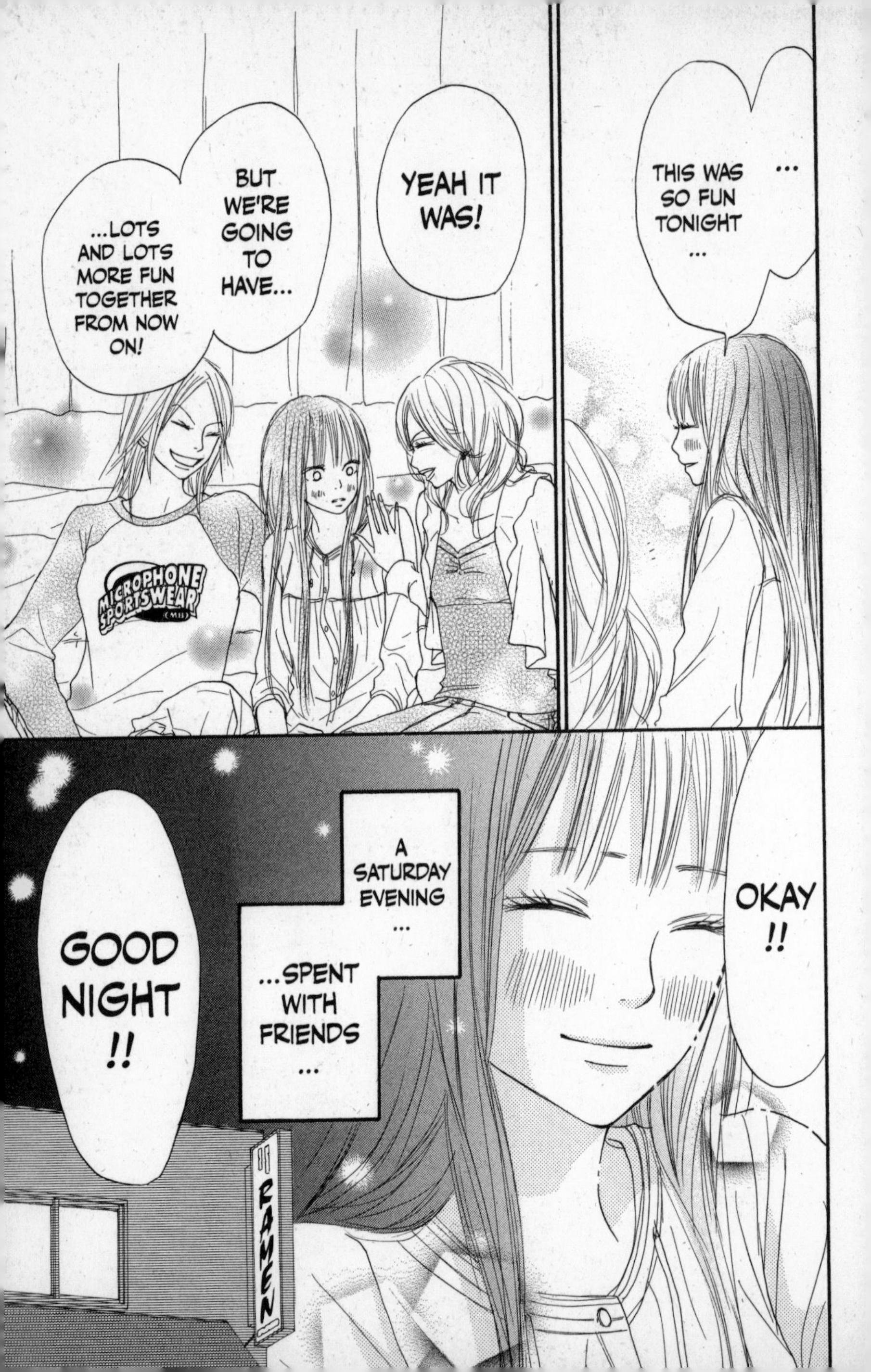
...
THIS WAS SO FUN TONIGHT ...
YEAH IT WAS!
BUT WE'RE GOING TO HAVE...
...LOTS AND LOTS MORE FUN TOGETHER FROM NOW ON!
MICROPHONE SPORTSWEAR
OKAY !!
A SATURDAY EVENING ...
...SPENT WITH FRIENDS ...
GOOD NIGHT !!
RAMEN

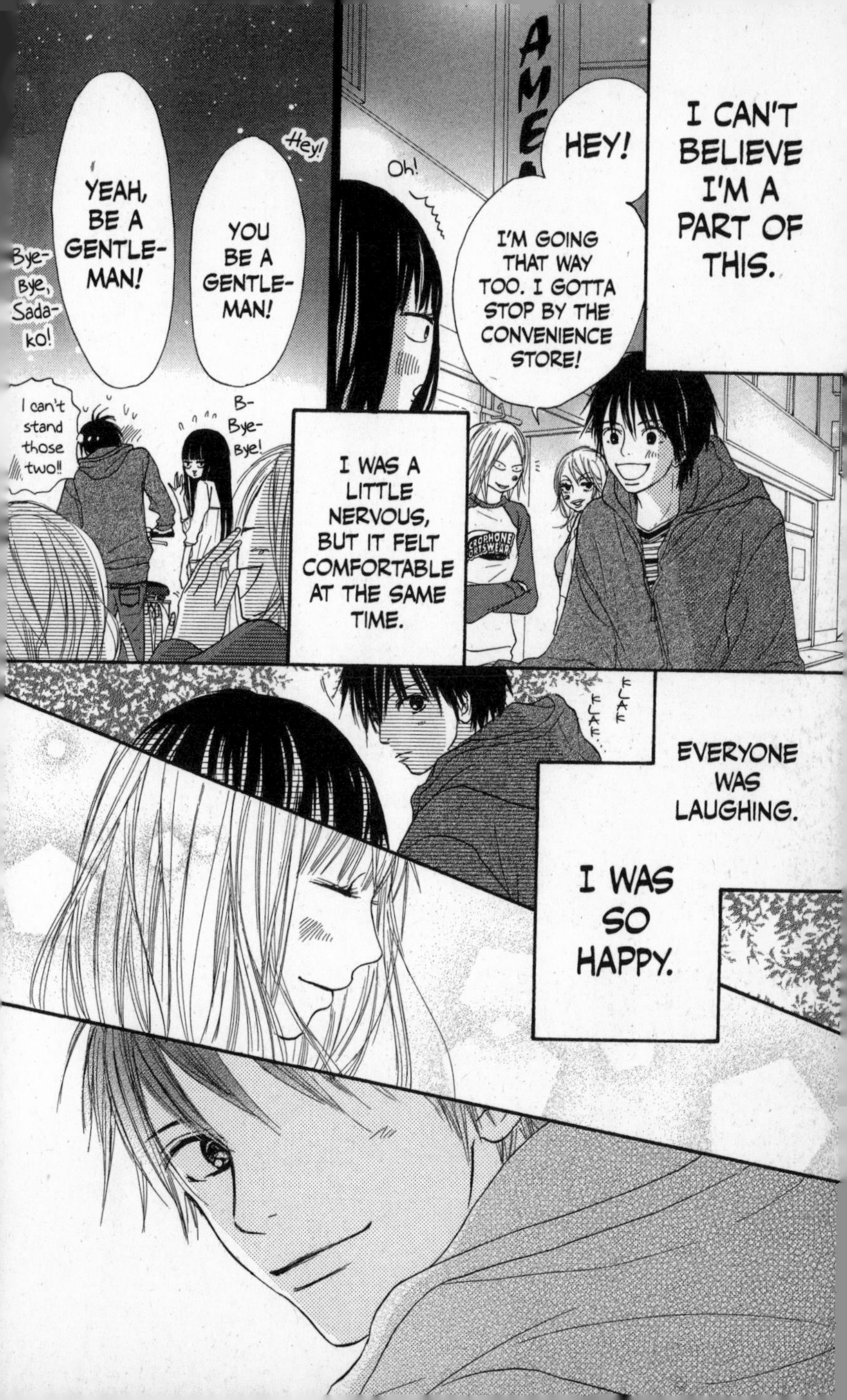
I CAN'T BELIEVE I'M A PART OF THIS.
HEY!
I'M GOING THAT WAY TOO. I GOTTA STOP BY THE CONVENIENCE STORE!
Oh!
I WAS A LITTLE NERVOUS, BUT IT FELT COMFORTABLE AT THE SAME TIME.
Hey!
YOU BE A GENTLEMAN!
YEAH, BE A GENTLEMAN!
Bye-Bye, Sadako!
B-Bye-Bye!
I can't stand those two!!
KLAK
KLAK...
EVERYONE WAS LAUGHING.
I WAS SO HAPPY.

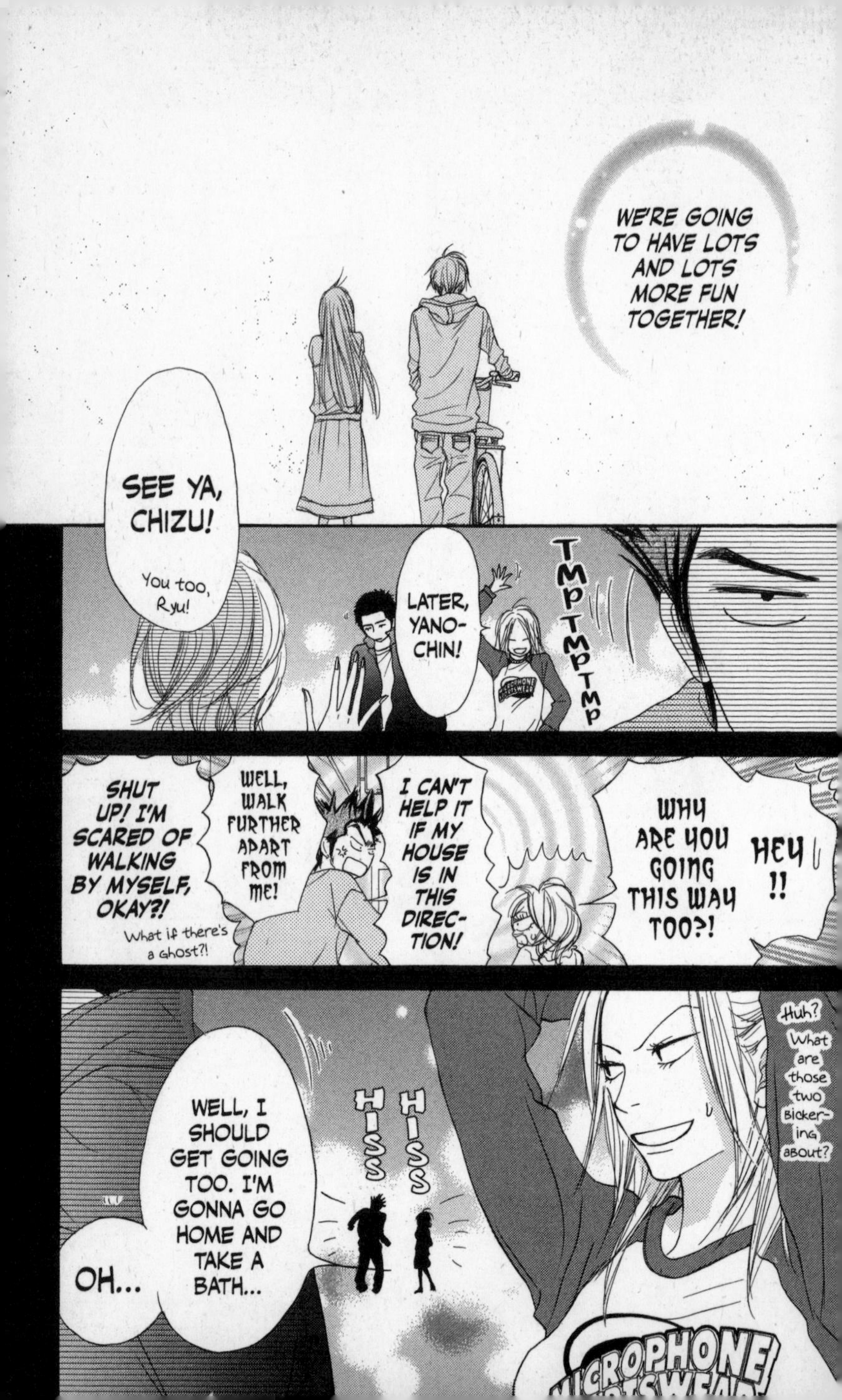
WE'RE GOING TO HAVE LOTS AND LOTS MORE FUN TOGETHER!
SEE YA, CHIZU!
You too, Ryu!
TMP TMP TMP TMP
LATER, YANO-CHIN!
HEY!!
WHY ARE YOU GOING THIS WAY TOO?!
I CAN'T HELP IT IF MY HOUSE IS IN THIS DIREC-TION!
WELL, WALK FURTHER APART FROM ME!
SHUT UP! I'M SCARED OF WALKING BY MYSELF, OKAY?!
What if there's a Ghost?!
Huh? What are those two Bicker-ing about?
HISS HISS
WELL, I SHOULD GET GOING TOO. I'M GONNA GO HOME AND TAKE A BATH...
OH...

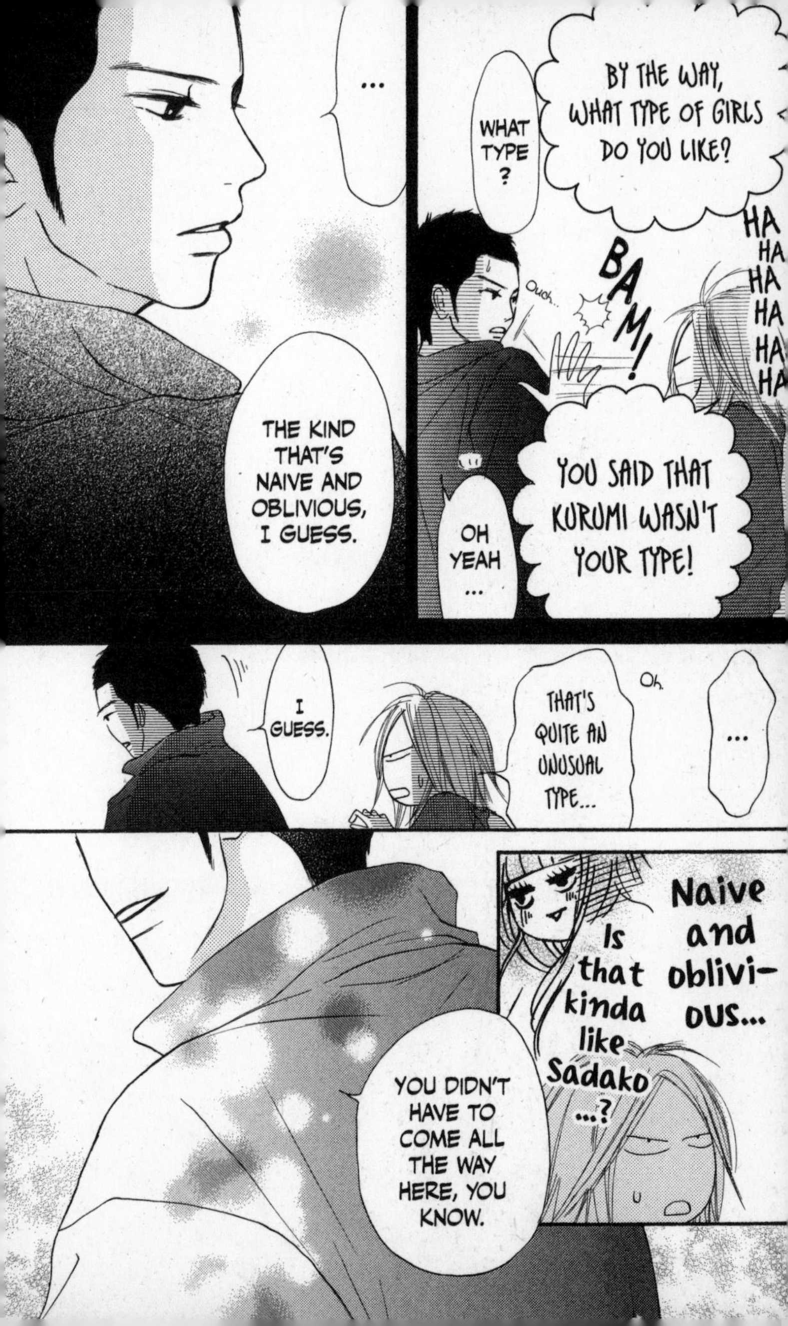
BY THE WAY, WHAT TYPE OF GIRLS DO YOU LIKE?
WHAT TYPE?
Ouch...
BAM!
HA HA HA HA HA HA
YOU SAID THAT KURUMI WASN'T YOUR TYPE!
OH YEAH...
...
THE KIND THAT'S NAIVE AND OBLIVIOUS, I GUESS.
...
Oh.
THAT'S QUITE AN UNUSUAL TYPE...
I GUESS.
Naive and oblivious...
Is that kinda like Sadako...?
YOU DIDN'T HAVE TO COME ALL THE WAY HERE, YOU KNOW.

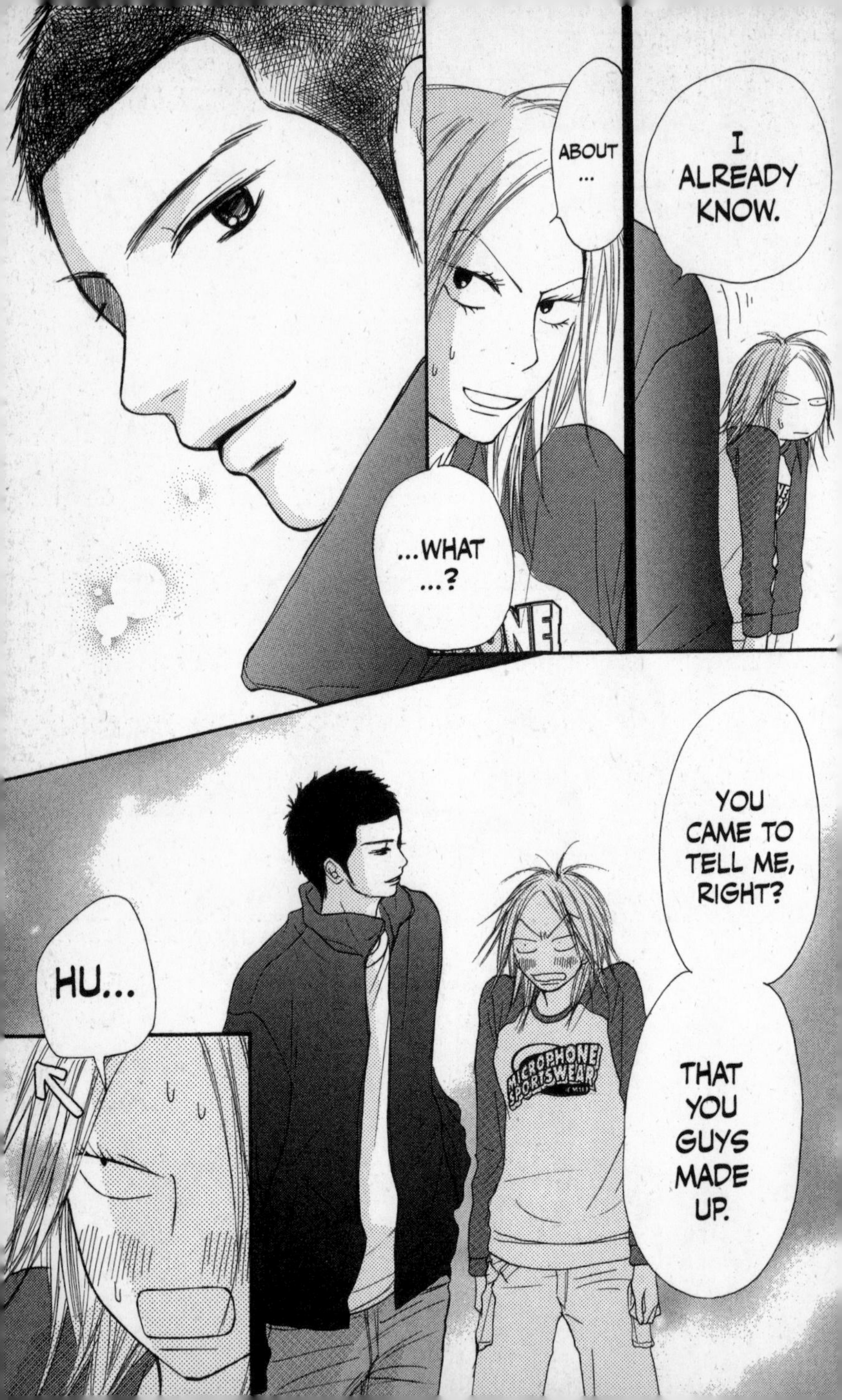
I ALREADY KNOW.
ABOUT ...
...WHAT ...?
YOU CAME TO TELL ME, RIGHT?
THAT YOU GUYS MADE UP.
MICROPHONE SPORTSWEAR
HU...

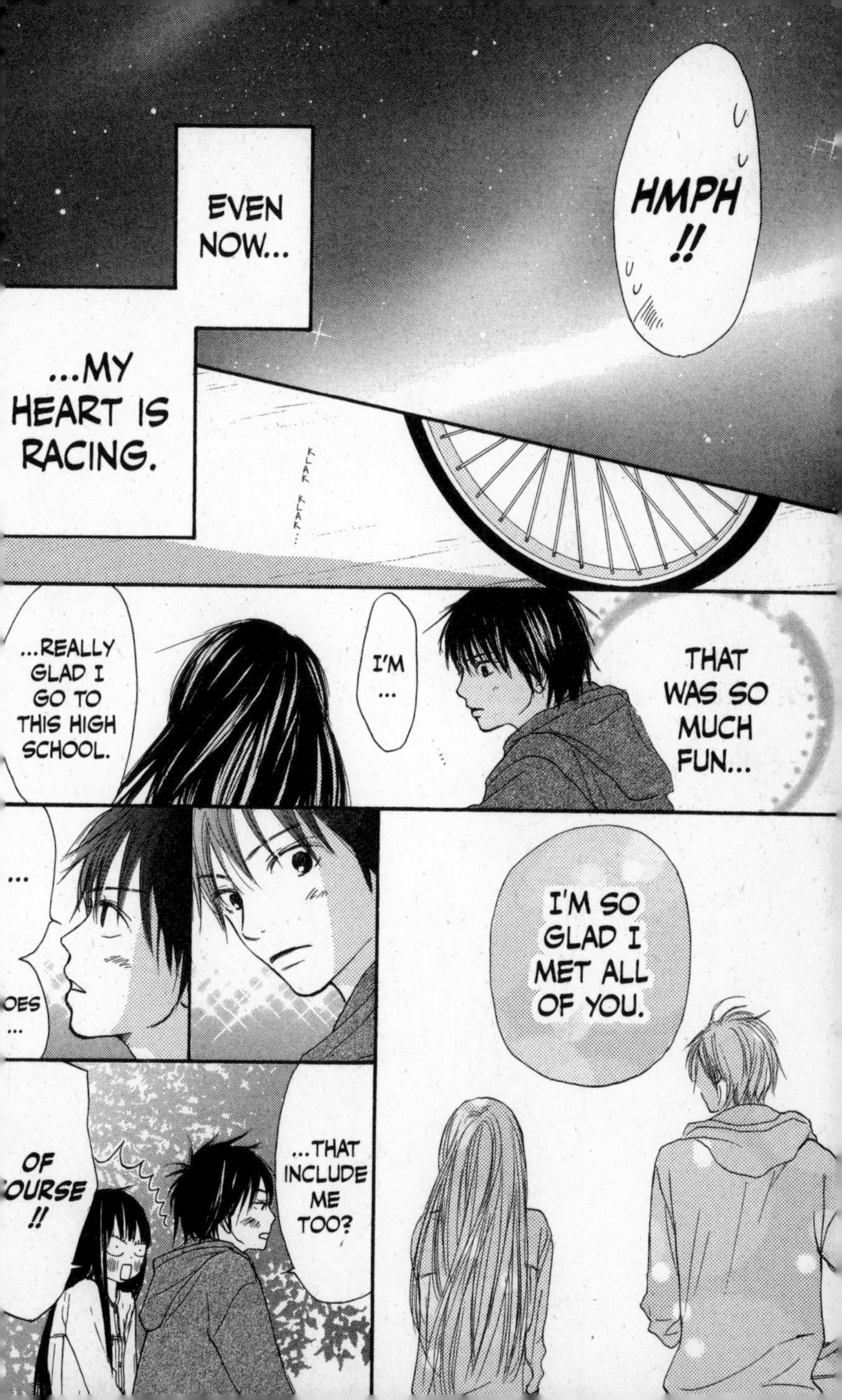
HMPH !!
EVEN NOW...
...MY HEART IS RACING.
KLAR KLAR...
THAT WAS SO MUCH FUN...
I'M ...
...REALLY GLAD I GO TO THIS HIGH SCHOOL.
I'M SO GLAD I MET ALL OF YOU.
...
OES ...
...THAT INCLUDE ME TOO?
OF OURSE !!

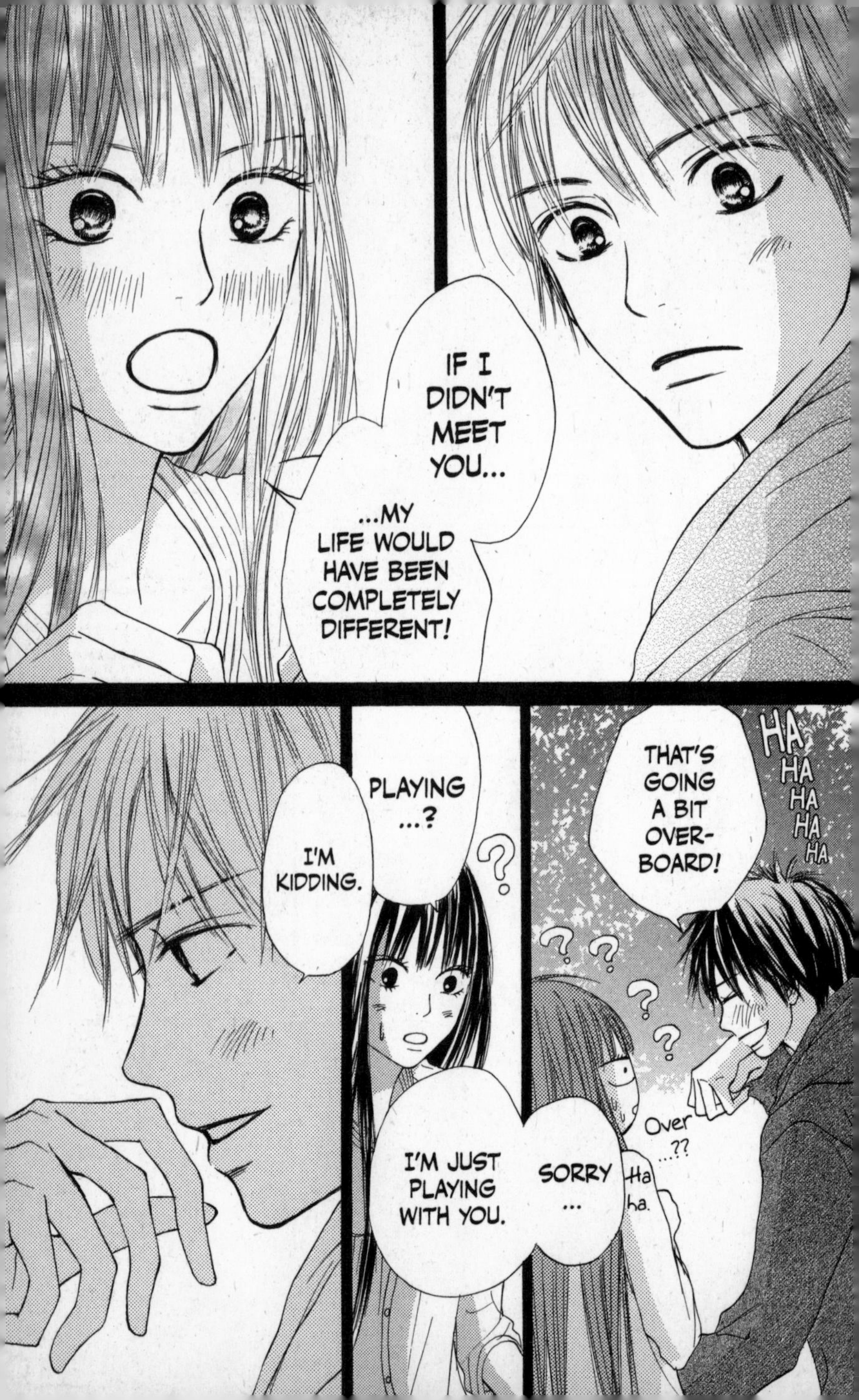
IF I DIDN'T MEET YOU...
...MY LIFE WOULD HAVE BEEN COMPLETELY DIFFERENT!
HA HA HA HA HA
THAT'S GOING A BIT OVER-BOARD!
Over ...??
Ha ha.
SORRY ...
I'M JUST PLAYING WITH YOU.
PLAYING ...?
I'M KIDDING.

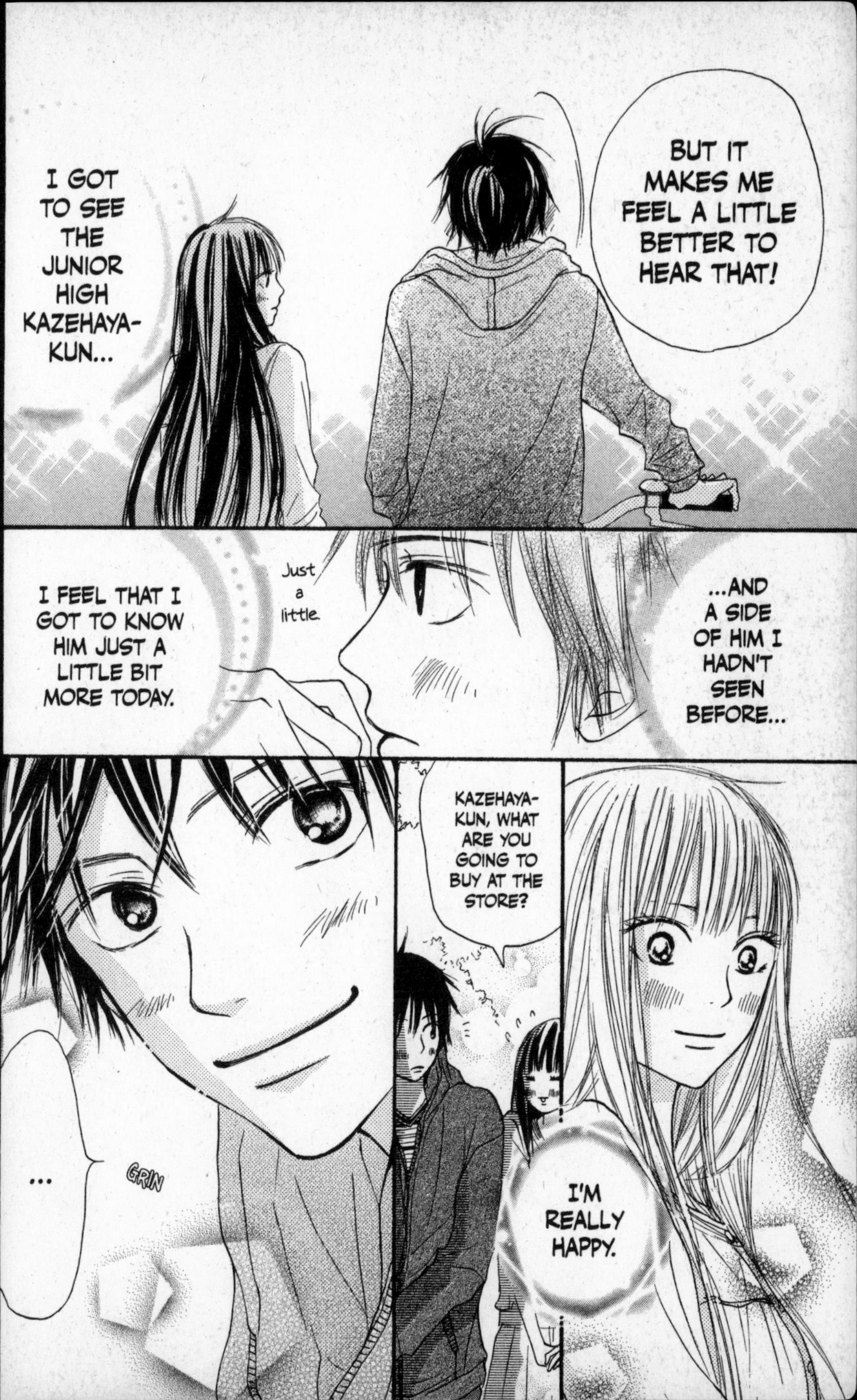
BUT IT MAKES ME FEEL A LITTLE BETTER TO HEAR THAT!
I GOT TO SEE THE JUNIOR HIGH KAZEHAYA-KUN...
...AND A SIDE OF HIM I HADN'T SEEN BEFORE...
Just a little.
I FEEL THAT I GOT TO KNOW HIM JUST A LITTLE BIT MORE TODAY.
I'M REALLY HAPPY.
KAZEHAYA-KUN, WHAT ARE YOU GOING TO BUY AT THE STORE?
...
GRIN

Hmm ...
WHAT SHOULD I GET?
HUH? WHAT ...?
AND HOPE-FULLY ...
I'LL GET TO KNOW A LOT MORE ABOUT HIM FROM NOW ON.

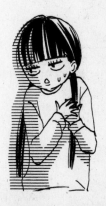

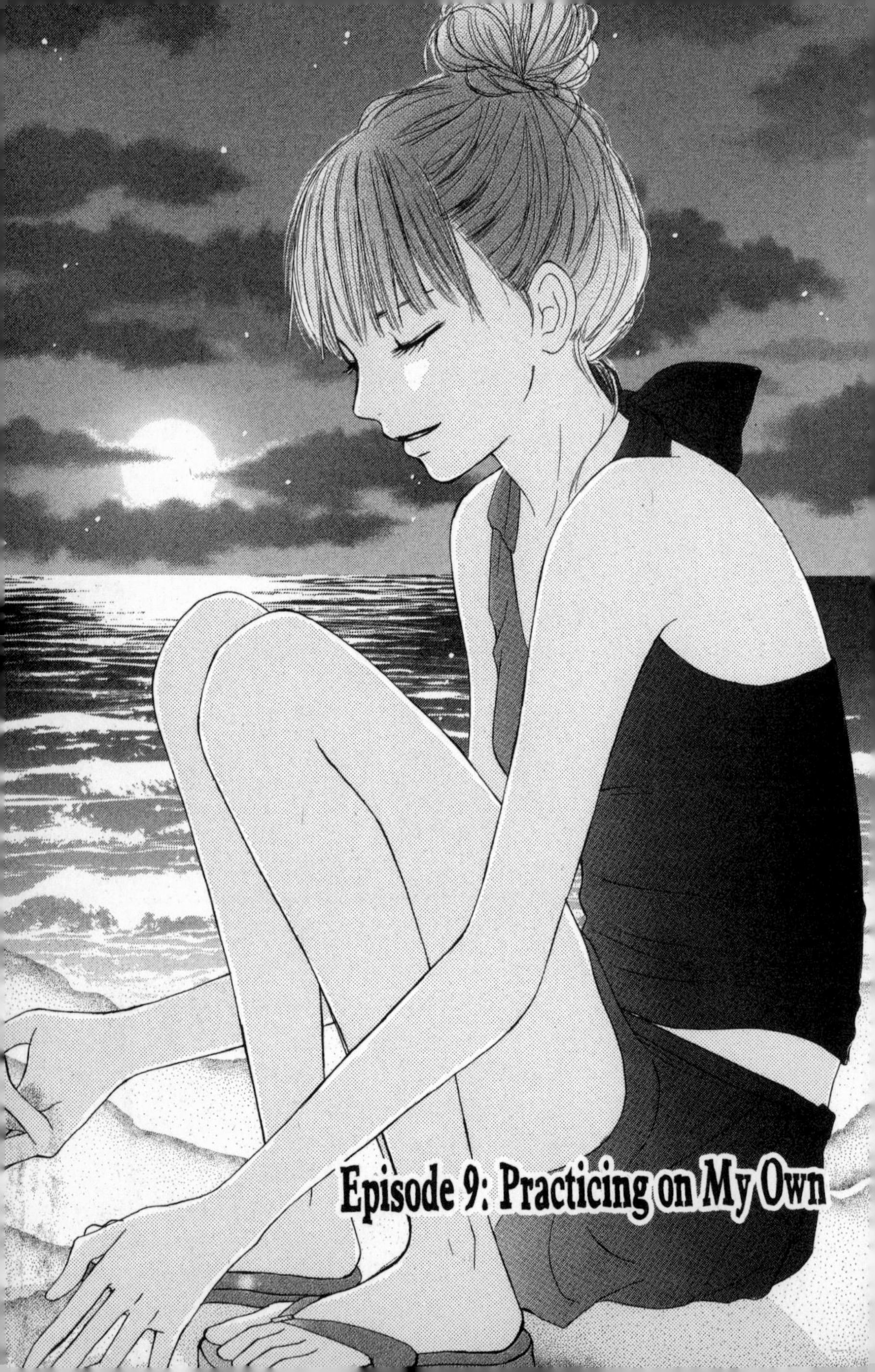
Episode 9: Practicing on My Own

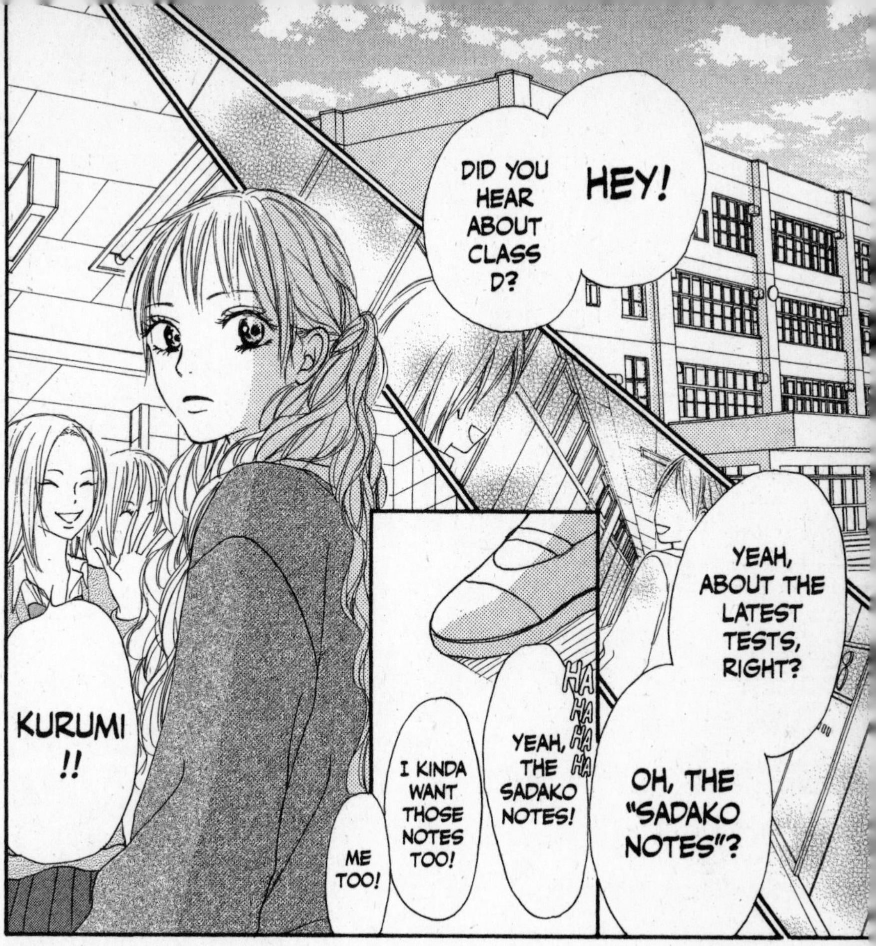
HEY!
DID YOU HEAR ABOUT CLASS D?
YEAH, ABOUT THE LATEST TESTS, RIGHT?
OH, THE "SADAKO NOTES"?
YEAH, THE SADAKO NOTES!
HA HA HA HA
I KINDA WANT THOSE NOTES TOO!
ME TOO!
KURUMI!!
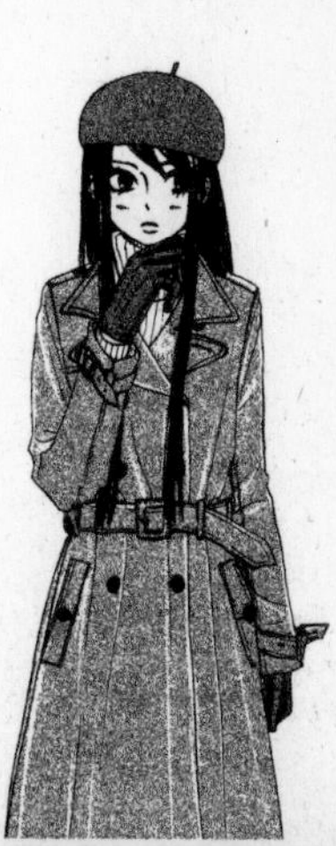

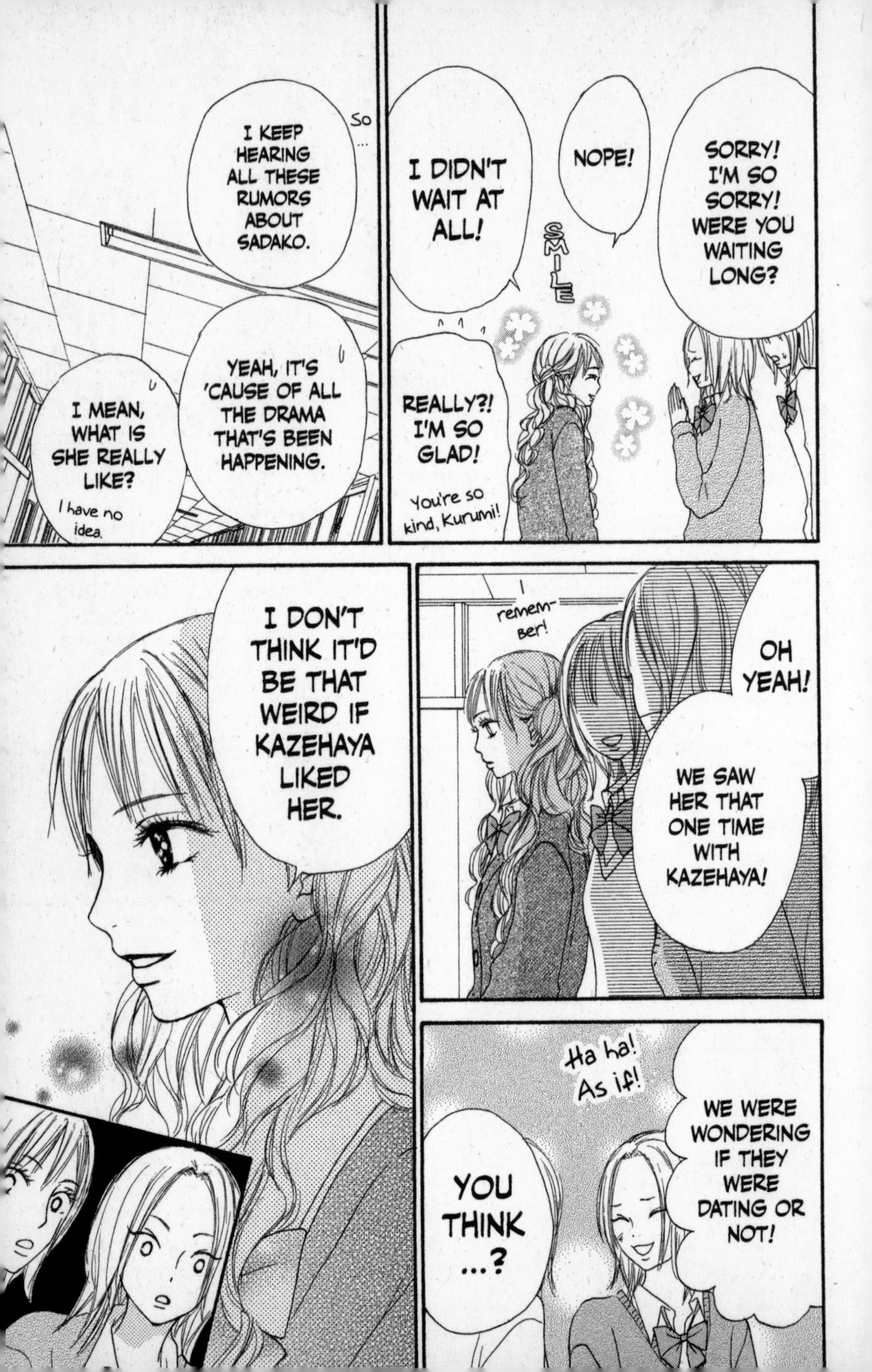
SORRY! I'M SO SORRY! WERE YOU WAITING LONG?
NOPE!
SMILE
I DIDN'T WAIT AT ALL!
REALLY?! I'M SO GLAD!
You're so kind, Kurumi!
So...
I KEEP HEARING ALL THESE RUMORS ABOUT SADAKO.
YEAH, IT'S 'CAUSE OF ALL THE DRAMA THAT'S BEEN HAPPENING.
I MEAN, WHAT IS SHE REALLY LIKE?
I have no idea.
OH YEAH!
I remember!
WE SAW HER THAT ONE TIME WITH KAZEHAYA!
WE WERE WONDERING IF THEY WERE DATING OR NOT!
Ha ha! As if!
YOU THINK ...?
I DON'T THINK IT'D BE THAT WEIRD IF KAZEHAYA LIKED HER.

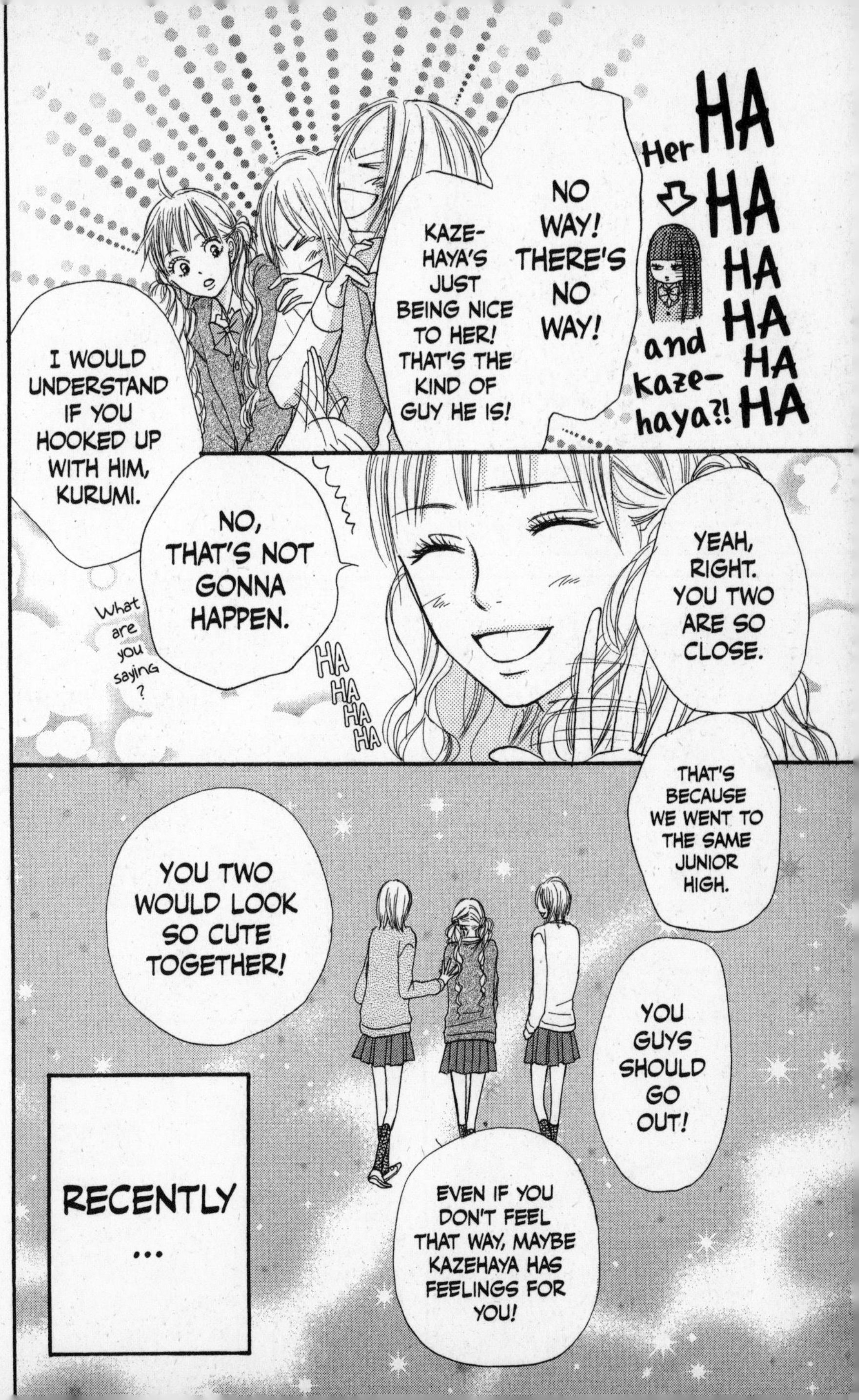
HA HA HA HA HA HA
Her and kaze-haya?!
NO WAY! THERE'S NO WAY!
KAZE-HAYA'S JUST BEING NICE TO HER! THAT'S THE KIND OF GUY HE IS!
I WOULD UNDERSTAND IF YOU HOOKED UP WITH HIM, KURUMI.
YEAH, RIGHT. YOU TWO ARE SO CLOSE.
HA HA HA HA
NO, THAT'S NOT GONNA HAPPEN.
What are you saying?
THAT'S BECAUSE WE WENT TO THE SAME JUNIOR HIGH.
YOU GUYS SHOULD GO OUT!
YOU TWO WOULD LOOK SO CUTE TOGETHER!
EVEN IF YOU DON'T FEEL THAT WAY, MAYBE KAZEHAYA HAS FEELINGS FOR YOU!
RECENTLY ...

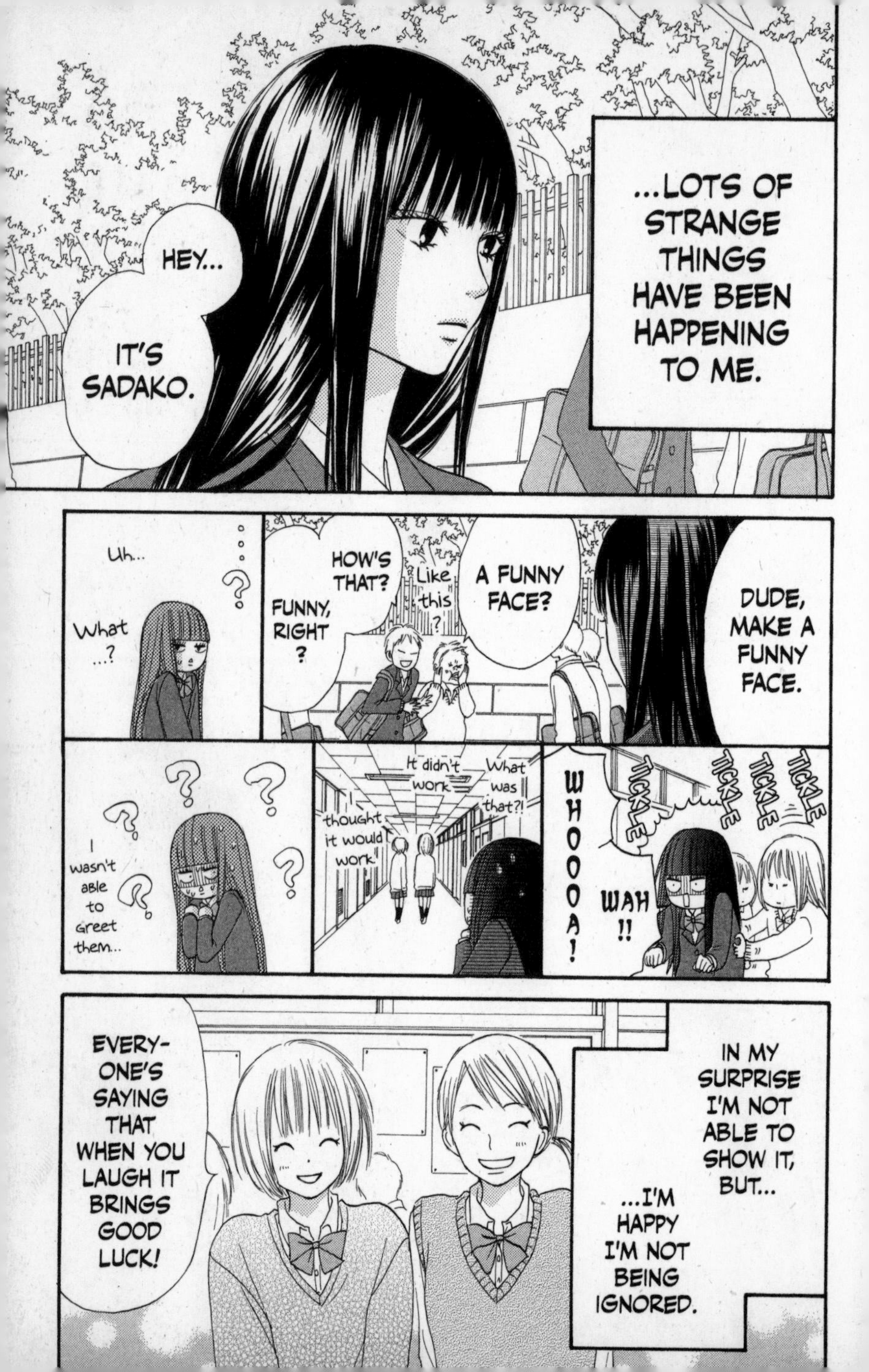
...LOTS OF STRANGE THINGS HAVE BEEN HAPPENING TO ME.
HEY...
IT'S SADAKO.
DUDE, MAKE A FUNNY FACE.
A FUNNY FACE?
Like this?
HOW'S THAT?
FUNNY, RIGHT?
...
?
Uh...
What...?
TICKLE
TICKLE
TICKLE
TICKLE
WHOOOA!
WAH!!
What was that?!
It didn't work
I thought it would work
I wasn't able to greet them...
IN MY SURPRISE I'M NOT ABLE TO SHOW IT, BUT...
...I'M HAPPY I'M NOT BEING IGNORED.
EVERY-ONE'S SAYING THAT WHEN YOU LAUGH IT BRINGS GOOD LUCK!

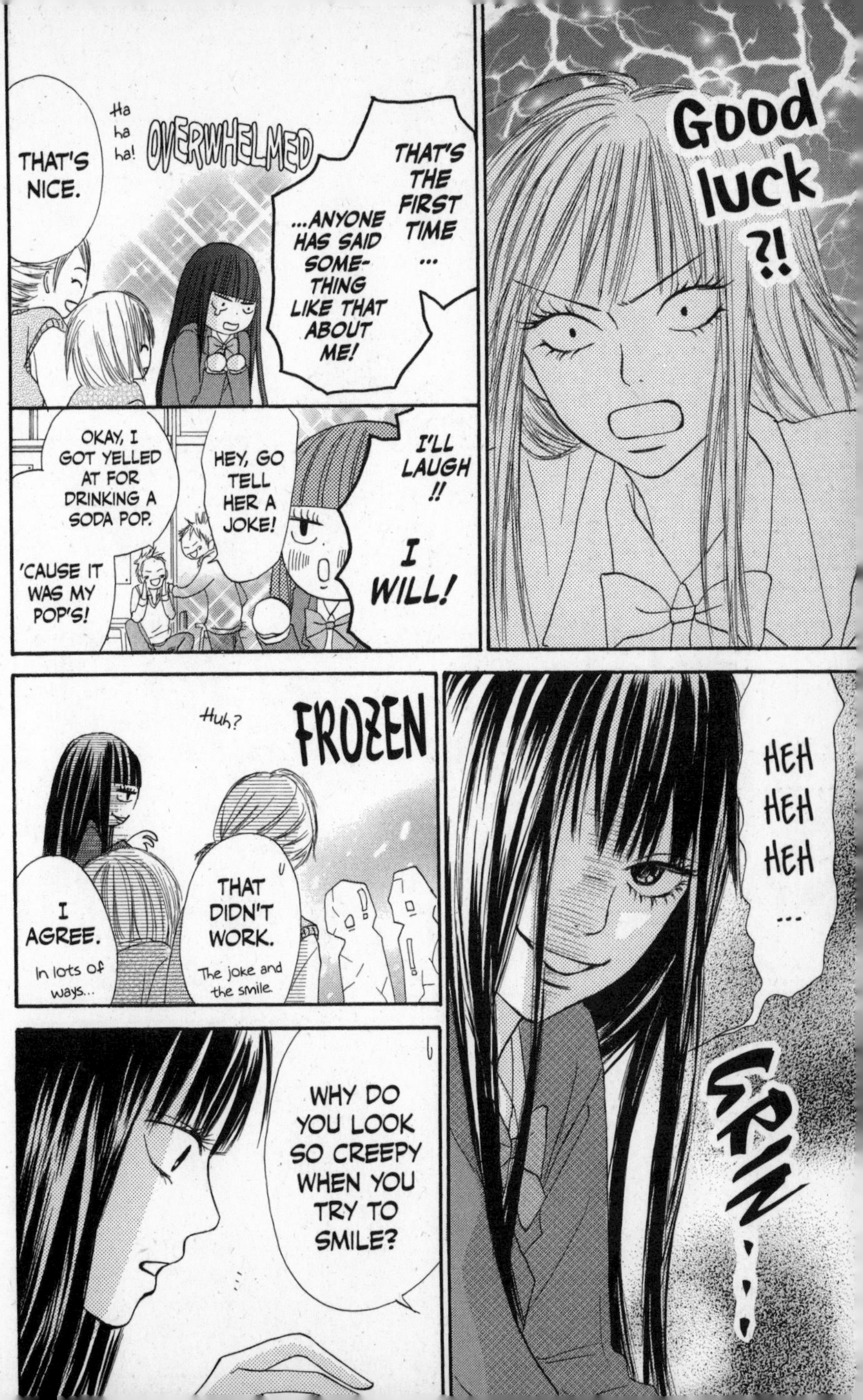
Good luck ?!
THAT'S THE FIRST TIME ...
...ANYONE HAS SAID SOME-THING LIKE THAT ABOUT ME!
OVERWHELMED
Ha ha ha!
THAT'S NICE.
I'LL LAUGH !!
I WILL!
HEY, GO TELL HER A JOKE!
OKAY, I GOT YELLED AT FOR DRINKING A SODA POP.
'CAUSE IT WAS MY POP'S!
HEH HEH HEH ...
GRIN...
FROZEN
Huh?
THAT DIDN'T WORK.
The joke and the smile.
I AGREE.
In lots of ways...
WHY DO YOU LOOK SO CREEPY WHEN YOU TRY TO SMILE?

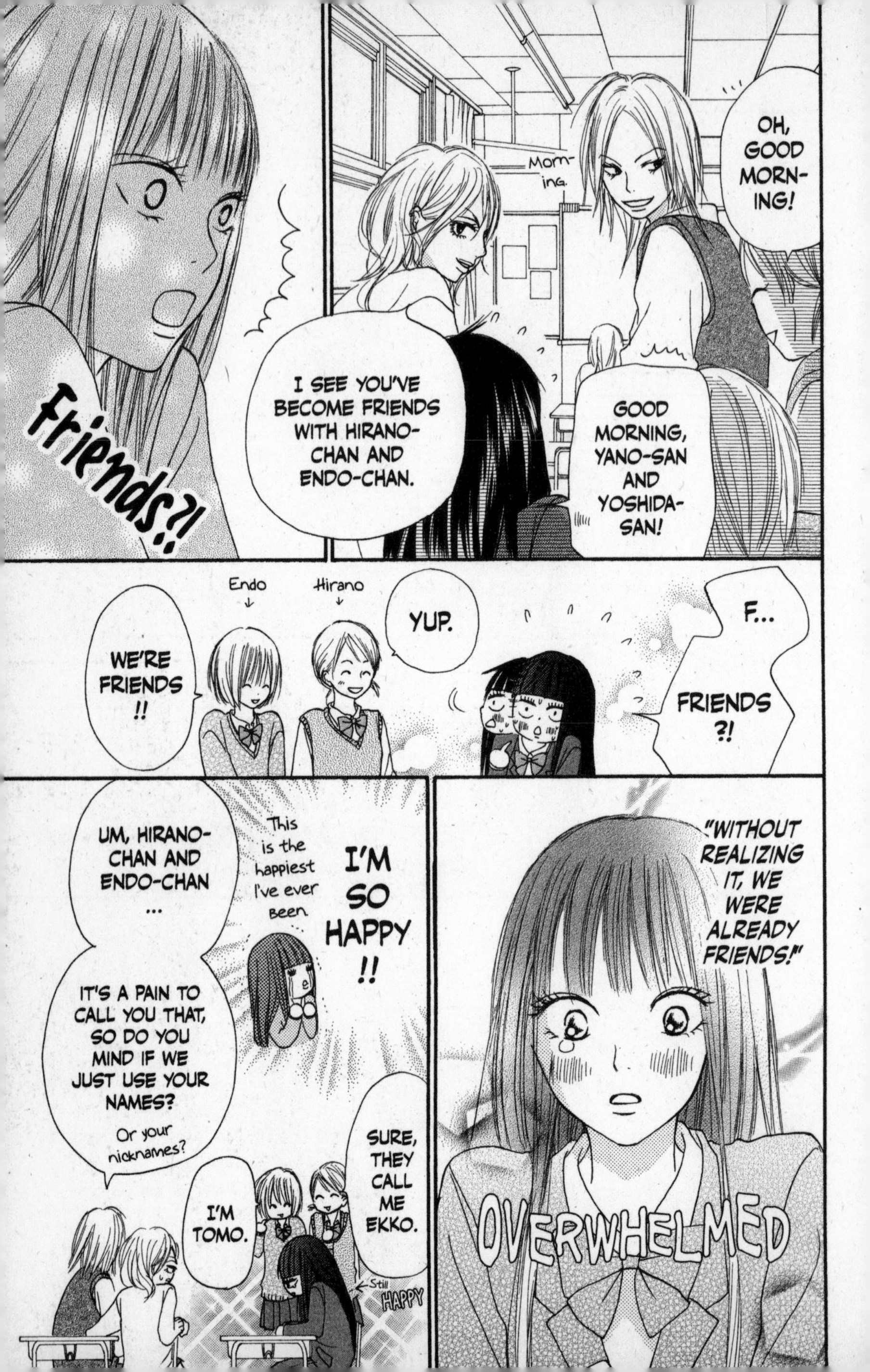
OH, GOOD MORNING!
Morn-ing.
GOOD MORNING, YANO-SAN AND YOSHIDA-SAN!
I SEE YOU'VE BECOME FRIENDS WITH HIRANO-CHAN AND ENDO-CHAN.
Friends?!
F... FRIENDS?!
YUP.
Hirano
Endo
WE'RE FRIENDS!!
"WITHOUT REALIZING IT, WE WERE ALREADY FRIENDS!"
OVERWHELMED
I'M SO HAPPY!!
This is the happiest I've ever been.
UM, HIRANO-CHAN AND ENDO-CHAN ...
IT'S A PAIN TO CALL YOU THAT, SO DO YOU MIND IF WE JUST USE YOUR NAMES?
Or your nicknames?
SURE, THEY CALL ME EKKO.
I'M TOMO.
Still HAPPY

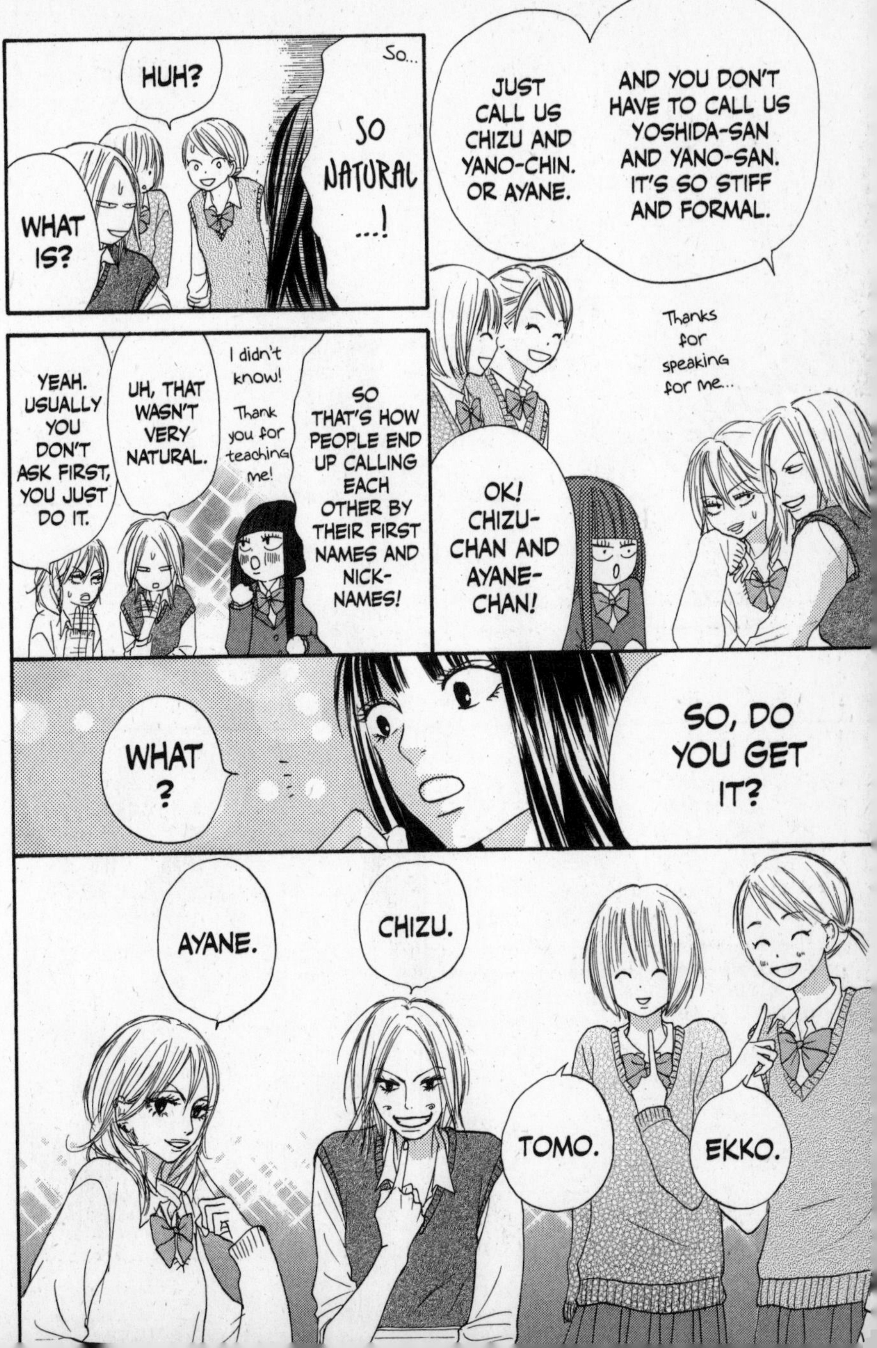
AND YOU DON'T HAVE TO CALL US YOSHIDA-SAN AND YANO-SAN. IT'S SO STIFF AND FORMAL.
JUST CALL US CHIZU AND YANO-CHIN. OR AYANE.
Thanks for speaking for me...
So...
SO NATURAL ...!
HUH?
WHAT IS?
OK! CHIZU-CHAN AND AYANE-CHAN!
SO THAT'S HOW PEOPLE END UP CALLING EACH OTHER BY THEIR FIRST NAMES AND NICK-NAMES!
I didn't know!
Thank you for teaching me!
UH, THAT WASN'T VERY NATURAL.
YEAH. USUALLY YOU DON'T ASK FIRST, YOU JUST DO IT.
SO, DO YOU GET IT?
WHAT ?
EKKO.
TOMO.
CHIZU.
AYANE.

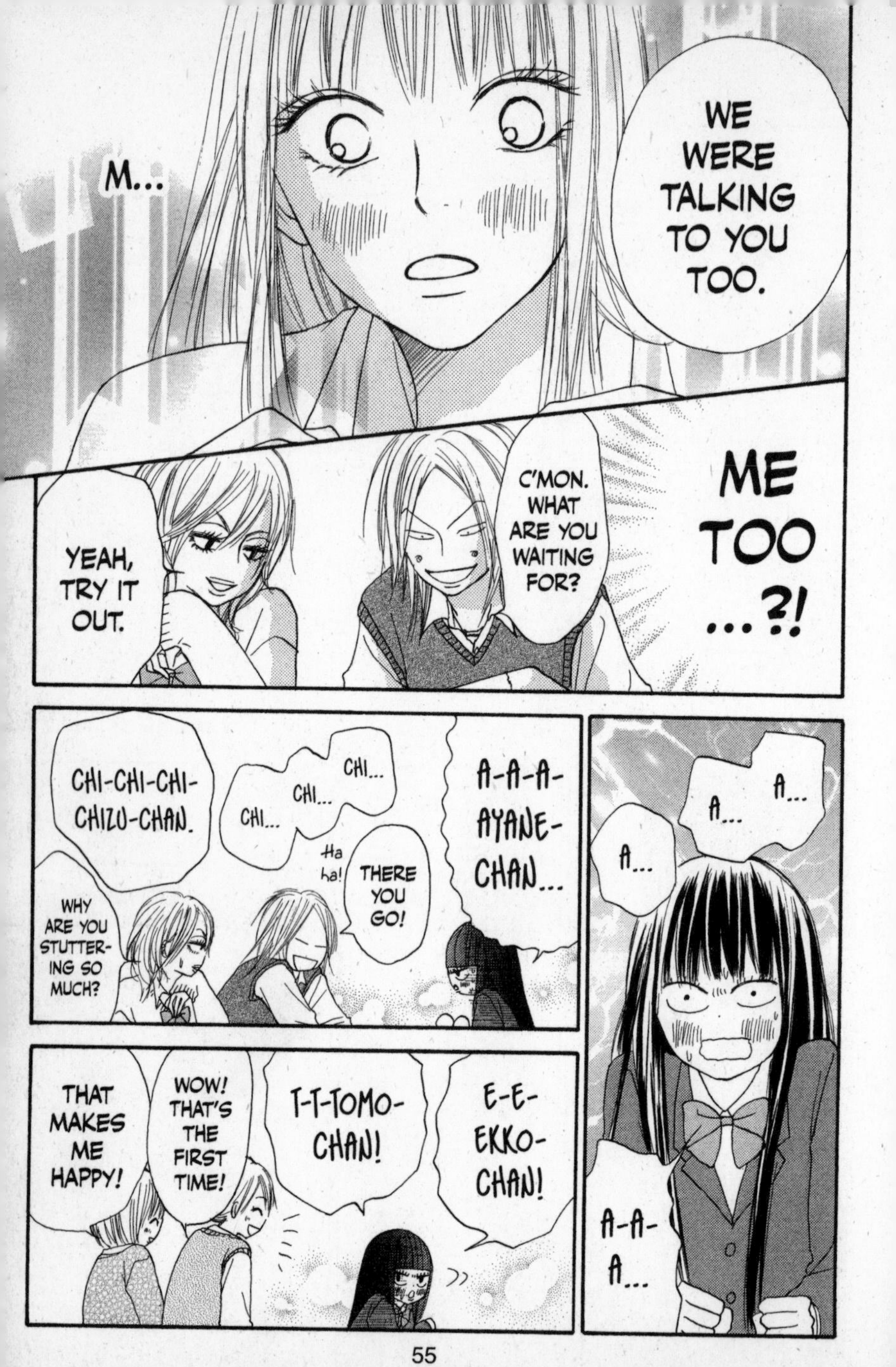

WE WERE TALKING TO YOU TOO.
M...
ME TOO ...?!
C'MON. WHAT ARE YOU WAITING FOR?
YEAH, TRY IT OUT.
A...
A...
A...
A-A-A-A...
A-A-A-AYANE-CHAN...
CHI...
CHI...
CHI...
THERE YOU GO!
Ha ha!
CHI-CHI-CHI-CHIZU-CHAN.
WHY ARE YOU STUTTER-ING SO MUCH?
E-E-EKKO-CHAN!
T-T-TOMO-CHAN!
WOW! THAT'S THE FIRST TIME!
THAT MAKES ME HAPPY!

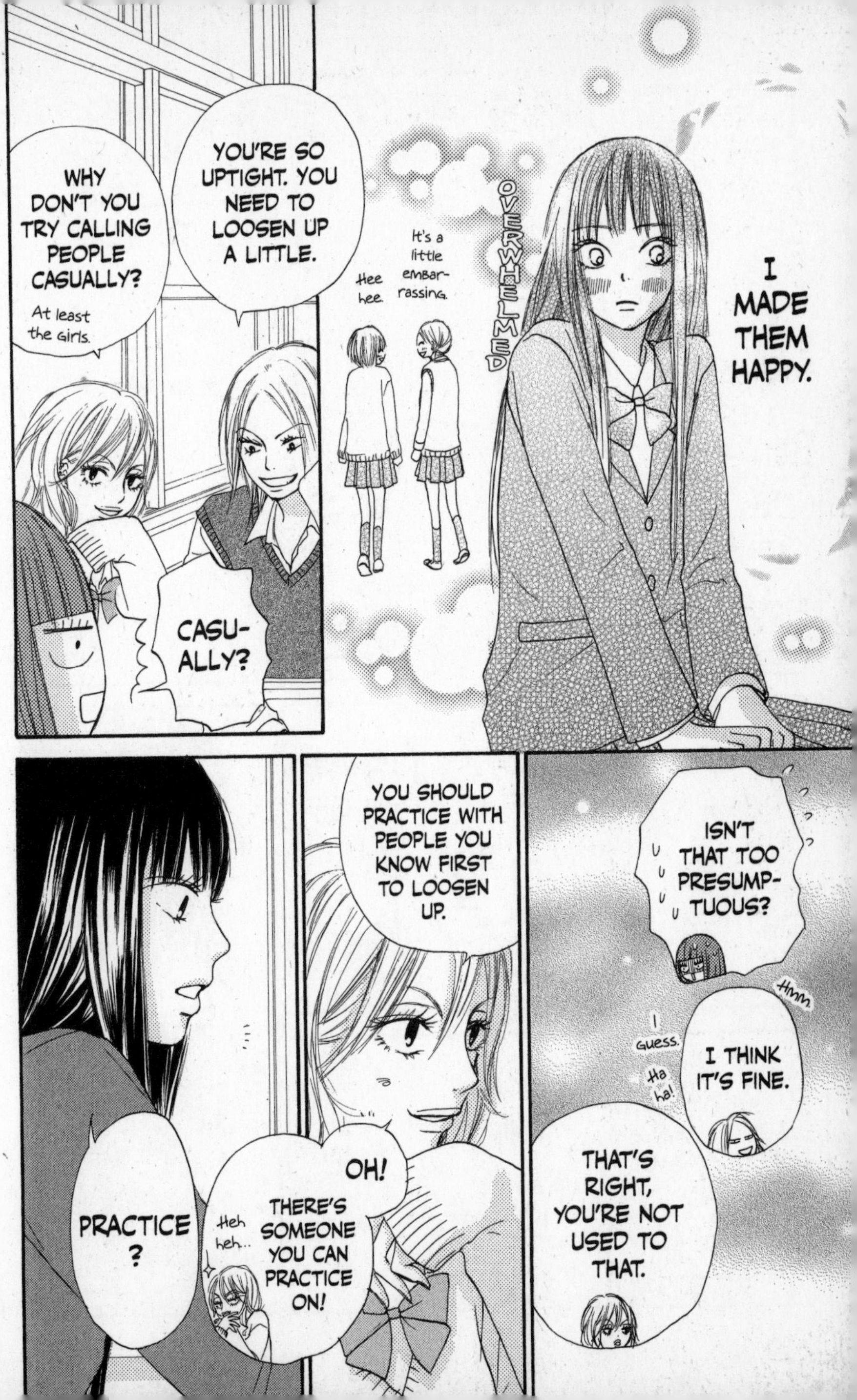
I MADE THEM HAPPY.
OVERWHELMED
It's a little embarrassing.
Hee hee.
YOU'RE SO UPTIGHT. YOU NEED TO LOOSEN UP A LITTLE.
WHY DON'T YOU TRY CALLING PEOPLE CASUALLY?
At least the girls.
CASU-ALLY?
ISN'T THAT TOO PRESUMP-TUOUS?
Hmm
I THINK IT'S FINE.
I guess.
Ha ha!
THAT'S RIGHT, YOU'RE NOT USED TO THAT.
YOU SHOULD PRACTICE WITH PEOPLE YOU KNOW FIRST TO LOOSEN UP.
PRACTICE?
OH!
THERE'S SOMEONE YOU CAN PRACTICE ON!
Heh heh...

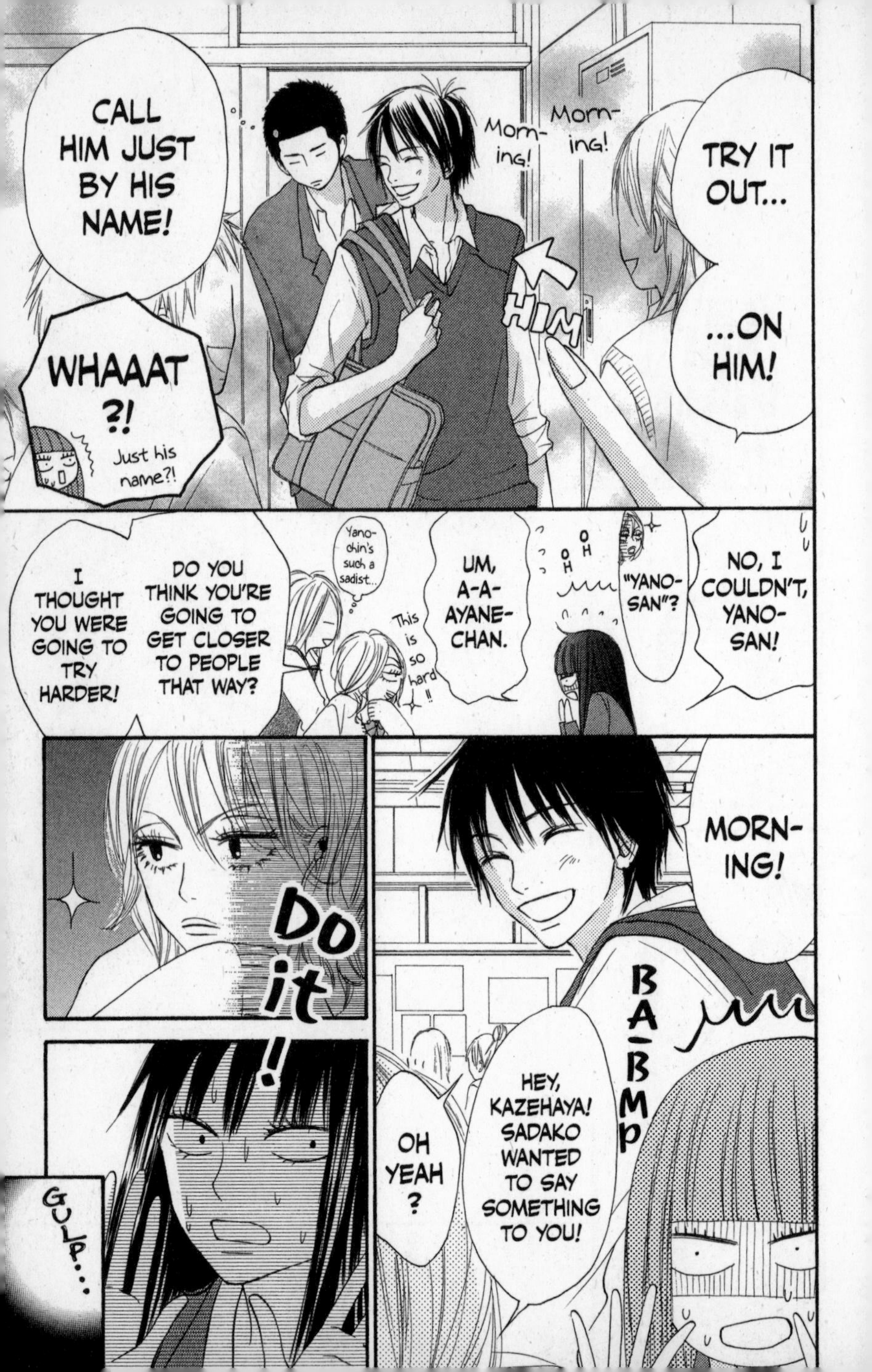
TRY IT OUT...
...ON HIM!
Morn-ing!
Morn-ing!
HIM
CALL HIM JUST BY HIS NAME!
WHAAAT ?!
Just his name?!
NO, I COULDN'T, YANO-SAN!
"YANO-SAN"?
OH OH
UM, A-A-AYANE-CHAN.
This is so hard!!
Yano-chin's such a sadist...
DO YOU THINK YOU'RE GOING TO GET CLOSER TO PEOPLE THAT WAY?
I THOUGHT YOU WERE GOING TO TRY HARDER!
MORN-ING!
BA-BMP
HEY, KAZEHAYA! SADAKO WANTED TO SAY SOMETHING TO YOU!
OH YEAH?
Do it!!
GULP...

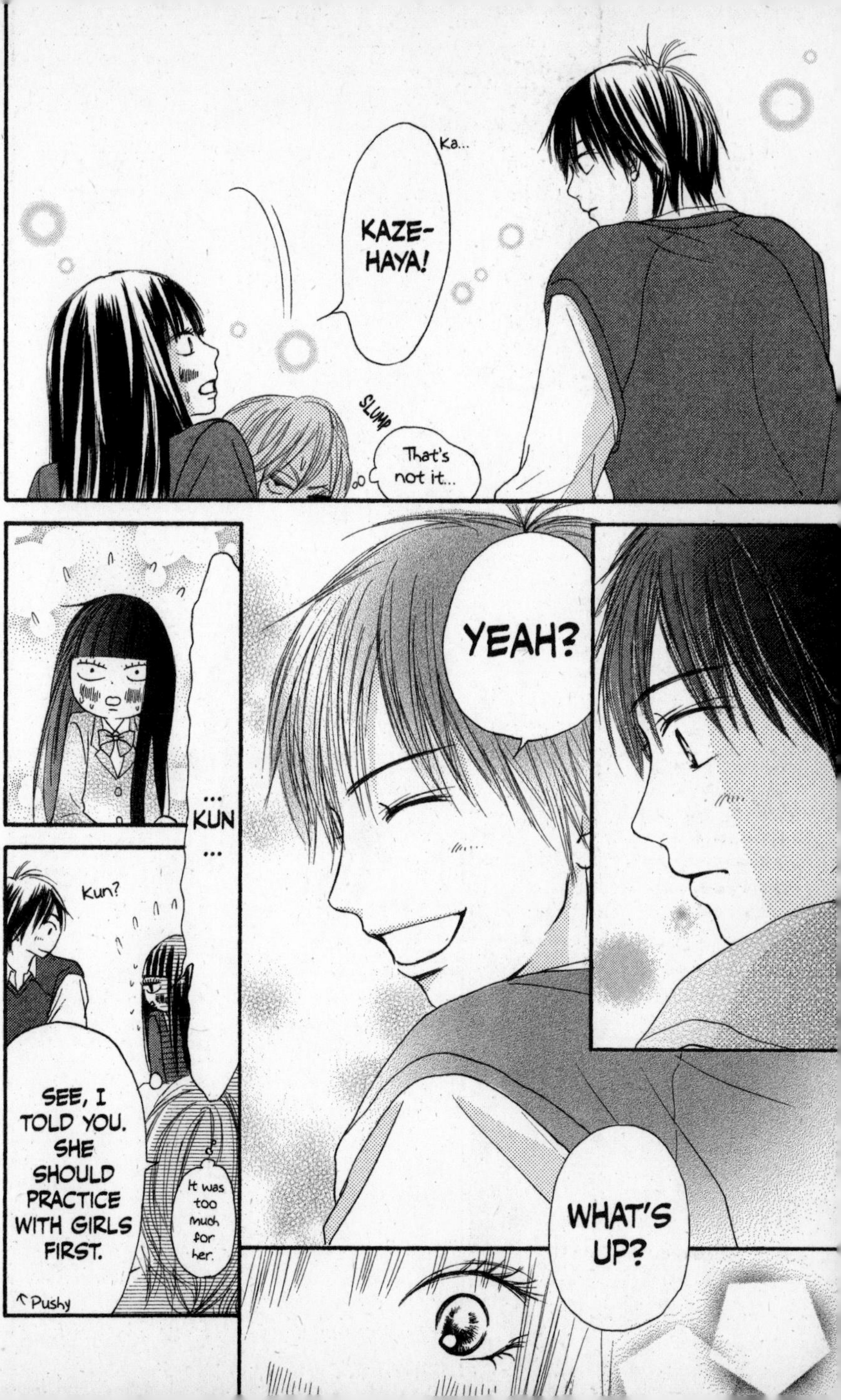
Ka...
KAZE-HAYA!
SLUMP
That's not it...
YEAH?
WHAT'S UP?
...KUN...
Kun?
SEE, I TOLD YOU. SHE SHOULD PRACTICE WITH GIRLS FIRST.
It was too much for her.
↑Pushy

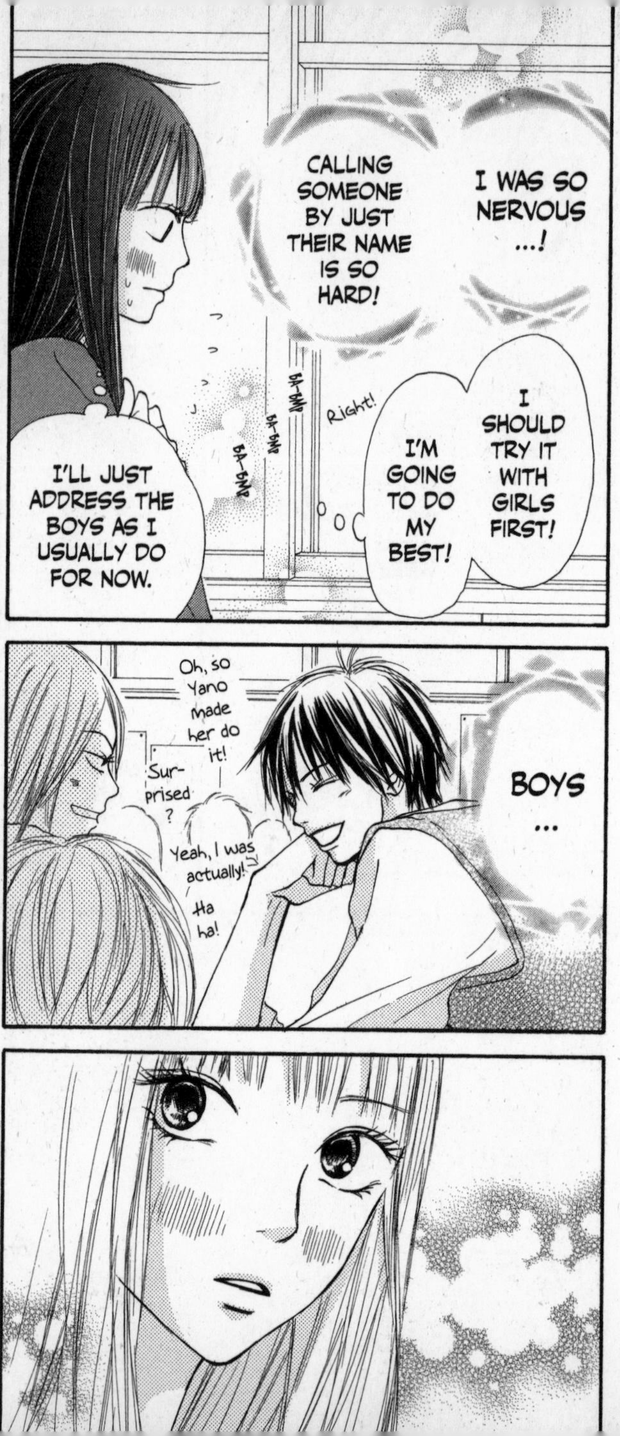
I WAS SO NERVOUS ...!
CALLING SOMEONE BY JUST THEIR NAME IS SO HARD!
I SHOULD TRY IT WITH GIRLS FIRST!
Right!
I'M GOING TO DO MY BEST!
BA-BMP BA-BMP BA-BMP
I'LL JUST ADDRESS THE BOYS AS I USUALLY DO FOR NOW.
BOYS ...
Oh, so Yano made her do it!
Sur-prised?
Yeah, I was actually!
Ha ha!

KARUPIN on JAPAN 2

The story where the little man says...

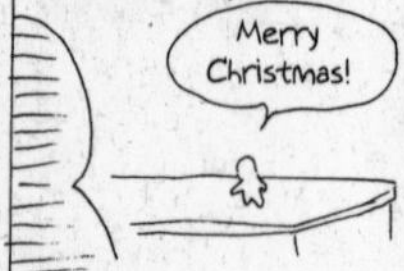
Merry Christmas!

...and then disappears is one of my favorites! It happened in the summer.

Ha ha ha! What's that all about?! That's so surreal!!

I also like the story where the little man has a megaphone while he's watching the baseball game on TV and the one where he's riding a Harley.

These little men doing whatever they want are ridiculously funny! (There are other stories too that I can't recall as I write this. My memory's so spotty.)

It's said that you can only see him if you have a pure heart. Or, only if you truly believe.

Oh, in that case, I don't know if I'll ever see him... Also, a reader wrote to me and said that on the Internet she found that most of the little men are about 20-30 cm (about 8"-12") tall.

Scary! I'm kinda glad I can't see him!

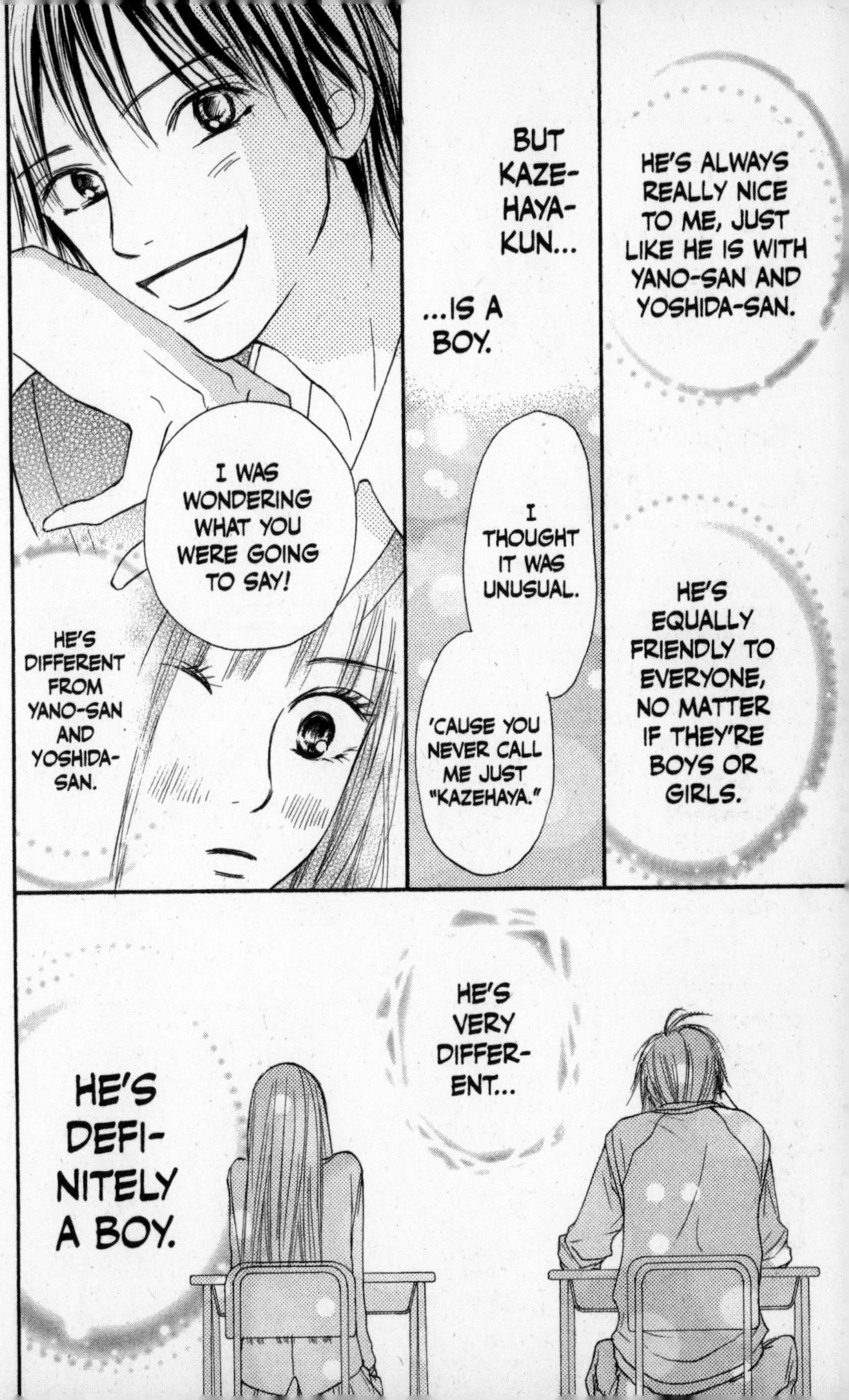
HE'S ALWAYS REALLY NICE TO ME, JUST LIKE HE IS WITH YANO-SAN AND YOSHIDA-SAN.
HE'S EQUALLY FRIENDLY TO EVERYONE, NO MATTER IF THEY'RE BOYS OR GIRLS.
BUT KAZEHAYA-KUN...
...IS A BOY.
I THOUGHT IT WAS UNUSUAL.
'CAUSE YOU NEVER CALL ME JUST "KAZEHAYA."
I WAS WONDERING WHAT YOU WERE GOING TO SAY!
HE'S DIFFERENT FROM YANO-SAN AND YOSHIDA-SAN.
HE'S VERY DIFFERENT...
HE'S DEFINITELY A BOY.

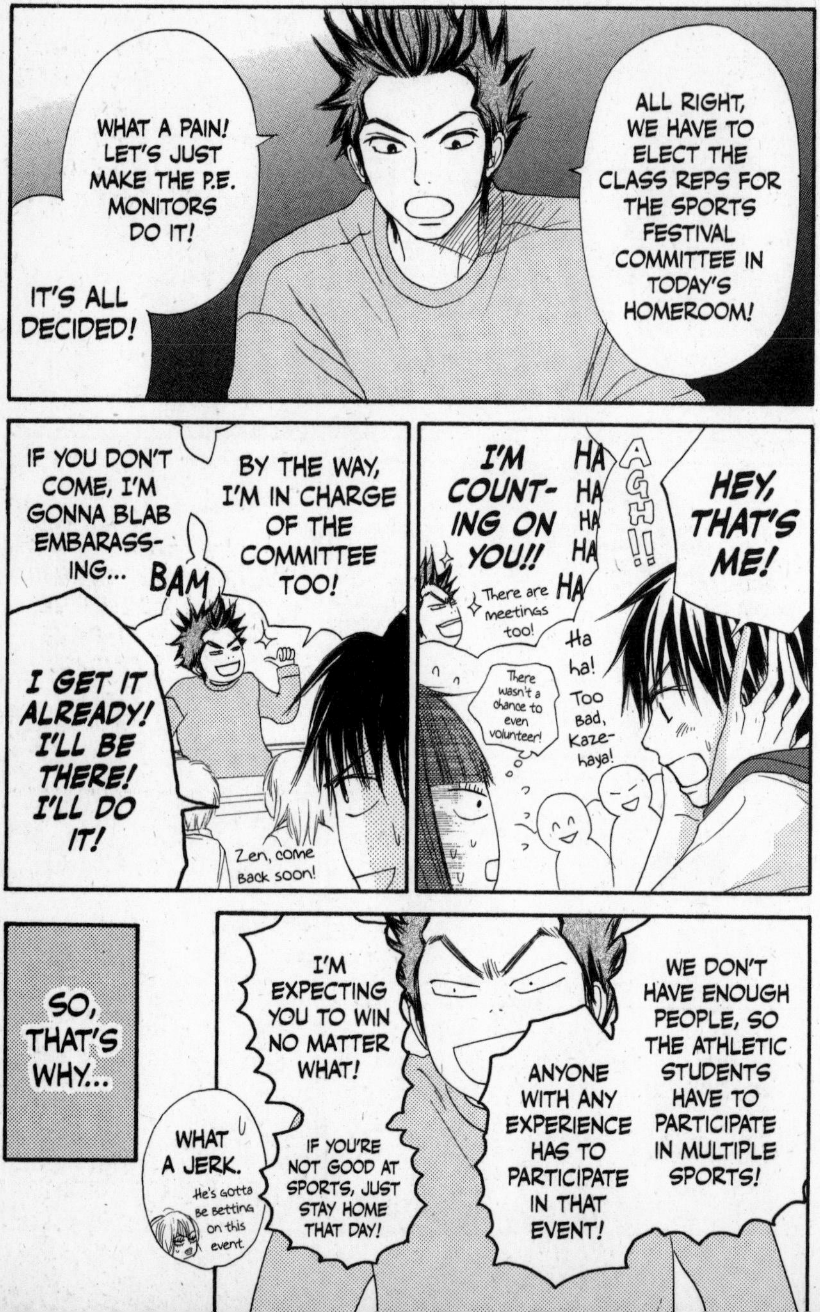
ALL RIGHT, WE HAVE TO ELECT THE CLASS REPS FOR THE SPORTS FESTIVAL COMMITTEE IN TODAY'S HOMEROOM!
WHAT A PAIN! LET'S JUST MAKE THE P.E. MONITORS DO IT!
IT'S ALL DECIDED!
HEY, THAT'S ME!
AGH!!
HA HA HA HA HA
I'M COUNTING ON YOU!!
There are meetings too!
Ha ha! Too bad, Kazehaya!
There wasn't a chance to even volunteer!
BY THE WAY, I'M IN CHARGE OF THE COMMITTEE TOO!
IF YOU DON'T COME, I'M GONNA BLAB EMBARASS-ING...
BAM
I GET IT ALREADY! I'LL BE THERE! I'LL DO IT!
Zen, come back soon!
WE DON'T HAVE ENOUGH PEOPLE, SO THE ATHLETIC STUDENTS HAVE TO PARTICIPATE IN MULTIPLE SPORTS!
ANYONE WITH ANY EXPERIENCE HAS TO PARTICIPATE IN THAT EVENT!
I'M EXPECTING YOU TO WIN NO MATTER WHAT!
IF YOU'RE NOT GOOD AT SPORTS, JUST STAY HOME THAT DAY!
WHAT A JERK.
He's gotta be betting on this event.
SO, THAT'S WHY...

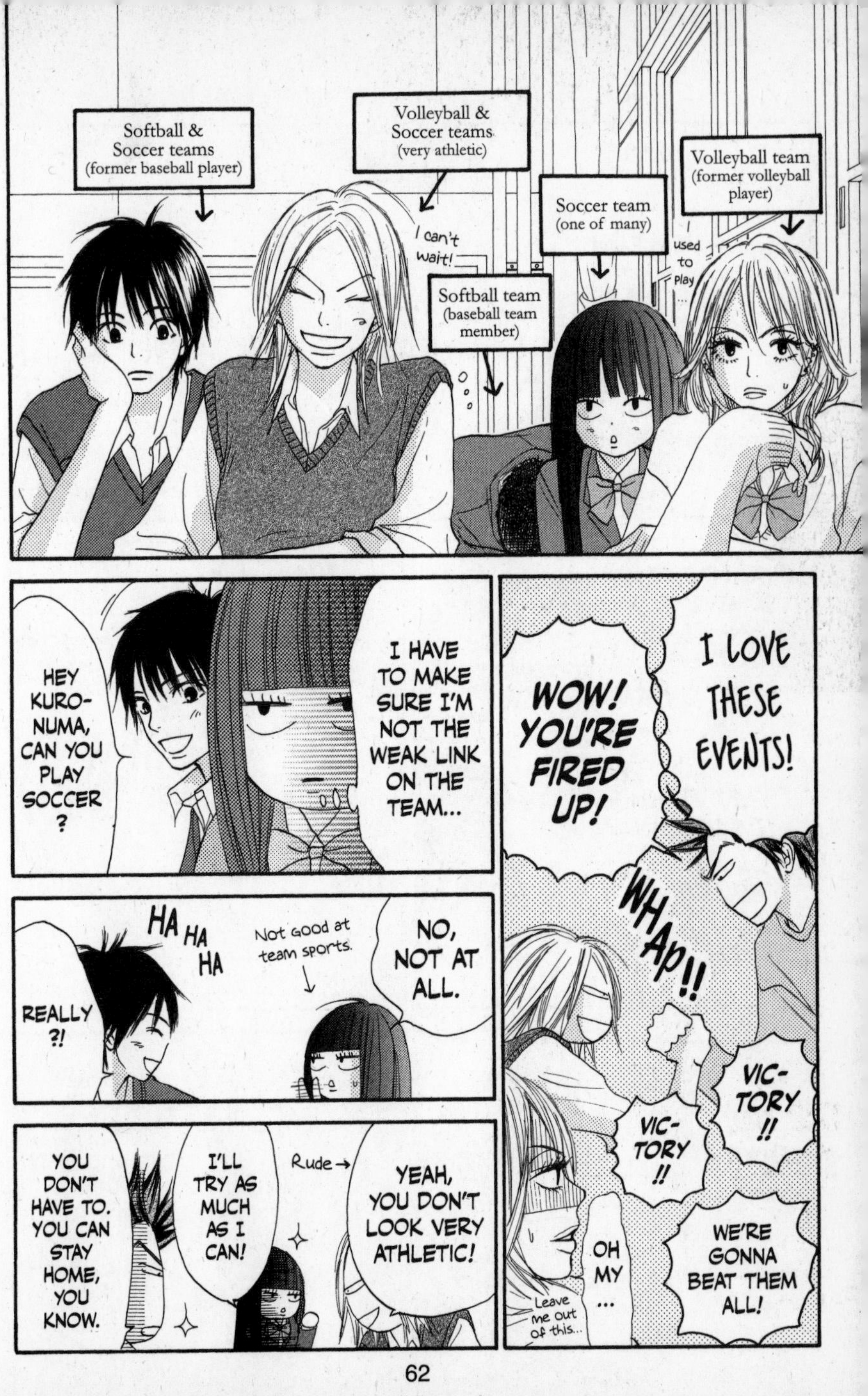
Volleyball team (former volleyball player)
I used to play...
Soccer team (one of many)
Softball team (baseball team member)
Volleyball & Soccer teams (very athletic)
I can't wait!
Softball & Soccer teams (former baseball player)
I LOVE THESE EVENTS!
WOW! YOU'RE FIRED UP!
WHAP!!
VICTORY!!
VICTORY!!
WE'RE GONNA BEAT THEM ALL!
OH MY...
Leave me out of this...
I HAVE TO MAKE SURE I'M NOT THE WEAK LINK ON THE TEAM...
HEY KURONUMA, CAN YOU PLAY SOCCER?
NO, NOT AT ALL.
Not good at team sports.
HA HA HA
REALLY?!
YEAH, YOU DON'T LOOK VERY ATHLETIC!
Rude
I'LL TRY AS MUCH AS I CAN!
YOU DON'T HAVE TO. YOU CAN STAY HOME, YOU KNOW.

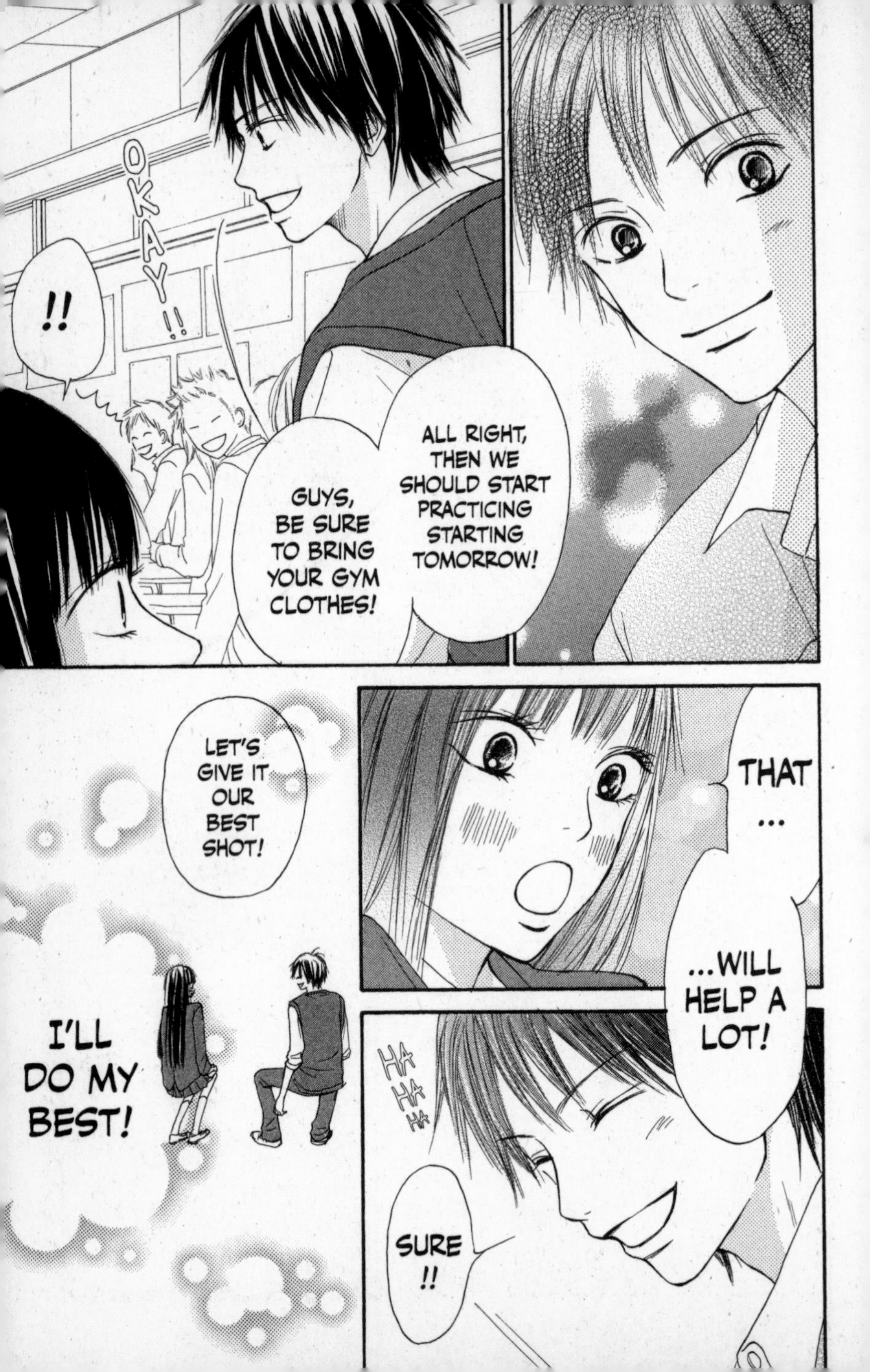
ALL RIGHT, THEN WE SHOULD START PRACTICING STARTING TOMORROW!
GUYS, BE SURE TO BRING YOUR GYM CLOTHES!
OKAY!!
!!
THAT ...
...WILL HELP A LOT!
HA HA HA
SURE !!
LET'S GIVE IT OUR BEST SHOT!
I'LL DO MY BEST!

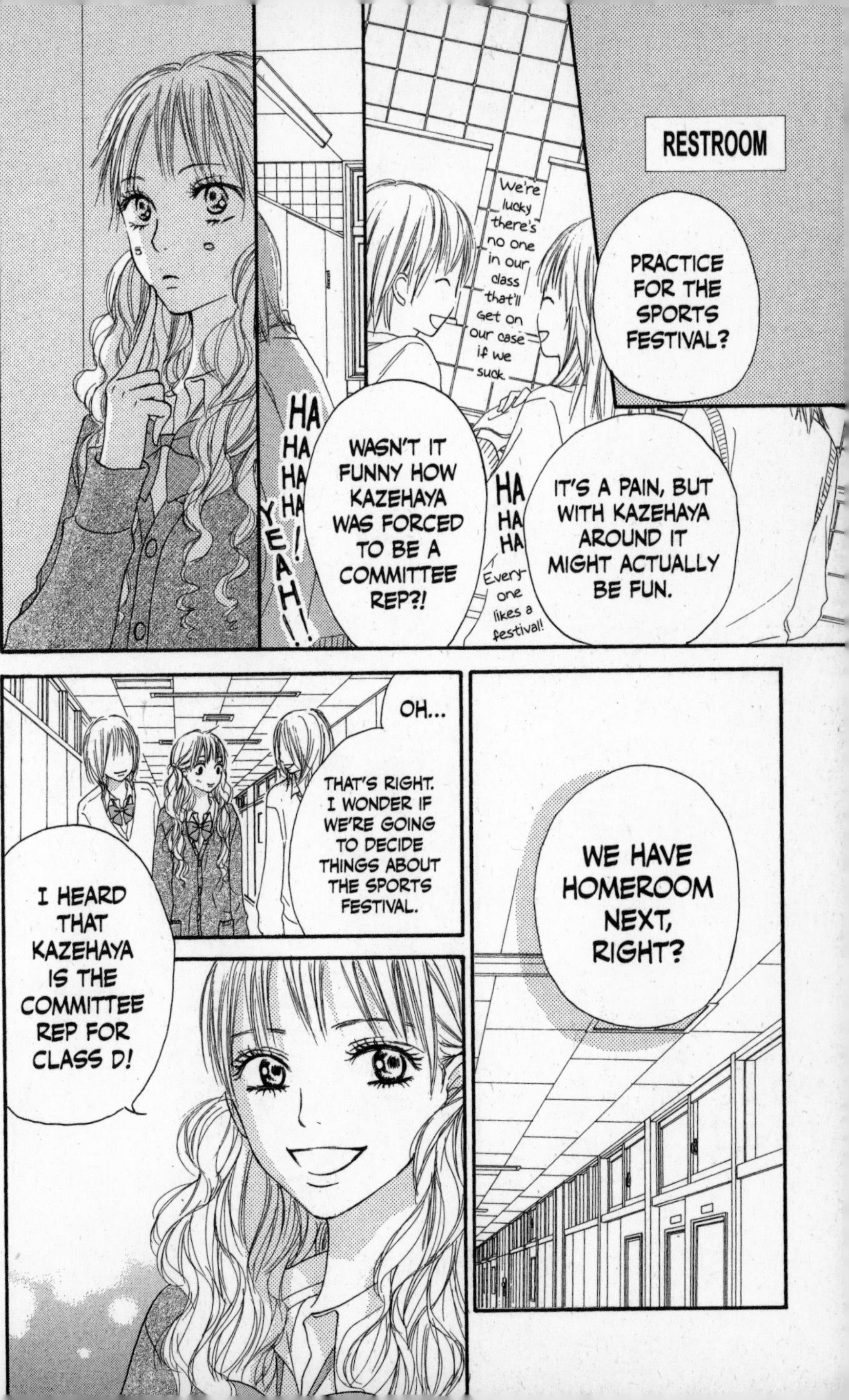
RESTROOM
PRACTICE FOR THE SPORTS FESTIVAL?
We're lucky there's no one in our class that'll get on our case if we suck.
IT'S A PAIN, BUT WITH KAZEHAYA AROUND IT MIGHT ACTUALLY BE FUN.
HA HA HA
Every-one likes a festival!
WASN'T IT FUNNY HOW KAZEHAYA WAS FORCED TO BE A COMMITTEE REP?!
HA HA HA HA!
YEAH!!
WE HAVE HOMEROOM NEXT, RIGHT?
OH...
THAT'S RIGHT. I WONDER IF WE'RE GOING TO DECIDE THINGS ABOUT THE SPORTS FESTIVAL.
I HEARD THAT KAZEHAYA IS THE COMMITTEE REP FOR CLASS D!

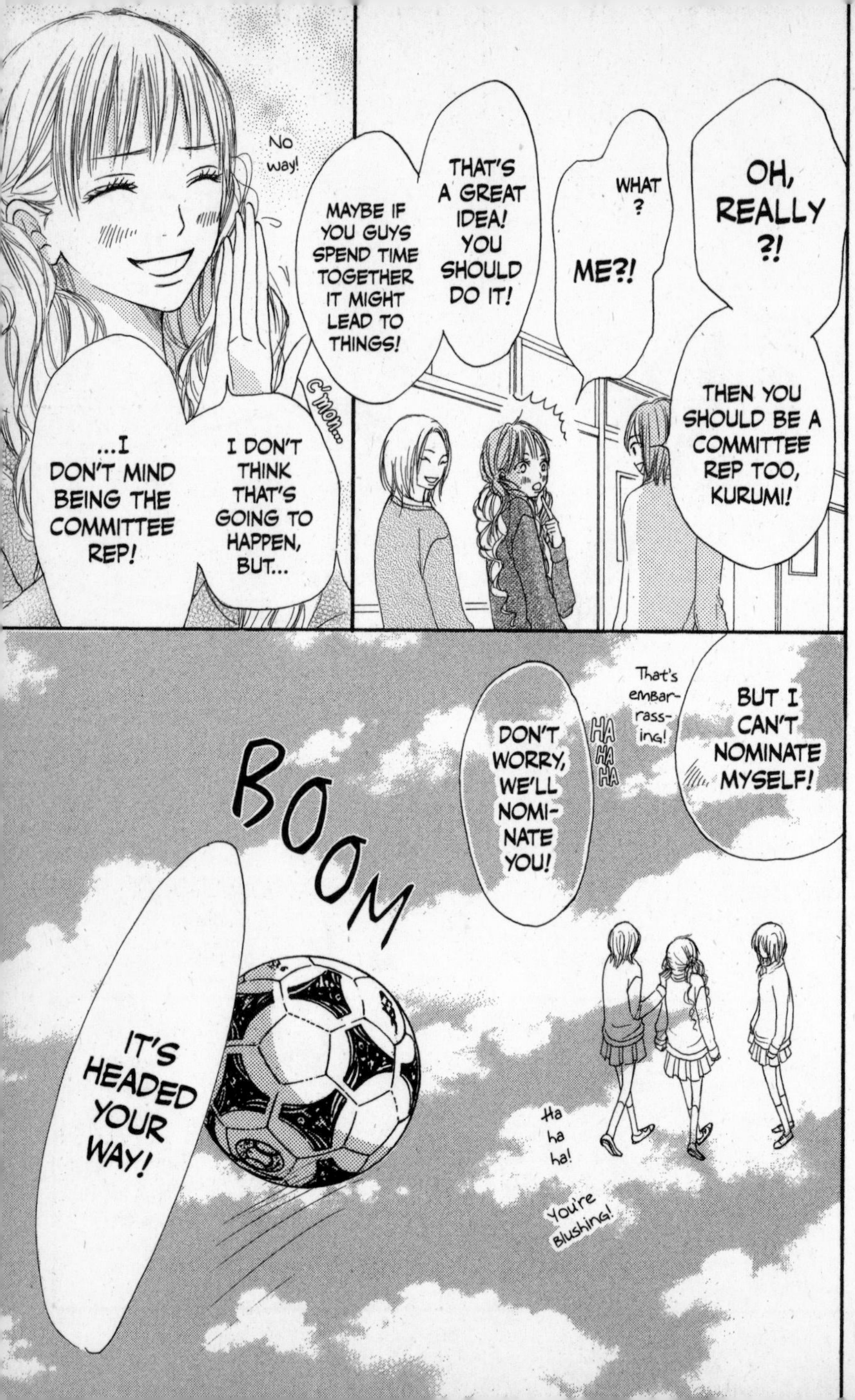

OH, REALLY?!
THEN YOU SHOULD BE A COMMITTEE REP TOO, KURUMI!
WHAT? ME?!
THAT'S A GREAT IDEA! YOU SHOULD DO IT!
MAYBE IF YOU GUYS SPEND TIME TOGETHER IT MIGHT LEAD TO THINGS!
No way!
C'mon...
I DON'T THINK THAT'S GOING TO HAPPEN, BUT...
...I DON'T MIND BEING THE COMMITTEE REP!
BUT I CAN'T NOMINATE MYSELF!
That's embarrassing!
HA HA HA
DON'T WORRY, WE'LL NOMINATE YOU!
Ha ha ha!
You're blushing!
BOOM
IT'S HEADED YOUR WAY!

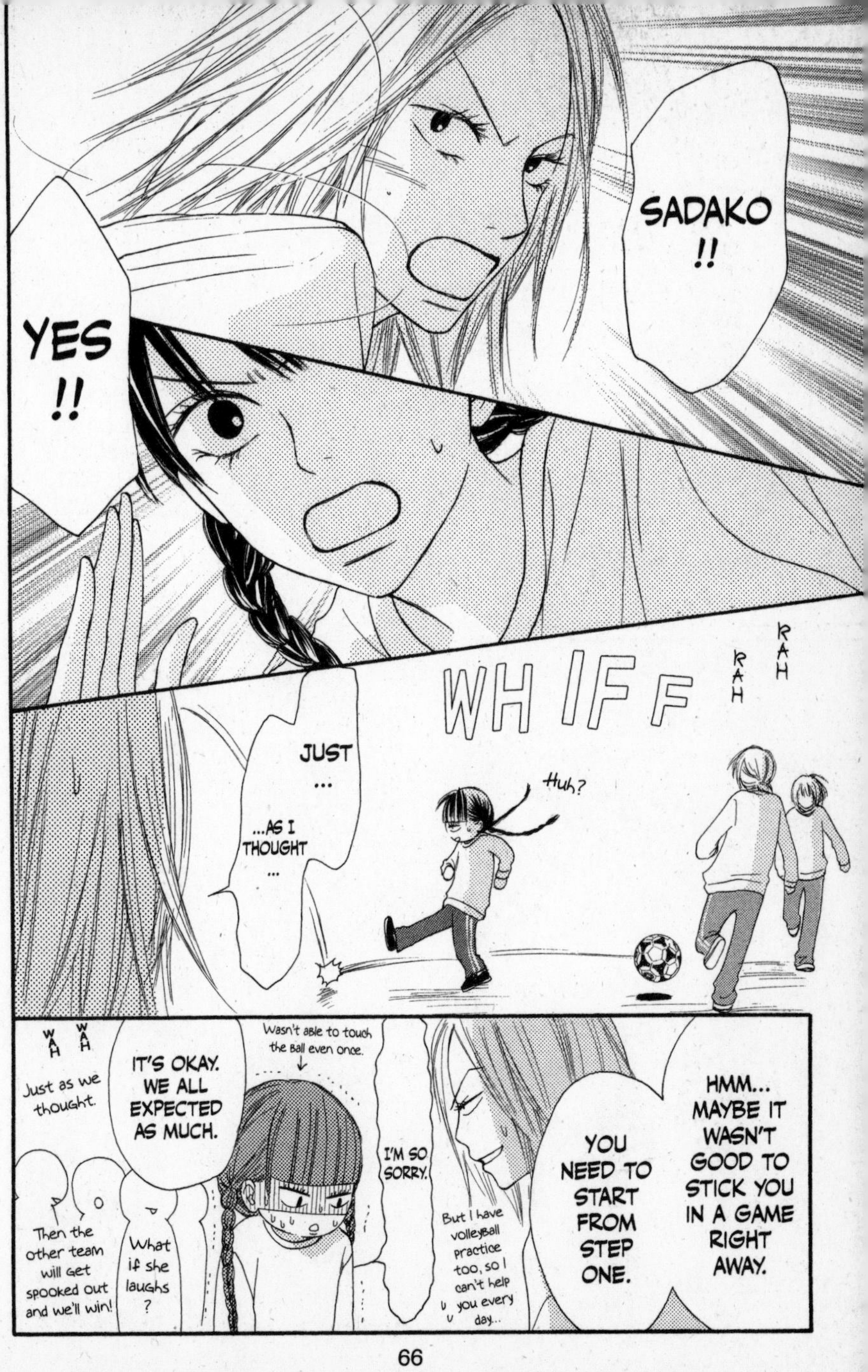

SADAKO !!
YES !!
RAH RAH
RAH
WHIFF
Huh?
JUST ...
...AS I THOUGHT ...
HMM... MAYBE IT WASN'T GOOD TO STICK YOU IN A GAME RIGHT AWAY.
YOU NEED TO START FROM STEP ONE.
But I have volleyball practice too, so I can't help you every day...
I'M SO SORRY.
Wasn't able to touch the ball even once.
IT'S OKAY. WE ALL EXPECTED AS MUCH.
WAH WAH
Just as we thought.
What if she laughs?
Then the other team will get spooked out and we'll win!

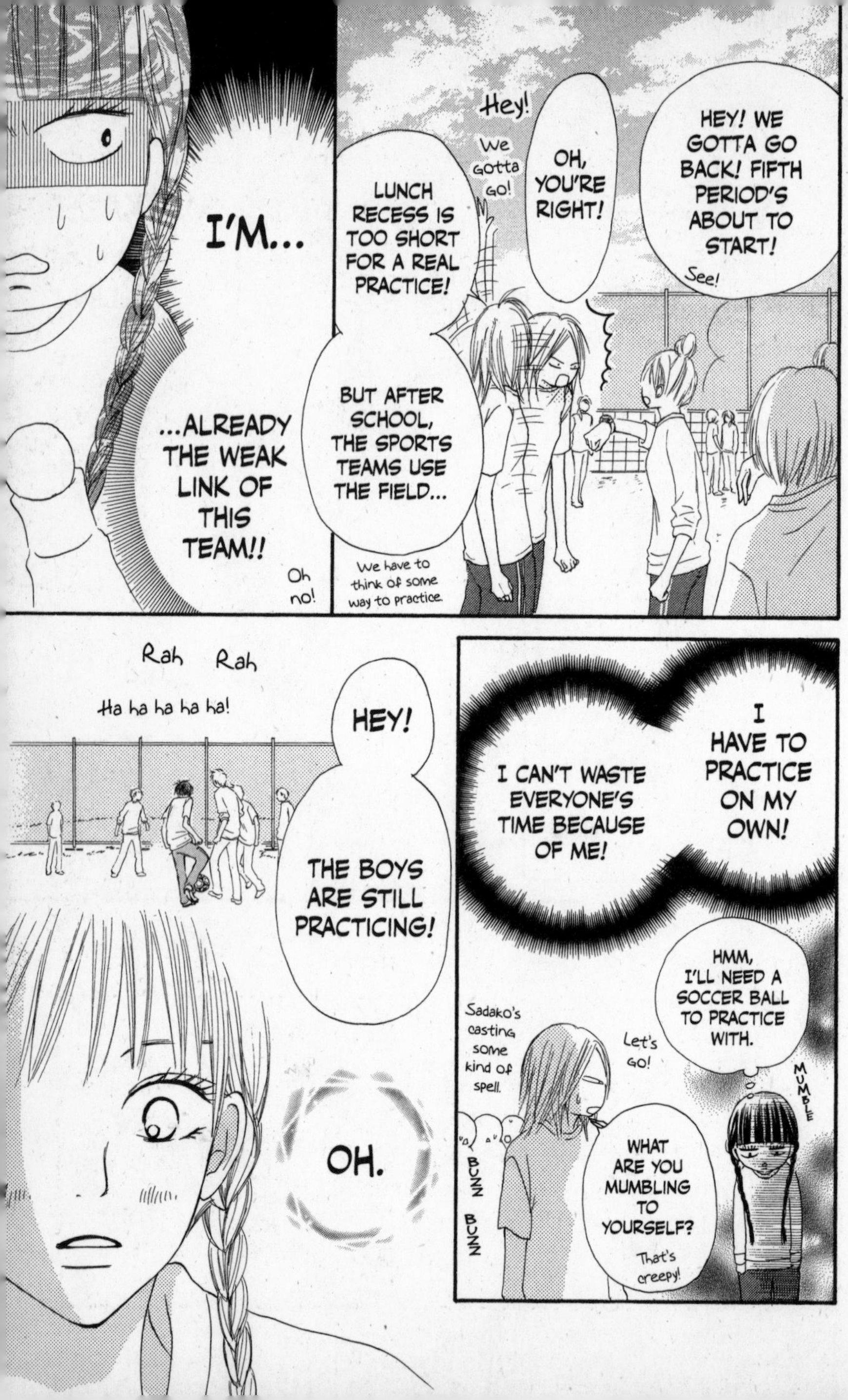
HEY! WE GOTTA GO BACK! FIFTH PERIOD'S ABOUT TO START!
See!
OH, YOU'RE RIGHT!
We gotta go!
Hey!
LUNCH RECESS IS TOO SHORT FOR A REAL PRACTICE!
BUT AFTER SCHOOL, THE SPORTS TEAMS USE THE FIELD...
We have to think of some way to practice
I'M...
...ALREADY THE WEAK LINK OF THIS TEAM!!
Oh no!
I HAVE TO PRACTICE ON MY OWN!
I CAN'T WASTE EVERYONE'S TIME BECAUSE OF ME!
HMM, I'LL NEED A SOCCER BALL TO PRACTICE WITH.
MUMBLE
Let's go!
Sadako's casting some kind of spell.
WHAT ARE YOU MUMBLING TO YOURSELF?
That's creepy!
BUZZ
BUZZ
HEY!
THE BOYS ARE STILL PRACTICING!
Rah Rah
Ha ha ha ha ha!
OH.

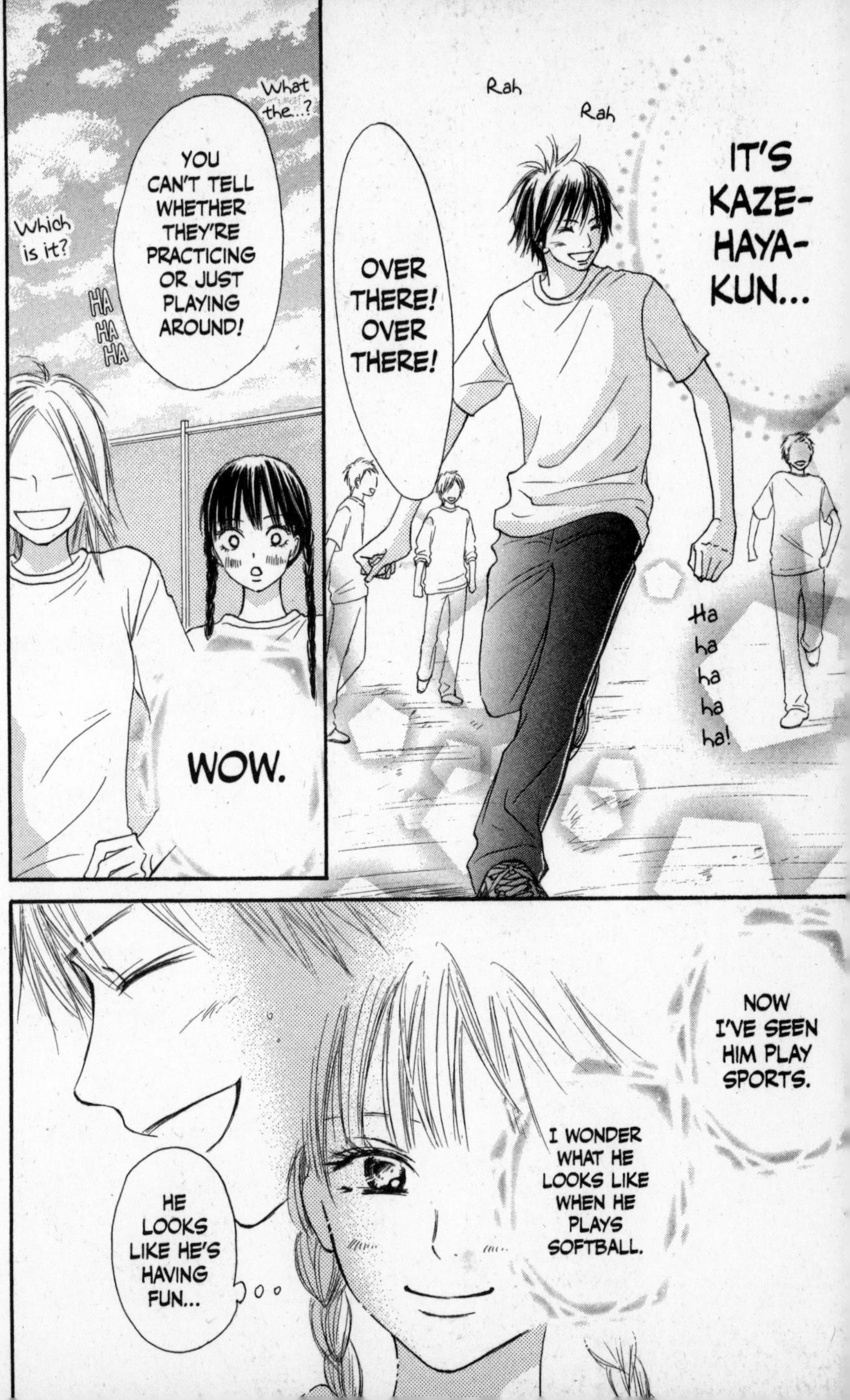
IT'S KAZE-HAYA-KUN...
Rah
Rah
OVER THERE! OVER THERE!
Ha ha ha ha ha!
What the...?
YOU CAN'T TELL WHETHER THEY'RE PRACTICING OR JUST PLAYING AROUND!
Which is it?
HA HA HA
WOW.
NOW I'VE SEEN HIM PLAY SPORTS.
I WONDER WHAT HE LOOKS LIKE WHEN HE PLAYS SOFTBALL.
HE LOOKS LIKE HE'S HAVING FUN...

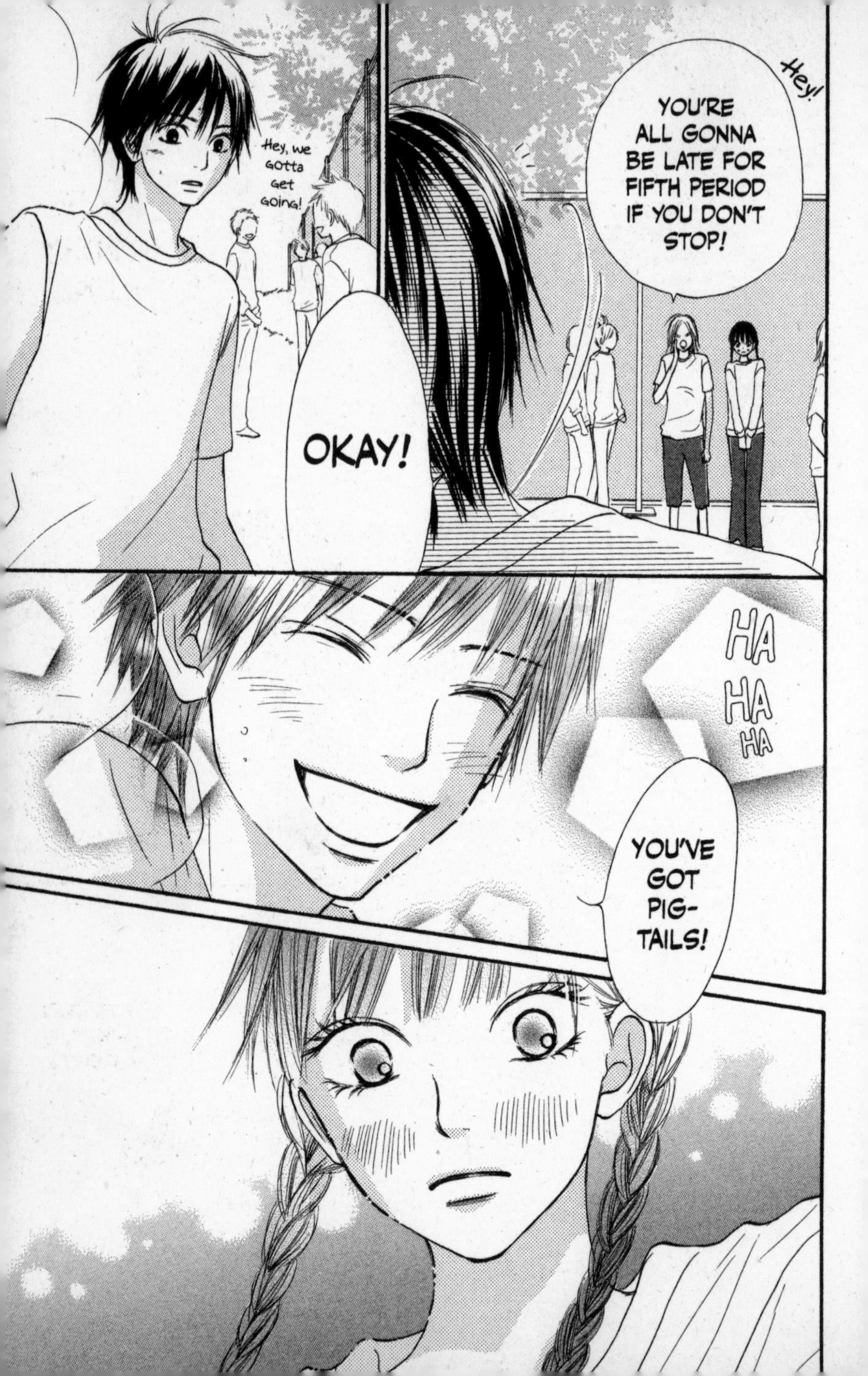
Hey!
YOU'RE ALL GONNA BE LATE FOR FIFTH PERIOD IF YOU DON'T STOP!
OKAY!
Hey, we gotta get going!
HA HA HA
YOU'VE GOT PIG-TAILS!

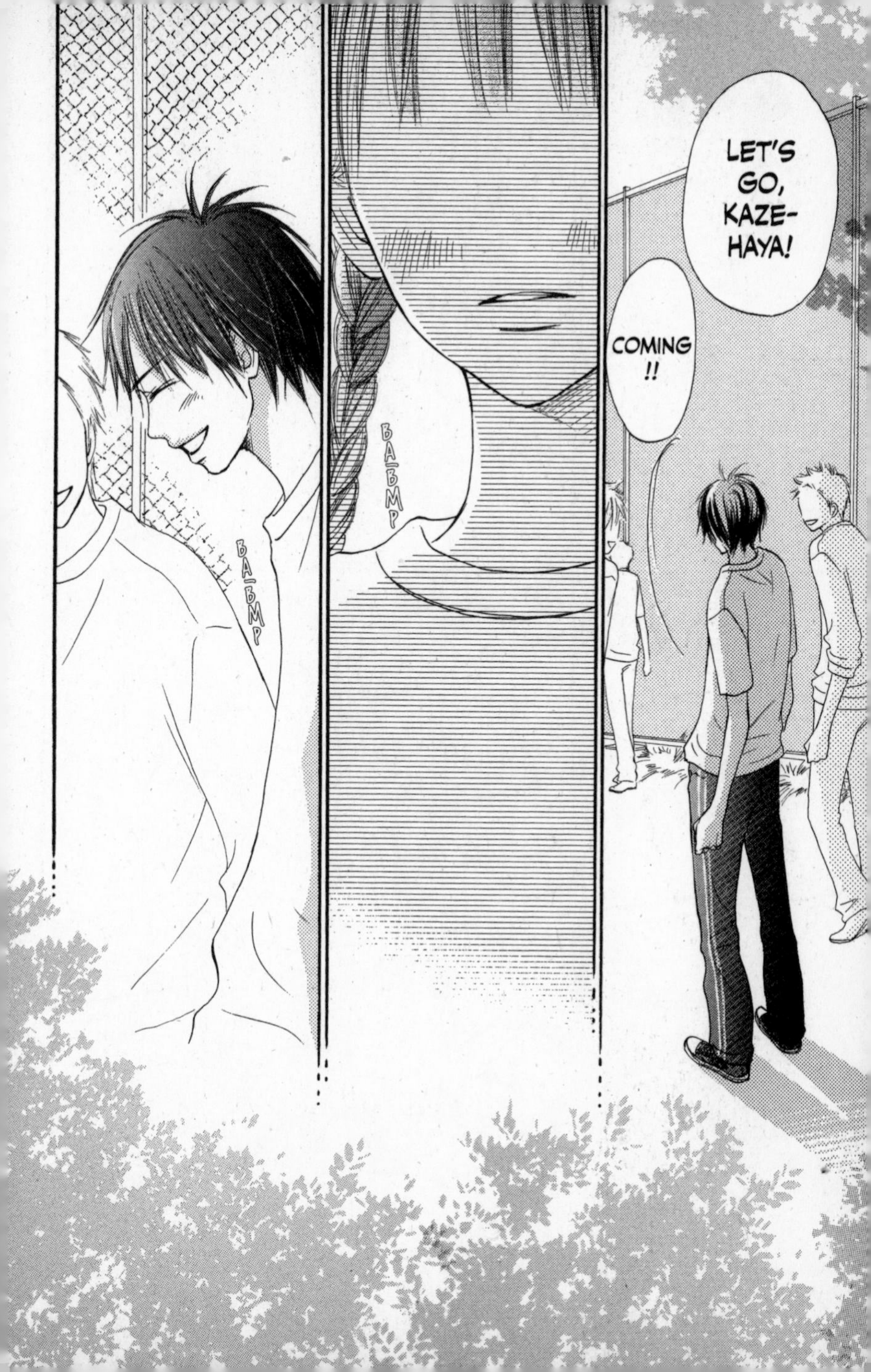
LET'S GO, KAZE-HAYA!
COMING!!
BA-BMP
BA-BMP

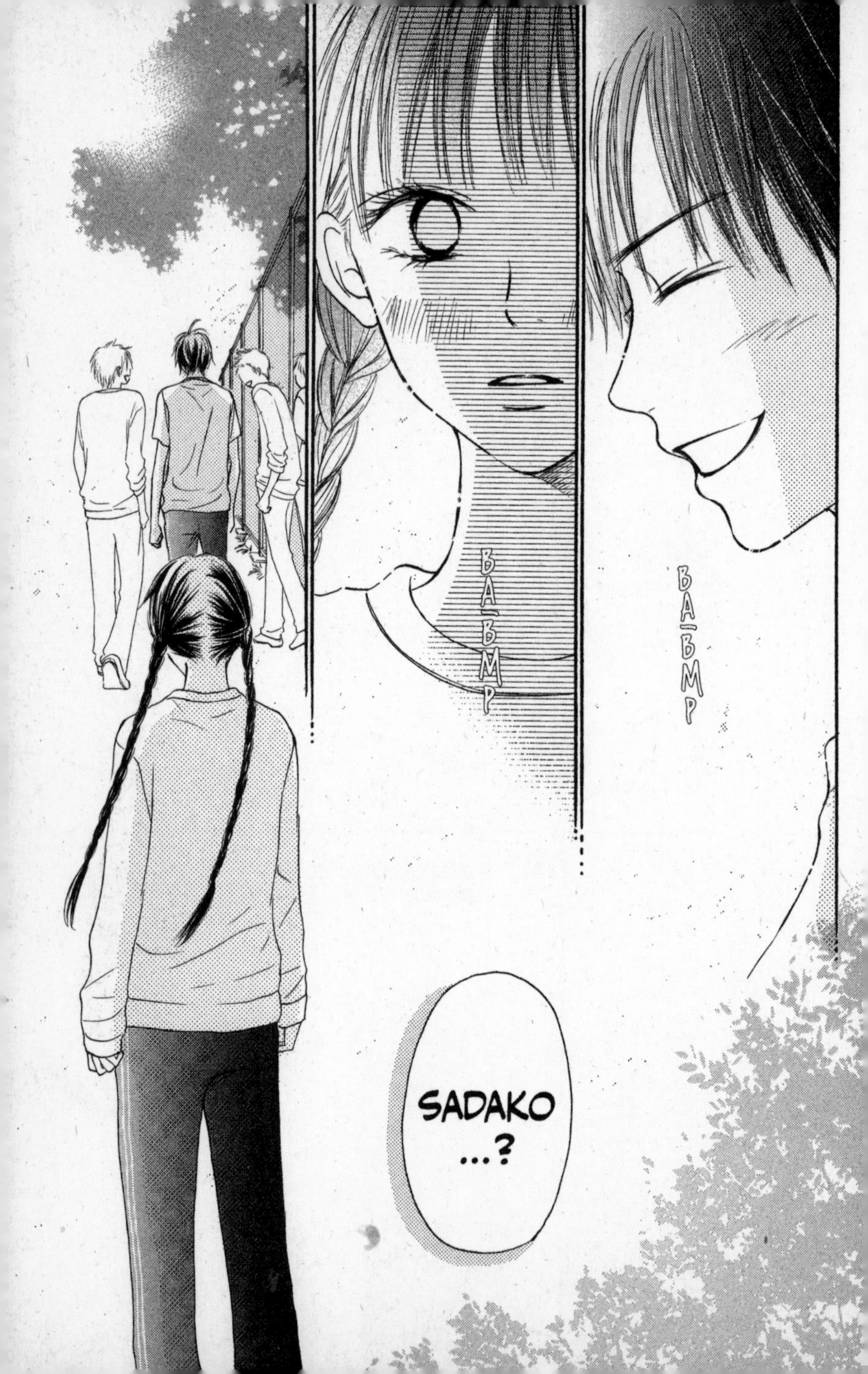
BA-BMP
BA-BMP
SADAKO ...?

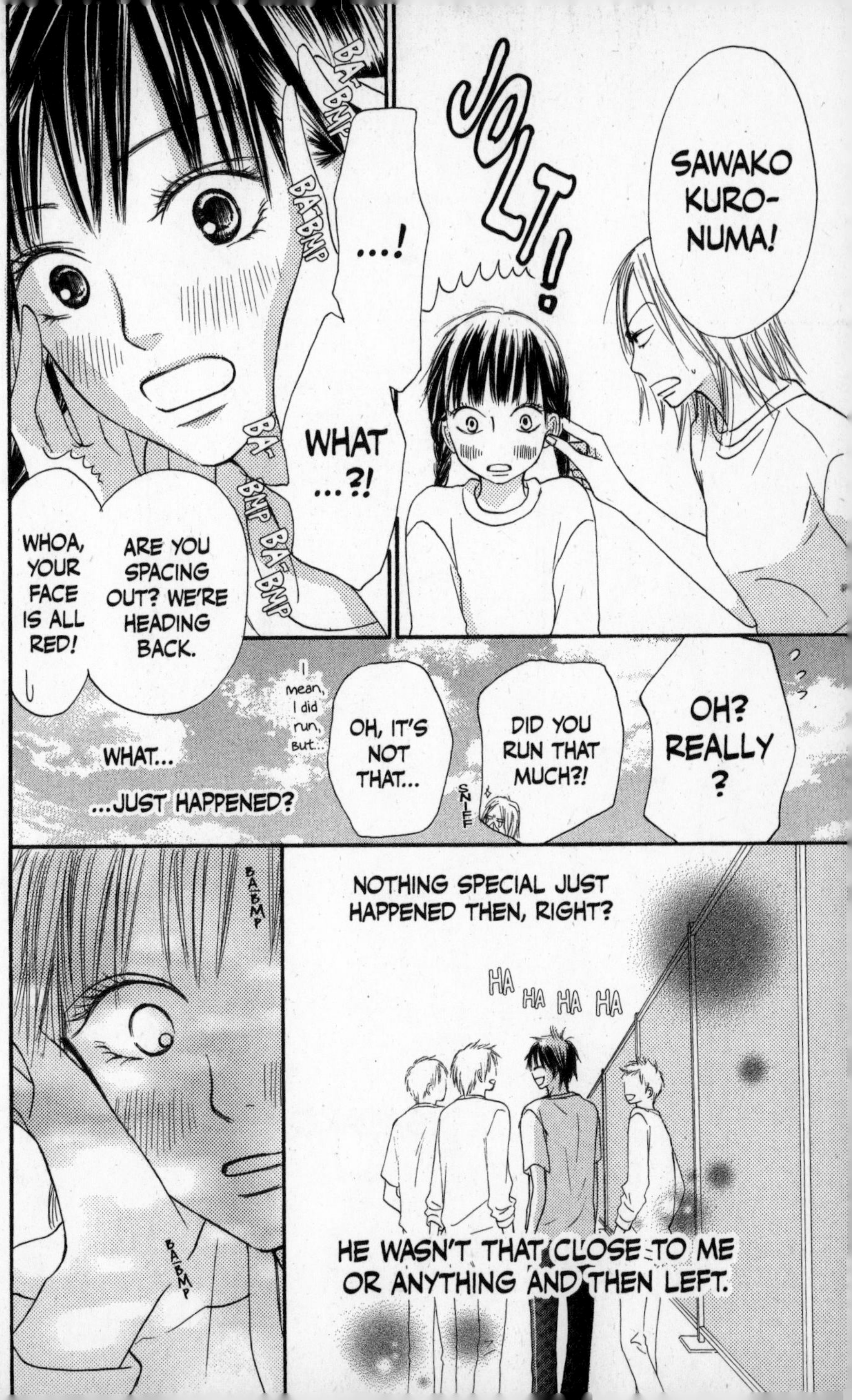
SAWAKO KURO-NUMA!
JOLT!
WHAT ...?!
...!
BA-BMP
BA-BMP
BA-BMP BA-BMP
ARE YOU SPACING OUT? WE'RE HEADING BACK.
WHOA, YOUR FACE IS ALL RED!
OH? REALLY?
DID YOU RUN THAT MUCH?!
SNIFF
OH, IT'S NOT THAT...
I mean, I did run, but...
WHAT...
...JUST HAPPENED?
NOTHING SPECIAL JUST HAPPENED THEN, RIGHT?
HA HA HA HA
HE WASN'T THAT CLOSE TO ME OR ANYTHING AND THEN LEFT.
BA-BMP
BA-BMP

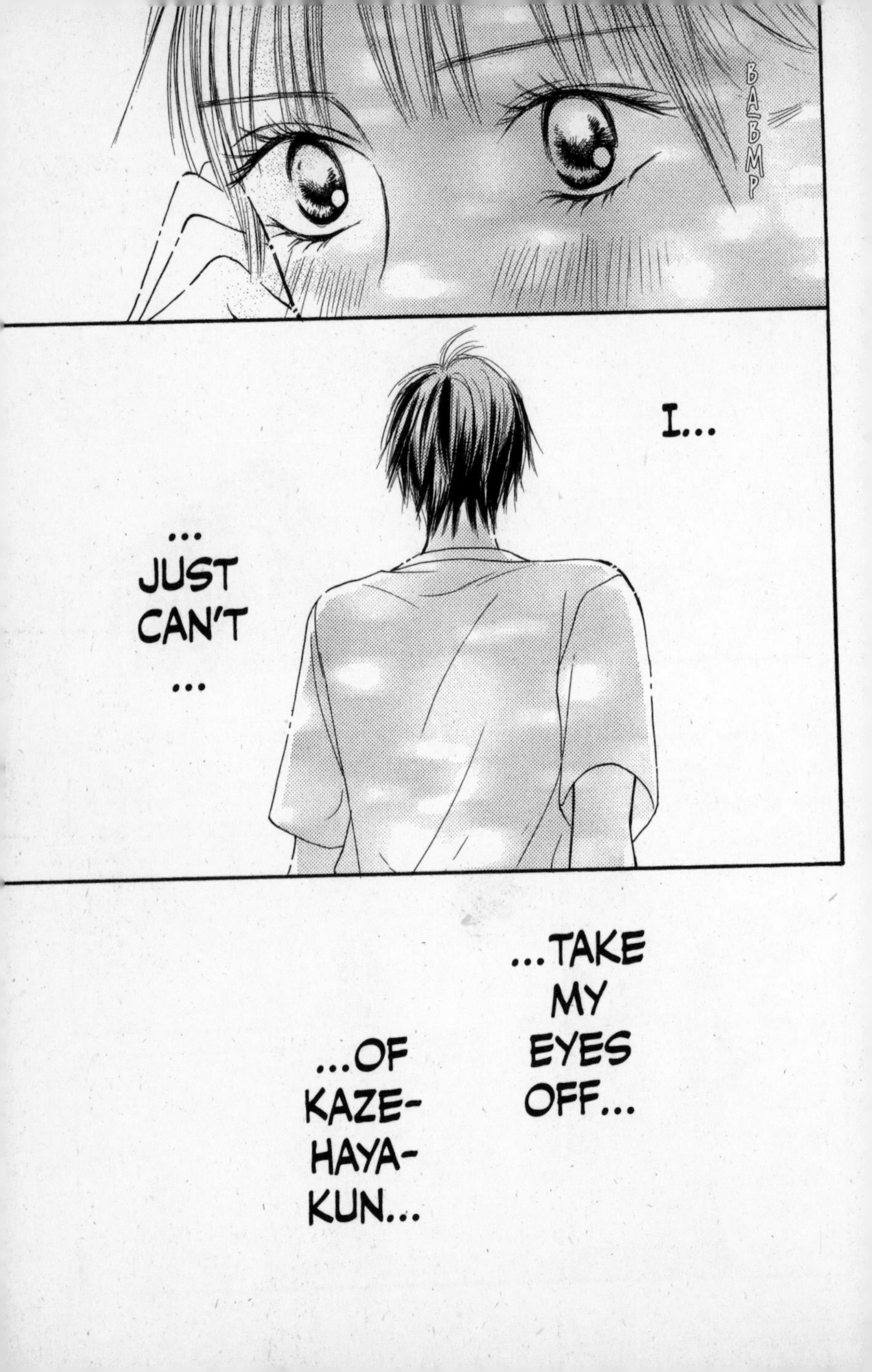
BA-BMP
I...
...JUST CAN'T...
...TAKE MY EYES OFF...
...OF KAZE-HAYA-KUN...

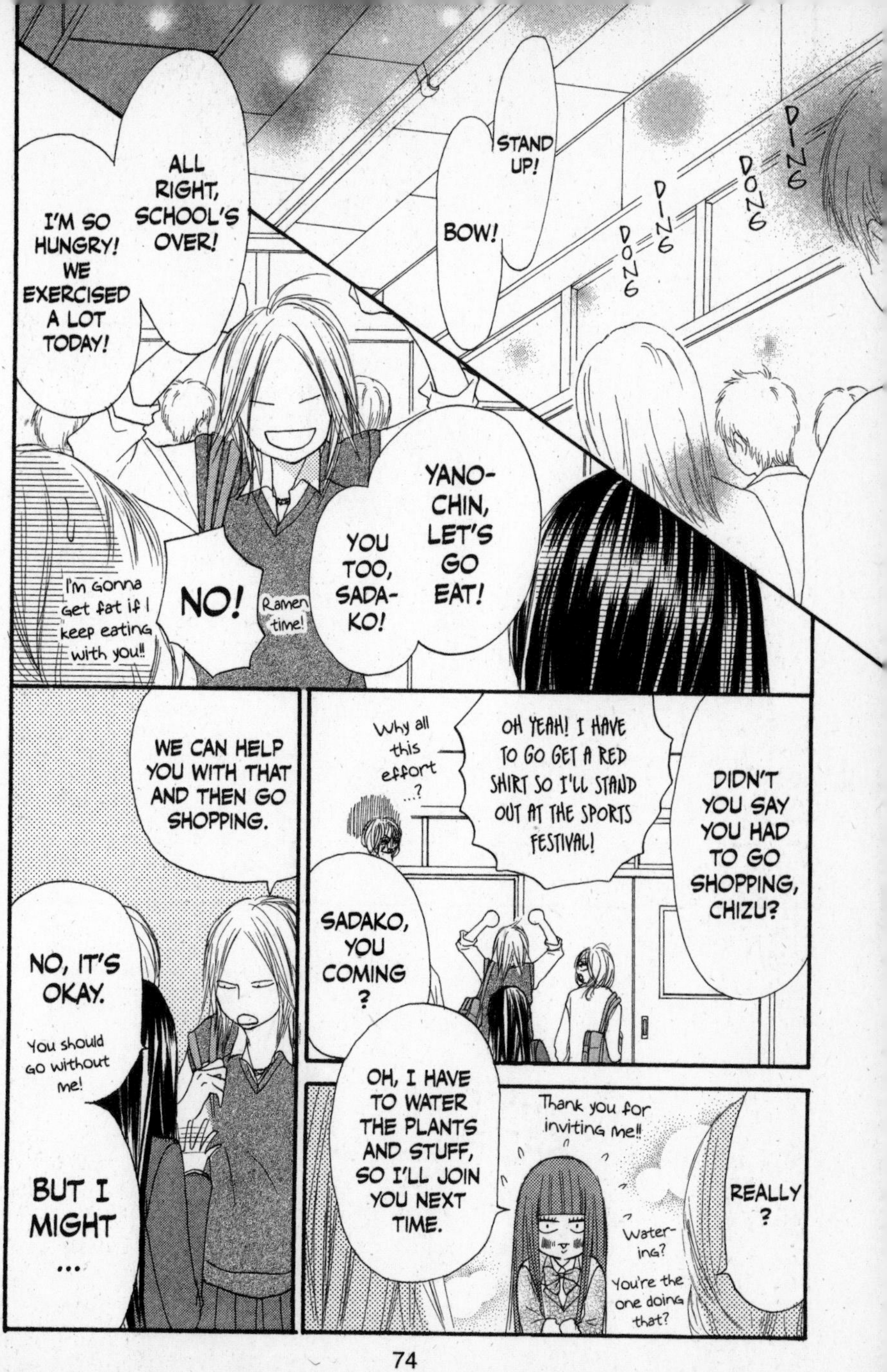
DING DONG
DING DONG
STAND UP!
BOW!
ALL RIGHT, SCHOOL'S OVER!
I'M SO HUNGRY! WE EXERCISED A LOT TODAY!
YANO-CHIN, LET'S GO EAT!
YOU TOO, SADAKO!
Ramen time!
NO!
I'm gonna get fat if I keep eating with you!!
DIDN'T YOU SAY YOU HAD TO GO SHOPPING, CHIZU?
OH YEAH! I HAVE TO GO GET A RED SHIRT SO I'LL STAND OUT AT THE SPORTS FESTIVAL!
Why all this effort ...?
SADAKO, YOU COMING ?
REALLY ?
Watering? You're the one doing that?
Thank you for inviting me!!
OH, I HAVE TO WATER THE PLANTS AND STUFF, SO I'LL JOIN YOU NEXT TIME.
WE CAN HELP YOU WITH THAT AND THEN GO SHOPPING.
NO, IT'S OKAY.
You should go without me!
BUT I MIGHT ...

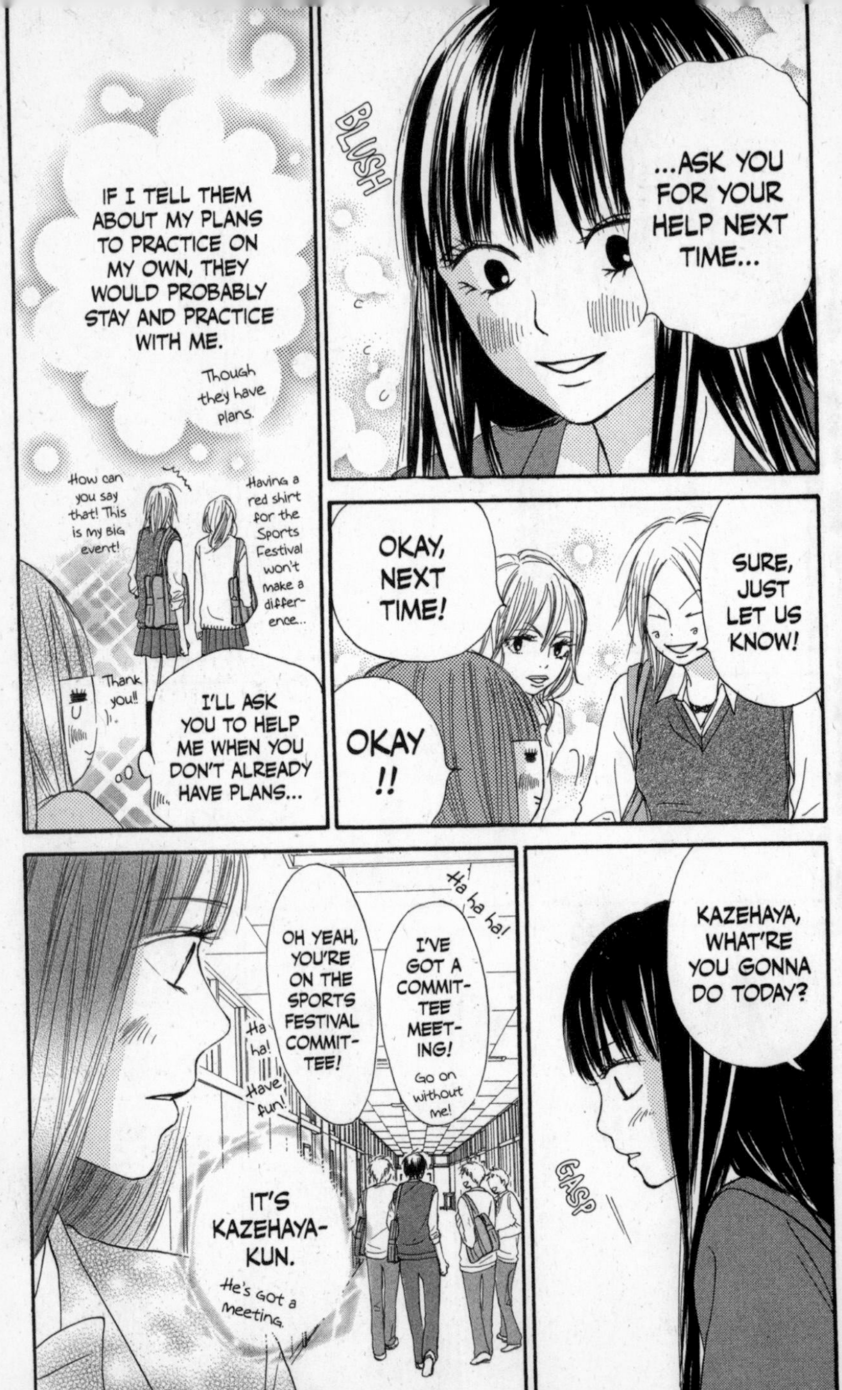
BLUSH
...ASK YOU FOR YOUR HELP NEXT TIME...
SURE, JUST LET US KNOW!
OKAY, NEXT TIME!
OKAY !!
IF I TELL THEM ABOUT MY PLANS TO PRACTICE ON MY OWN, THEY WOULD PROBABLY STAY AND PRACTICE WITH ME.
Though they have plans.
Having a red shirt for the Sports Festival won't make a difference...
How can you say that! This is my BIG event!
I'LL ASK YOU TO HELP ME WHEN YOU DON'T ALREADY HAVE PLANS...
Thank you!!
KAZEHAYA, WHAT'RE YOU GONNA DO TODAY?
GASP
Ha ha ha!
I'VE GOT A COMMITTEE MEETING!
Go on without me!
OH YEAH, YOU'RE ON THE SPORTS FESTIVAL COMMITTEE!
Ha ha! Have fun!
IT'S KAZEHAYA-KUN.
He's got a meeting.

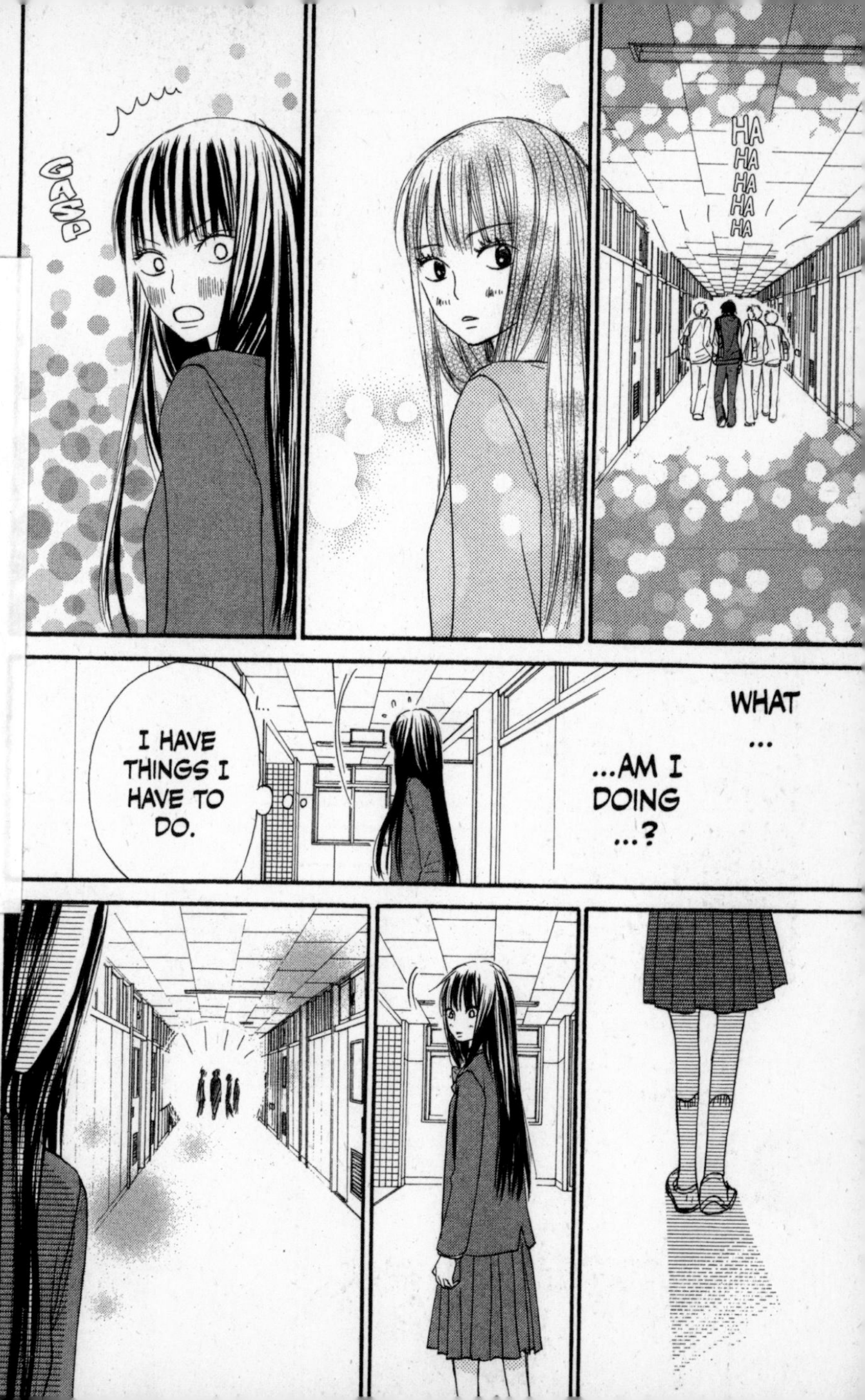
HA HA HA HA HA HA
GASP
WHAT ...
...AM I DOING ...?
I HAVE THINGS I HAVE TO DO.

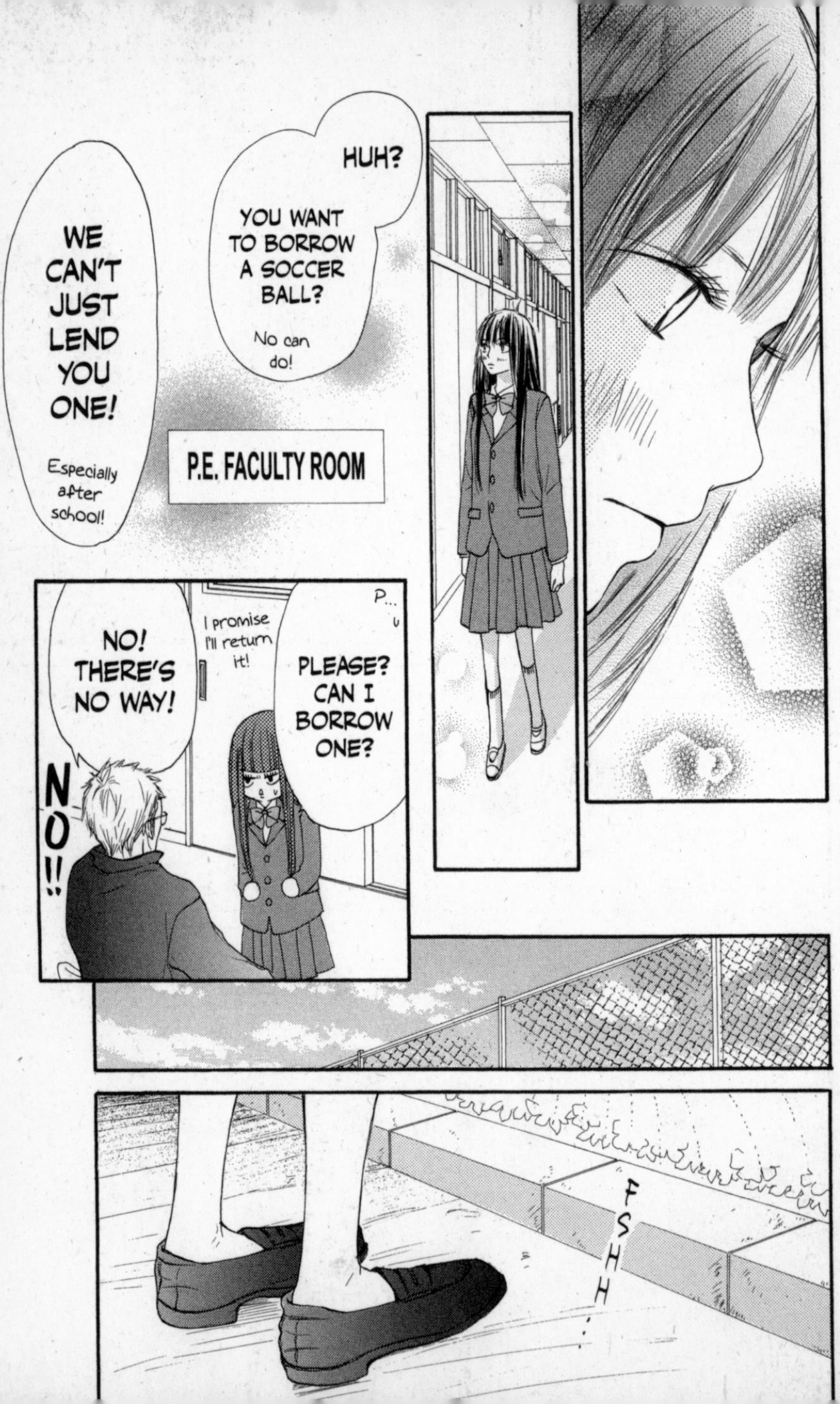
HUH? YOU WANT TO BORROW A SOCCER BALL?
No can do!
WE CAN'T JUST LEND YOU ONE!
Especially after school!
P.E. FACULTY ROOM
P...
PLEASE? CAN I BORROW ONE?
I promise I'll return it!
NO! THERE'S NO WAY!
NO!!
FSHH..

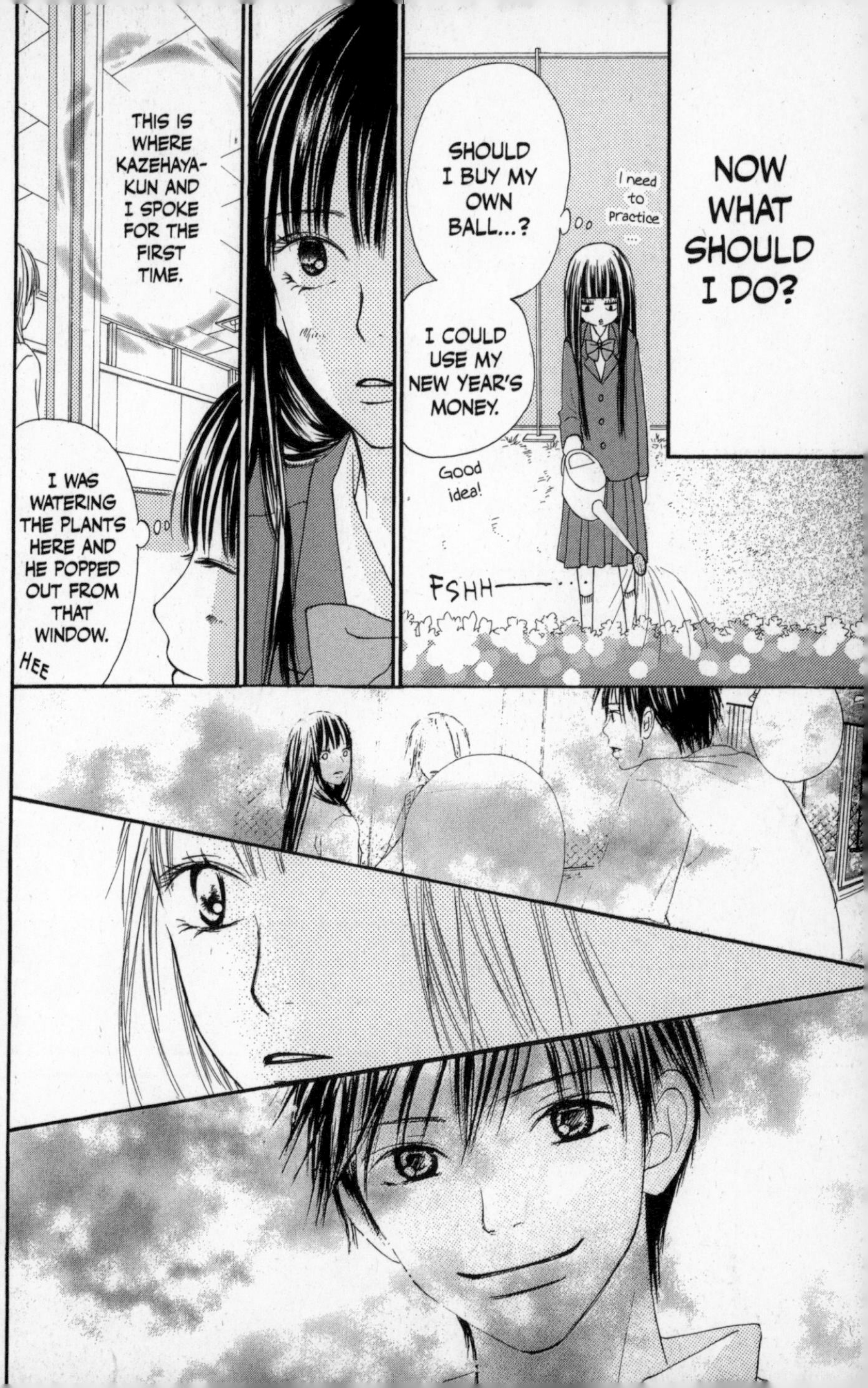
NOW WHAT SHOULD I DO?
I need to Practice ...
SHOULD I BUY MY OWN BALL...?
I COULD USE MY NEW YEAR'S MONEY.
Good idea!
FSHH—...
THIS IS WHERE KAZEHAYA-KUN AND I SPOKE FOR THE FIRST TIME.
I WAS WATERING THE PLANTS HERE AND HE POPPED OUT FROM THAT WINDOW.
HEE

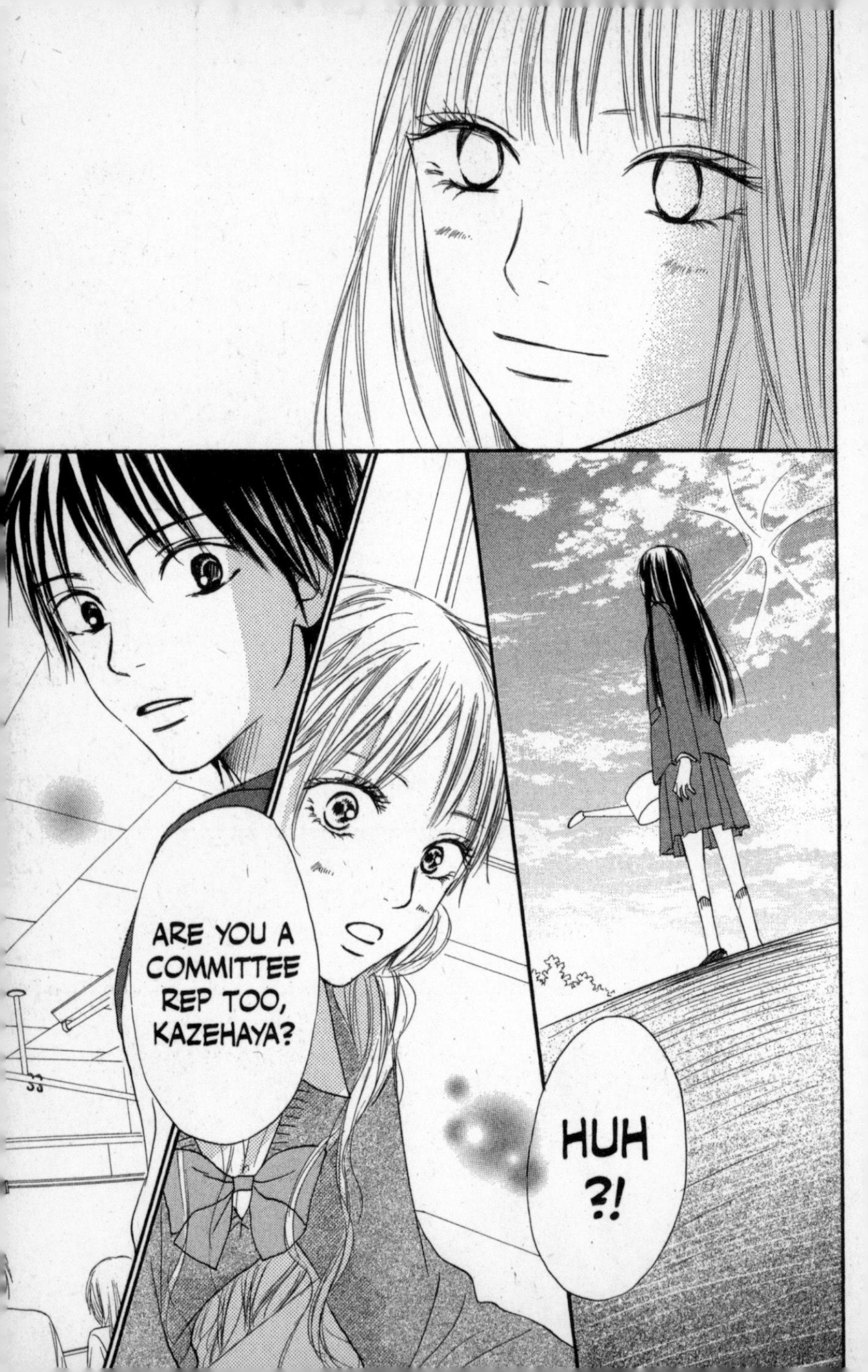
ARE YOU A COMMITTEE REP TOO, KAZEHAYA?
HUH ?!

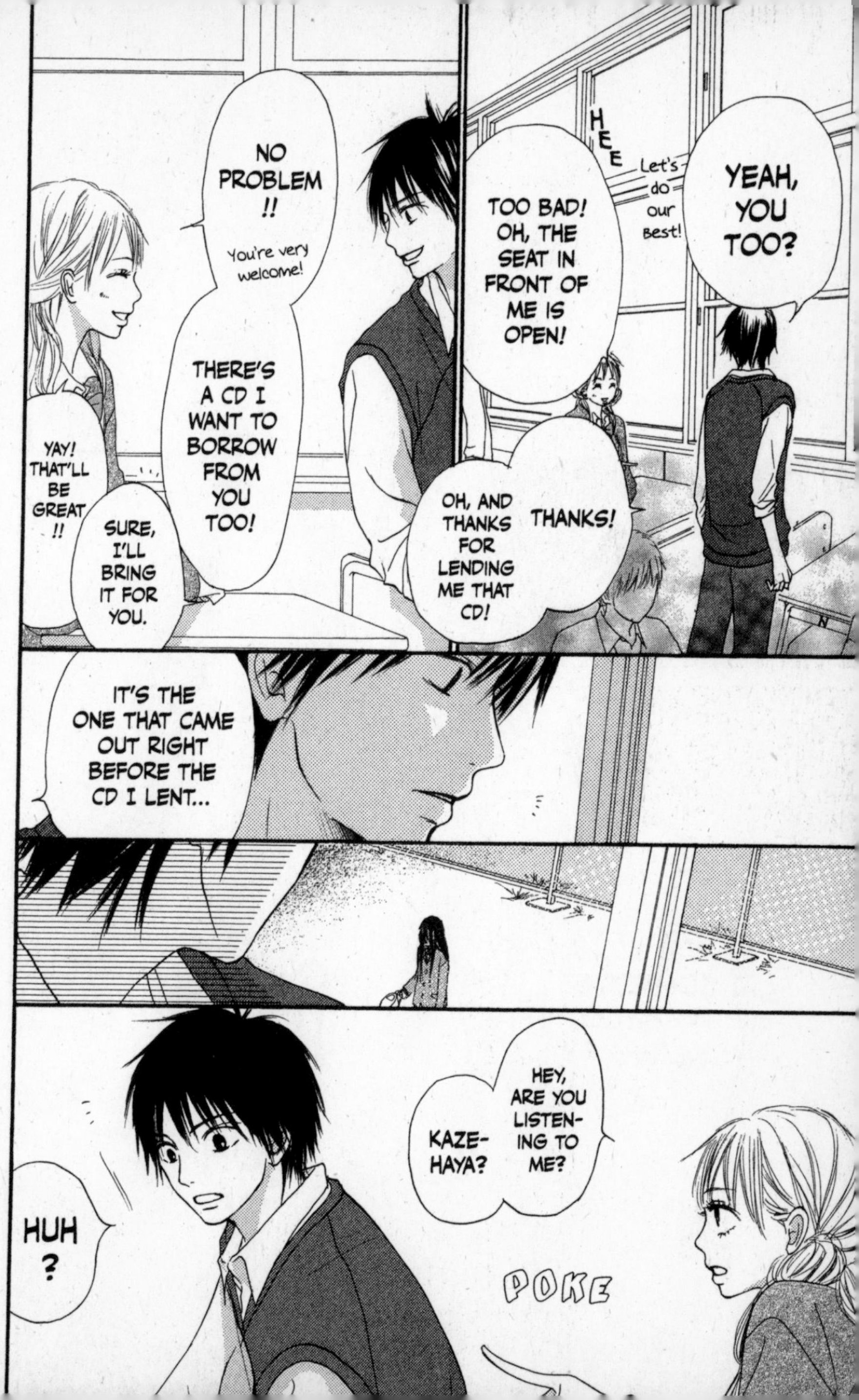
YEAH, YOU TOO?
Let's do our best!
HEE
TOO BAD! OH, THE SEAT IN FRONT OF ME IS OPEN!
THANKS!
OH, AND THANKS FOR LENDING ME THAT CD!
NO PROBLEM !!
You're very welcome!
THERE'S A CD I WANT TO BORROW FROM YOU TOO!
SURE, I'LL BRING IT FOR YOU.
YAY! THAT'LL BE GREAT !!
IT'S THE ONE THAT CAME OUT RIGHT BEFORE THE CD I LENT...
HEY, ARE YOU LISTENING TO ME?
KAZE-HAYA?
POKE
HUH ?

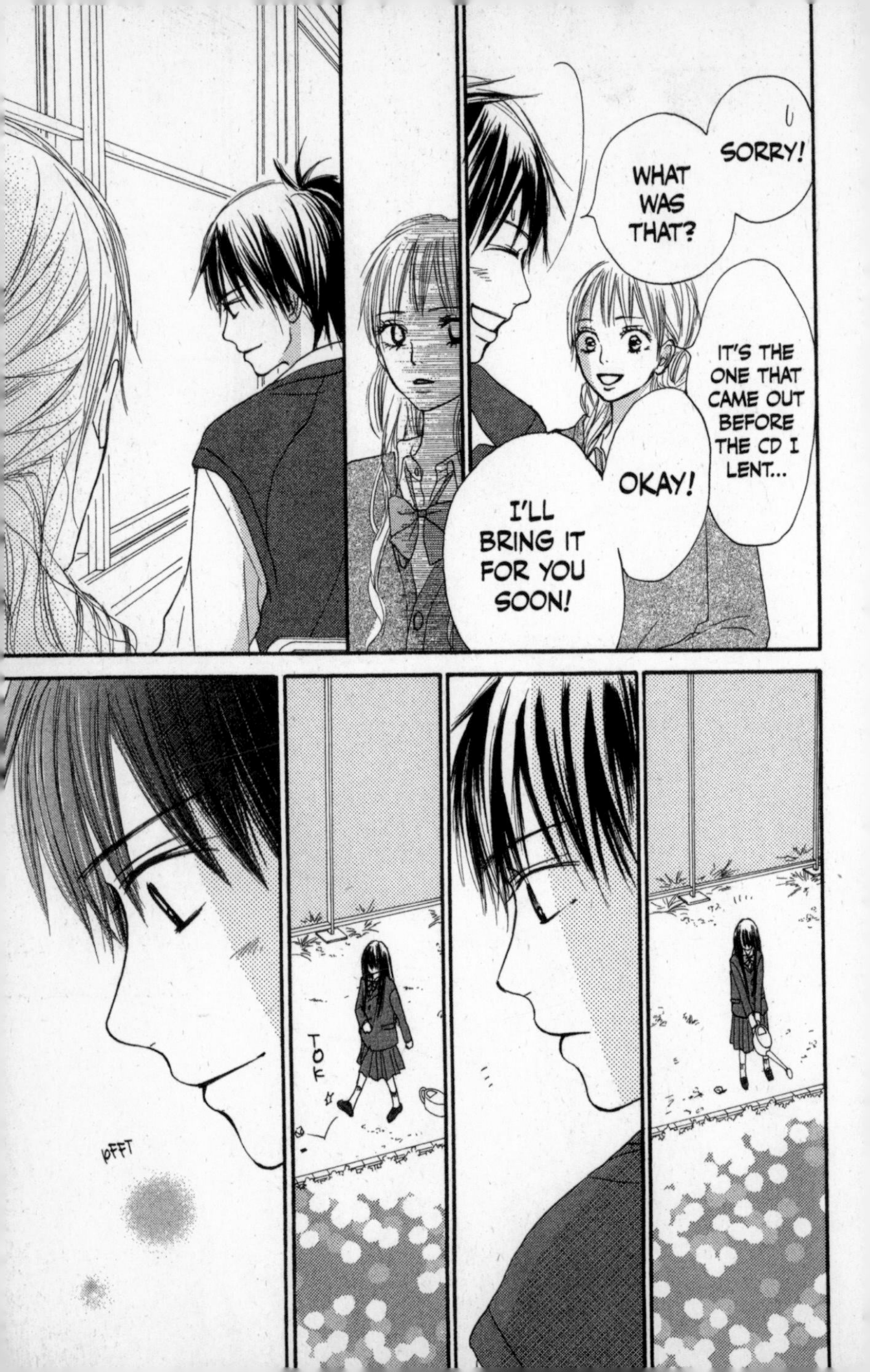
SORRY! WHAT WAS THAT?
IT'S THE ONE THAT CAME OUT BEFORE THE CD I LENT...
OKAY!
I'LL BRING IT FOR YOU SOON!
TOK
POFFT

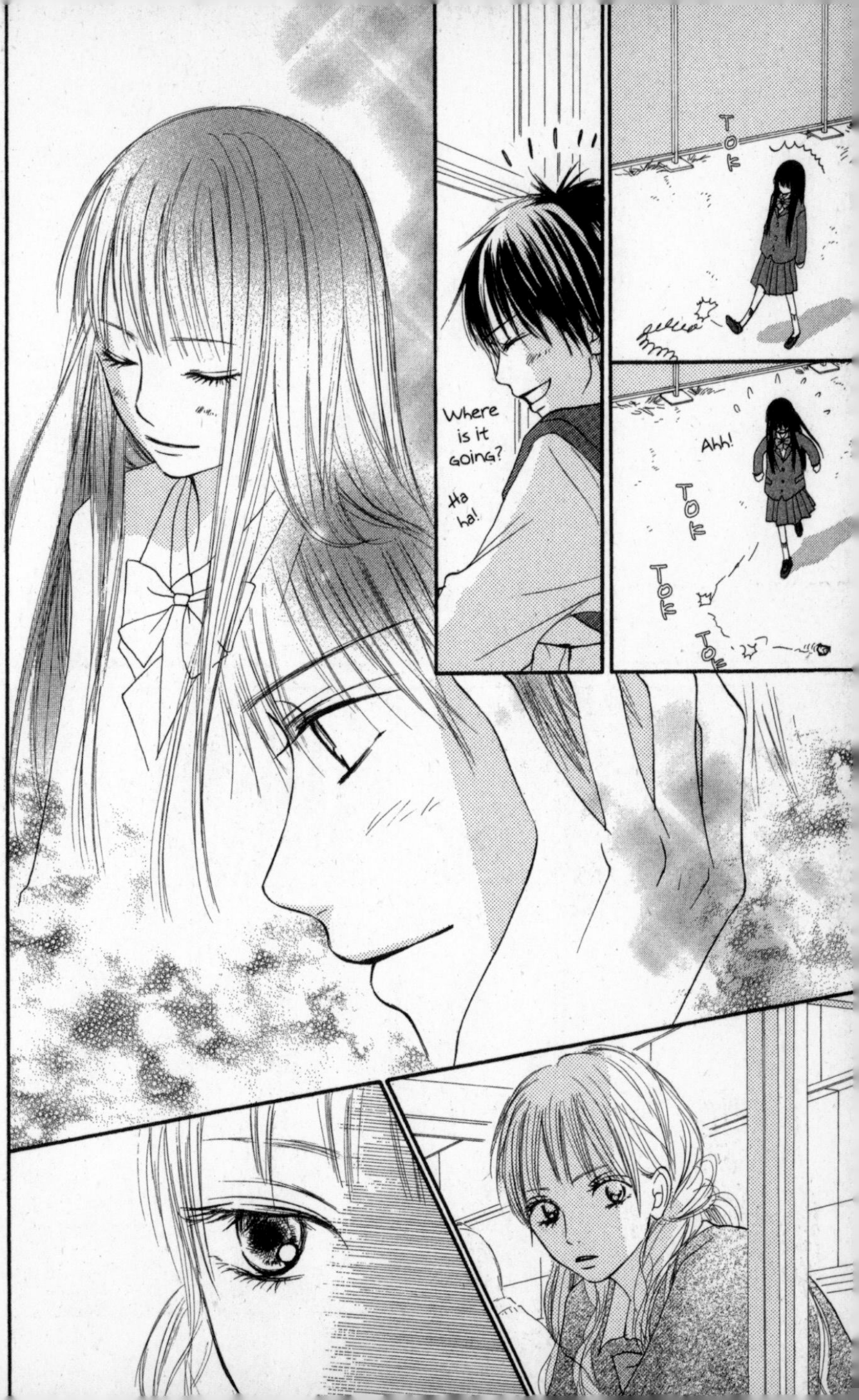
TOK
Ahh!
TOK
TOK
TOK
Where is it going?
Ha ha!

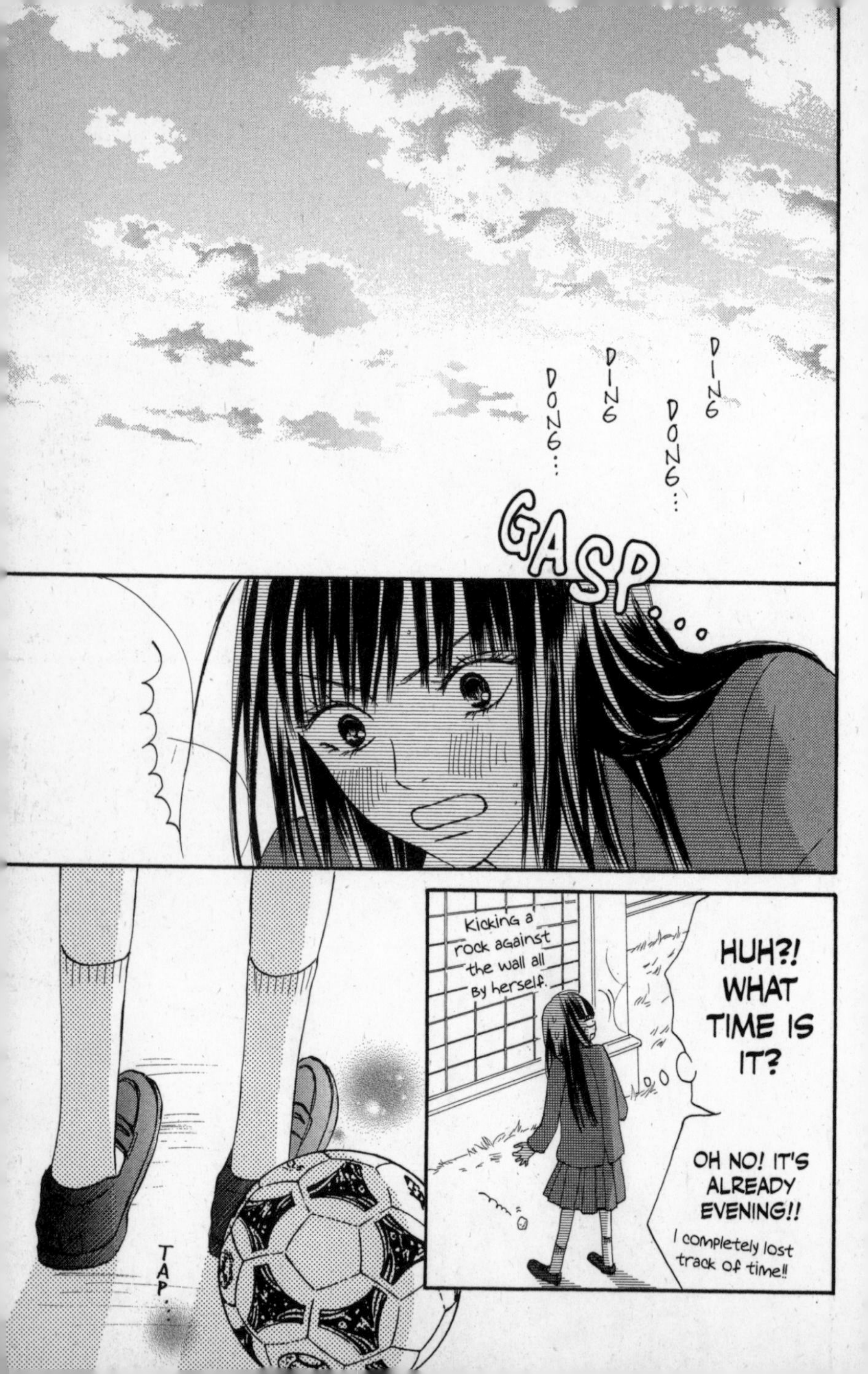
DING DONG...
DING DONG...
GASP...
HUH?! WHAT TIME IS IT?
OH NO! IT'S ALREADY EVENING!!
I completely lost track of time!!
Kicking a rock against the wall all by herself.
TAP...

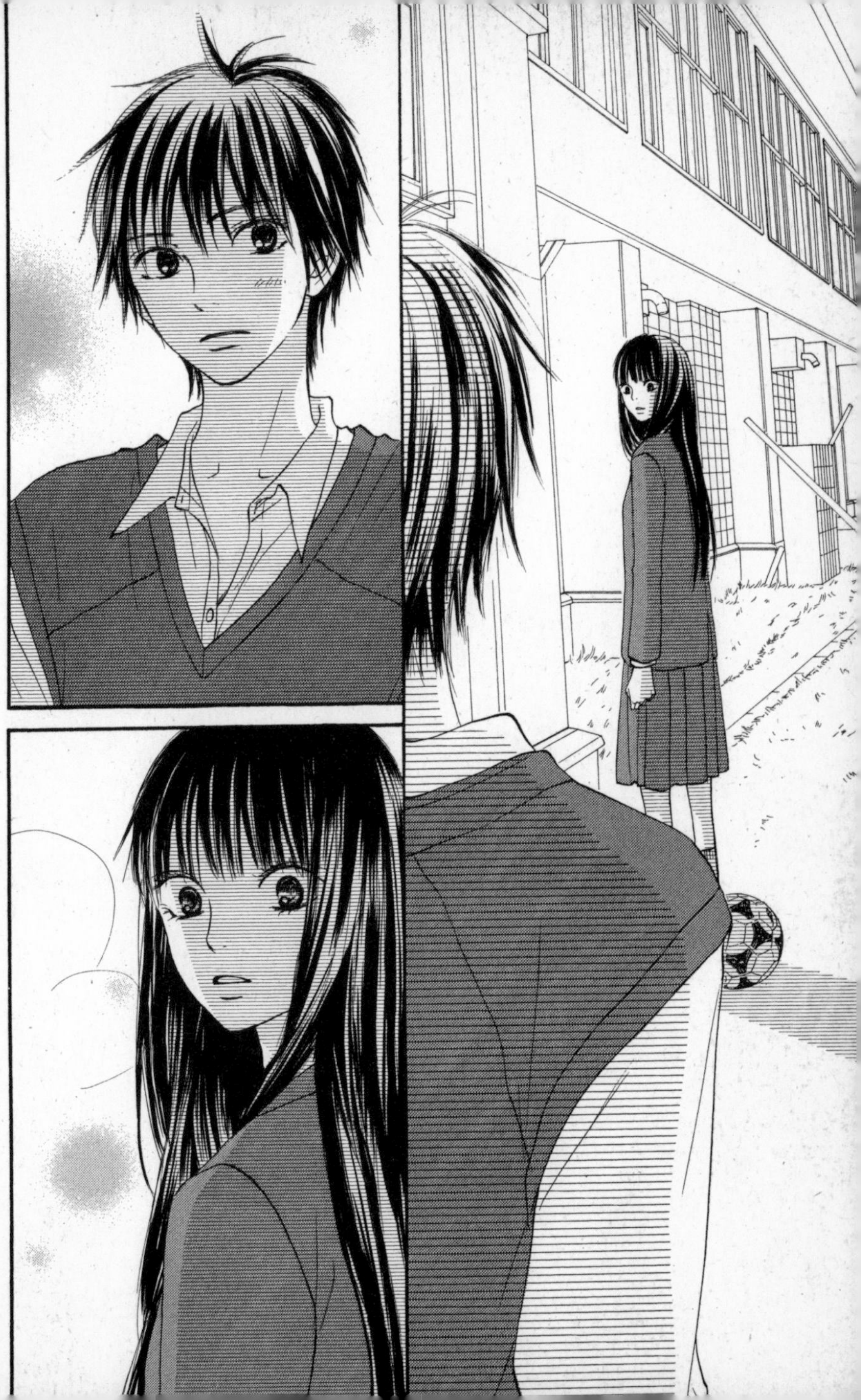

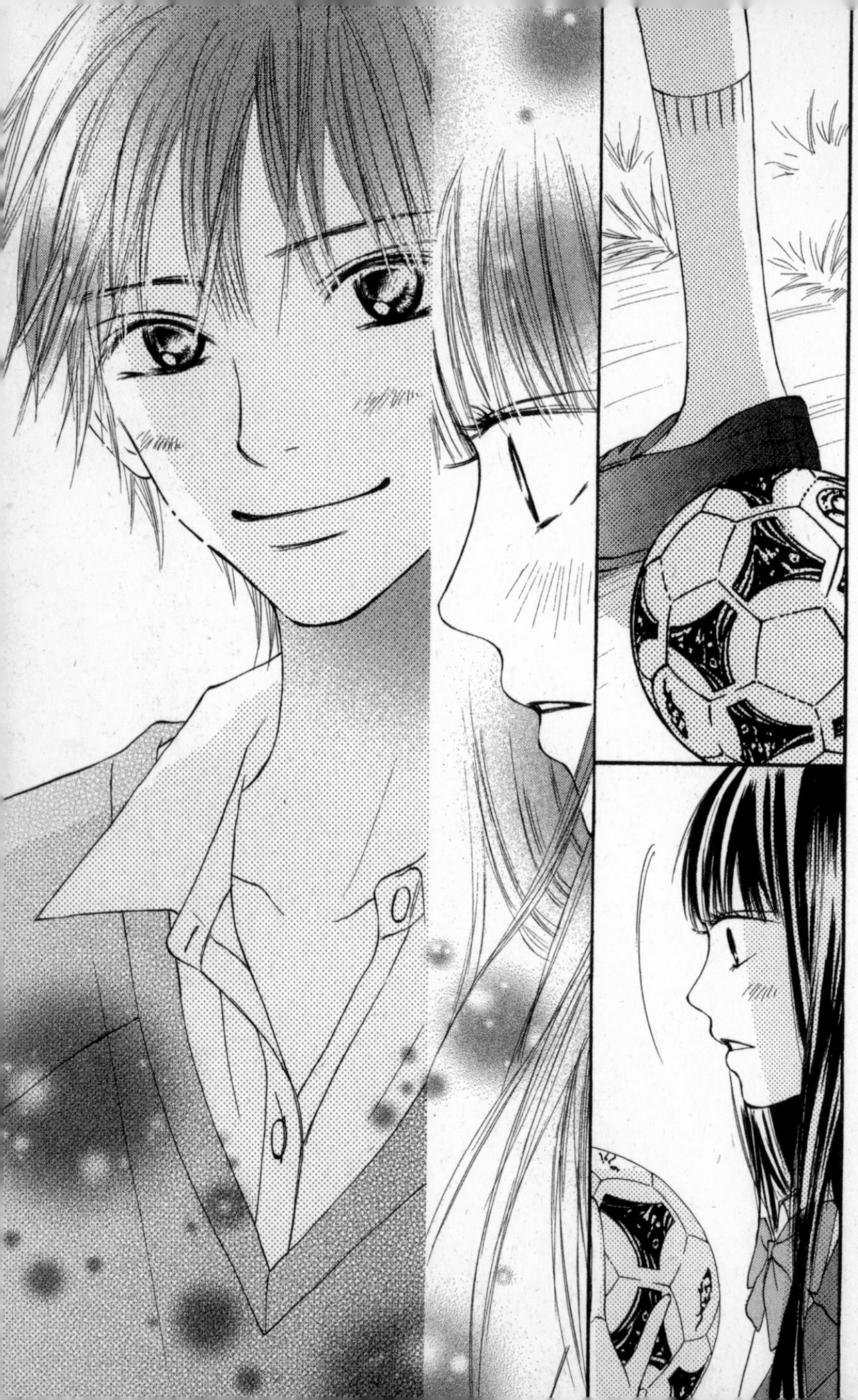

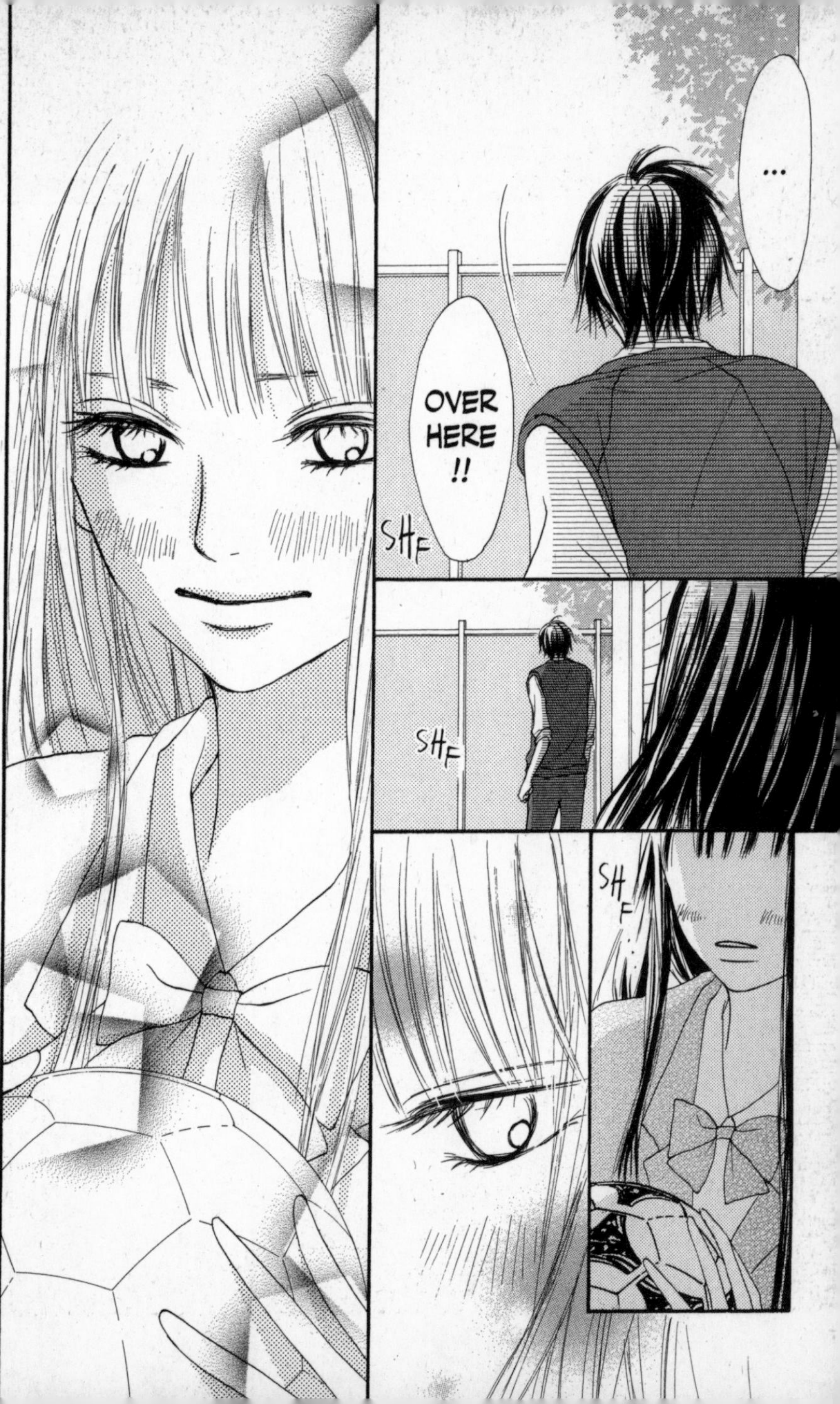
...
OVER HERE !!
SHF
SHF
SHF

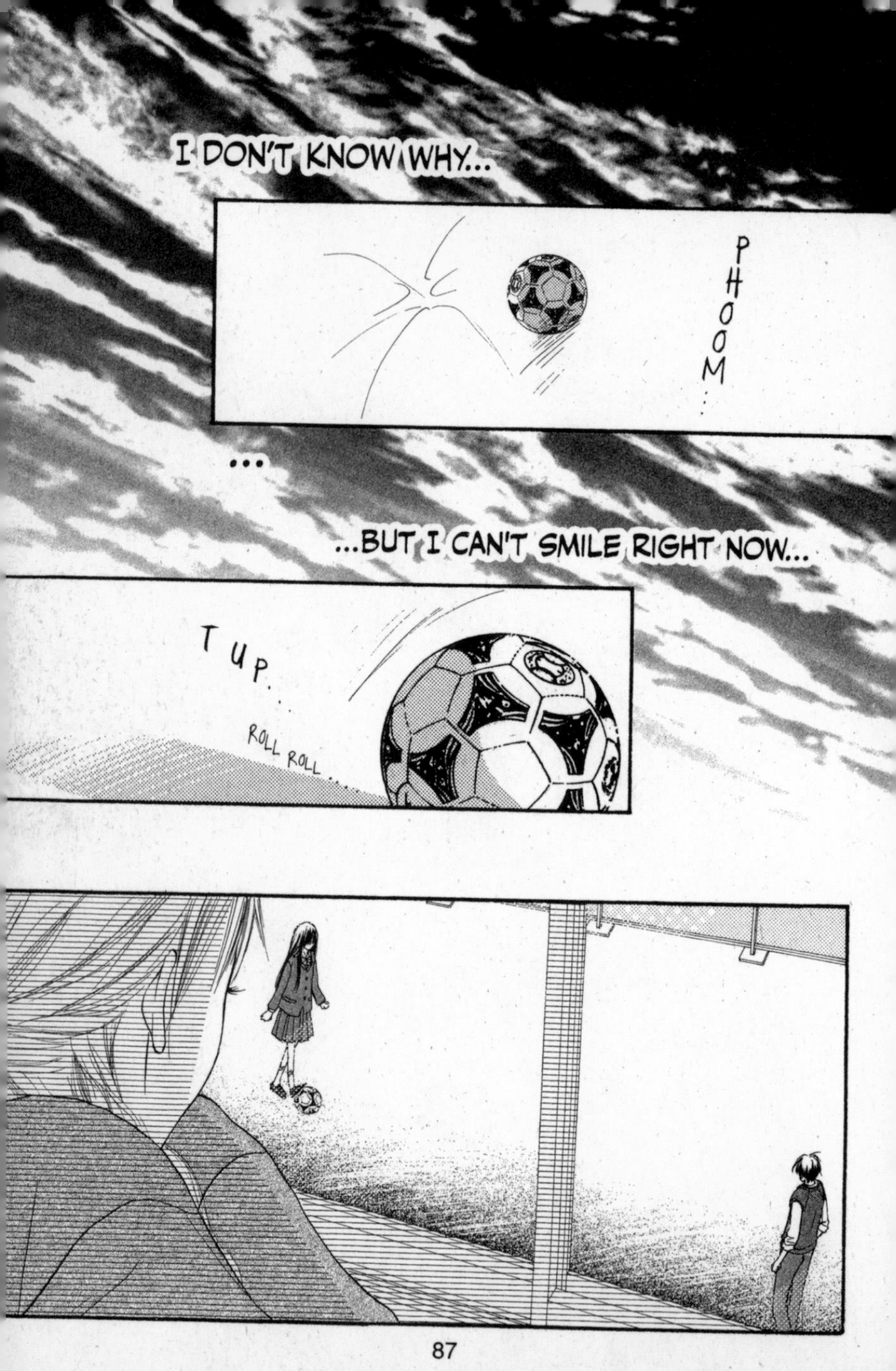
I DON'T KNOW WHY...
PHOOM...
...
...BUT I CAN'T SMILE RIGHT NOW...
TUP...
ROLL ROLL...

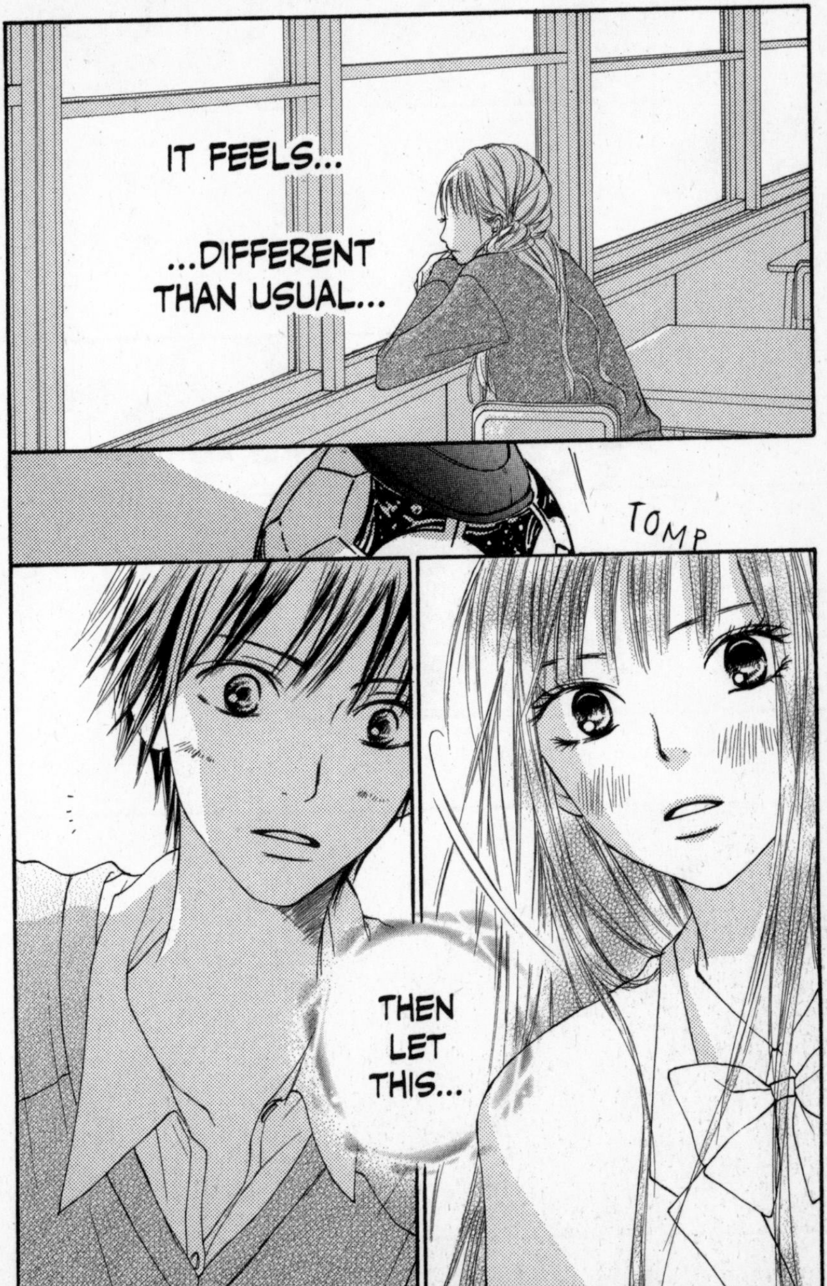
IT FEELS...
...DIFFERENT THAN USUAL...
TOMP
THEN LET THIS...

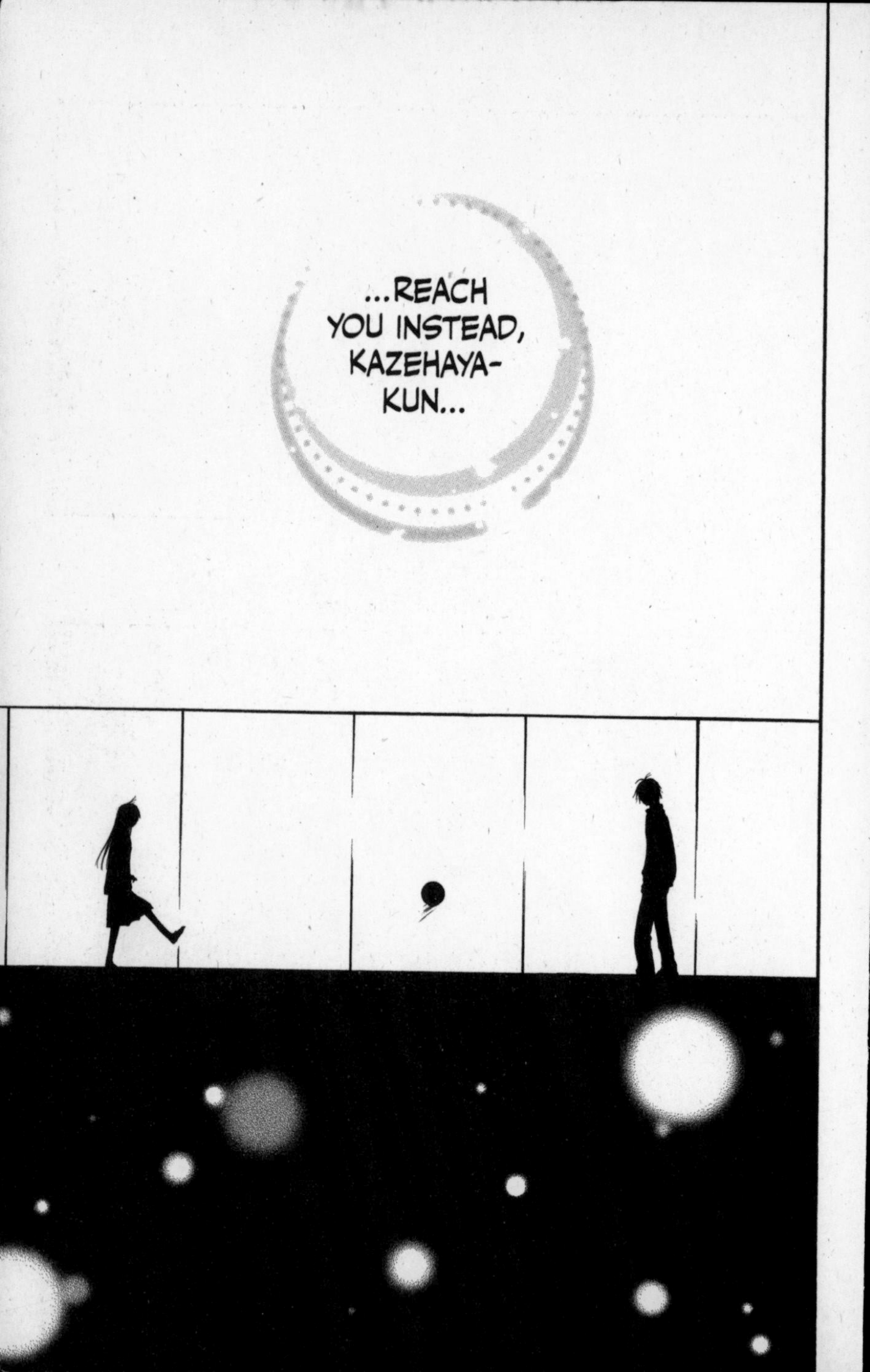
...REACH YOU INSTEAD, KAZEHAYA-KUN...

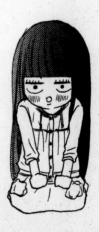

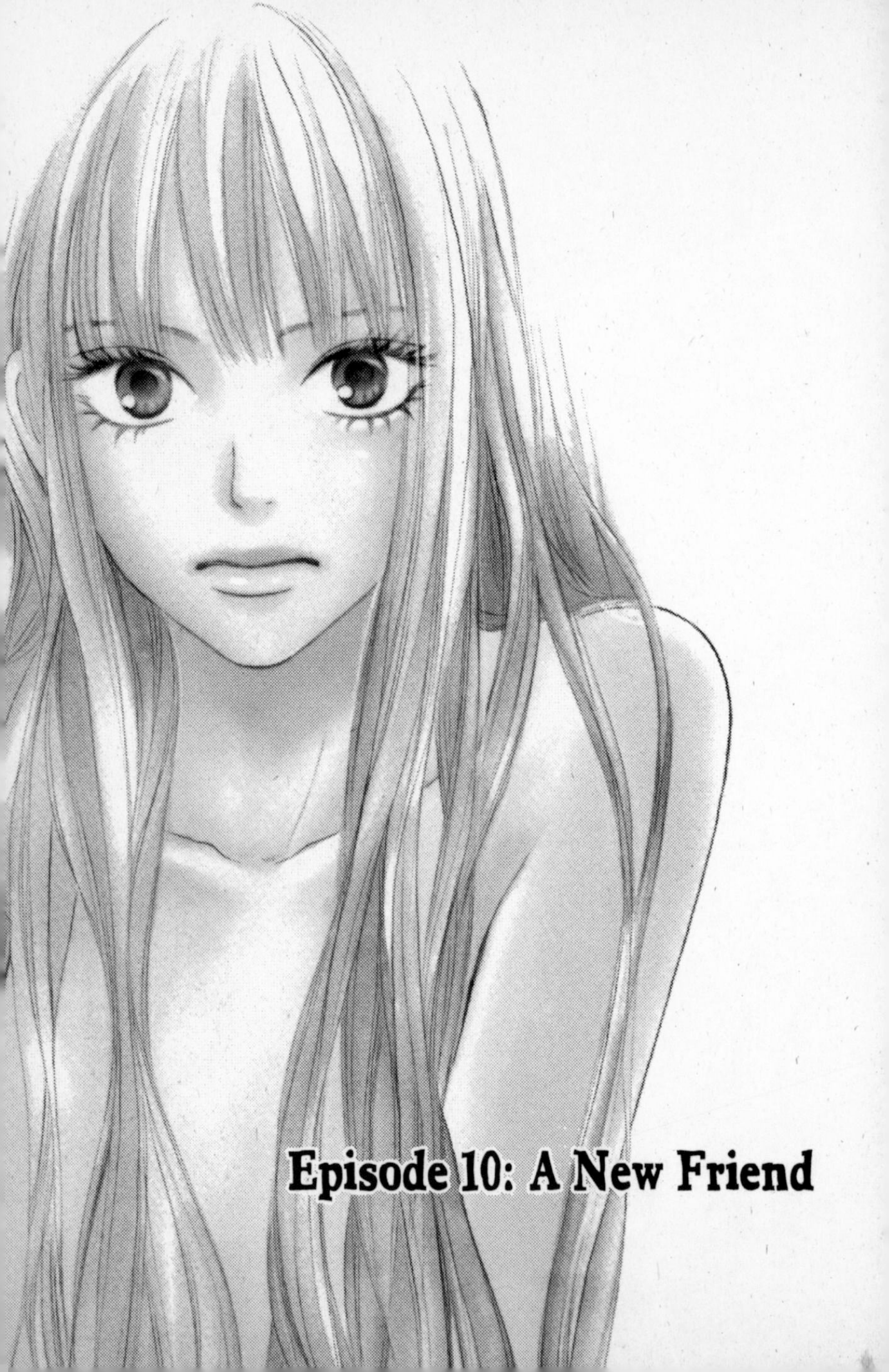
Episode 10: A New Friend

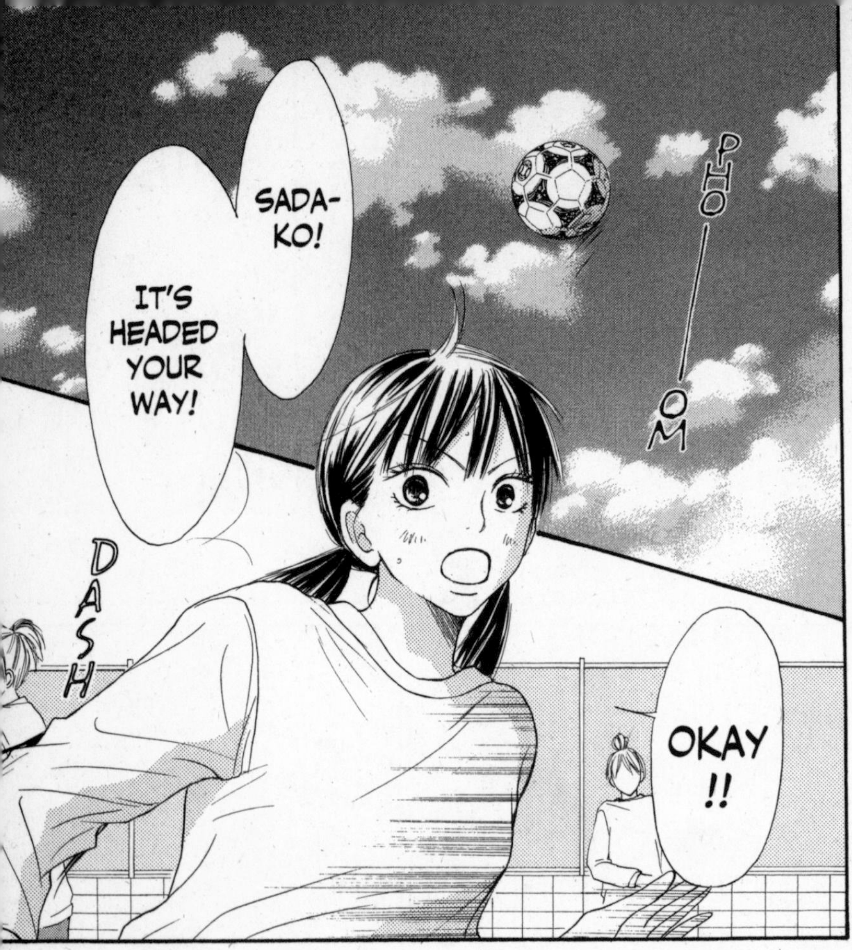
PHO—OM
SADA-KO!
IT'S HEADED YOUR WAY!
OKAY!!
DASH

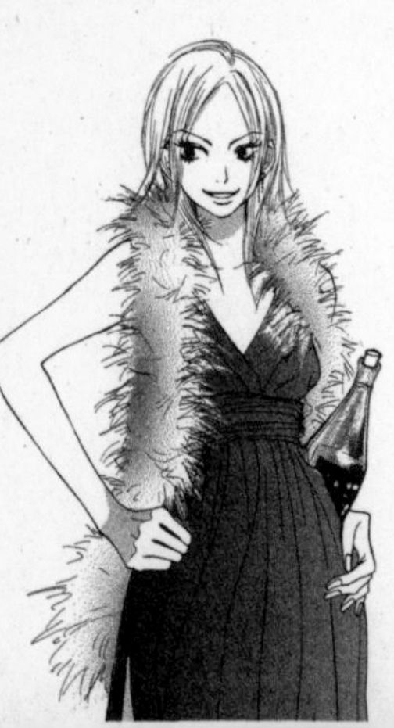

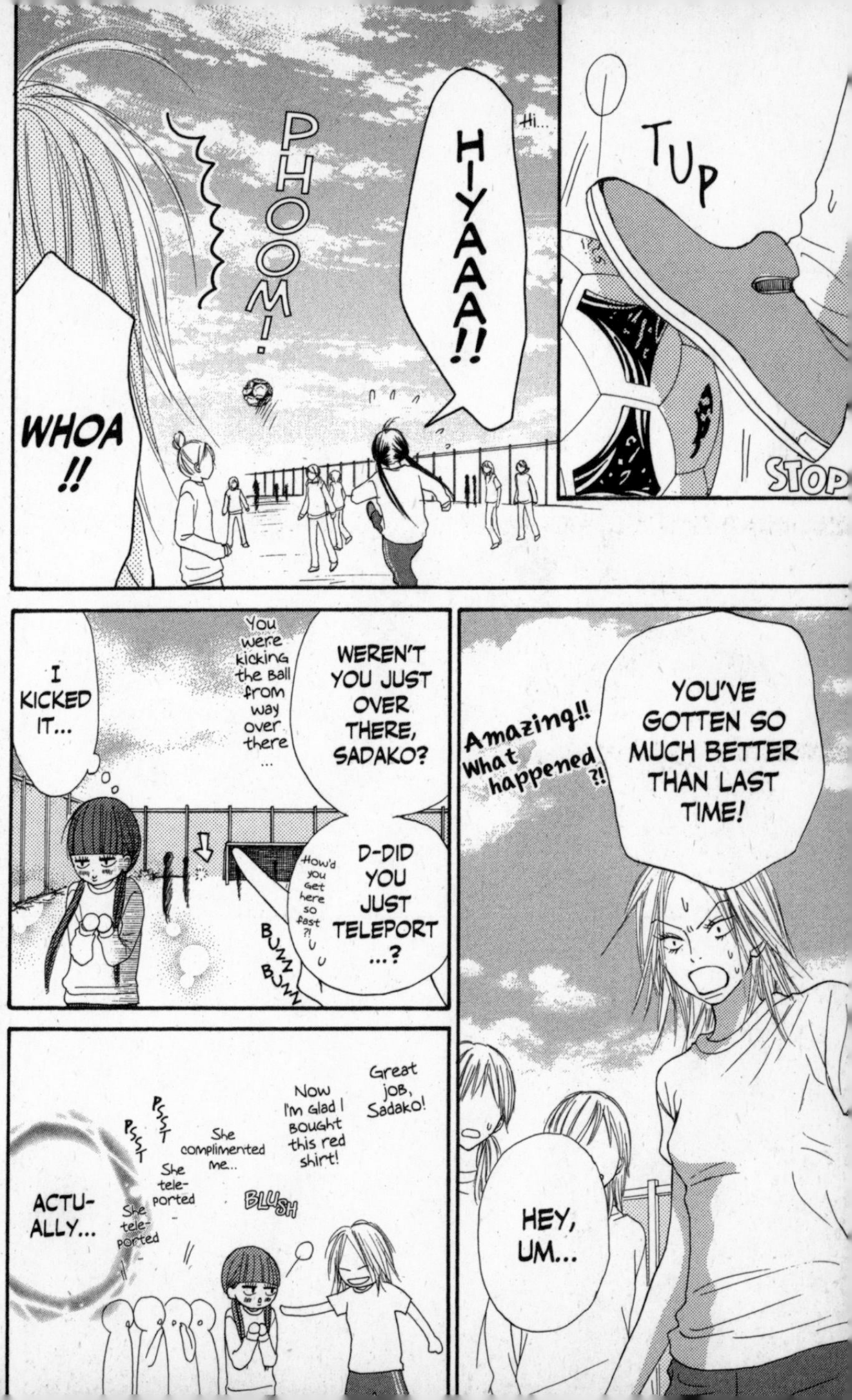
TUP
STOP
Hi...
HIYAAA!!
PHOOOM!
WHOA!!
YOU'VE GOTTEN SO MUCH BETTER THAN LAST TIME!
Amazing!! What happened?!
HEY, UM...
WEREN'T YOU JUST OVER THERE, SADAKO?
You were kicking the ball from way over there...
D-DID YOU JUST TELEPORT...?
How'd you get here so fast?!
BUZZ BUZZ
I KICKED IT...
Great job, Sadako!
Now I'm glad I bought this red shirt!
She complimented me..
BLUSH
PSSST
PSSST
She teleported
She teleported
ACTU-ALLY...

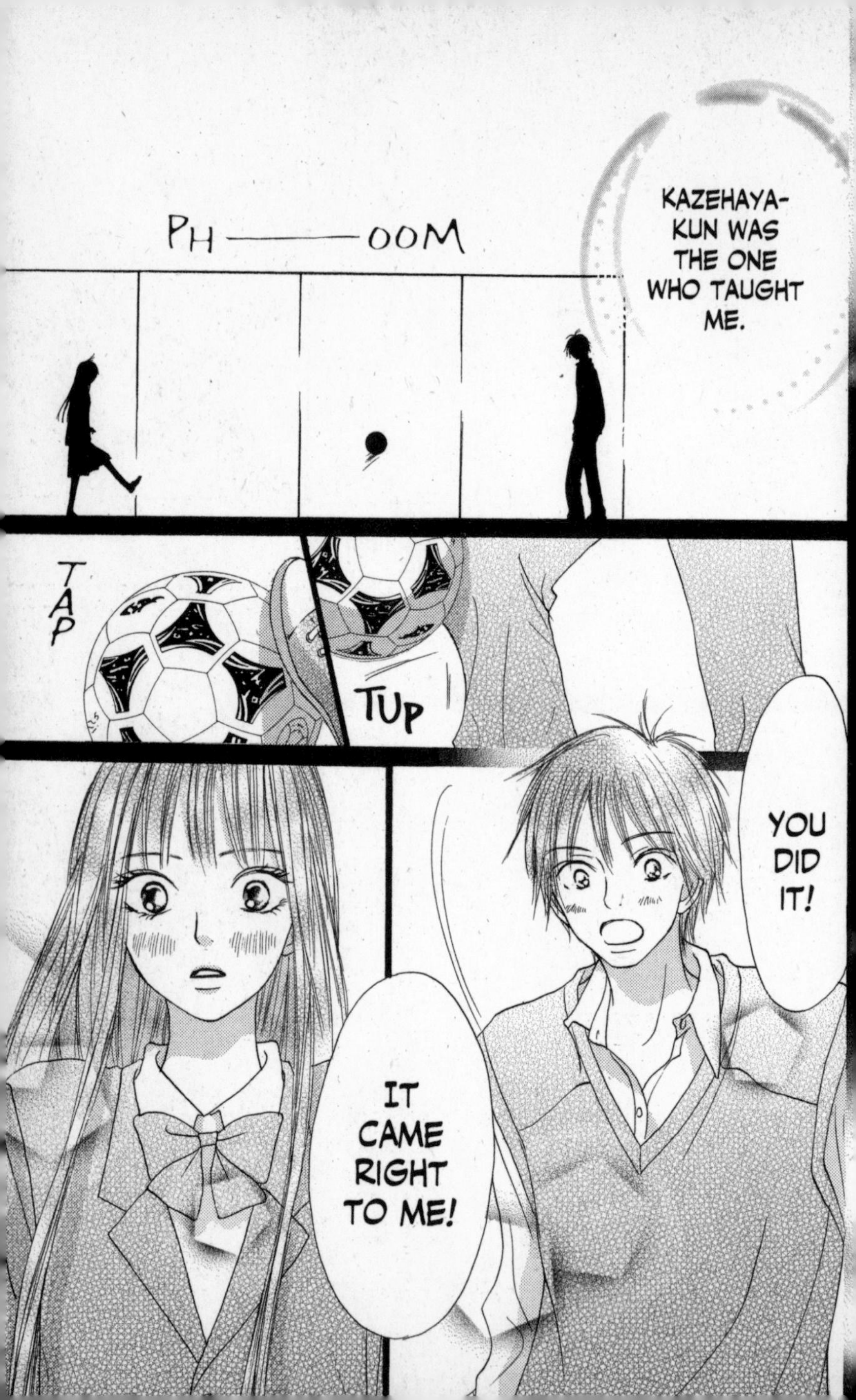
KAZEHAYA-KUN WAS THE ONE WHO TAUGHT ME.
PH——OOM
TUP
TAP
YOU DID IT!
IT CAME RIGHT TO ME!

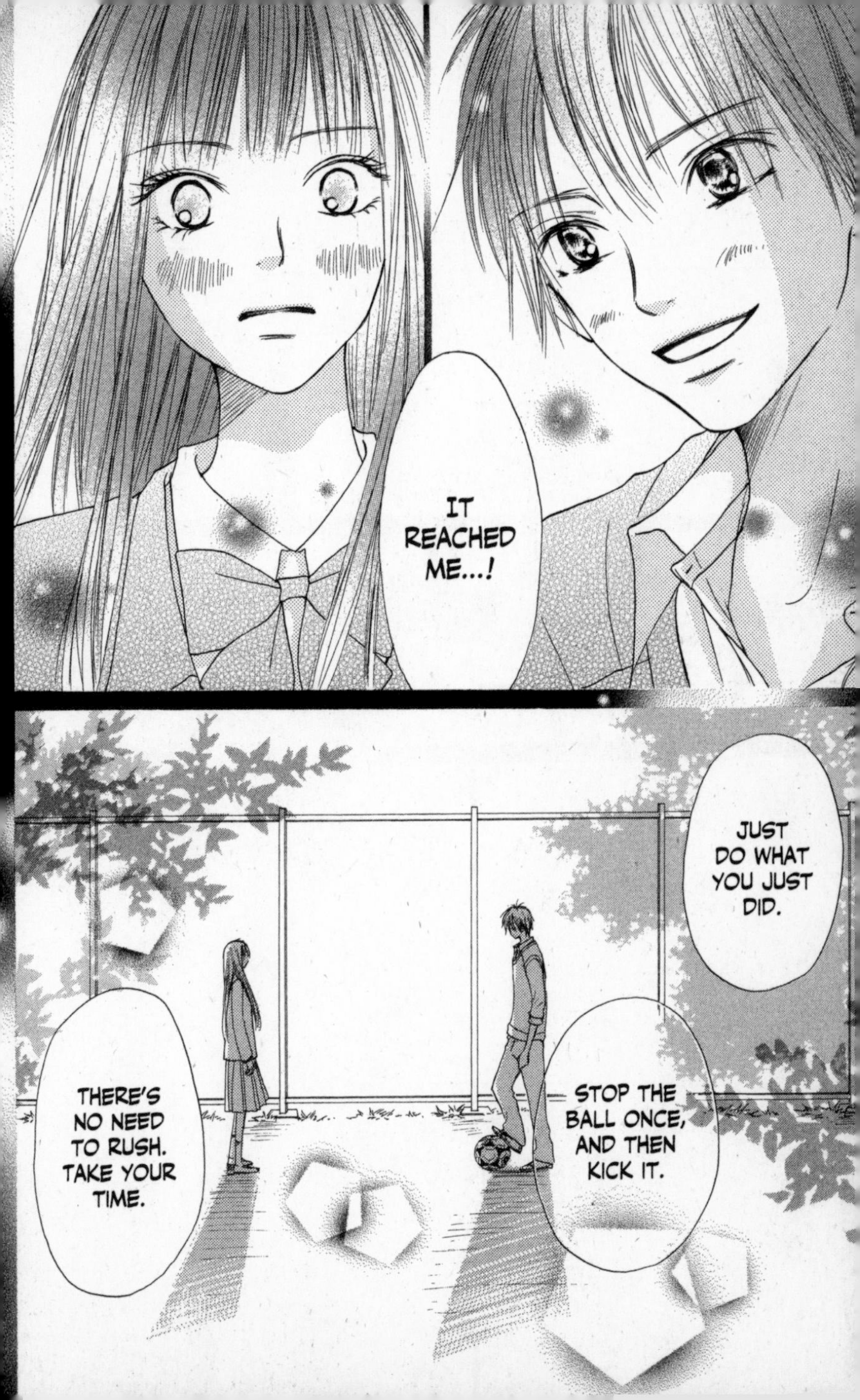
IT REACHED ME...!
JUST DO WHAT YOU JUST DID.
STOP THE BALL ONCE, AND THEN KICK IT.
THERE'S NO NEED TO RUSH. TAKE YOUR TIME.

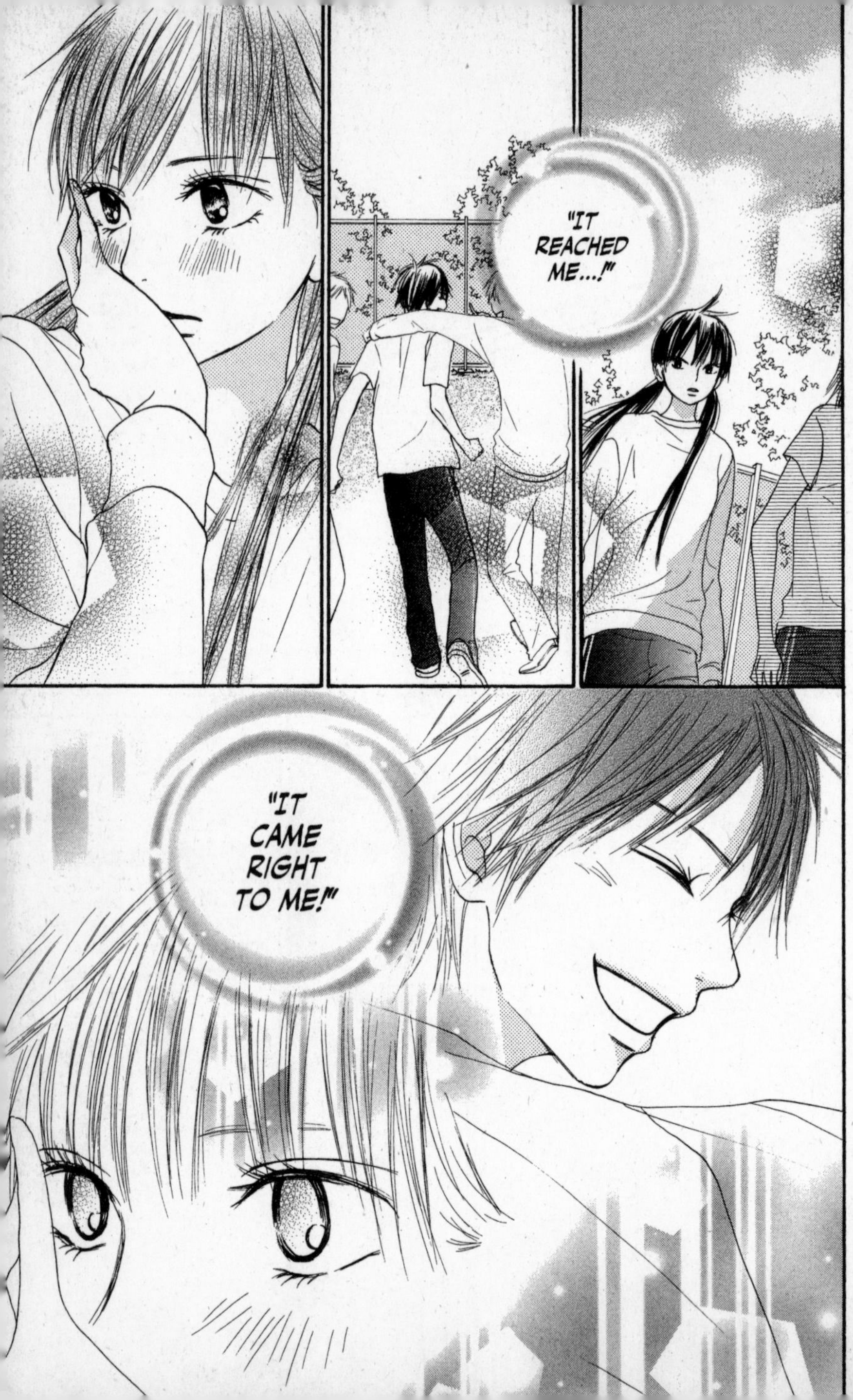
"IT REACHED ME...!"
"IT CAME RIGHT TO ME!"

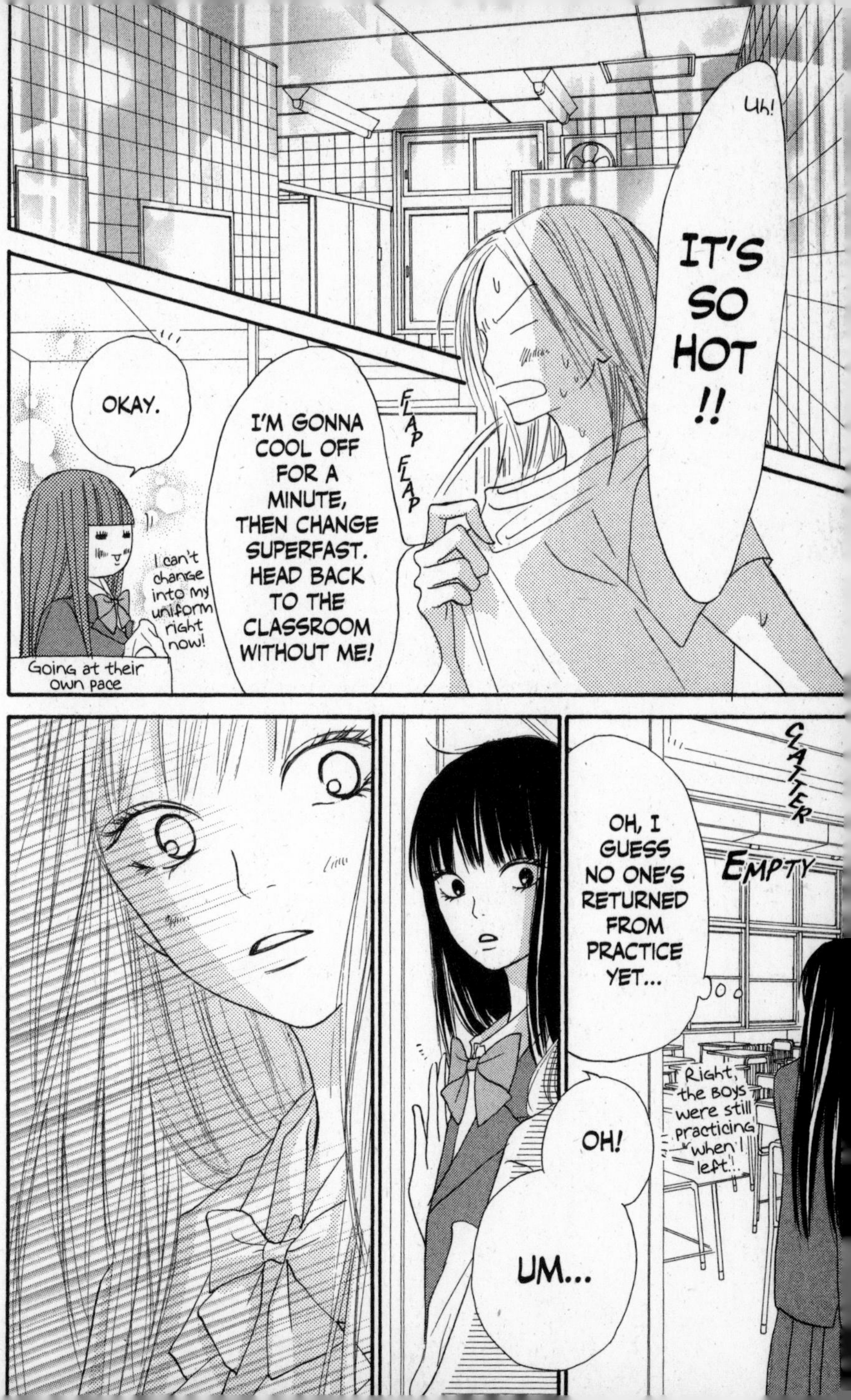

Uh!
IT'S SO HOT!!
FLAP FLAP
I'M GONNA COOL OFF FOR A MINUTE, THEN CHANGE SUPERFAST. HEAD BACK TO THE CLASSROOM WITHOUT ME!
OKAY.
I can't change into my uniform right now!
Going at their own pace
CLATTER
EMPTY
OH, I GUESS NO ONE'S RETURNED FROM PRACTICE YET...
Right, the boys were still practicing when I left...
OH!
UM...

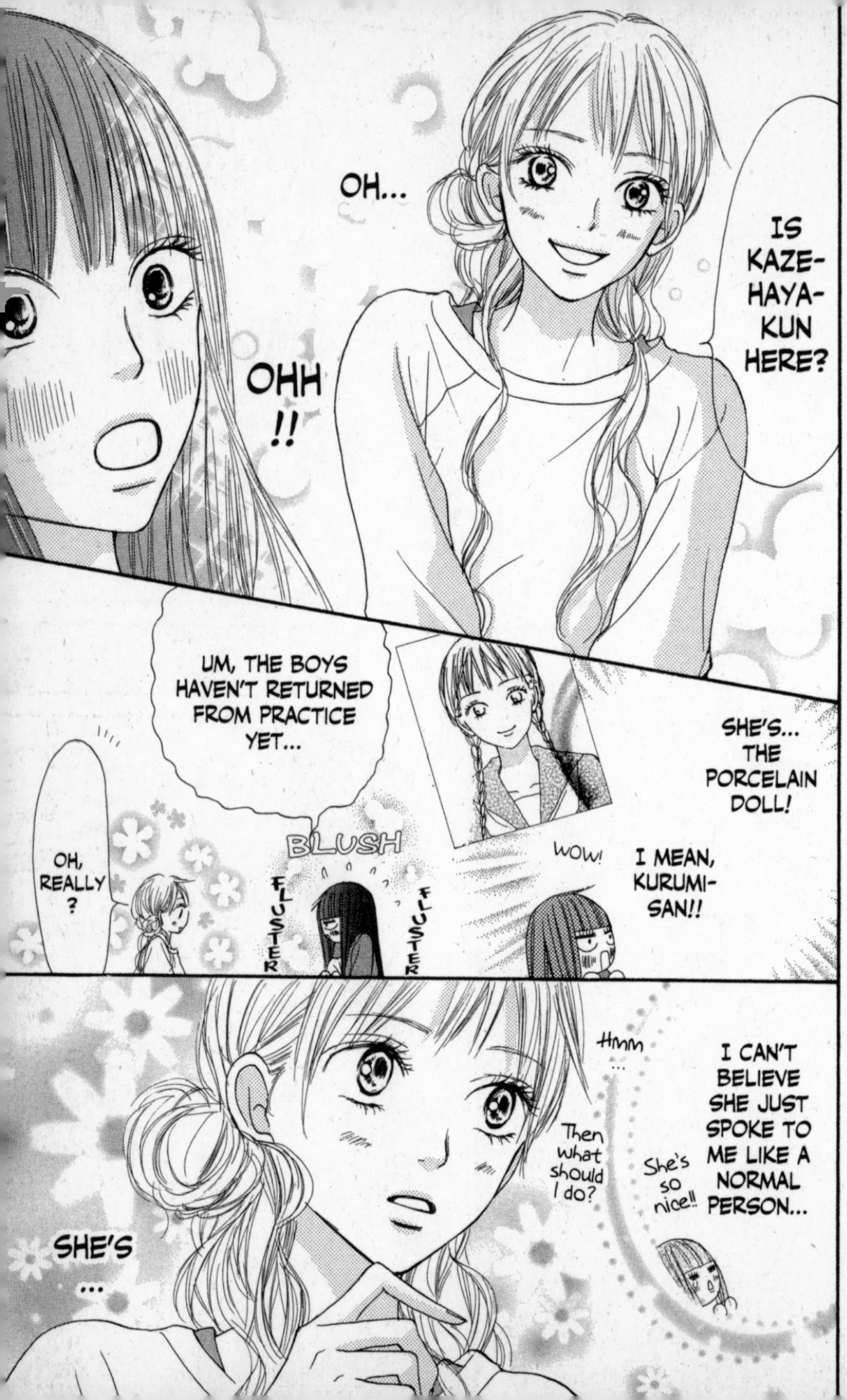
IS KAZE-HAYA-KUN HERE?
OH...
OHH !!
SHE'S... THE PORCELAIN DOLL!
I MEAN, KURUMI-SAN!!
WOW!
UM, THE BOYS HAVEN'T RETURNED FROM PRACTICE YET...
BLUSH
FLUSTER
FLUSTER
OH, REALLY ?
I CAN'T BELIEVE SHE JUST SPOKE TO ME LIKE A NORMAL PERSON...
She's so nice!!
Hmm ...
Then what should I do?
SHE'S ...

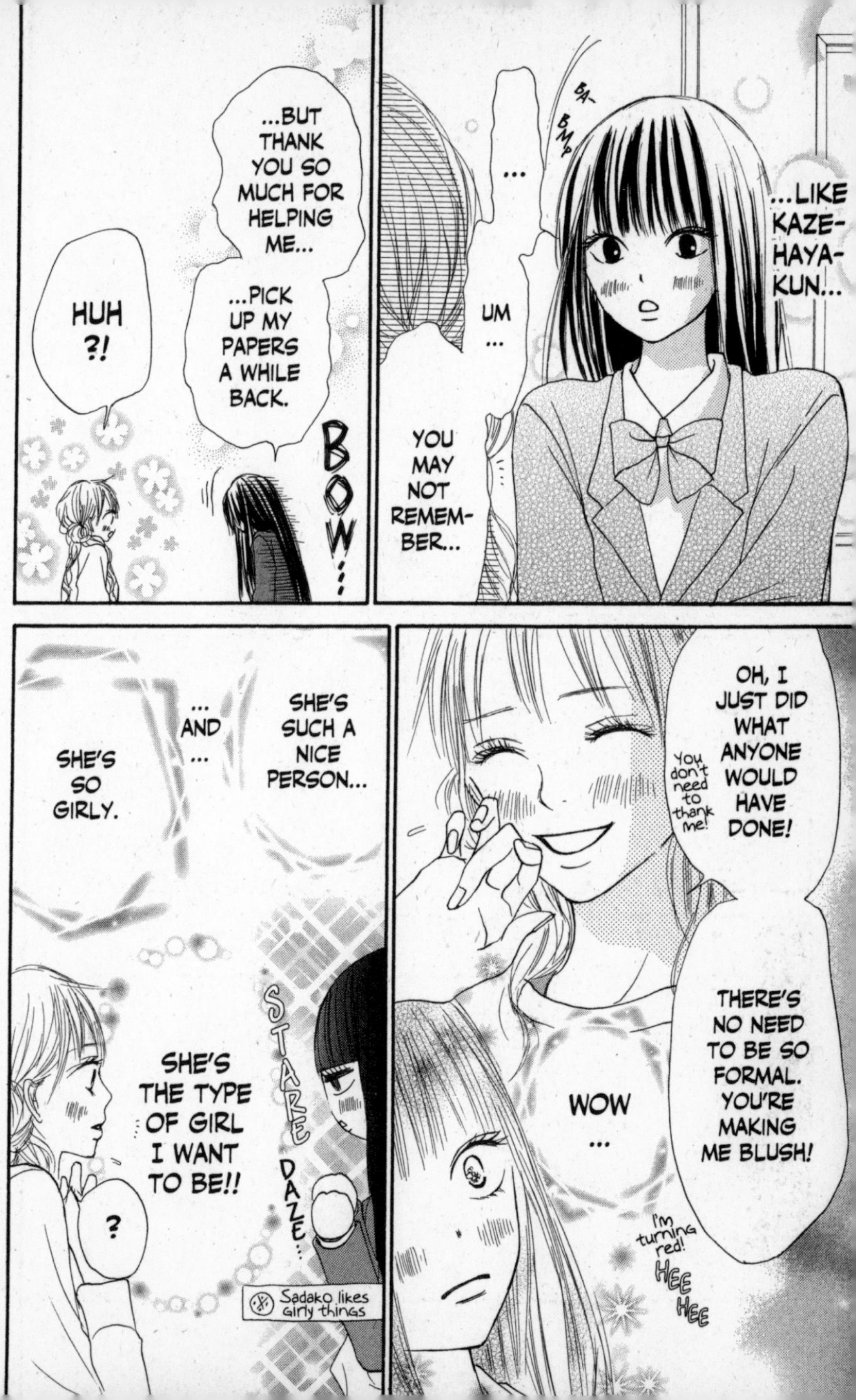
...LIKE KAZE-HAYA-KUN...
BA-BMP
UM...
...
YOU MAY NOT REMEMBER...
...BUT THANK YOU SO MUCH FOR HELPING ME...
...PICK UP MY PAPERS A WHILE BACK.
BOW...
HUH?!
OH, I JUST DID WHAT ANYONE WOULD HAVE DONE!
You don't need to thank me!
THERE'S NO NEED TO BE SO FORMAL. YOU'RE MAKING ME BLUSH!
WOW...
I'm turning red!
HEE HEE
SHE'S SUCH A NICE PERSON...
...AND...
SHE'S SO GIRLY.
SHE'S THE TYPE OF GIRL I WANT TO BE!!
STARE
DAZE...
?
Sadako likes girly things

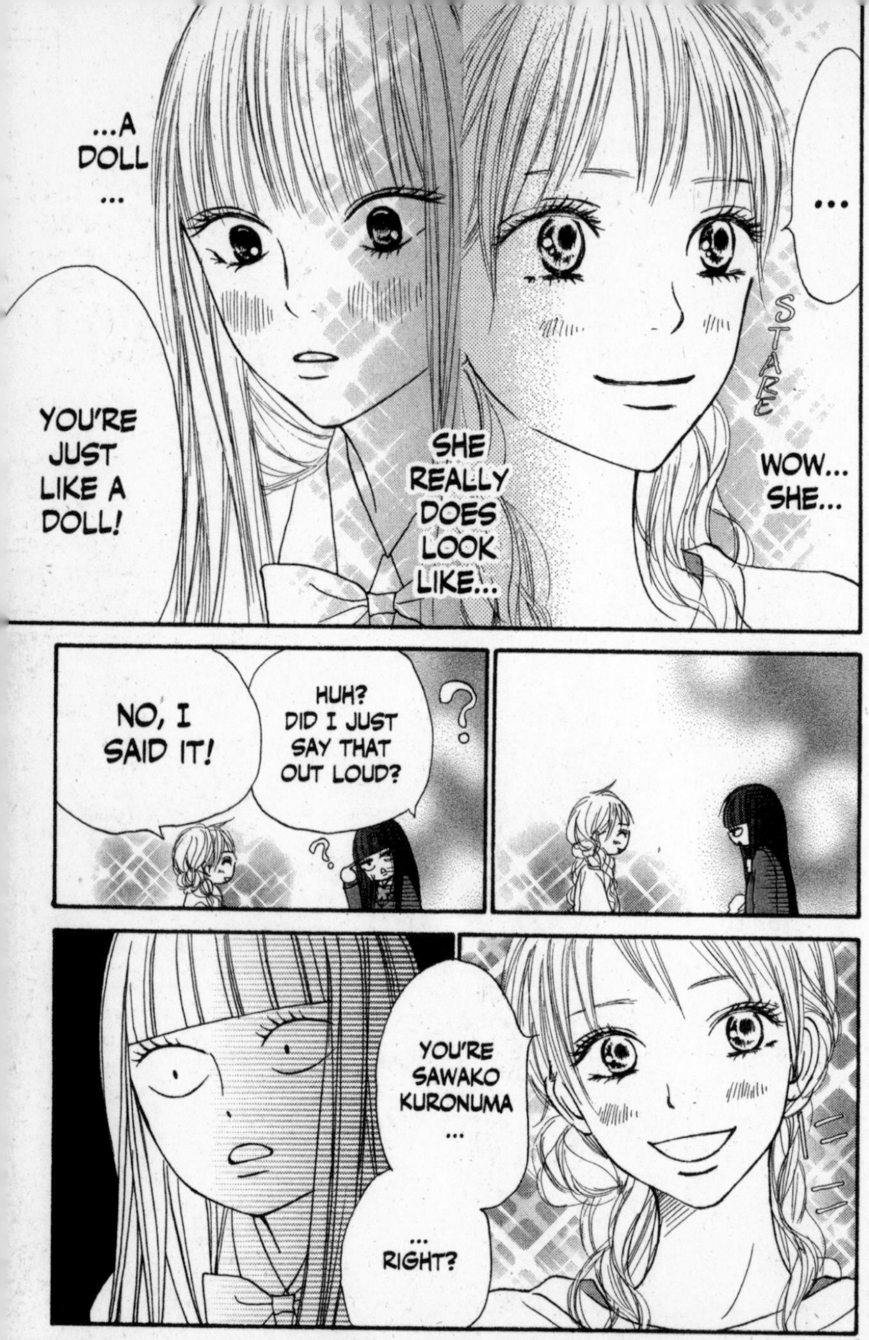
...
STARE
WOW... SHE...
SHE REALLY DOES LOOK LIKE...
...A DOLL ...
YOU'RE JUST LIKE A DOLL!
HUH? DID I JUST SAY THAT OUT LOUD?
NO, I SAID IT!
YOU'RE SAWAKO KURONUMA ...
... RIGHT?

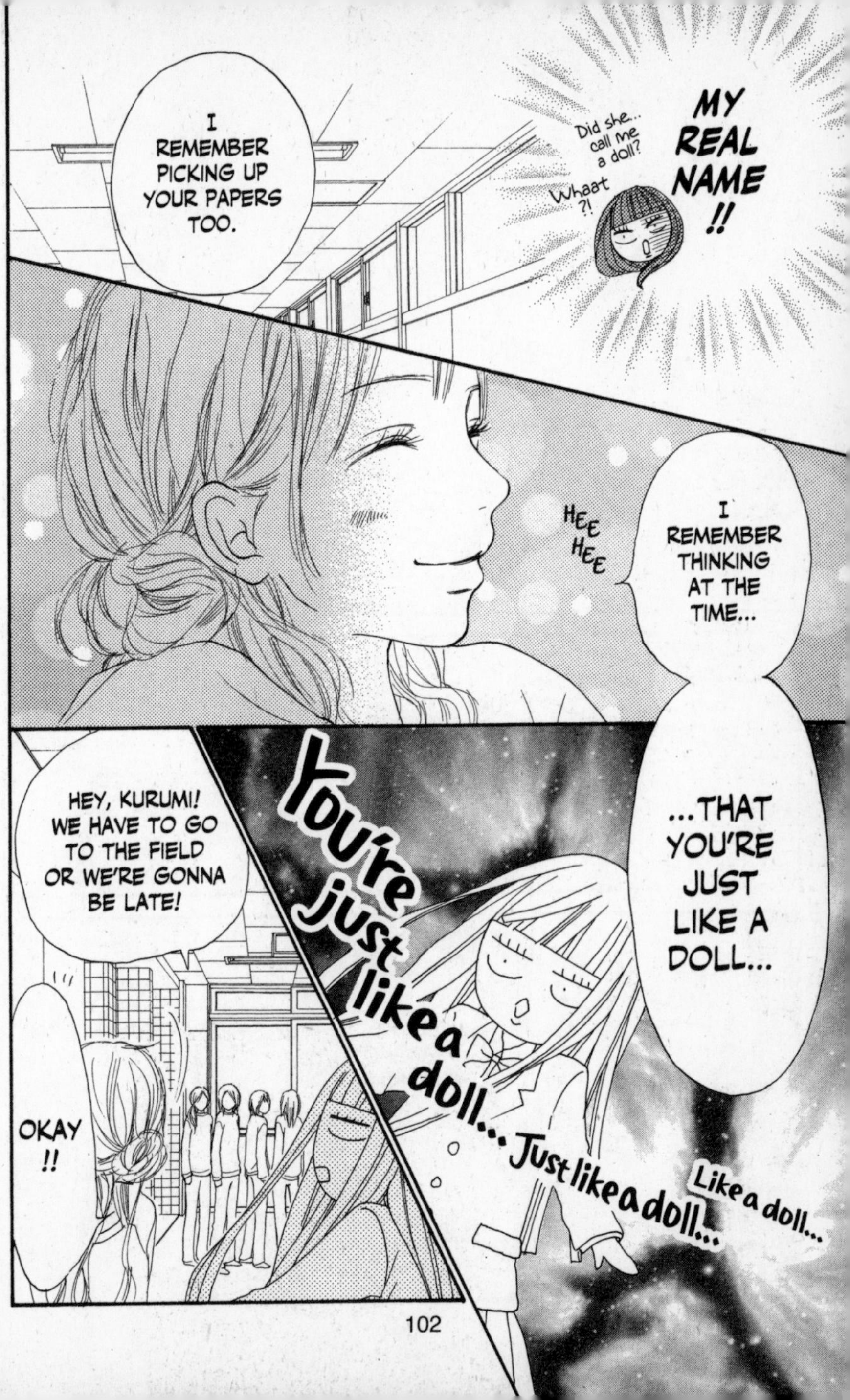
MY REAL NAME !!
Did she... call me a doll?
Whaat ?!
I REMEMBER PICKING UP YOUR PAPERS TOO.
HEE HEE
I REMEMBER THINKING AT THE TIME...
...THAT YOU'RE JUST LIKE A DOLL...
You're just like a doll...
Just like a doll...
Like a doll...
HEY, KURUMI! WE HAVE TO GO TO THE FIELD OR WE'RE GONNA BE LATE!
OKAY !!

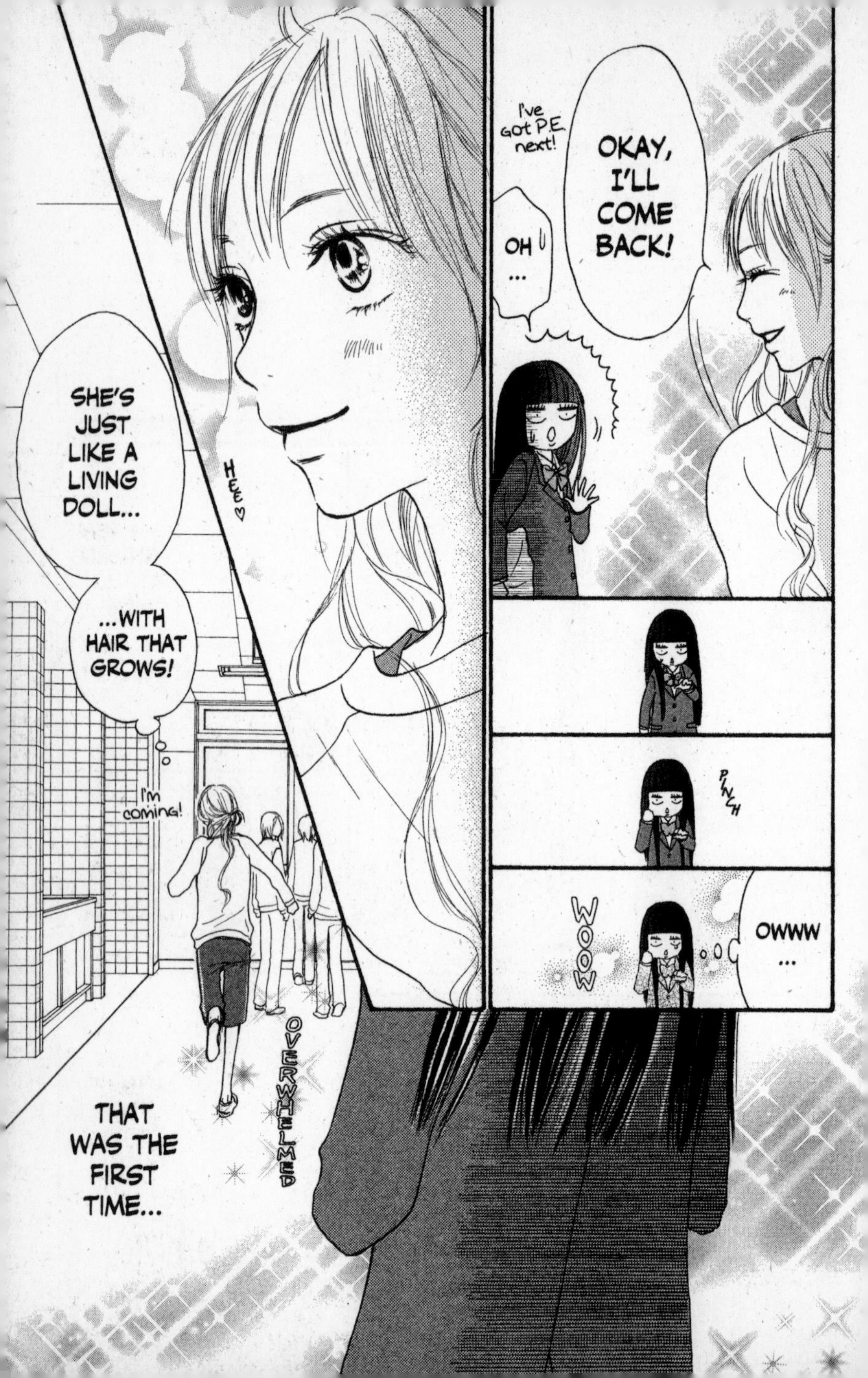
OKAY, I'LL COME BACK!
I've got P.E. next!
OH ...
PINCH
OWWW ...
WOOW
HEE♥
SHE'S JUST LIKE A LIVING DOLL...
...WITH HAIR THAT GROWS!
I'm coming!
OVERWHELMED
THAT WAS THE FIRST TIME...

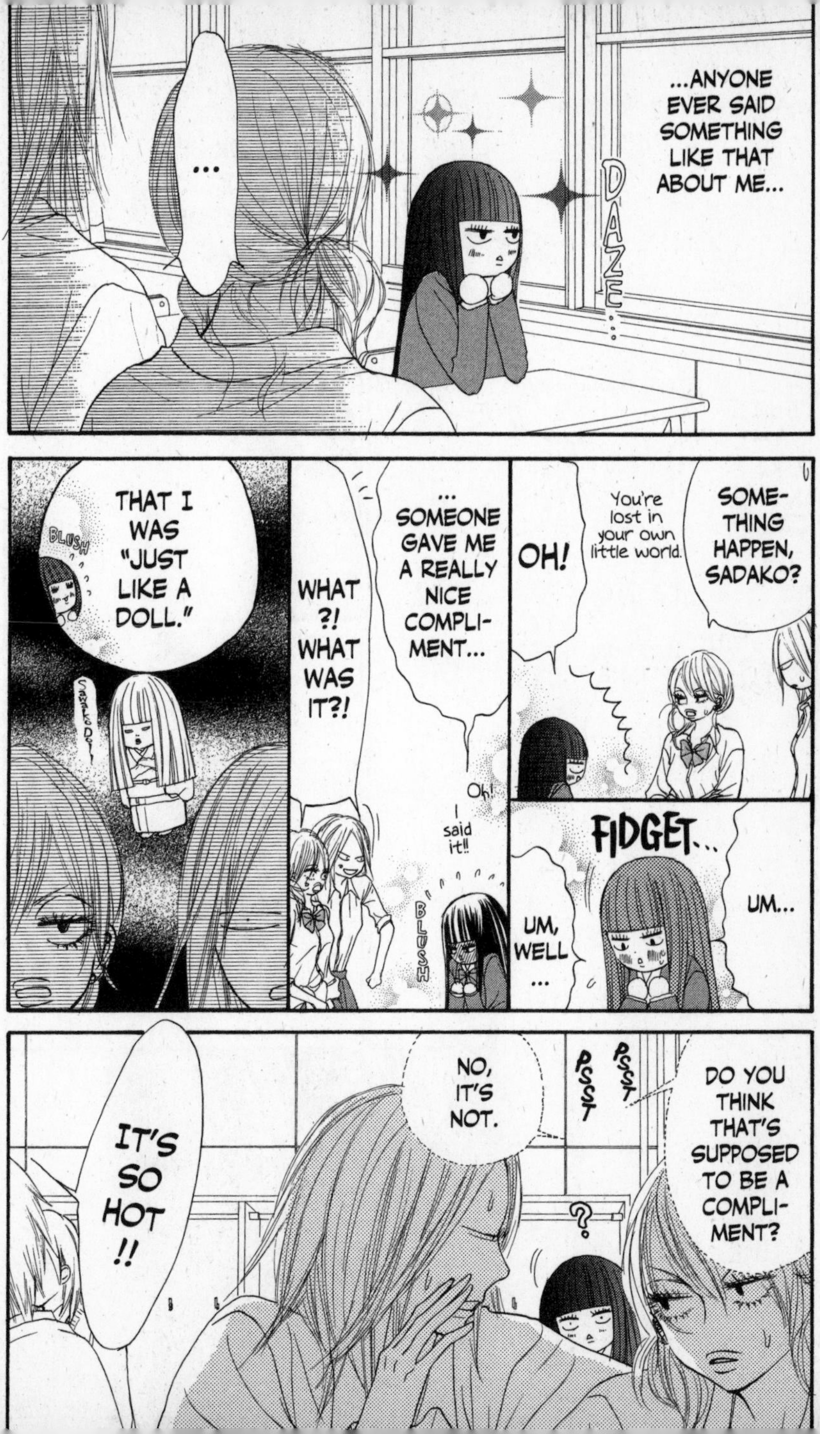
...ANYONE EVER SAID SOMETHING LIKE THAT ABOUT ME...
DAZE...
...
SOME-THING HAPPEN, SADAKO?
You're lost in your own little world.
OH!
UM...
FIDGET...
UM, WELL ...
... SOMEONE GAVE ME A REALLY NICE COMPLI-MENT...
WHAT?! WHAT WAS IT?!
Oh! I said it!!
BLUSH
THAT I WAS "JUST LIKE A DOLL."
BLUSH
DO YOU THINK THAT'S SUPPOSED TO BE A COMPLI-MENT?
PSST PSST
NO, IT'S NOT.
?
IT'S SO HOT!!

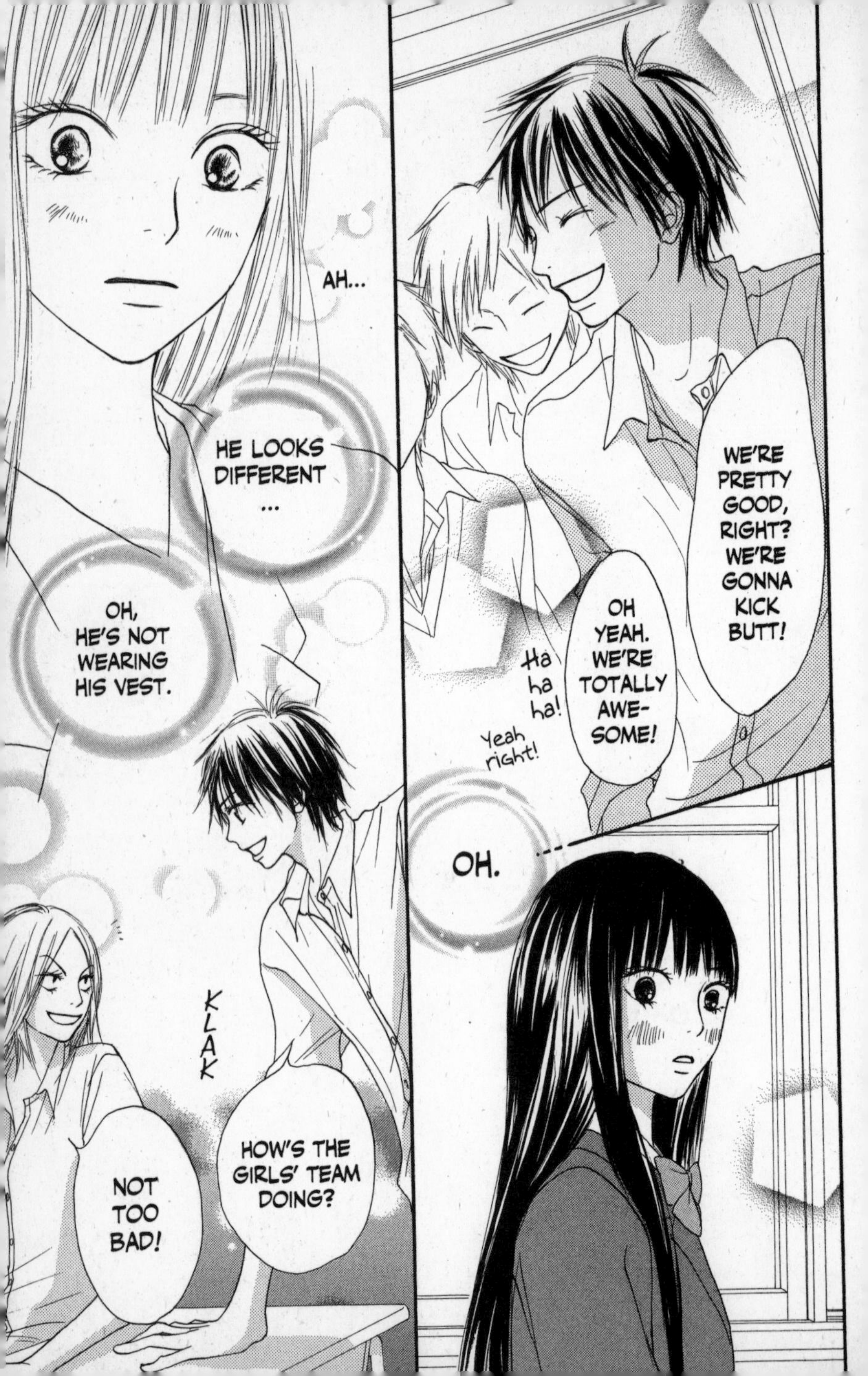
WE'RE PRETTY GOOD, RIGHT? WE'RE GONNA KICK BUTT!
OH YEAH. WE'RE TOTALLY AWE-SOME!
Ha ha ha!
Yeah right!
OH.
AH...
HE LOOKS DIFFERENT ...
OH, HE'S NOT WEARING HIS VEST.
KLAK
HOW'S THE GIRLS' TEAM DOING?
NOT TOO BAD!

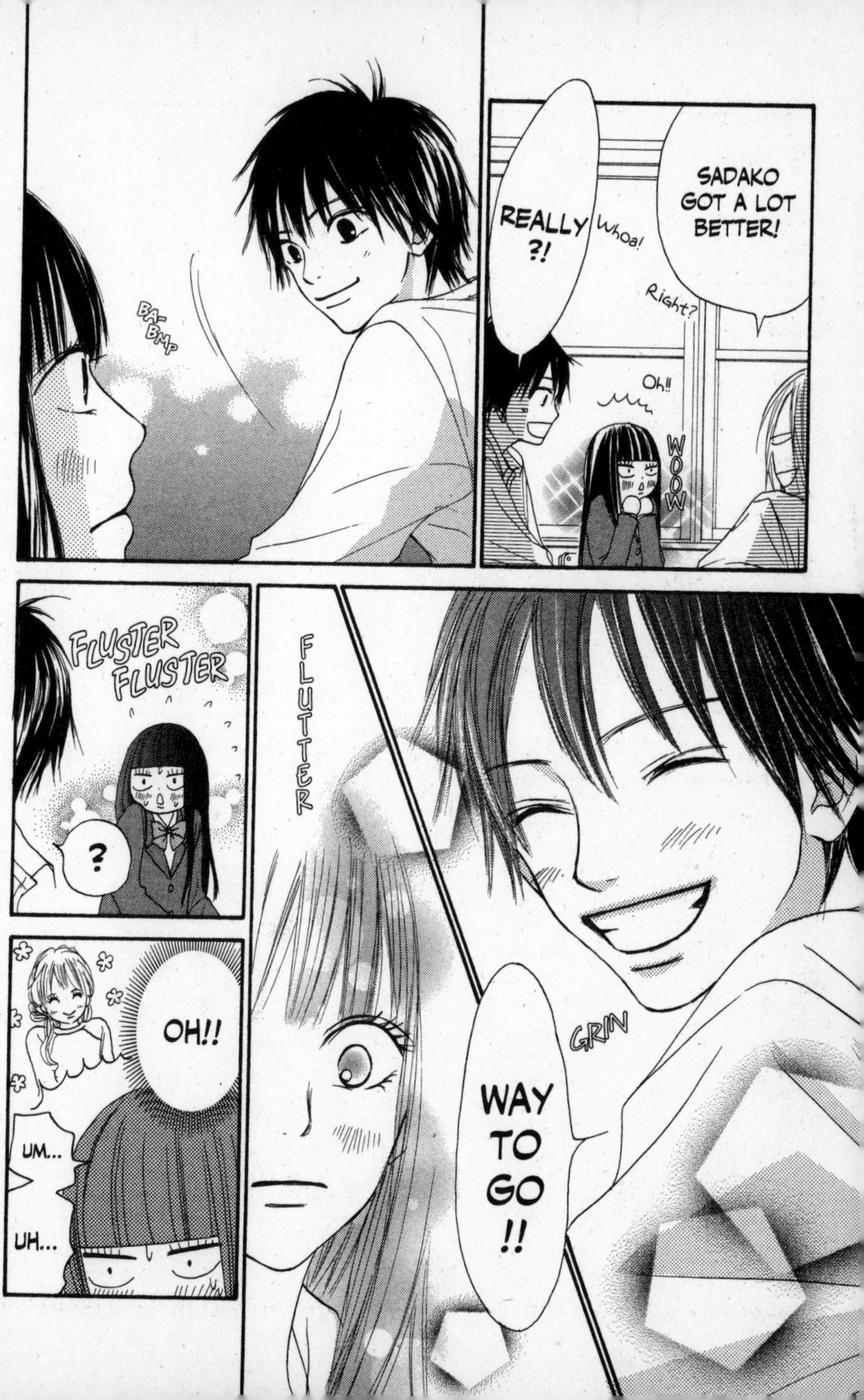
SADAKO GOT A LOT BETTER!
Right?
REALLY ?!
Whoa!
Oh!!
WOOW
BA-BMP
GRIN
FLUTTER
WAY TO GO !!
FLUSTER FLUSTER
?
OH!!
UM...
UH...

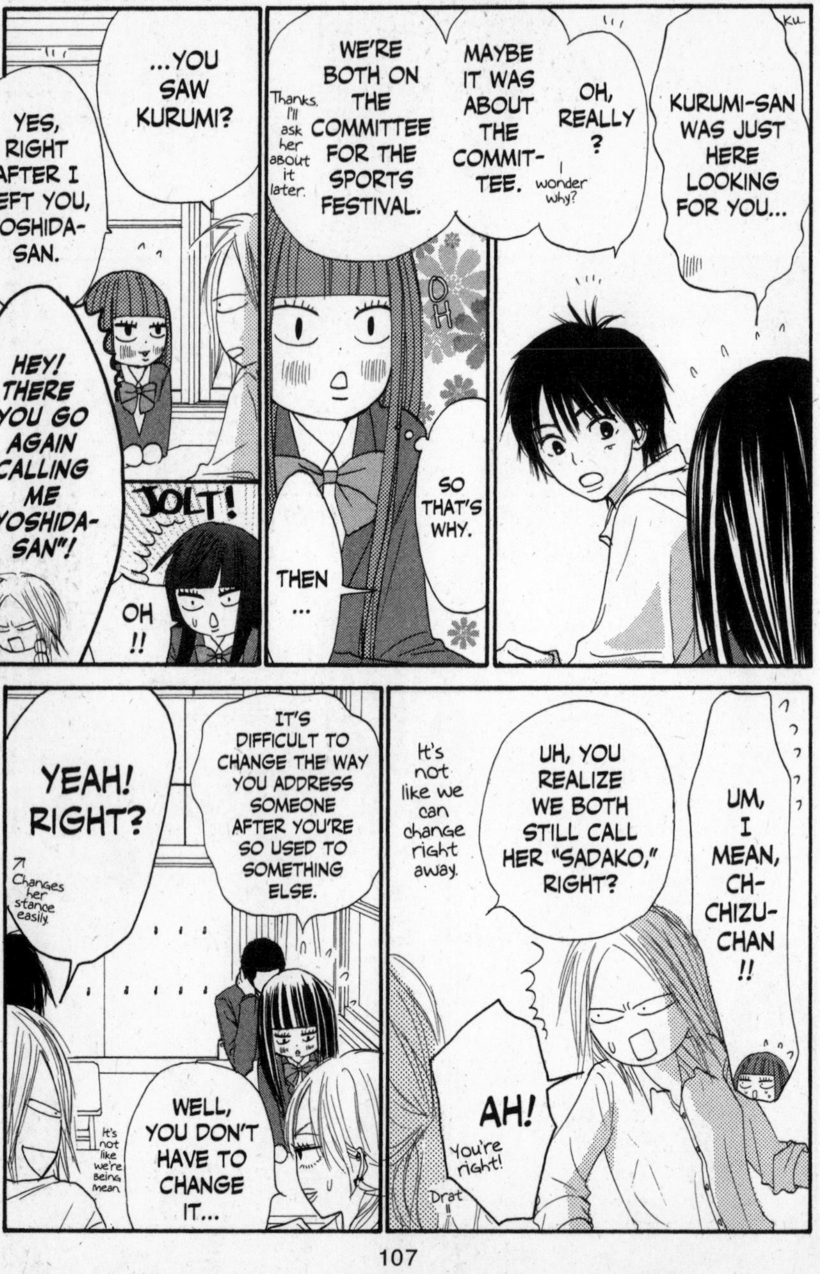

Ku...
KURUMI-SAN WAS JUST HERE LOOKING FOR YOU...
OH, REALLY?
I wonder why?
MAYBE IT WAS ABOUT THE COMMIT-TEE.
WE'RE BOTH ON THE COMMITTEE FOR THE SPORTS FESTIVAL.
Thanks. I'll ask her about it later.
OH
SO THAT'S WHY.
THEN...
...YOU SAW KURUMI?
YES, RIGHT AFTER I LEFT YOU, YOSHIDA-SAN.
HEY! THERE YOU GO AGAIN CALLING ME "YOSHIDA-SAN"!
JOLT!
OH !!
UM, I MEAN, CH-CHIZU-CHAN !!
UH, YOU REALIZE WE BOTH STILL CALL HER "SADAKO," RIGHT?
It's not like we can change right away.
AH!
You're right!
Drat !!
IT'S DIFFICULT TO CHANGE THE WAY YOU ADDRESS SOMEONE AFTER YOU'RE SO USED TO SOMETHING ELSE.
YEAH! RIGHT?
Changes her stance easily.
WELL, YOU DON'T HAVE TO CHANGE IT...
It's not like we're being mean.

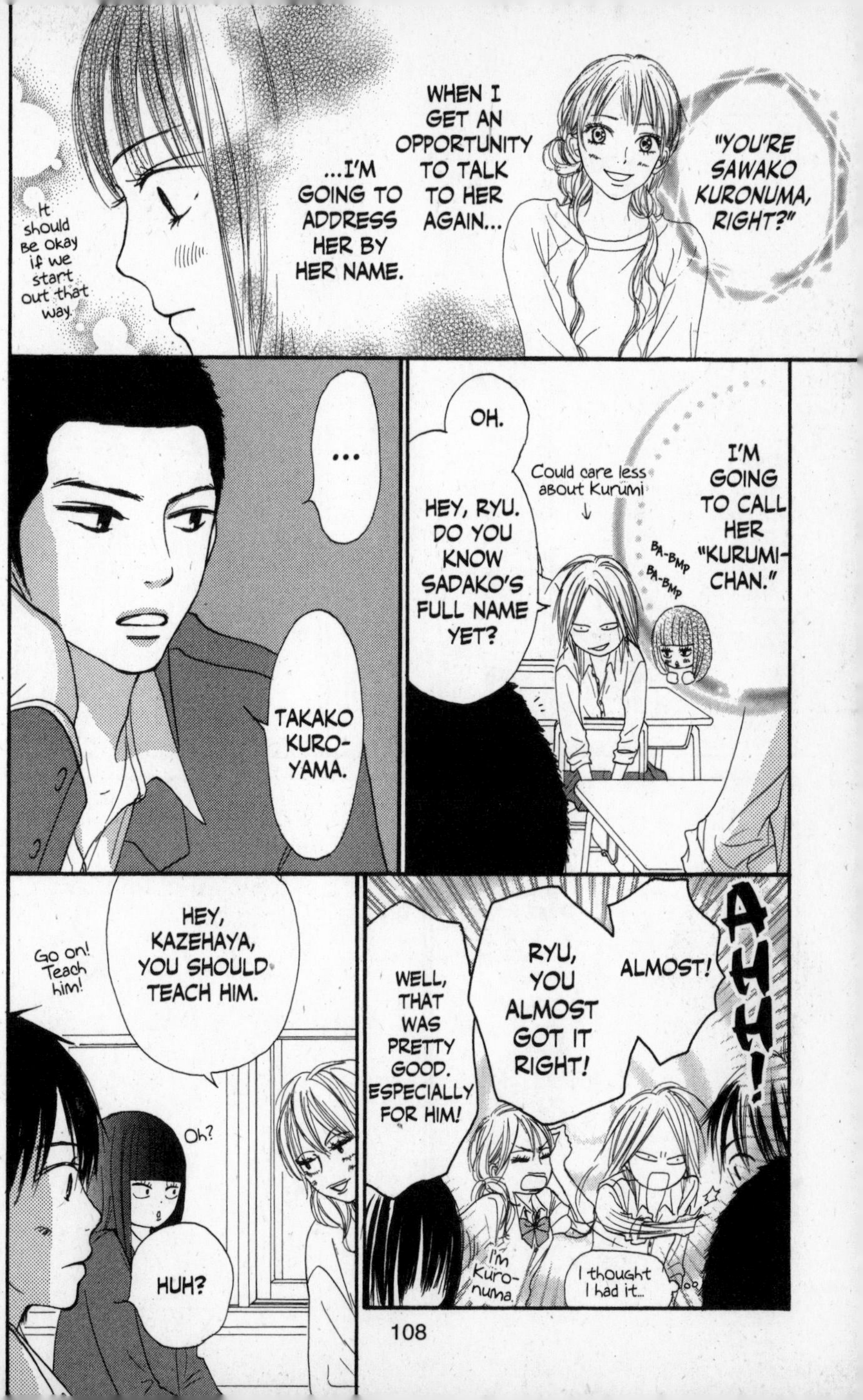
"YOU'RE SAWAKO KURONUMA, RIGHT?"
WHEN I GET AN OPPORTUNITY TO TALK TO HER AGAIN...
...I'M GOING TO ADDRESS HER BY HER NAME.
It should be okay if we start out that way.
I'M GOING TO CALL HER "KURUMI-CHAN."
BA-BMP BA-BMP
OH.
Could care less about Kurumi
HEY, RYU. DO YOU KNOW SADAKO'S FULL NAME YET?
...
TAKAKO KURO-YAMA.
AHH!
ALMOST!
RYU, YOU ALMOST GOT IT RIGHT!
WELL, THAT WAS PRETTY GOOD. ESPECIALLY FOR HIM!
I thought I had it...
I'm Kuro-numa.
HEY, KAZEHAYA, YOU SHOULD TEACH HIM.
Go on! Teach him!
Oh?
HUH?

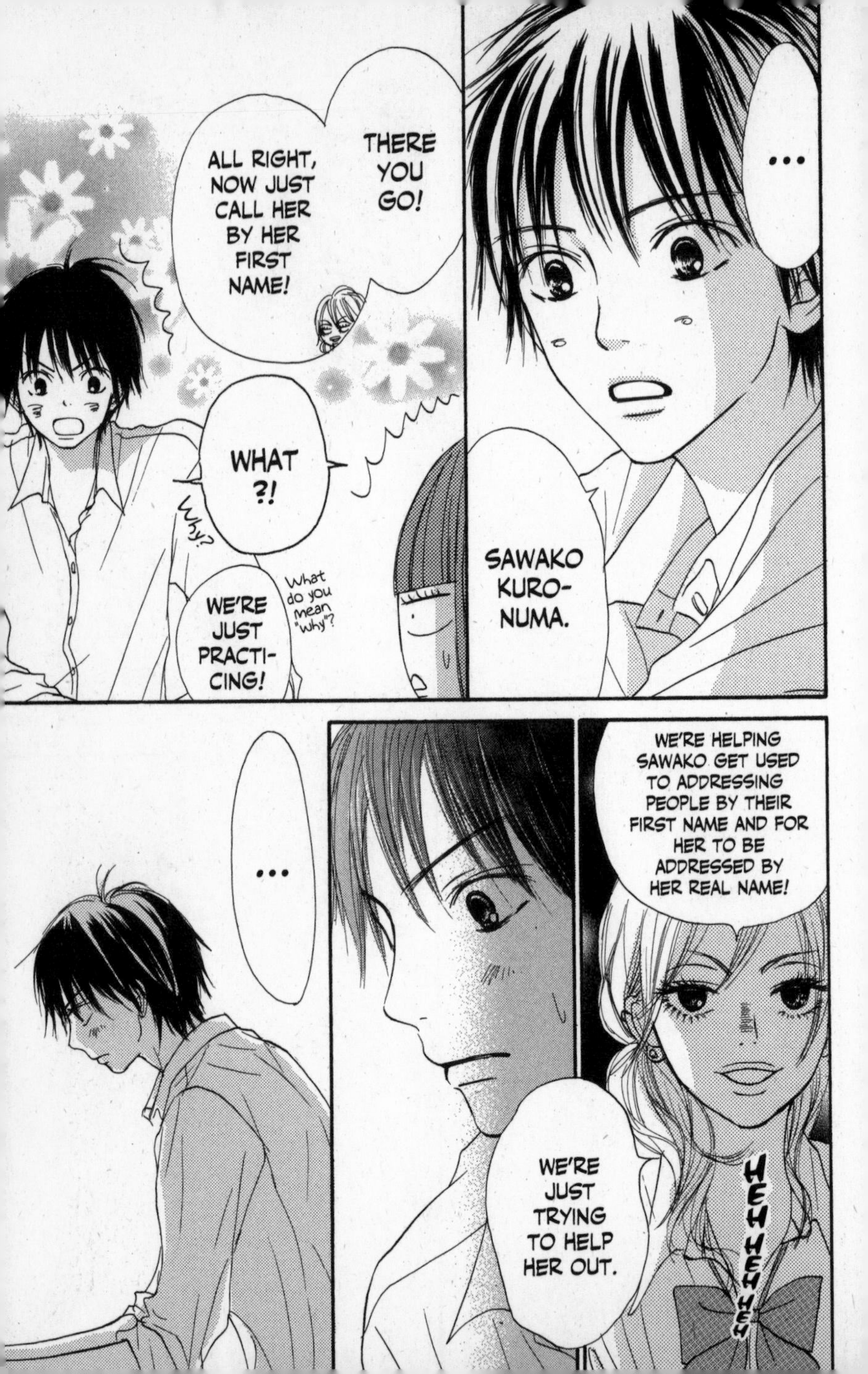
...
SAWAKO KURO-NUMA.
THERE YOU GO!
ALL RIGHT, NOW JUST CALL HER BY HER FIRST NAME!
WHAT?!
Why?
What do you mean "why"?
WE'RE JUST PRACTICING!
WE'RE HELPING SAWAKO GET USED TO ADDRESSING PEOPLE BY THEIR FIRST NAME AND FOR HER TO BE ADDRESSED BY HER REAL NAME!
WE'RE JUST TRYING TO HELP HER OUT.
HEH HEH HEH
...

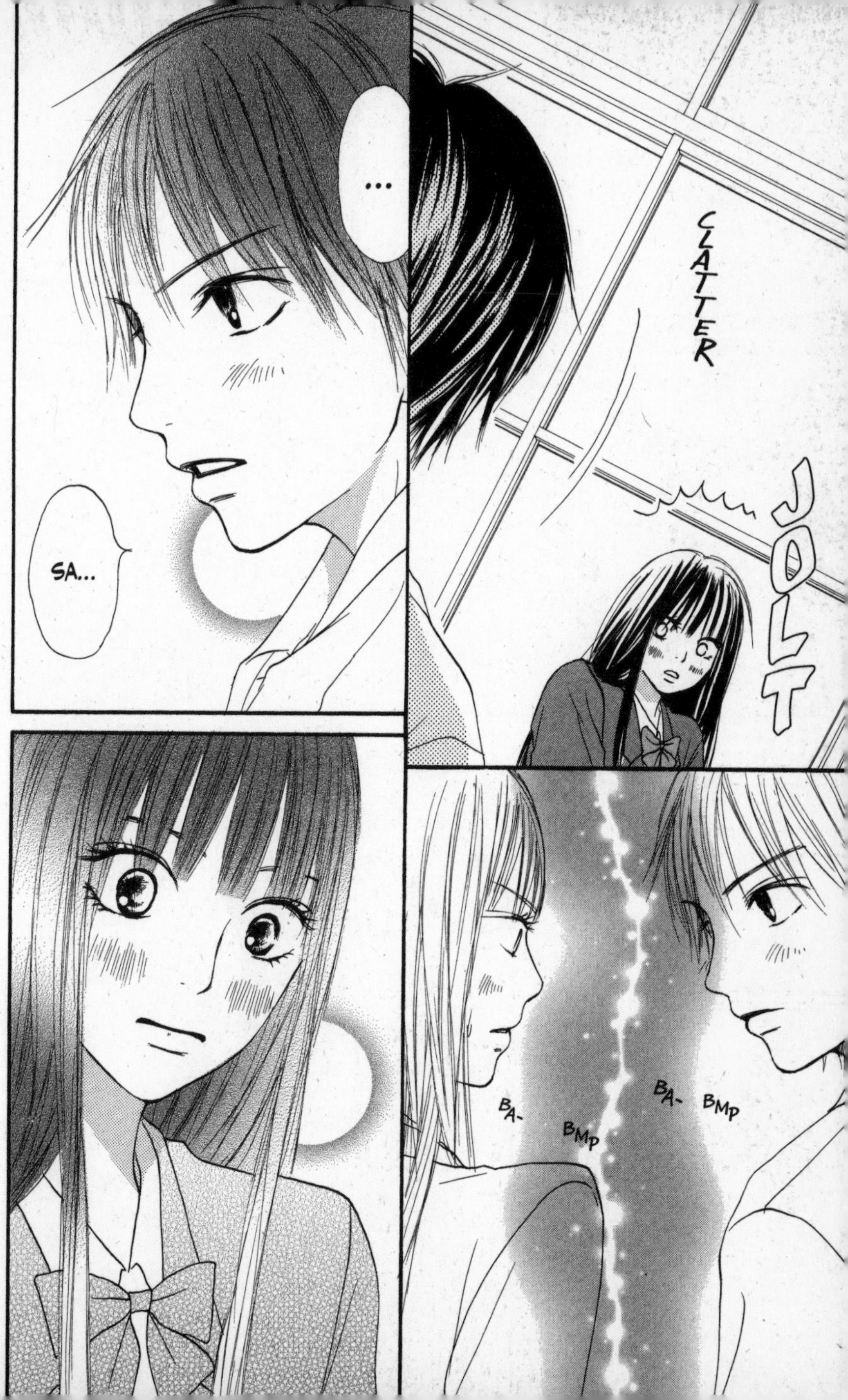
CLATTER
JOLT
...
SA...
BA- BMP
BA- BMP

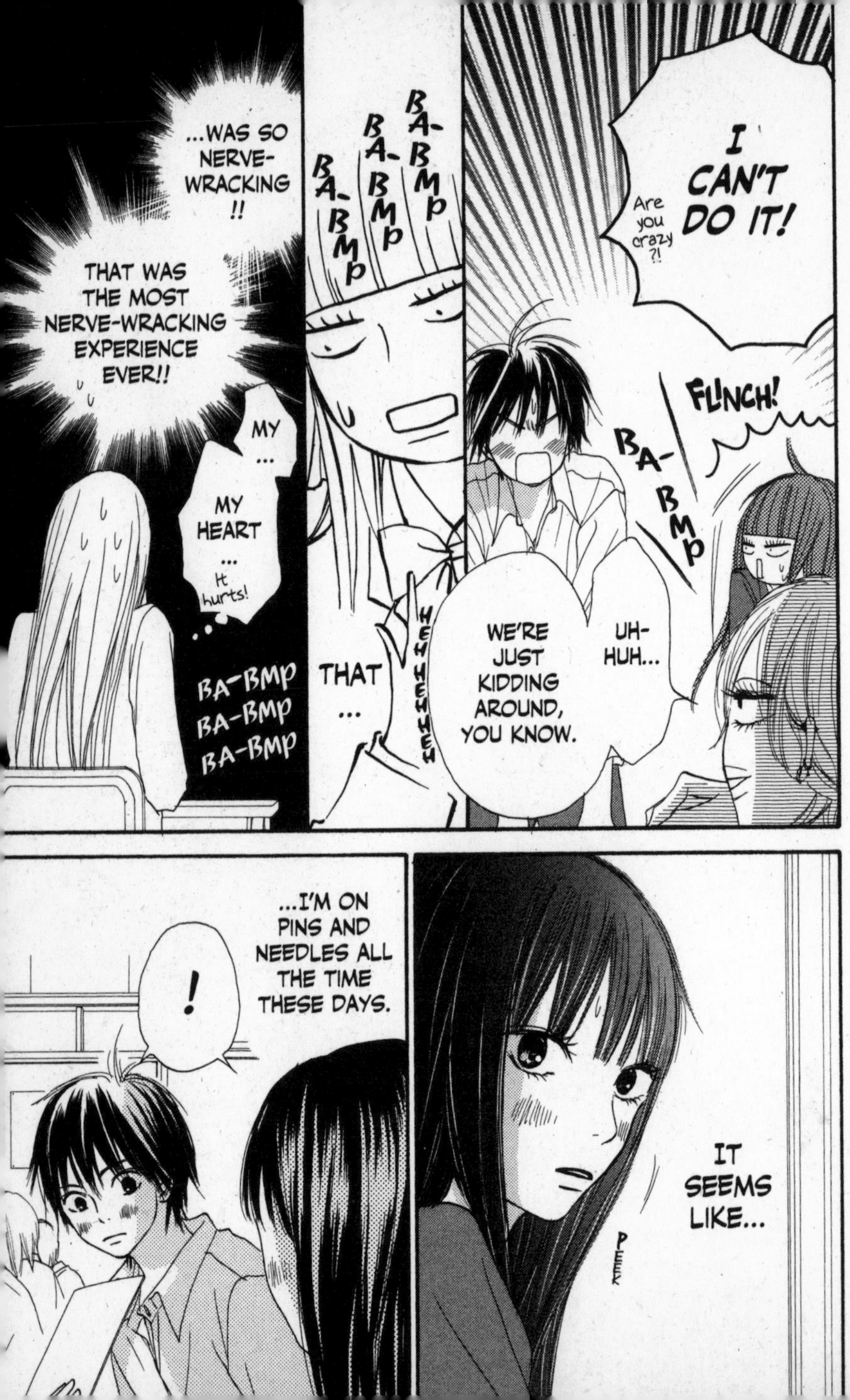
I CAN'T DO IT!
Are you crazy?!
FLINCH!
BA-BMP
UH-HUH...
WE'RE JUST KIDDING AROUND, YOU KNOW.
BA-BMP BA-BMP BA-BMP
THAT...
HEH HEH HEH
...WAS SO NERVE-WRACKING!!
THAT WAS THE MOST NERVE-WRACKING EXPERIENCE EVER!!
MY...
MY HEART... It hurts!
BA-BMP BA-BMP BA-BMP
IT SEEMS LIKE...
PEEK
...I'M ON PINS AND NEEDLES ALL THE TIME THESE DAYS.
!

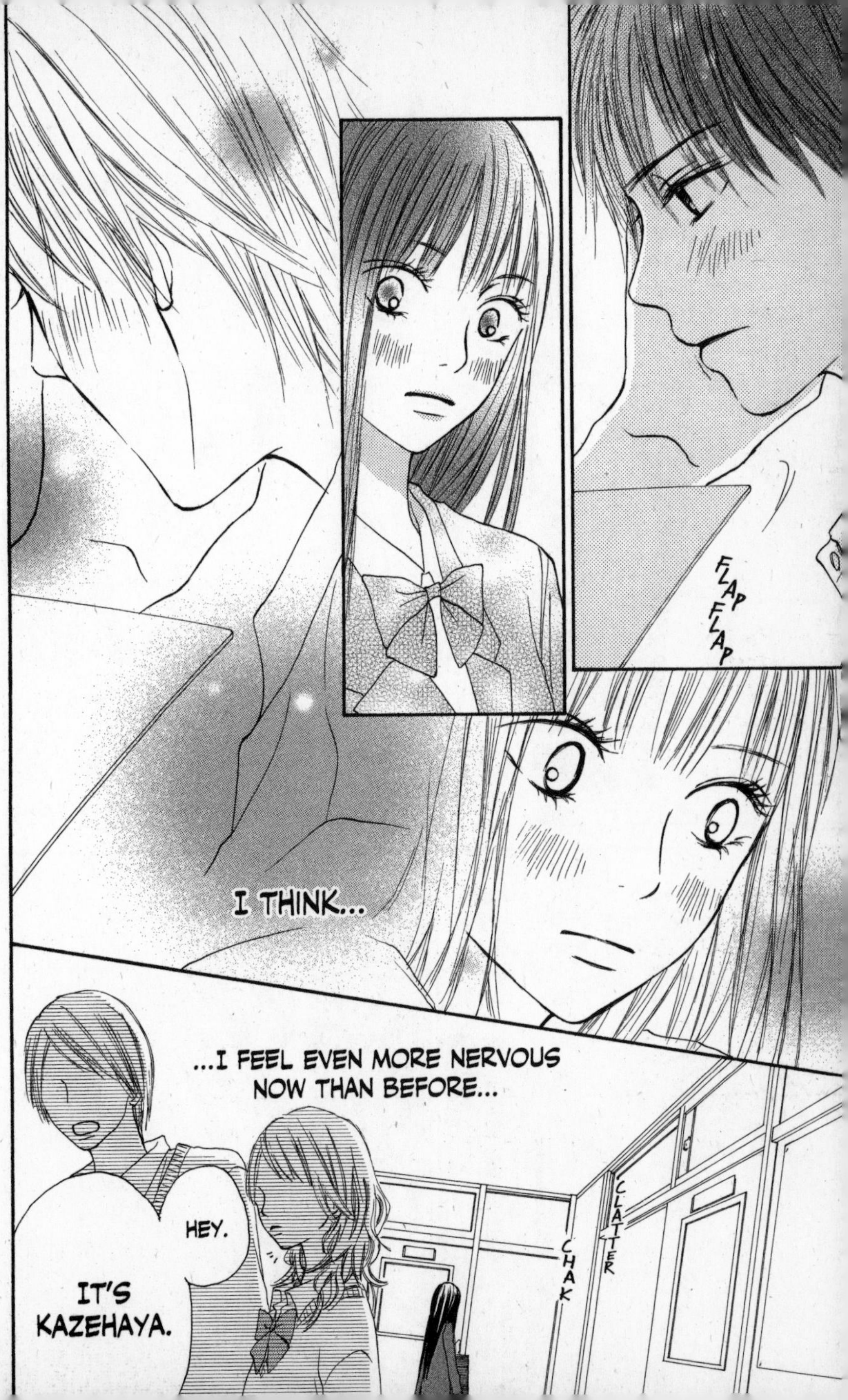
FLAP FLAP
I THINK...
...I FEEL EVEN MORE NERVOUS NOW THAN BEFORE...
CLATTER
CHAK
HEY.
IT'S KAZEHAYA.

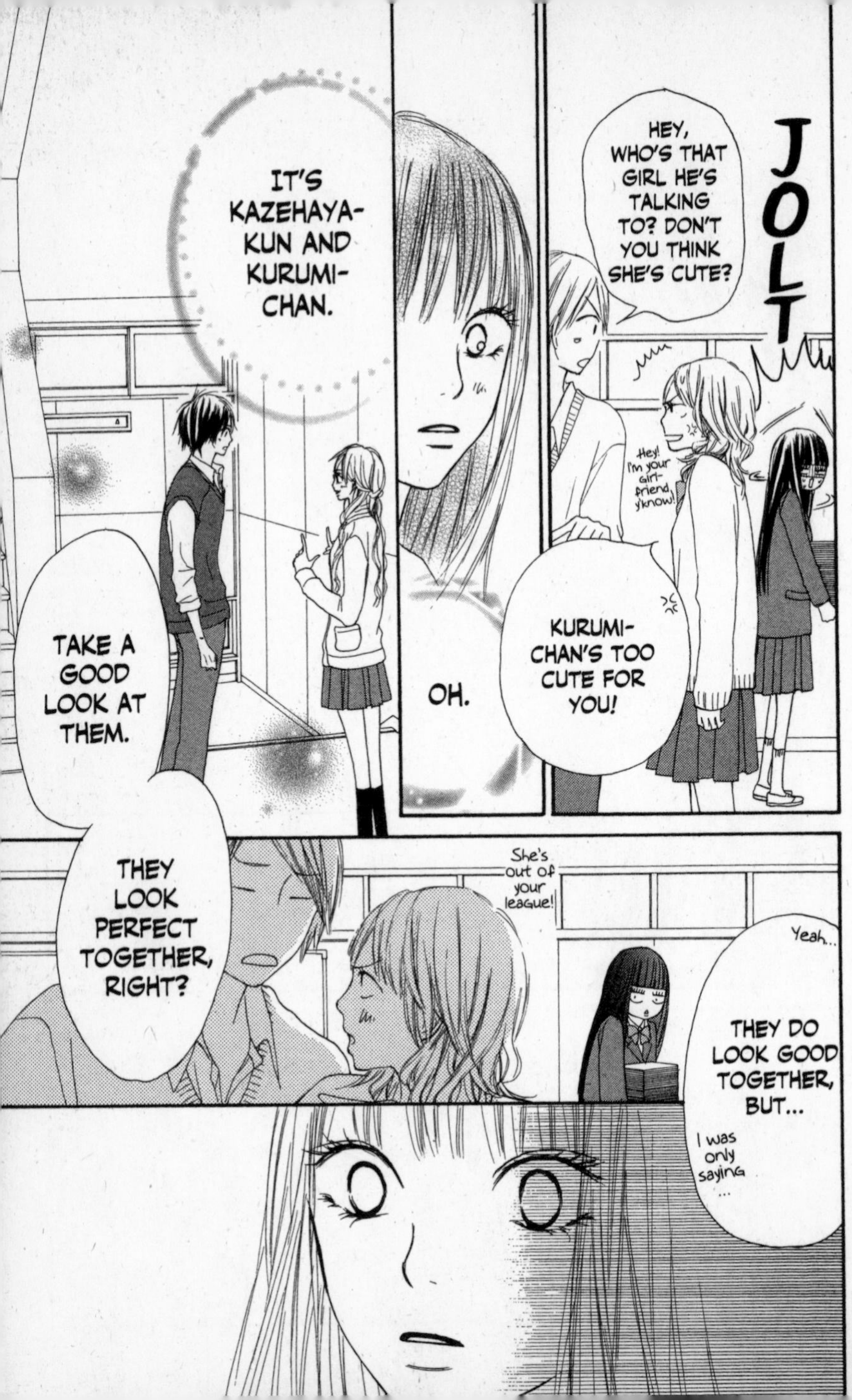
HEY, WHO'S THAT GIRL HE'S TALKING TO? DON'T YOU THINK SHE'S CUTE?
JOLT
Hey! I'm your girl-friend, y'know!
KURUMI-CHAN'S TOO CUTE FOR YOU!
OH.
IT'S KAZEHAYA-KUN AND KURUMI-CHAN.
TAKE A GOOD LOOK AT THEM.
THEY LOOK PERFECT TOGETHER, RIGHT?
She's out of your league!
Yeah...
THEY DO LOOK GOOD TOGETHER, BUT...
I was only saying ...

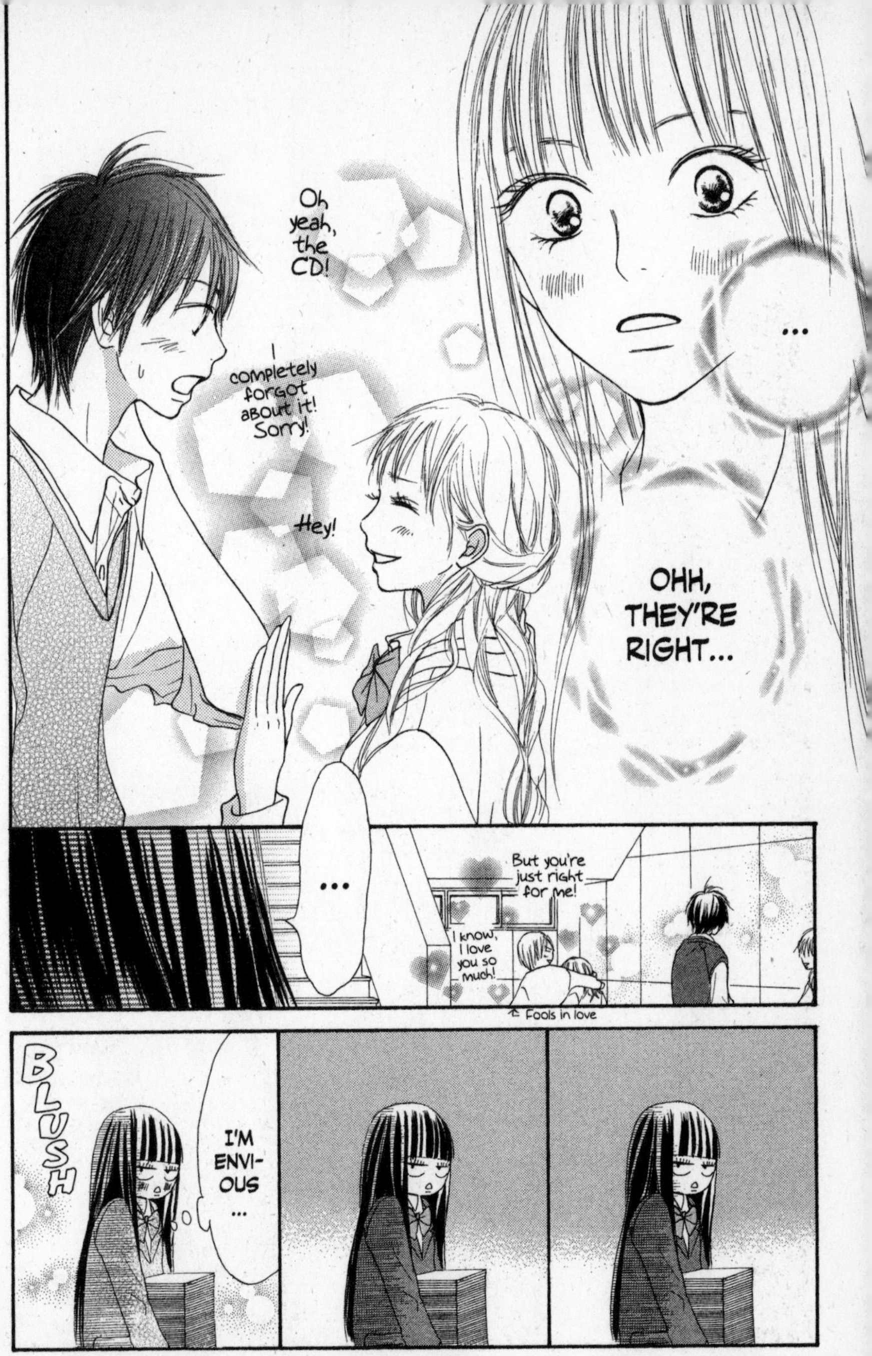
...
OHH, THEY'RE RIGHT...
Oh yeah, the CD!
I completely forgot about it! Sorry!
Hey!
But you're just right for me!
I know, I love you so much!
Fools in love
...
I'M ENVIOUS ...
BLUSH

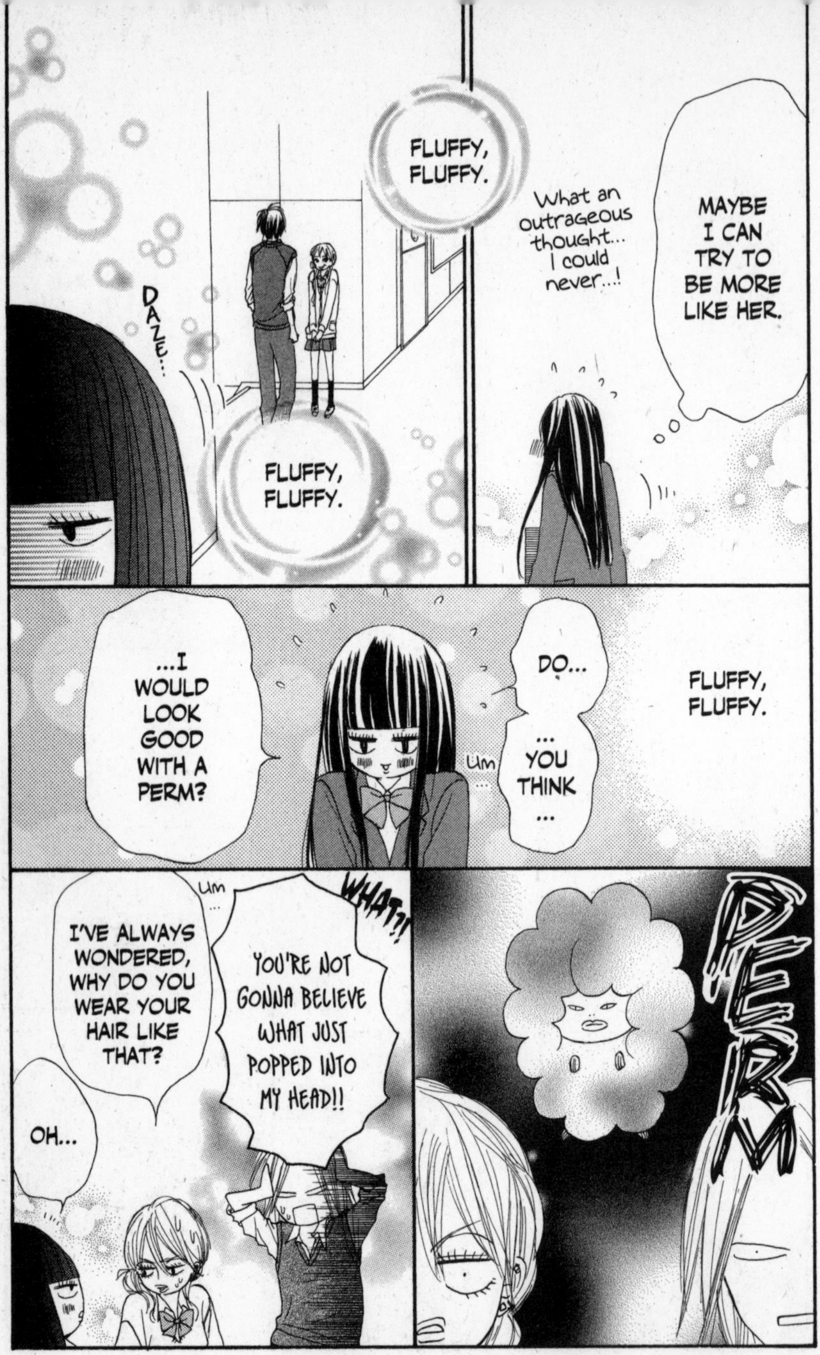
MAYBE I CAN TRY TO BE MORE LIKE HER.
What an outrageous thought... I could never...!
FLUFFY, FLUFFY.
DAZE...
FLUFFY, FLUFFY.
FLUFFY, FLUFFY.
DO... ...YOU THINK ...
Um...
...I WOULD LOOK GOOD WITH A PERM?
PERM
WHAT?!
YOU'RE NOT GONNA BELIEVE WHAT JUST POPPED INTO MY HEAD!!
Um...
I'VE ALWAYS WONDERED, WHY DO YOU WEAR YOUR HAIR LIKE THAT?
OH...

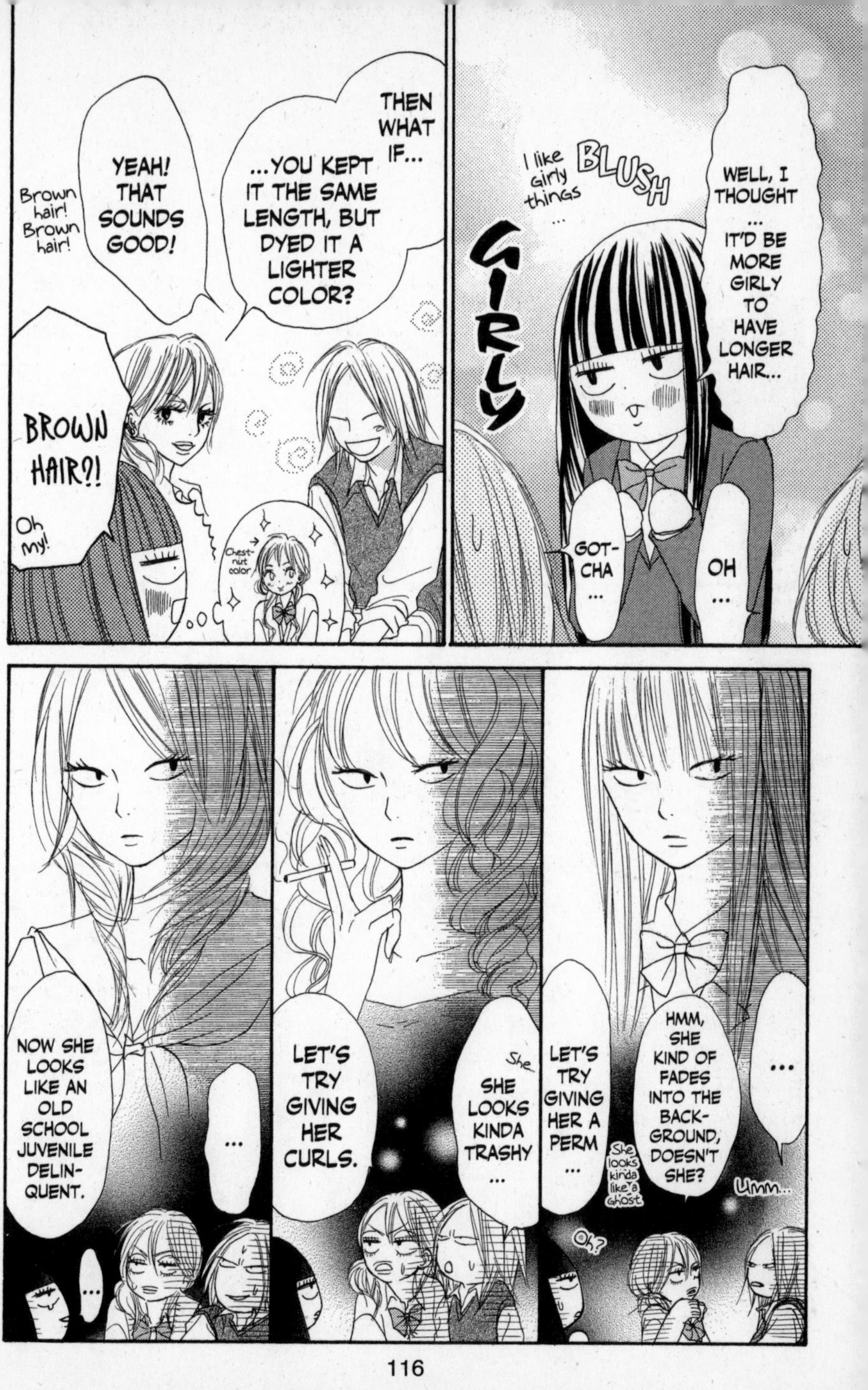

WELL, I THOUGHT ... IT'D BE MORE GIRLY TO HAVE LONGER HAIR...
BLUSH
I like Girly things ...
GIRLY
OH ...
GOT-CHA ...
THEN WHAT IF...
...YOU KEPT IT THE SAME LENGTH, BUT DYED IT A LIGHTER COLOR?
YEAH! THAT SOUNDS GOOD!
Brown hair! Brown hair!
Chest-nut color
BROWN HAIR?!
Oh my!
...
HMM, SHE KIND OF FADES INTO THE BACK-GROUND, DOESN'T SHE?
Umm...
She looks kinda like a ghost
LET'S TRY GIVING HER A PERM ...
Oh?
She...
SHE LOOKS KINDA TRASHY ...
LET'S TRY GIVING HER CURLS.
...
NOW SHE LOOKS LIKE AN OLD SCHOOL JUVENILE DELIN-QUENT.
...

KARUPIN on JAPAN 3

I really enjoyed hearing about everyone's little men stories.

I'm so happy✿ Thank you so much!!

I've enjoyed reading all the letters readers have sent me!!

However, I've been so busy the past couple of years that I don't have time to reply. I keep getting and getting and haven't returned anything.

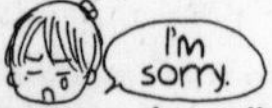
I'm sorry.

For anyone that still wants to write me, you don't need to include return postage!

It's really heartwarming to see everyone's cute drawings of the characters. Thank you!

And to the middle school girl who was kind enough to send me a Bo Jo Bo wishing doll and others who sent me a strawberry and a ball and stuff made out of beads... Thank you, everyone!

I tied the legs of the doll together!

Also, I've been receiving letters recently from people who had written to me once before a long time ago. It makes me so happy!

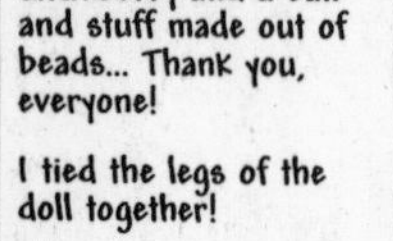
Oh! re-member this per-son!
Congrats on your wedding!
WOW!
Oh! They've grown up!
They didn't write their name. Who is it?!

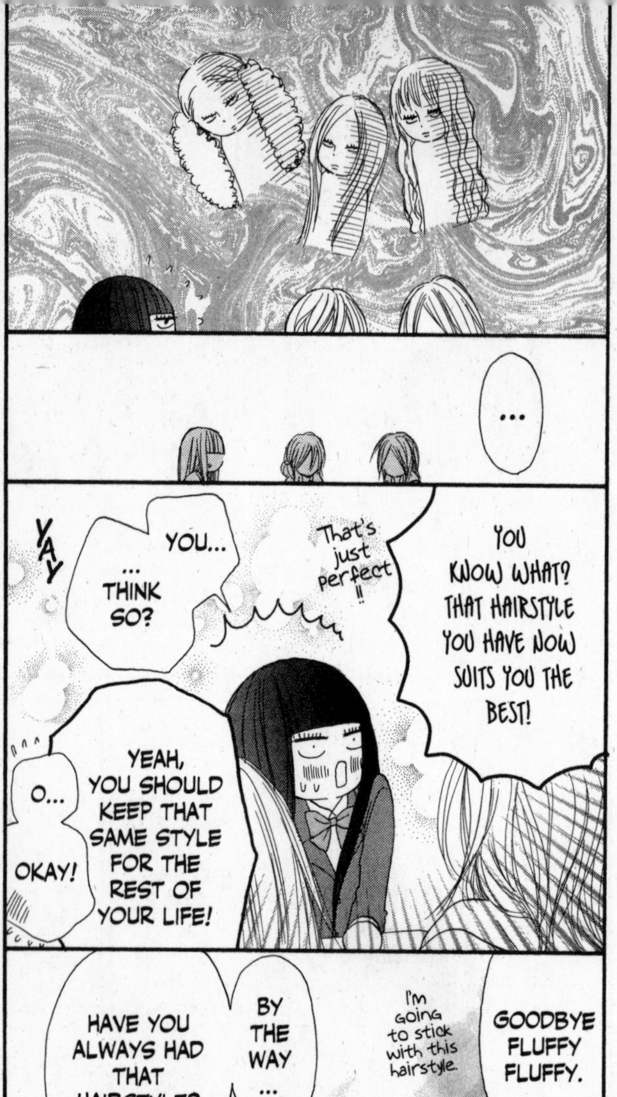
...
YOU KNOW WHAT? THAT HAIRSTYLE YOU HAVE NOW SUITS YOU THE BEST!
That's just perfect !!
YOU... ...THINK SO?
YAY
YEAH, YOU SHOULD KEEP THAT SAME STYLE FOR THE REST OF YOUR LIFE!
O... OKAY!
GOODBYE FLUFFY FLUFFY.
I'm going to stick with this hairstyle.
BY THE WAY...
HAVE YOU ALWAYS HAD THAT HAIRSTYLE?

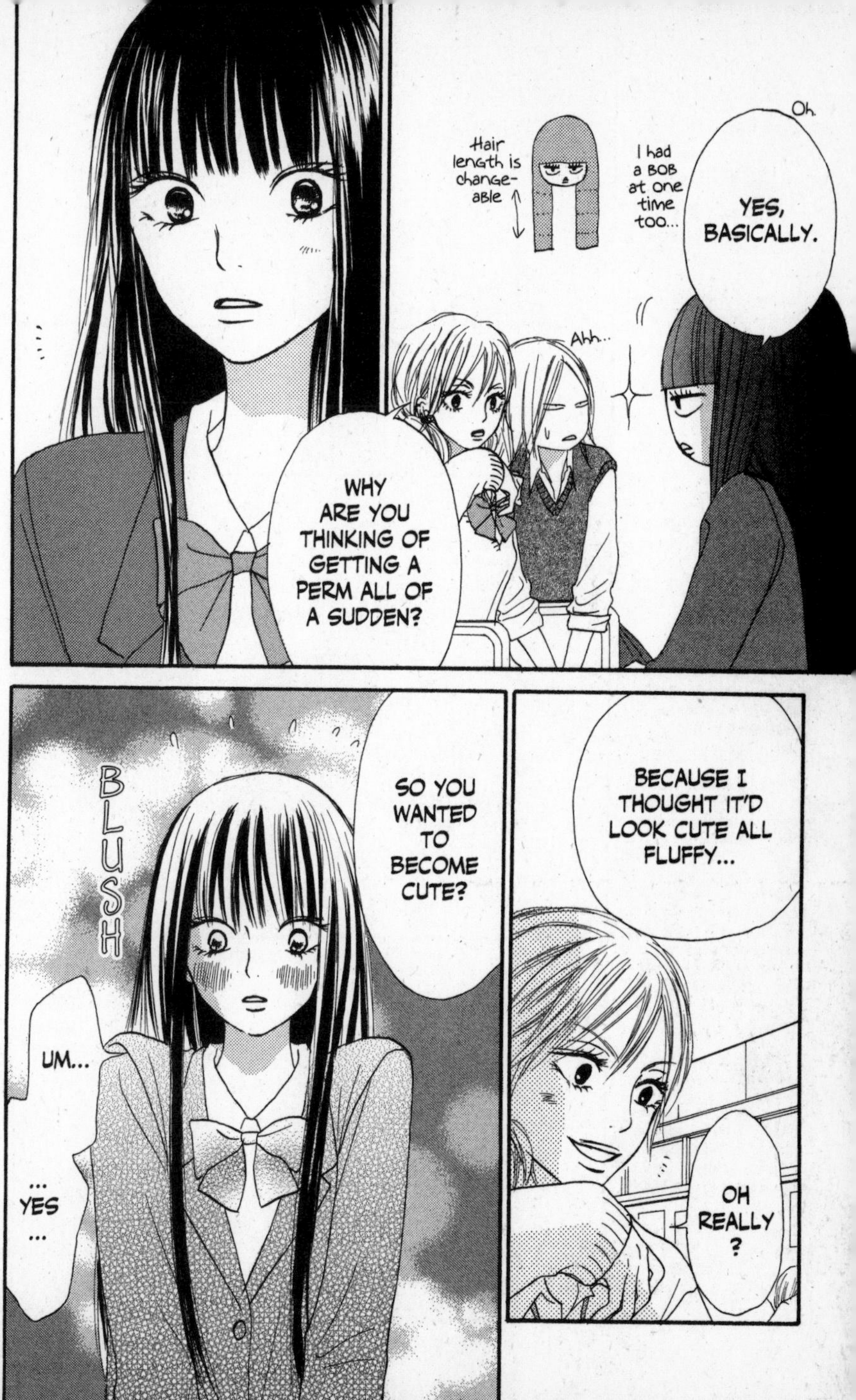
Oh.
YES, BASICALLY.
I had a BOB at one time too...
Hair length is changeable
Ahh...
WHY ARE YOU THINKING OF GETTING A PERM ALL OF A SUDDEN?
BECAUSE I THOUGHT IT'D LOOK CUTE ALL FLUFFY...
OH REALLY?
SO YOU WANTED TO BECOME CUTE?
BLUSH
UM...
...YES...

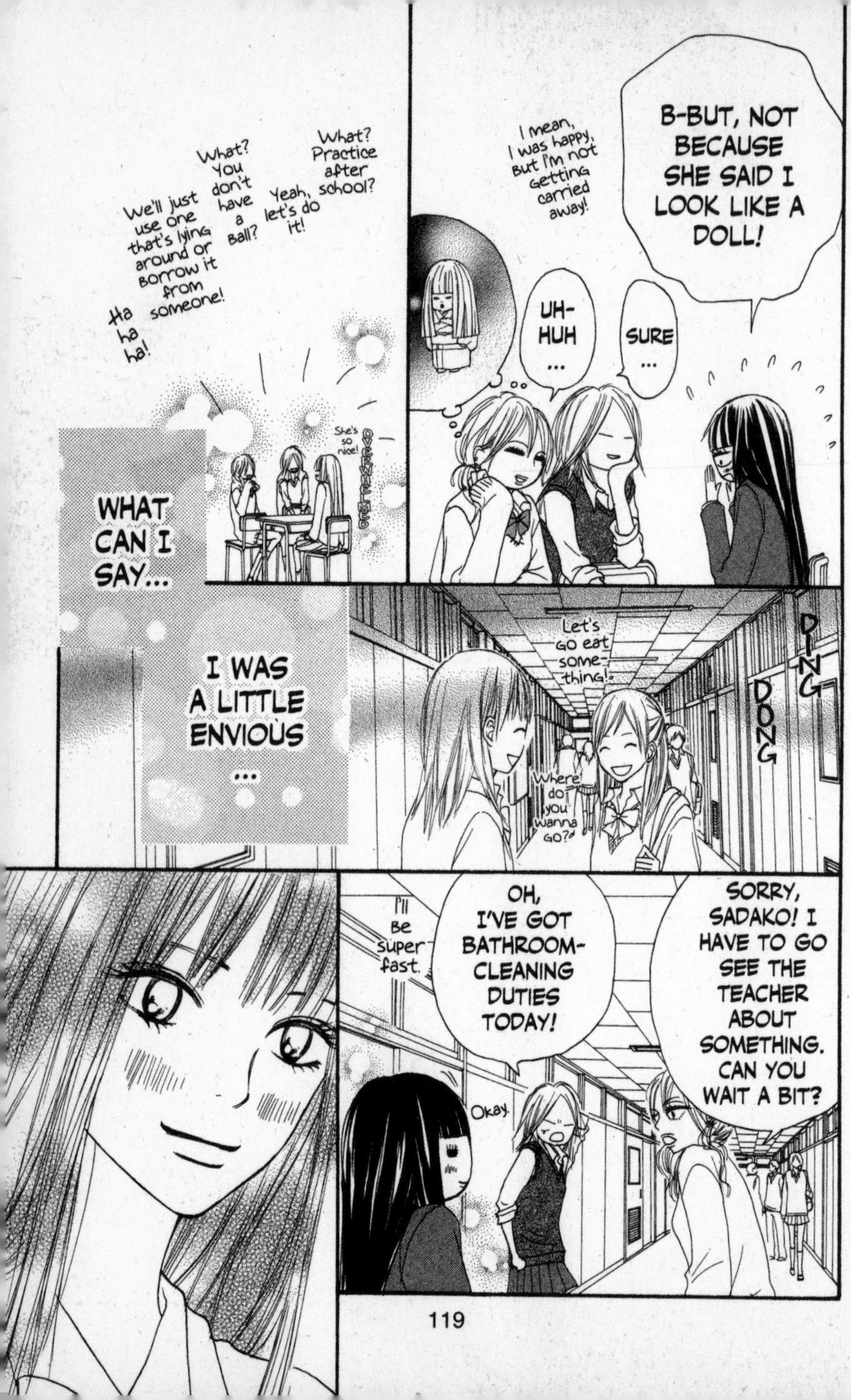
B-BUT, NOT BECAUSE SHE SAID I LOOK LIKE A DOLL!
SURE...
UH-HUH...
I mean, I was happy, but I'm not getting carried away!
What? Practice after school?
Yeah, let's do it!
What? You don't have a ball?
We'll just use one that's lying around or borrow it from someone!
Ha ha ha!
She's so nice!
OVERWHELMED
WHAT CAN I SAY...
DING
DONG
Let's go eat some-thing!
Where do you wanna go?
I WAS A LITTLE ENVIOUS...
SORRY, SADAKO! I HAVE TO GO SEE THE TEACHER ABOUT SOMETHING. CAN YOU WAIT A BIT?
OH, I'VE GOT BATHROOM-CLEANING DUTIES TODAY!
I'll be super fast.
Okay.

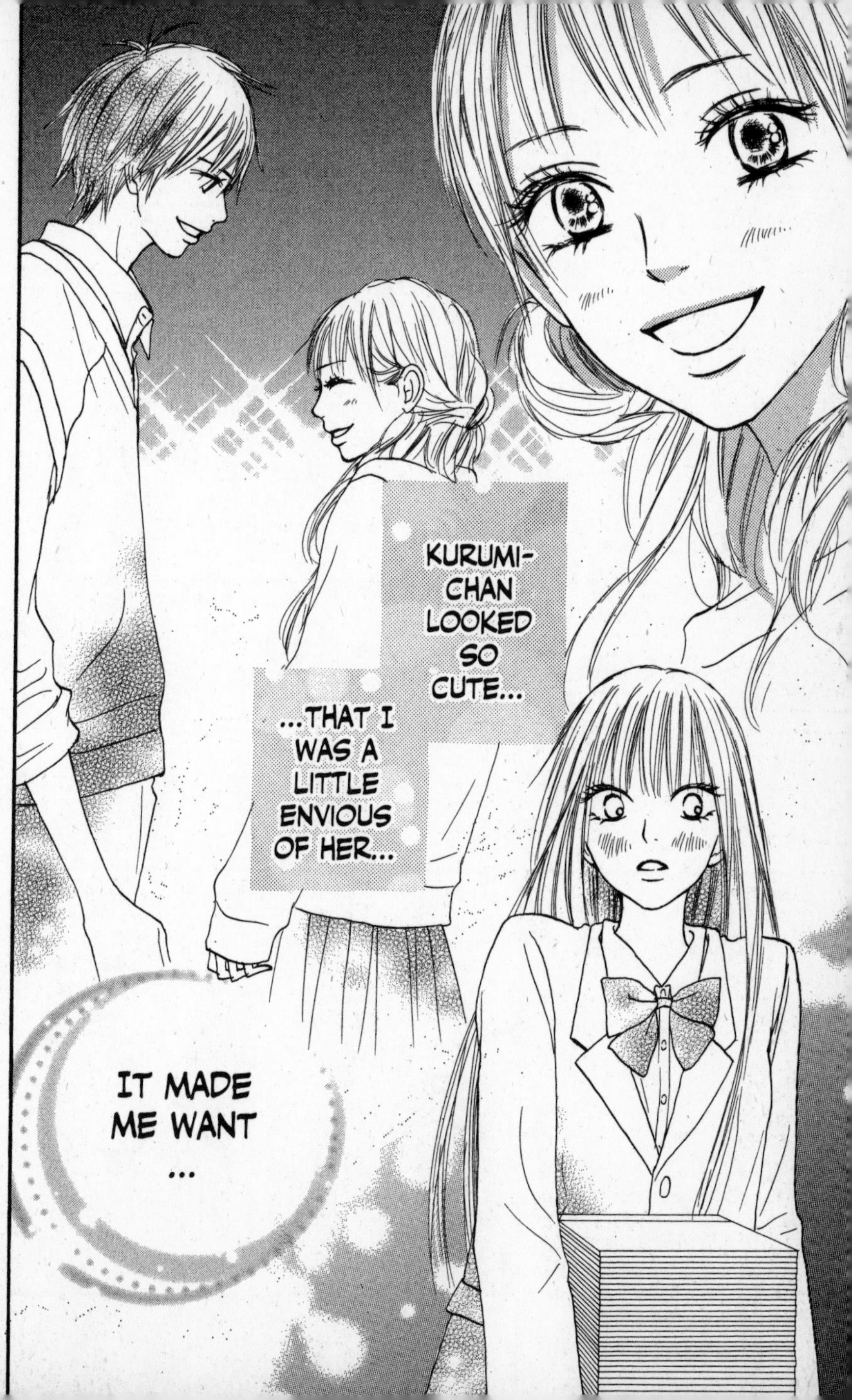
KURUMI-CHAN LOOKED SO CUTE...
...THAT I WAS A LITTLE ENVIOUS OF HER...
IT MADE ME WANT ...

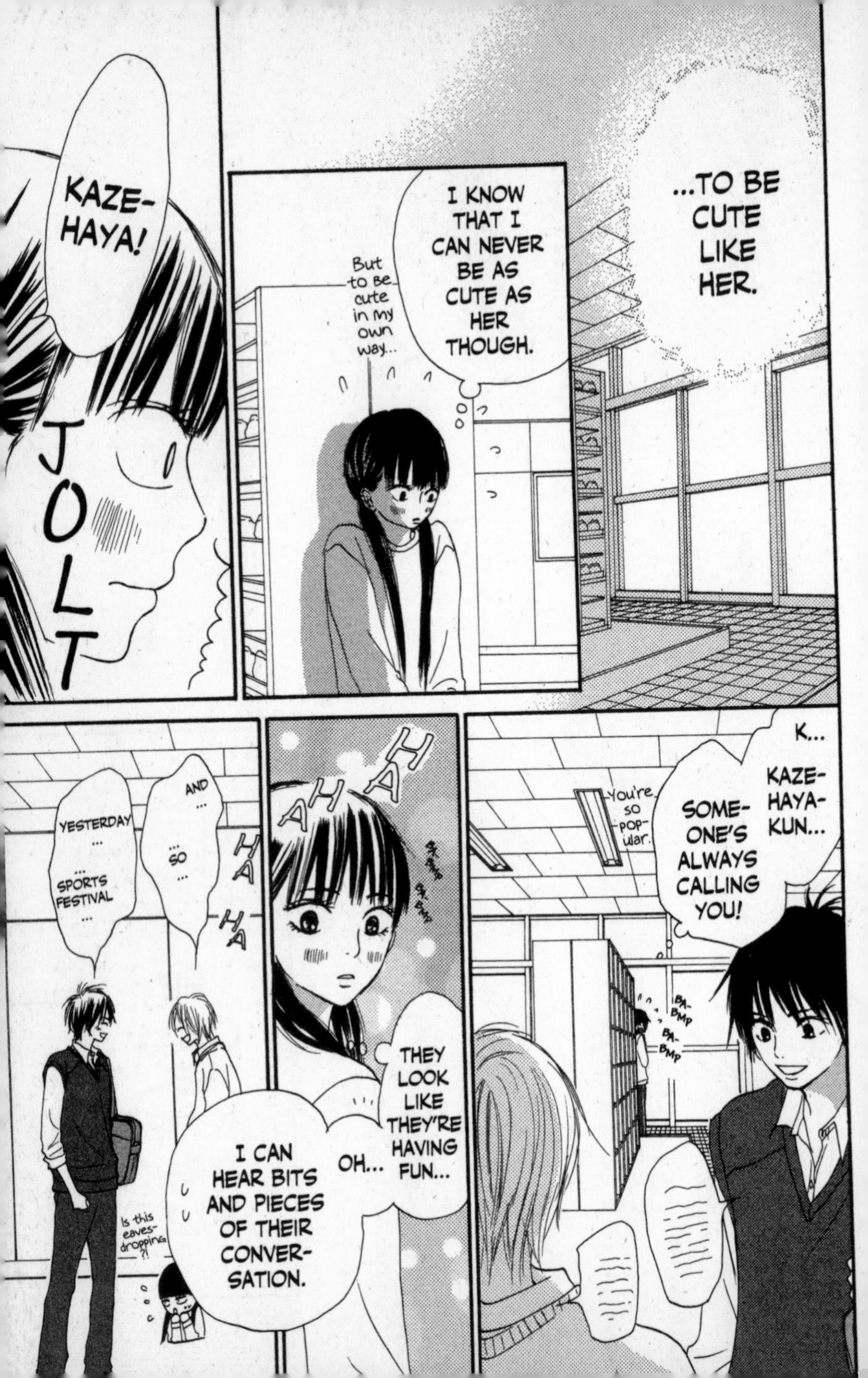
...TO BE CUTE LIKE HER.
I KNOW THAT I CAN NEVER BE AS CUTE AS HER THOUGH.
But to be cute in my own way...
KAZE-HAYA!
JOLT
K... KAZE-HAYA-KUN...
SOME-ONE'S ALWAYS CALLING YOU!
You're so pop-ular.
BA-BMP BA-BMP
HA HA HA HA HA HA
THEY LOOK LIKE THEY'RE HAVING FUN...
OH...
I CAN HEAR BITS AND PIECES OF THEIR CONVER-SATION.
AND ... ... SO ...
YESTERDAY ... ... SPORTS FESTIVAL ...
Is this eaves-dropping?!

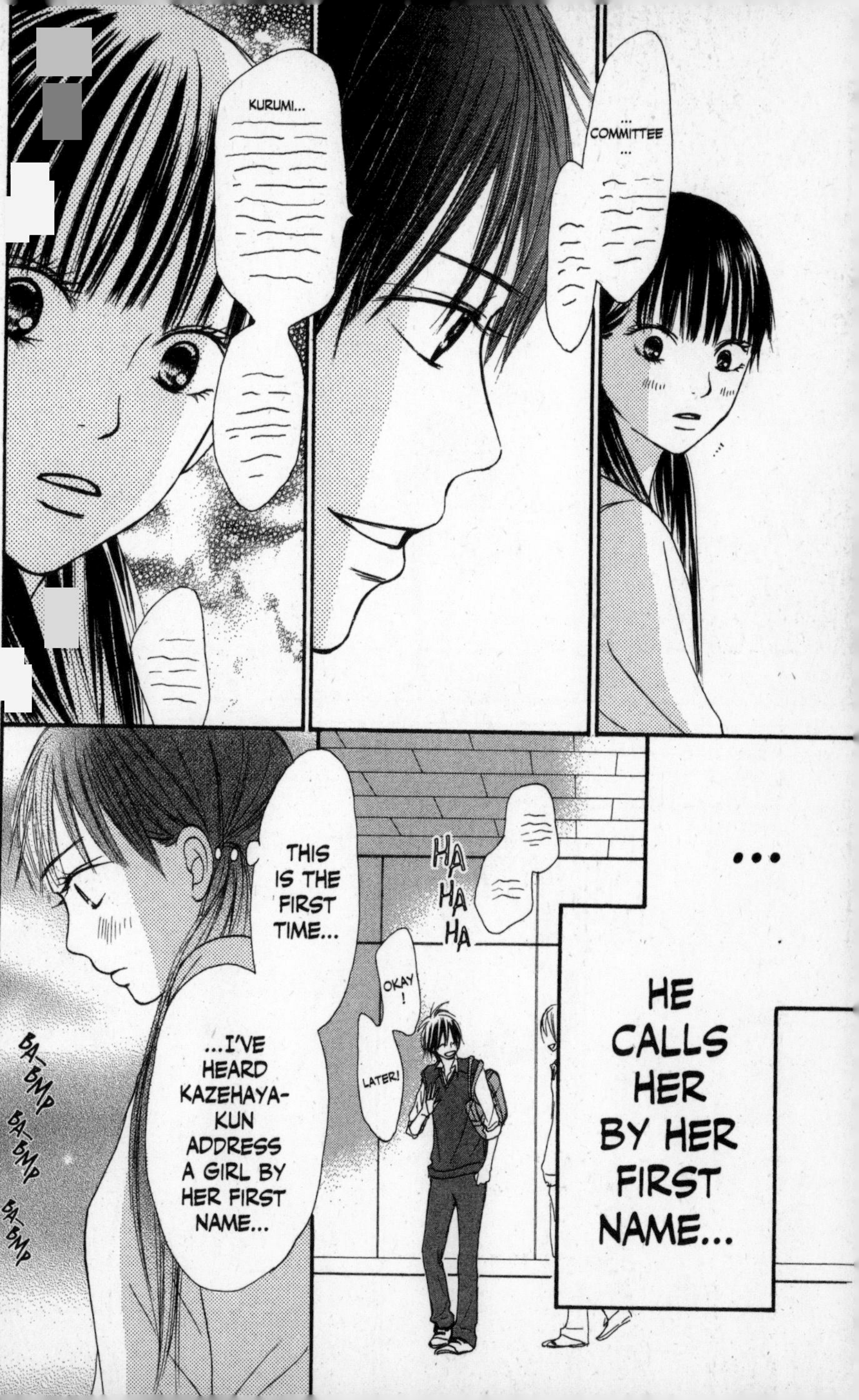
... COMMITTEE ...
KURUMI...
...
HE CALLS HER BY HER FIRST NAME...
HA HA HA
OKAY!
LATER!
THIS IS THE FIRST TIME...
...I'VE HEARD KAZEHAYA-KUN ADDRESS A GIRL BY HER FIRST NAME...
BA-BMP BA-BMP BA-BMP

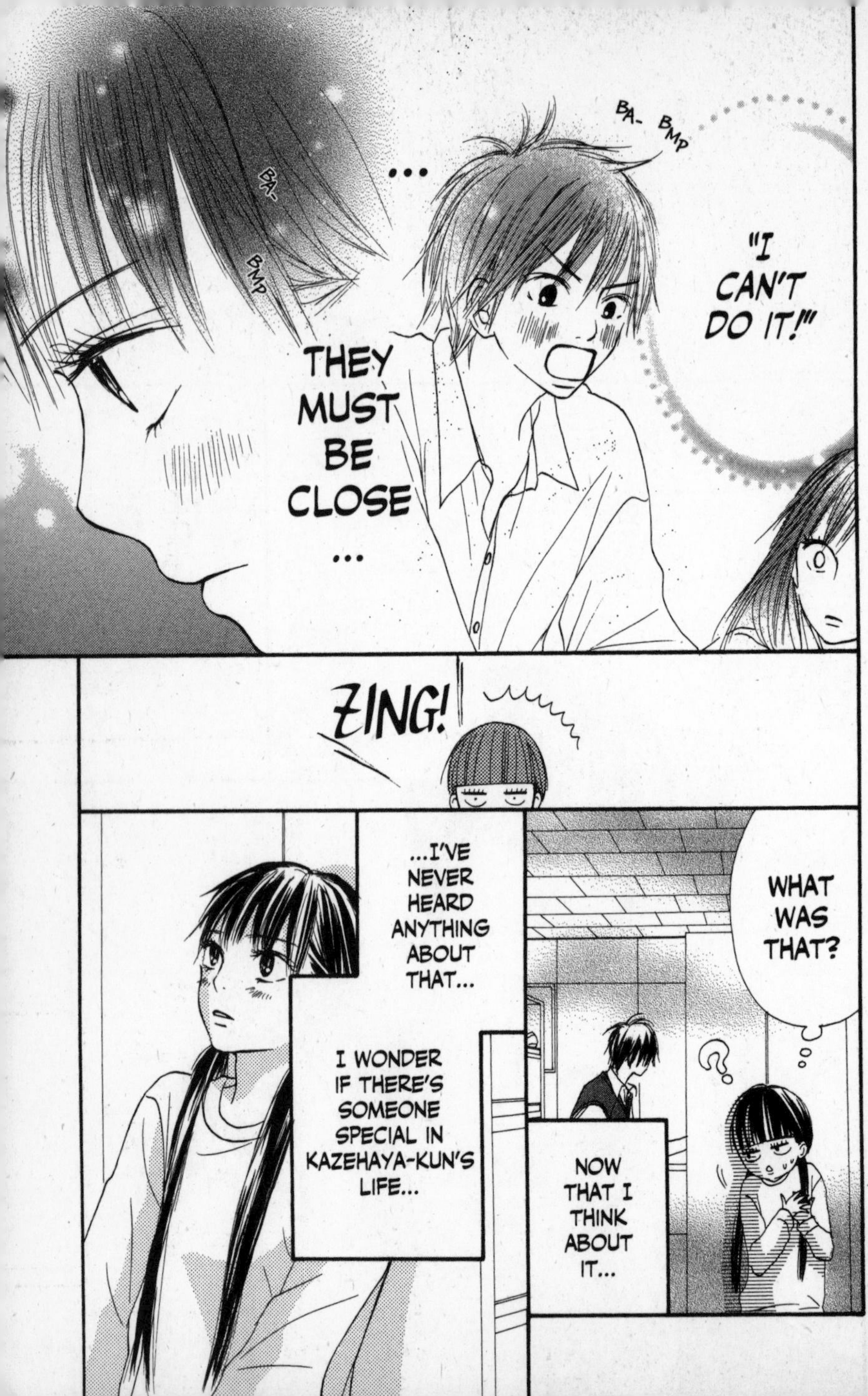

BA- BMP
"I CAN'T DO IT!"
...
BA- BMP
THEY MUST BE CLOSE...
ZING!
WHAT WAS THAT?
?
NOW THAT I THINK ABOUT IT...
...I'VE NEVER HEARD ANYTHING ABOUT THAT...
I WONDER IF THERE'S SOMEONE SPECIAL IN KAZEHAYA-KUN'S LIFE...

IF YOU CALL SOMEONE BY THEIR FIRST NAME ...
...IS THAT PERSON SPECIAL?
ZING ZING!!
?
?
MY ...
MY CHEST HURTS !!
...
UGHH

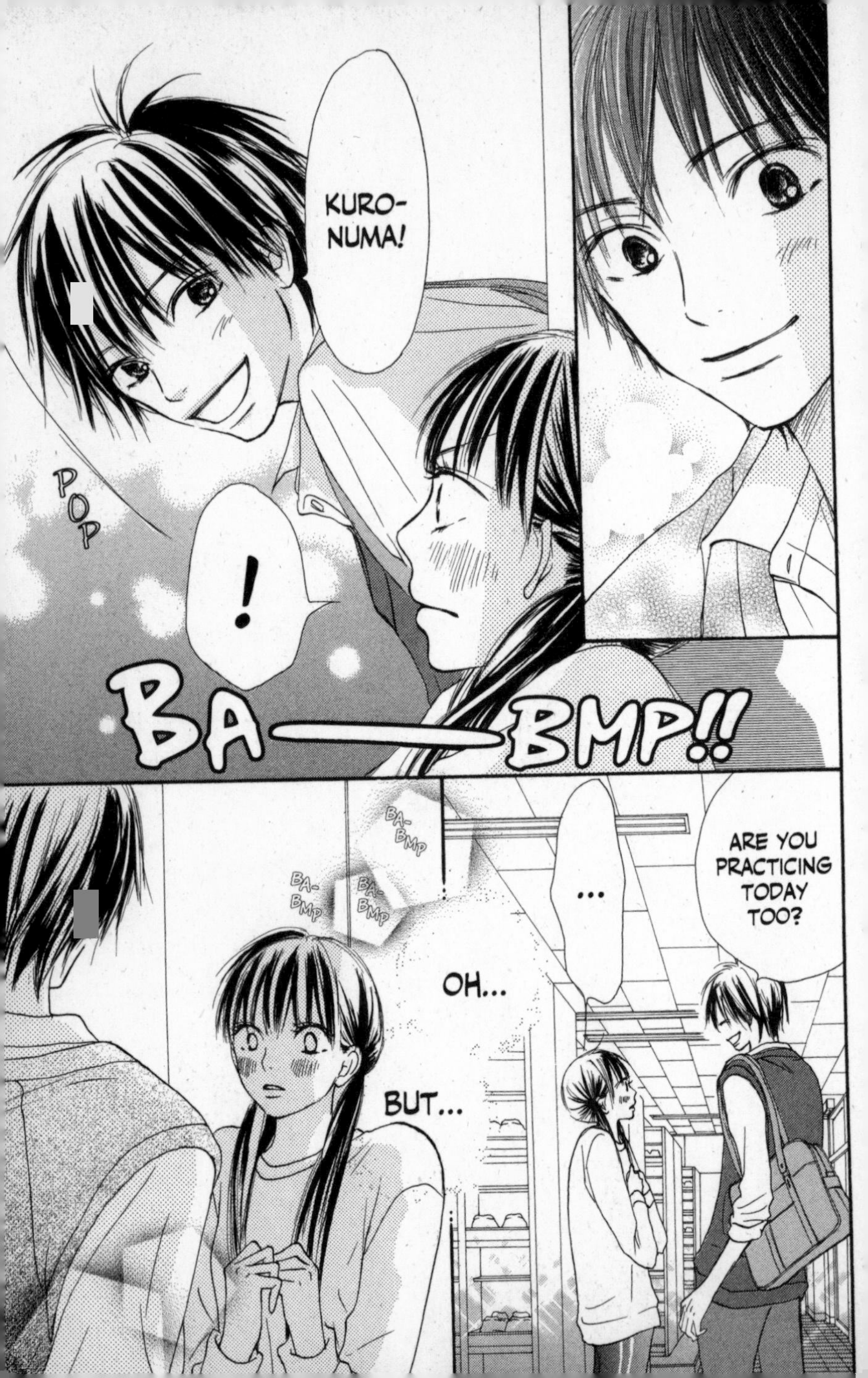
KURO-
NUMA!
POP
!
BA—BMP!!
ARE YOU PRACTICING TODAY TOO?
...
OH...
BUT...
BA-BMP
BA-BMP
BA-BMP

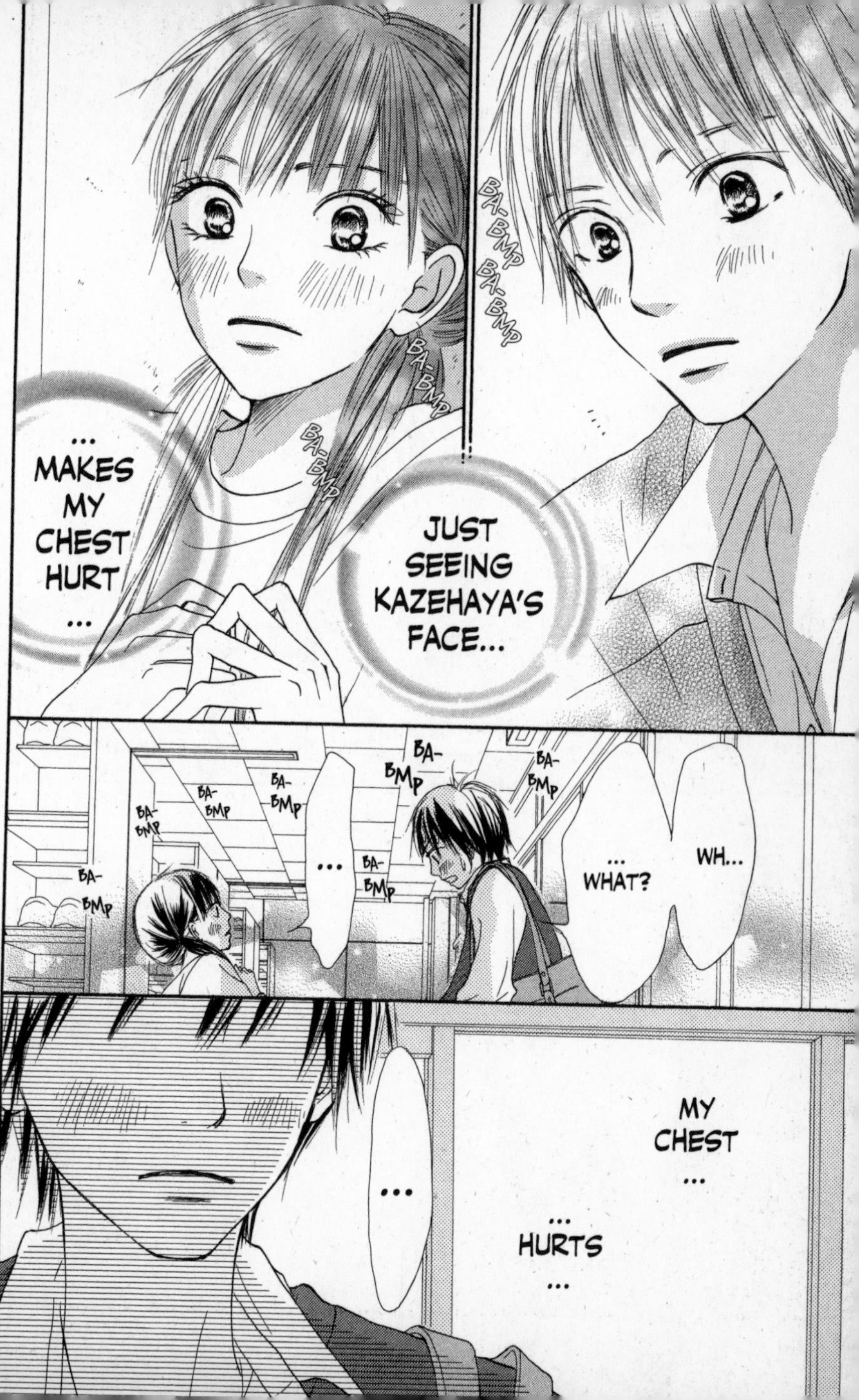
BA-BMP BA-BMP
JUST SEEING KAZEHAYA'S FACE...
BA-BMP
BA-BMP
... MAKES MY CHEST HURT ...
WH...
... WHAT?
BA-BMP
BA-BMP
BA-BMP
...
BA-BMP
BA-BMP
BA-BMP
BA-BMP
MY CHEST ...
... HURTS ...
...

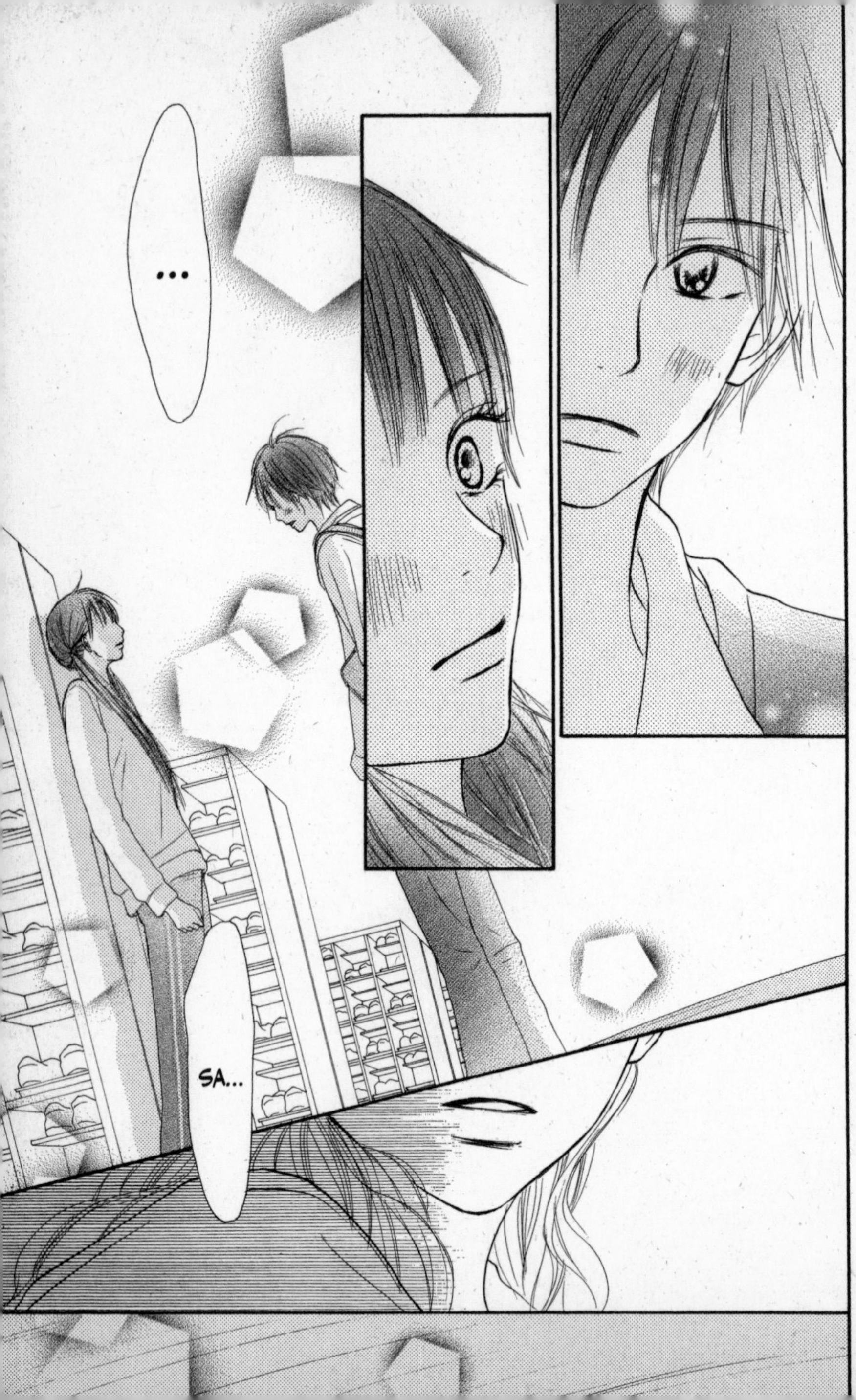
...
SA...

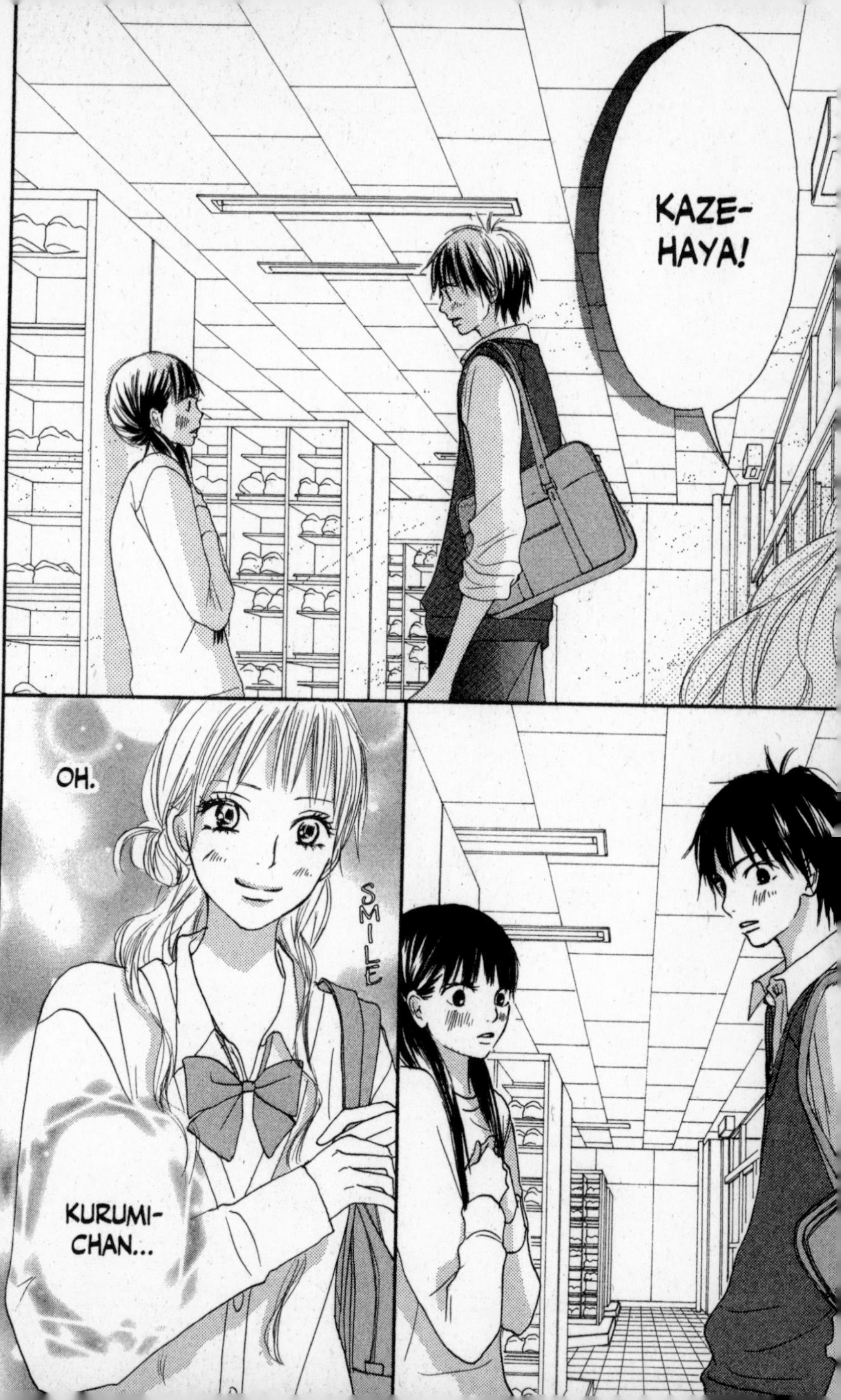
KAZE-HAYA!
OH.
SMILE
KURUMI-CHAN...

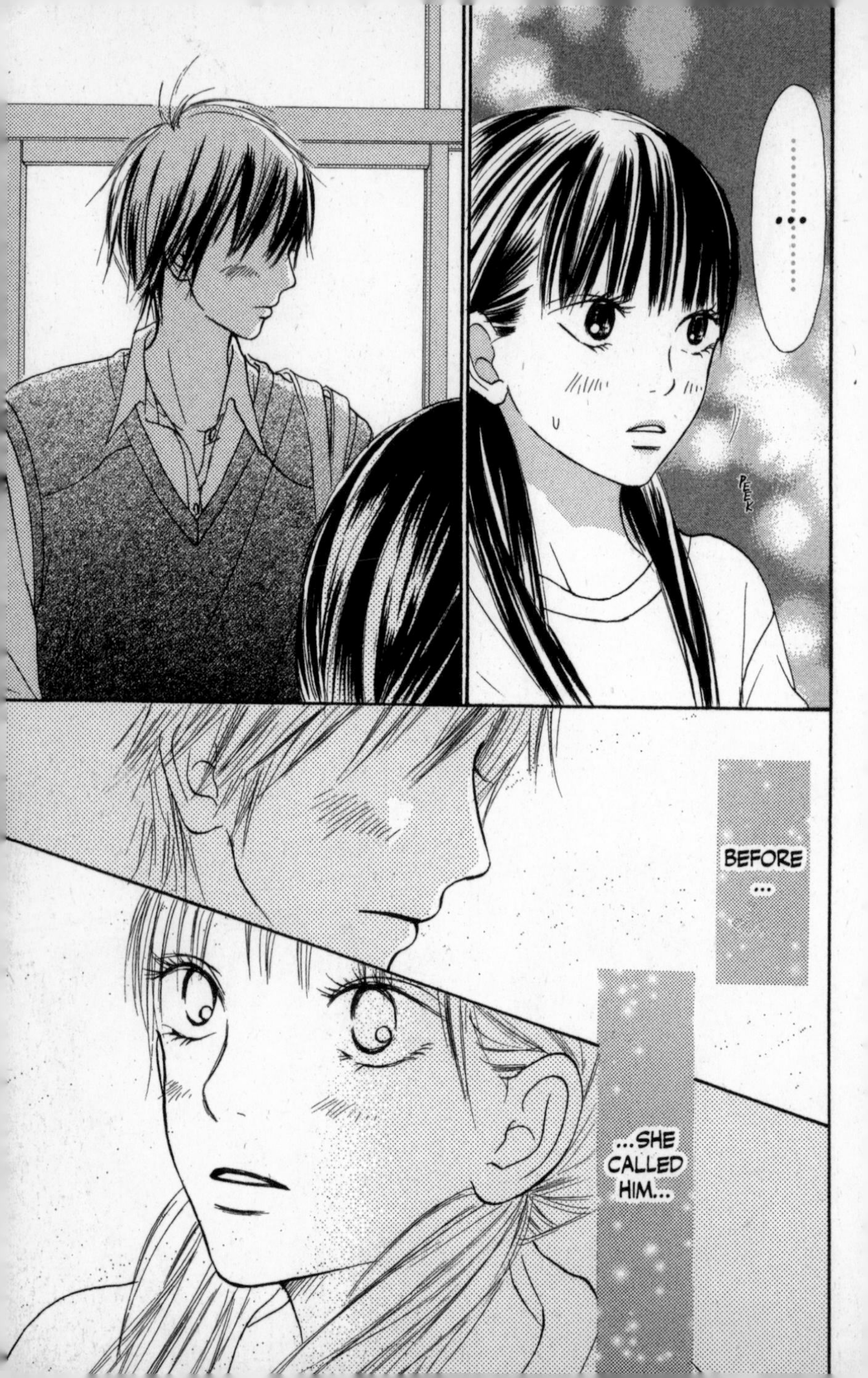

....
PEEK
BEFORE ...
...SHE CALLED HIM...

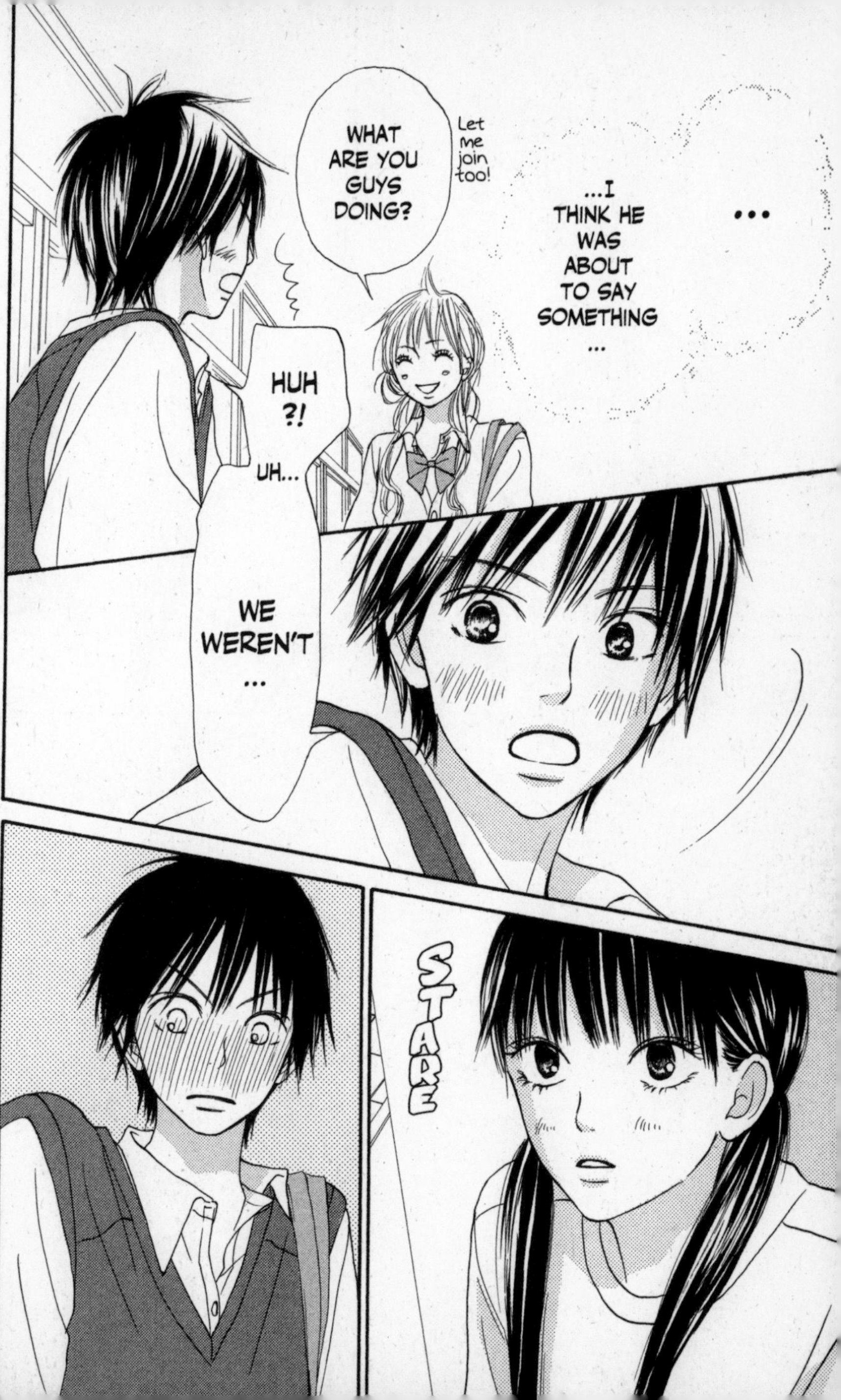
...
...I THINK HE WAS ABOUT TO SAY SOMETHING...
WHAT ARE YOU GUYS DOING?
Let me join too!
HUH ?!
UH...
WE WEREN'T...
STARE

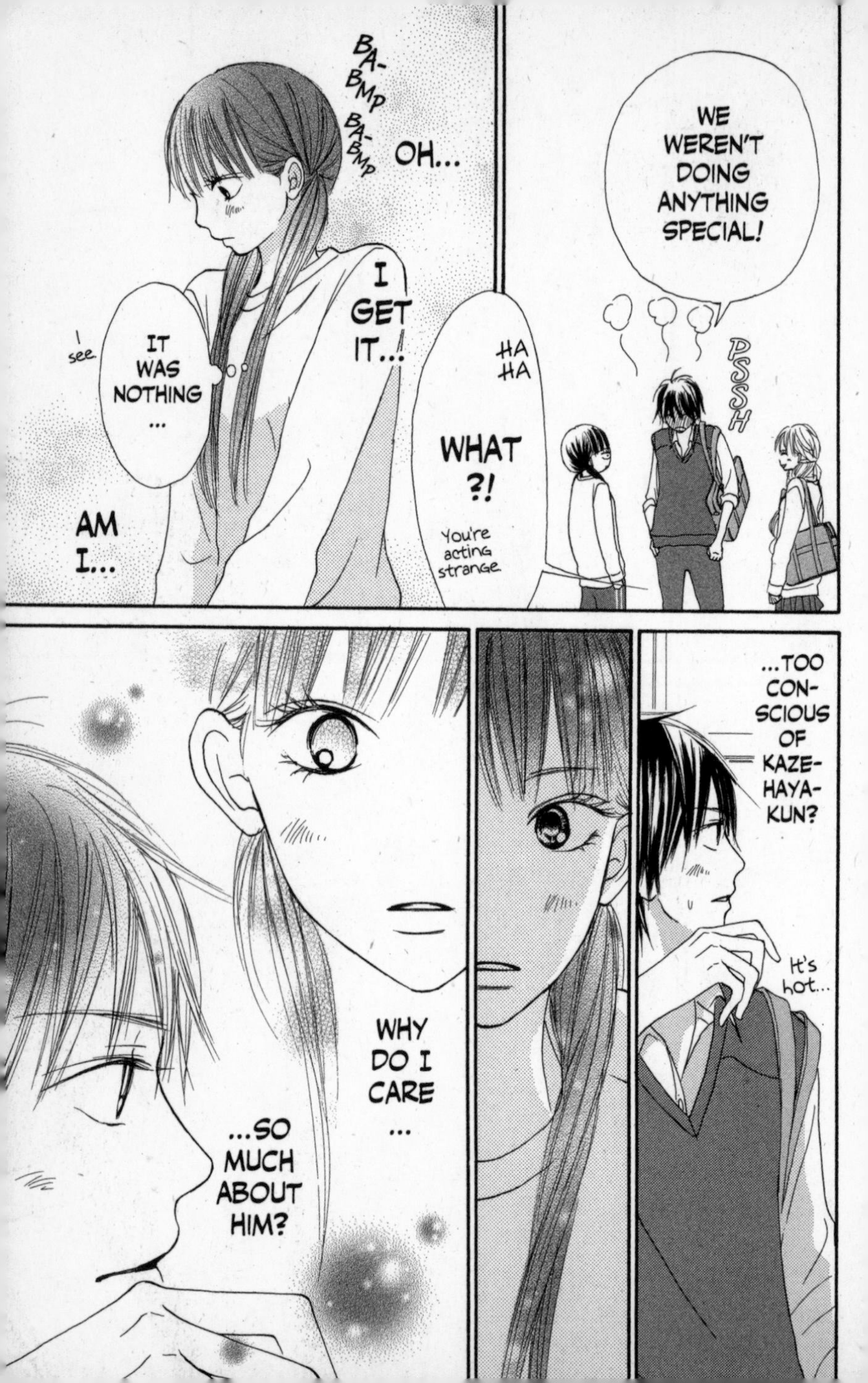
WE WEREN'T DOING ANYTHING SPECIAL!
PSSH
HA HA
WHAT ?!
You're acting strange.
BA-BMP BA-BMP
OH...
I GET IT...
IT WAS NOTHING ...
I see.
AM I...
...TOO CONSCIOUS OF KAZE-HAYA-KUN?
It's hot...
WHY DO I CARE ...
...SO MUCH ABOUT HIM?

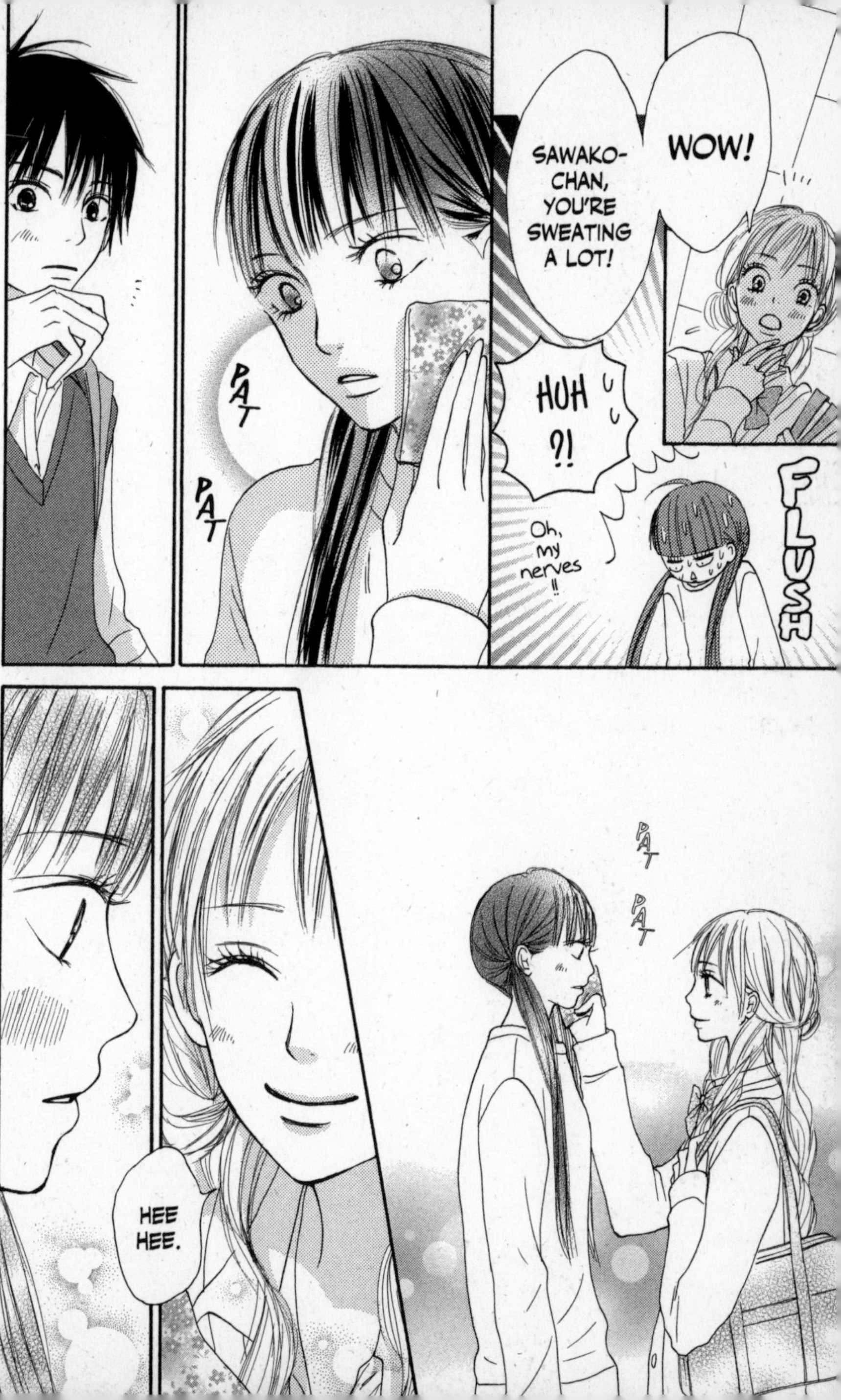
WOW!
SAWAKO-CHAN, YOU'RE SWEATING A LOT!
HUH?!
Oh, my nerves!!
FLUSH
PAT
PAT
PAT
PAT
HEE HEE.

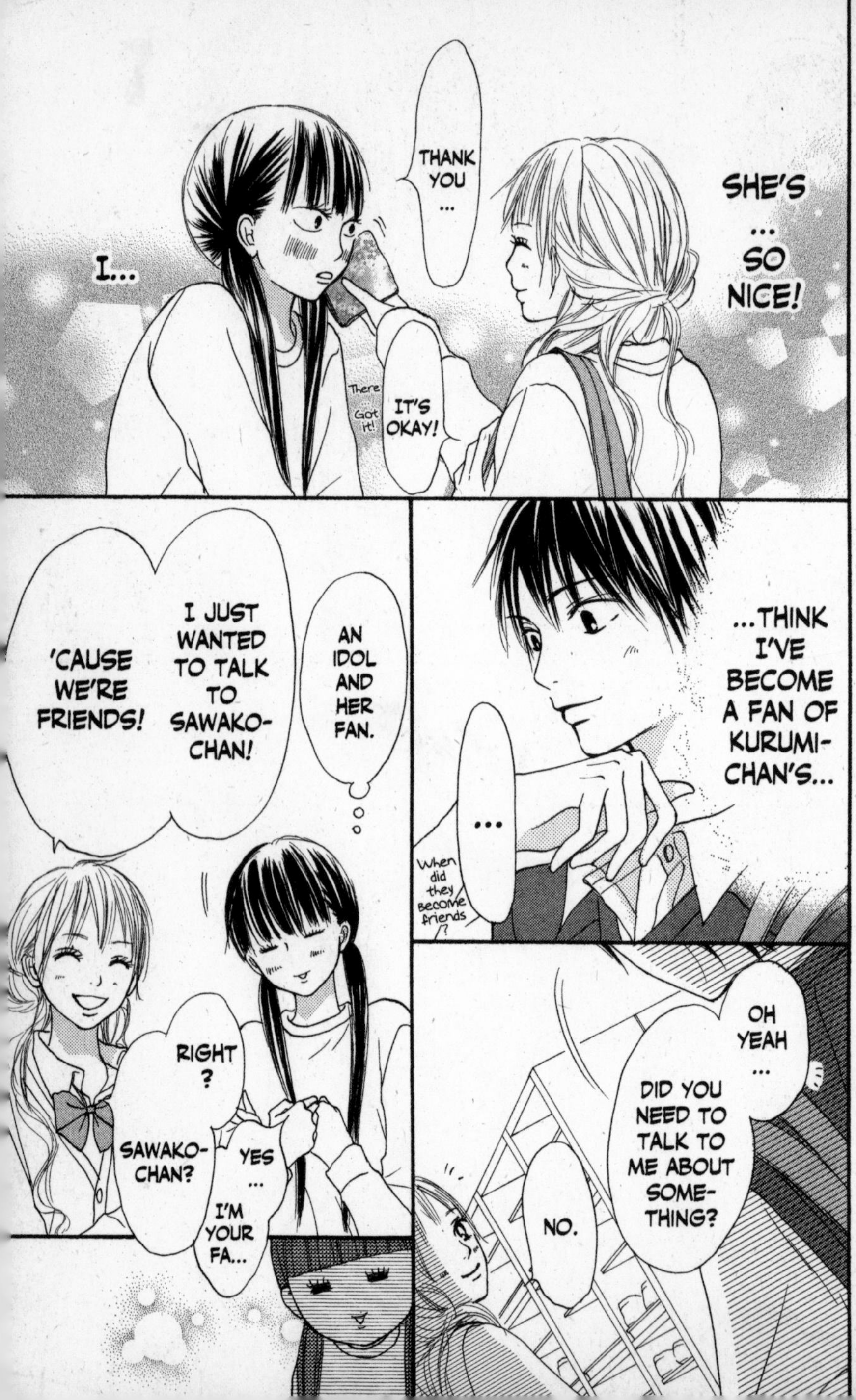
SHE'S ... SO NICE!
THANK YOU ...
There ... Got it!
IT'S OKAY!
I...
...THINK I'VE BECOME A FAN OF KURUMI-CHAN'S...
...
When did they become friends?
AN IDOL AND HER FAN.
I JUST WANTED TO TALK TO SAWAKO-CHAN!
'CAUSE WE'RE FRIENDS!
RIGHT? SAWAKO-CHAN?
YES ... I'M YOUR FA...
OH YEAH ...
DID YOU NEED TO TALK TO ME ABOUT SOME-THING?
NO.

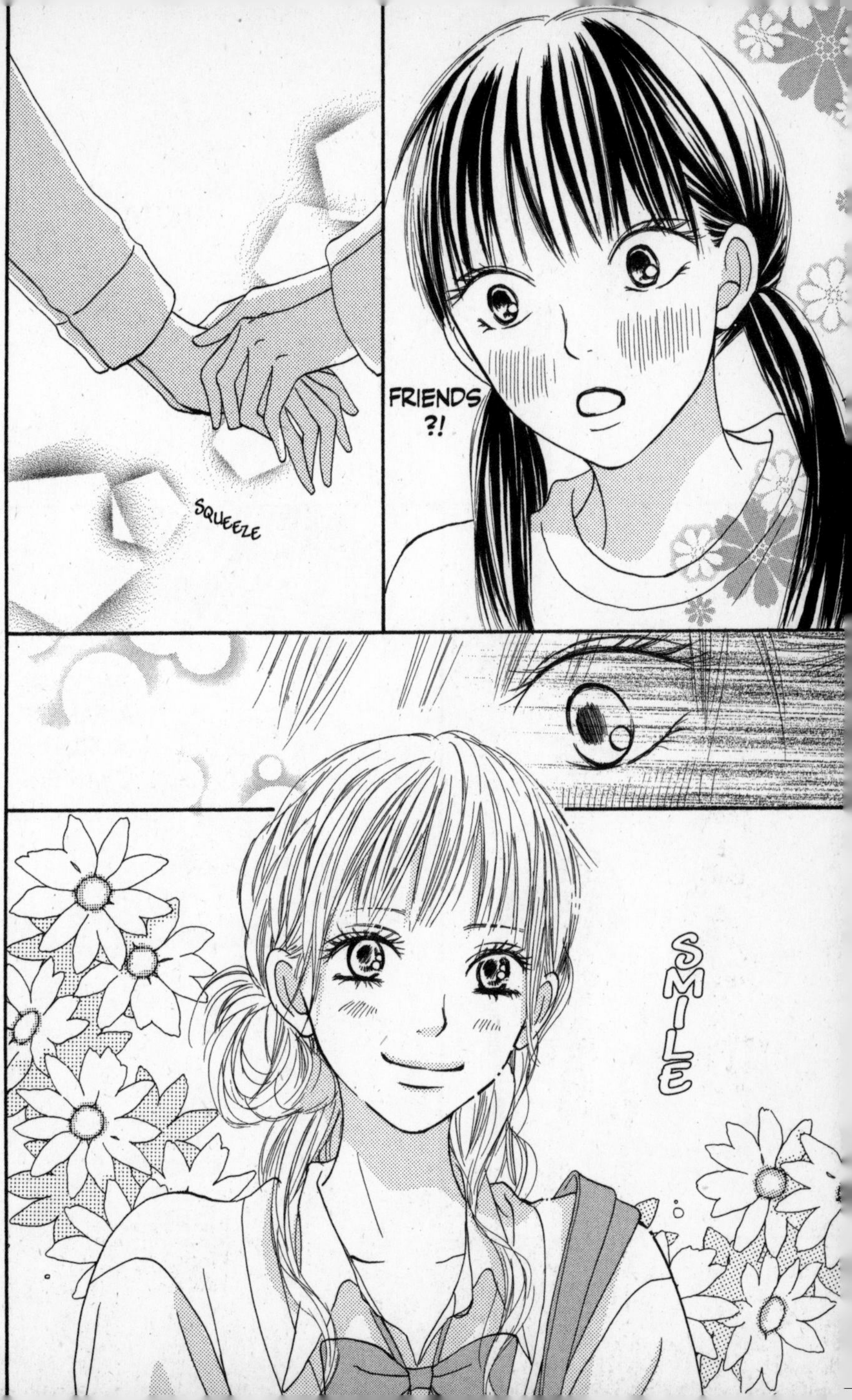
FRIENDS ?!
SQUEEZE
SMILE

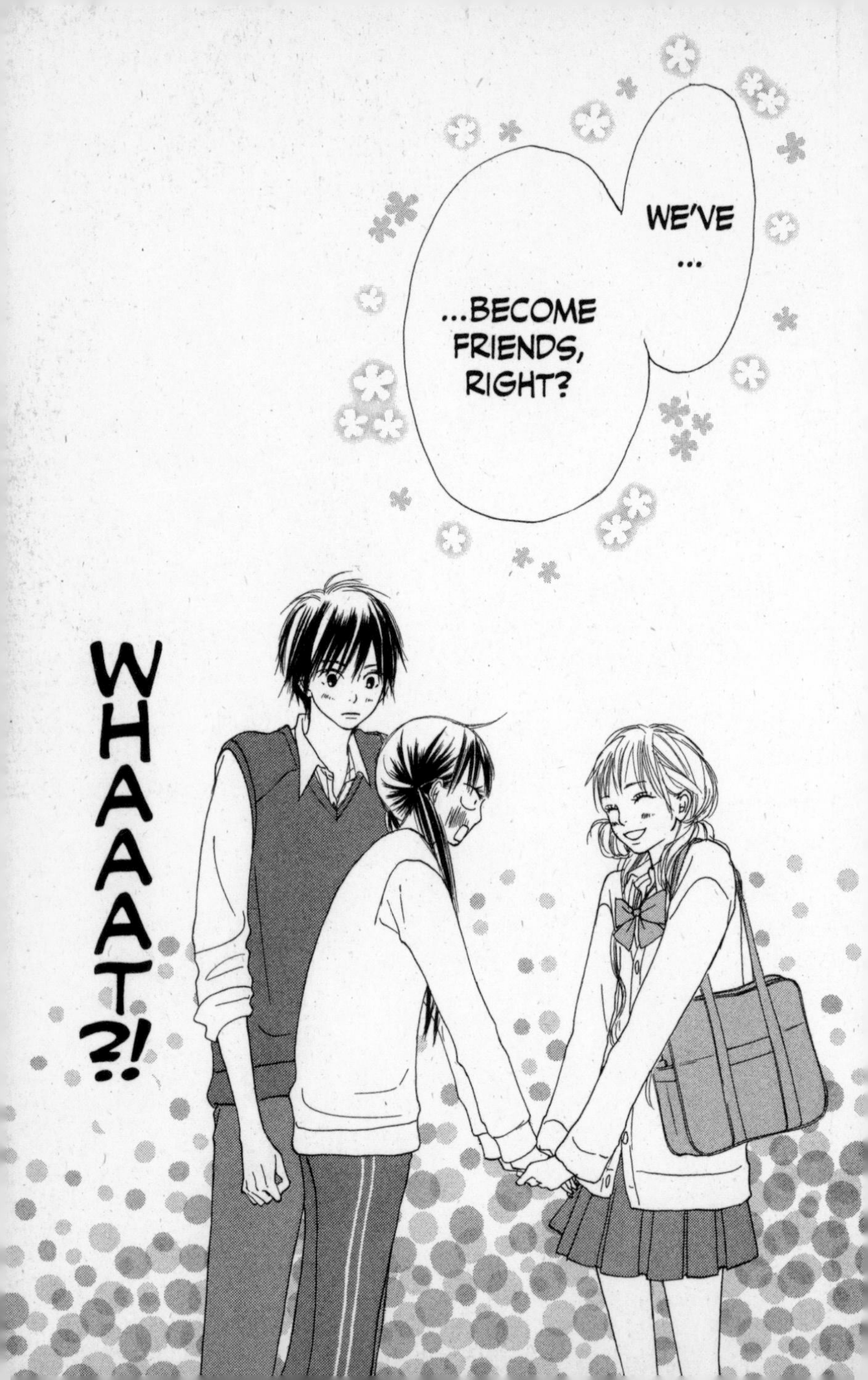
WE'VE
...
...BECOME FRIENDS, RIGHT?
WHAAAT?!

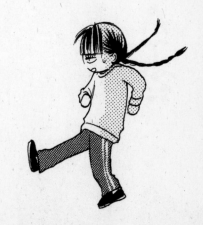

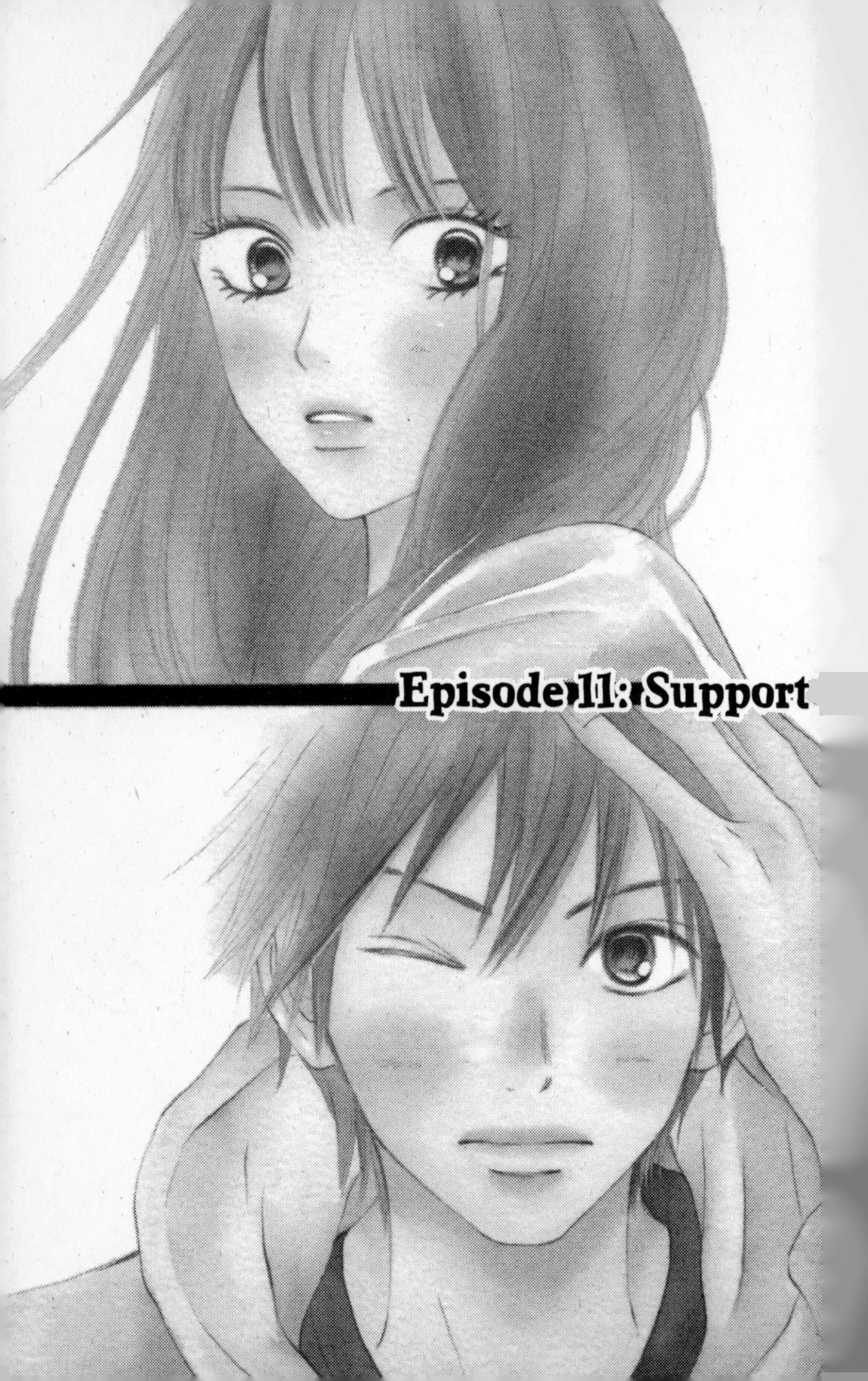
Episode 11: Support

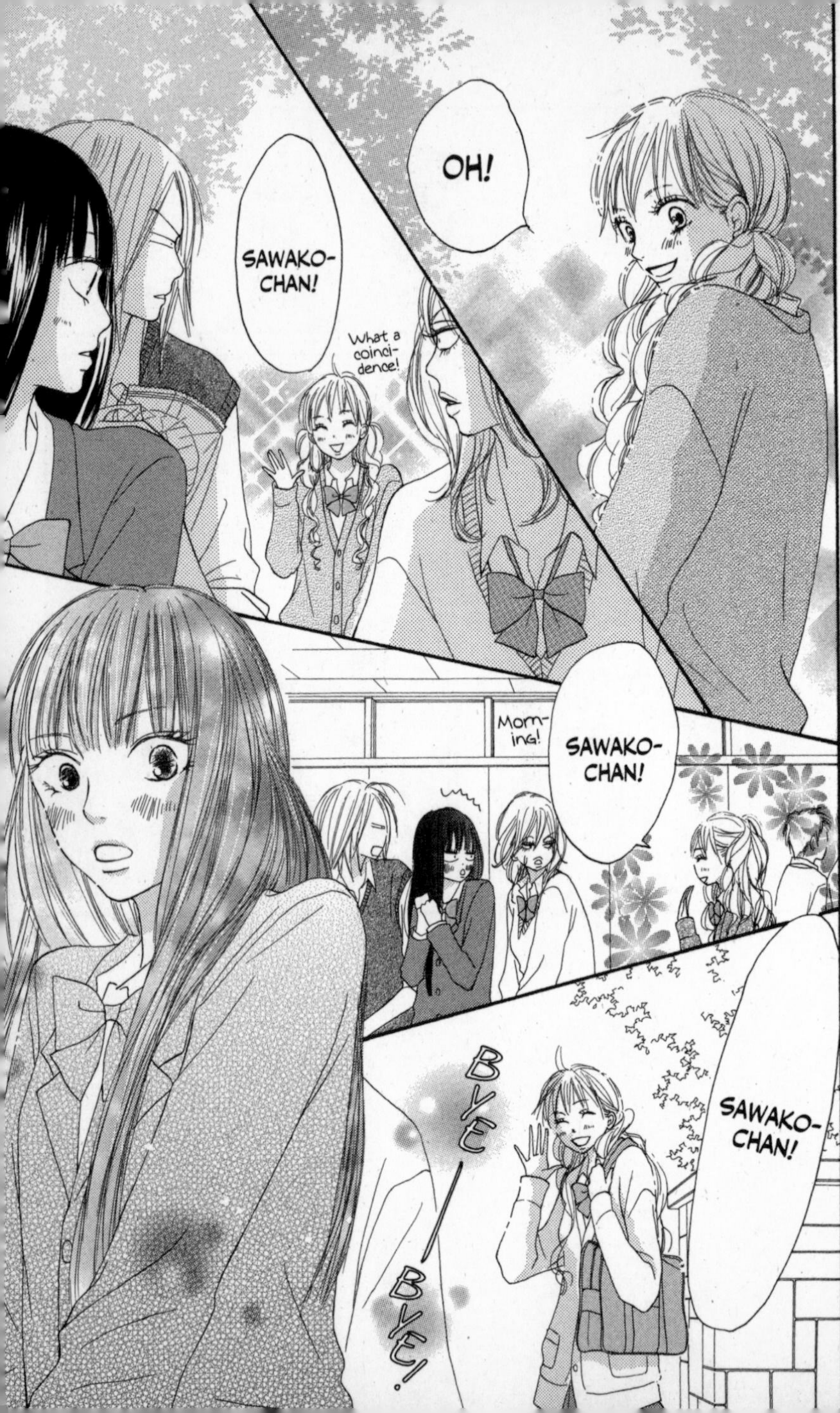
OH!
SAWAKO-CHAN!
What a coincidence!
SAWAKO-CHAN!
Morning!
SAWAKO-CHAN!
BYE-BYE!

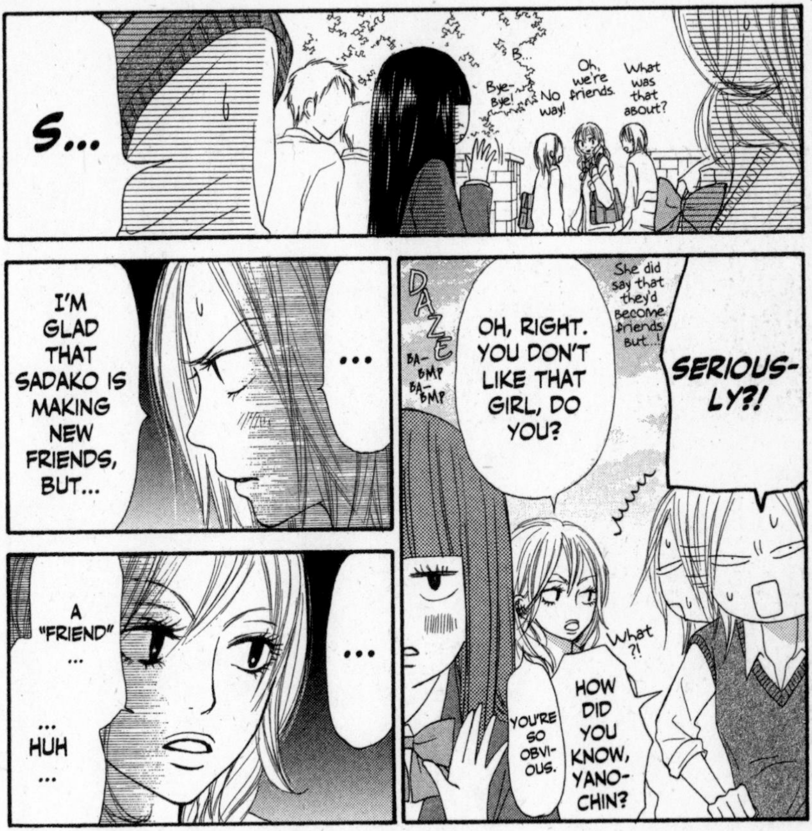
What was that about?
Oh, we're friends.
No way!
Bye-Bye!
B...
S...
SERIOUS-LY?!
She did say that they'd become friends but...!
OH, RIGHT. YOU DON'T LIKE THAT GIRL, DO YOU?
DAZE
BA-BMP BA-BMP
What?!
HOW DID YOU KNOW, YANO-CHIN?
YOU'RE SO OBVI-OUS.
...
I'M GLAD THAT SADAKO IS MAKING NEW FRIENDS, BUT...
...
A "FRIEND" ...
... HUH ...

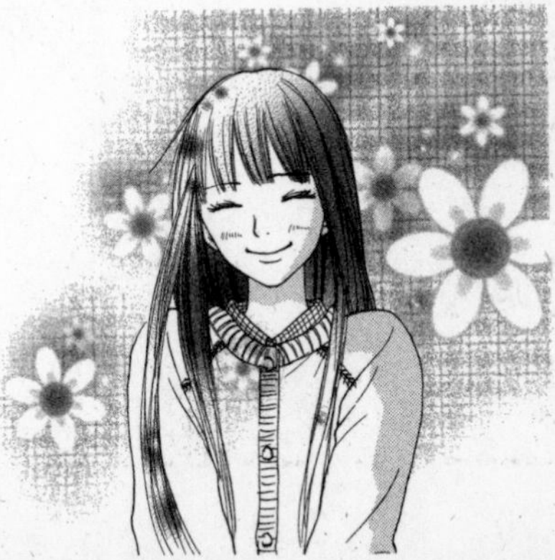

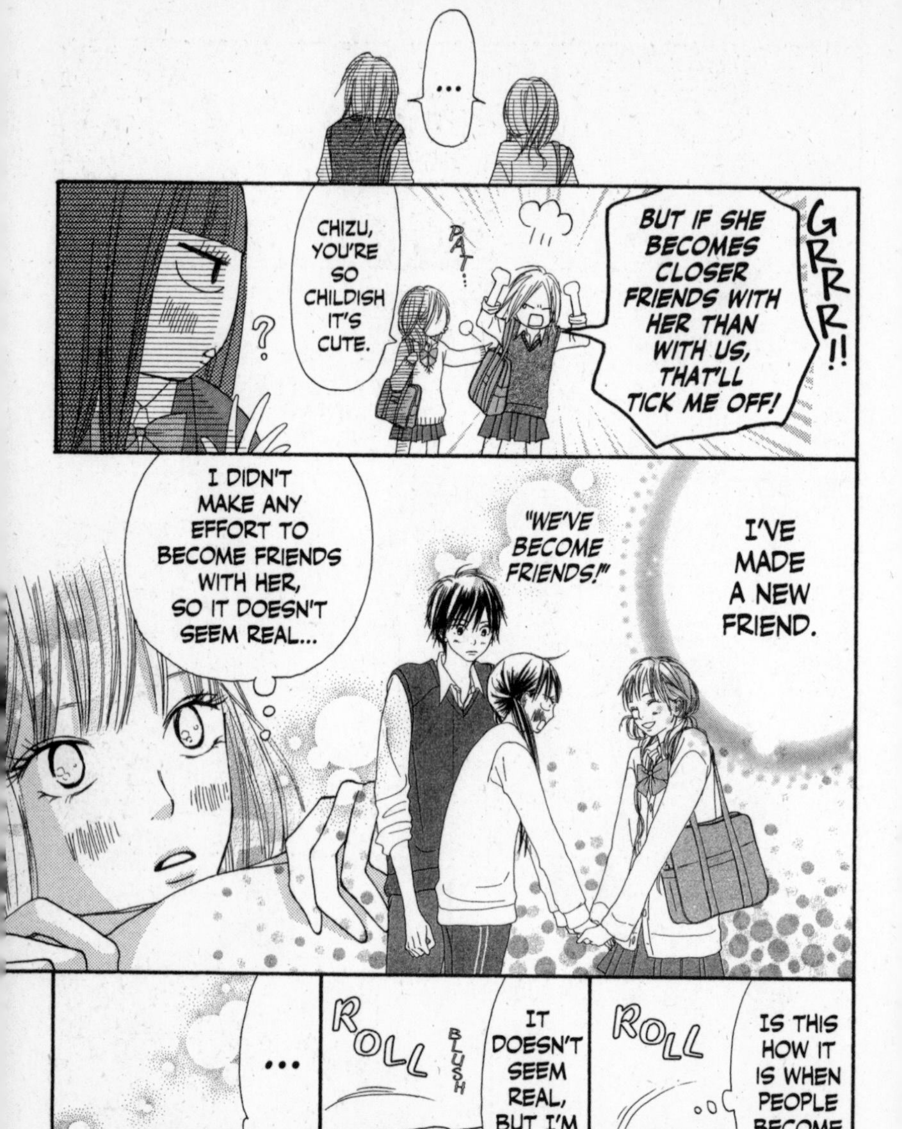
...
GRRR!!
BUT IF SHE BECOMES CLOSER FRIENDS WITH HER THAN WITH US, THAT'LL TICK ME OFF!
PAT...
CHIZU, YOU'RE SO CHILDISH IT'S CUTE.
?
I'VE MADE A NEW FRIEND.
"WE'VE BECOME FRIENDS!"
I DIDN'T MAKE ANY EFFORT TO BECOME FRIENDS WITH HER, SO IT DOESN'T SEEM REAL...
ROLL
IS THIS HOW IT IS WHEN PEOPLE BECOME FRIENDS ?
IT DOESN'T SEEM REAL, BUT I'M REALLY HAPPY.
BLUSH
ROLL
...

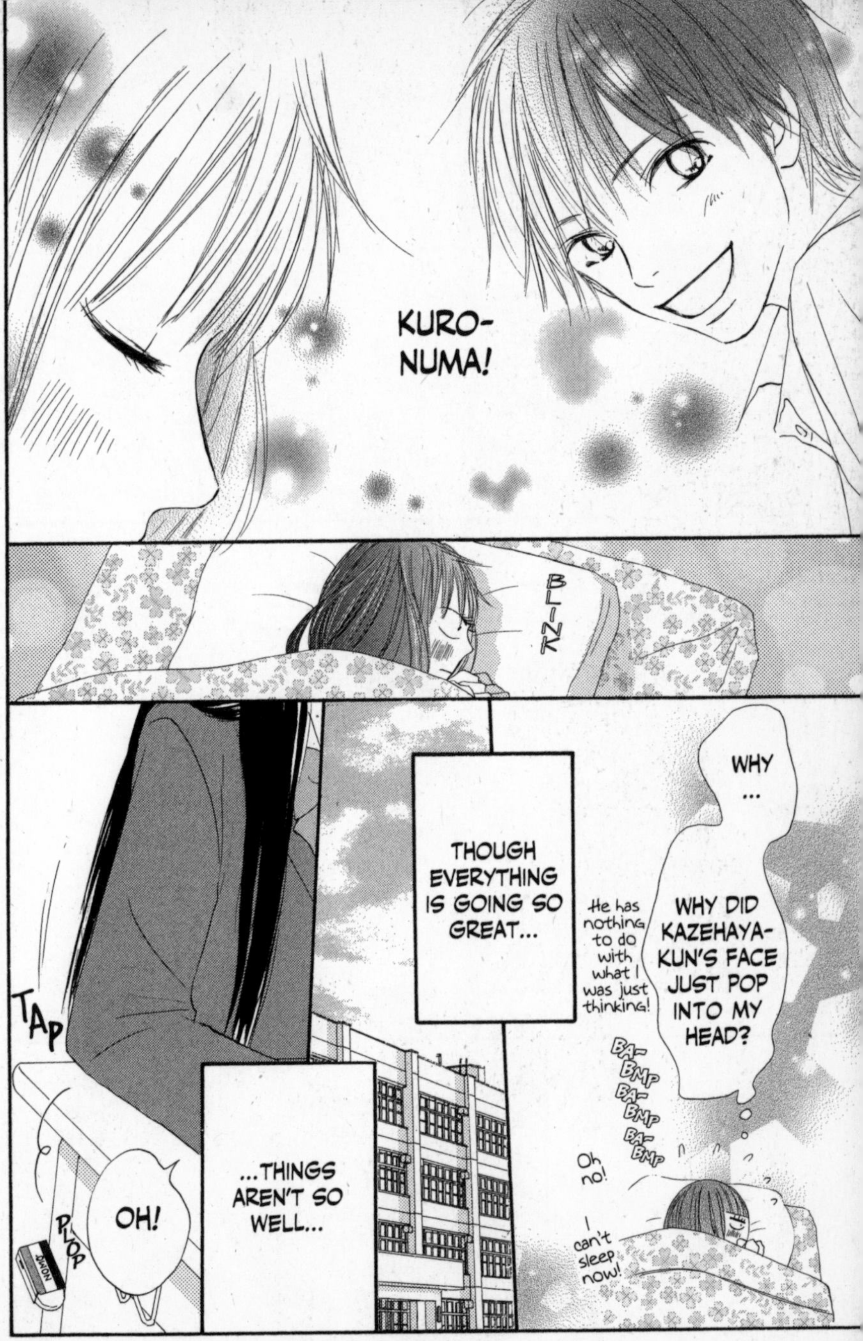
KURO-
NUMA!
BLINK
WHY
...
WHY DID KAZEHAYA-KUN'S FACE JUST POP INTO MY HEAD?
He has nothing to do with what I was just thinking!
BA-BMP BA-BMP BA-BMP
Oh no!
I can't sleep now!
THOUGH EVERYTHING IS GOING SO GREAT...
...THINGS AREN'T SO WELL...
TAP
OH!
PLOP

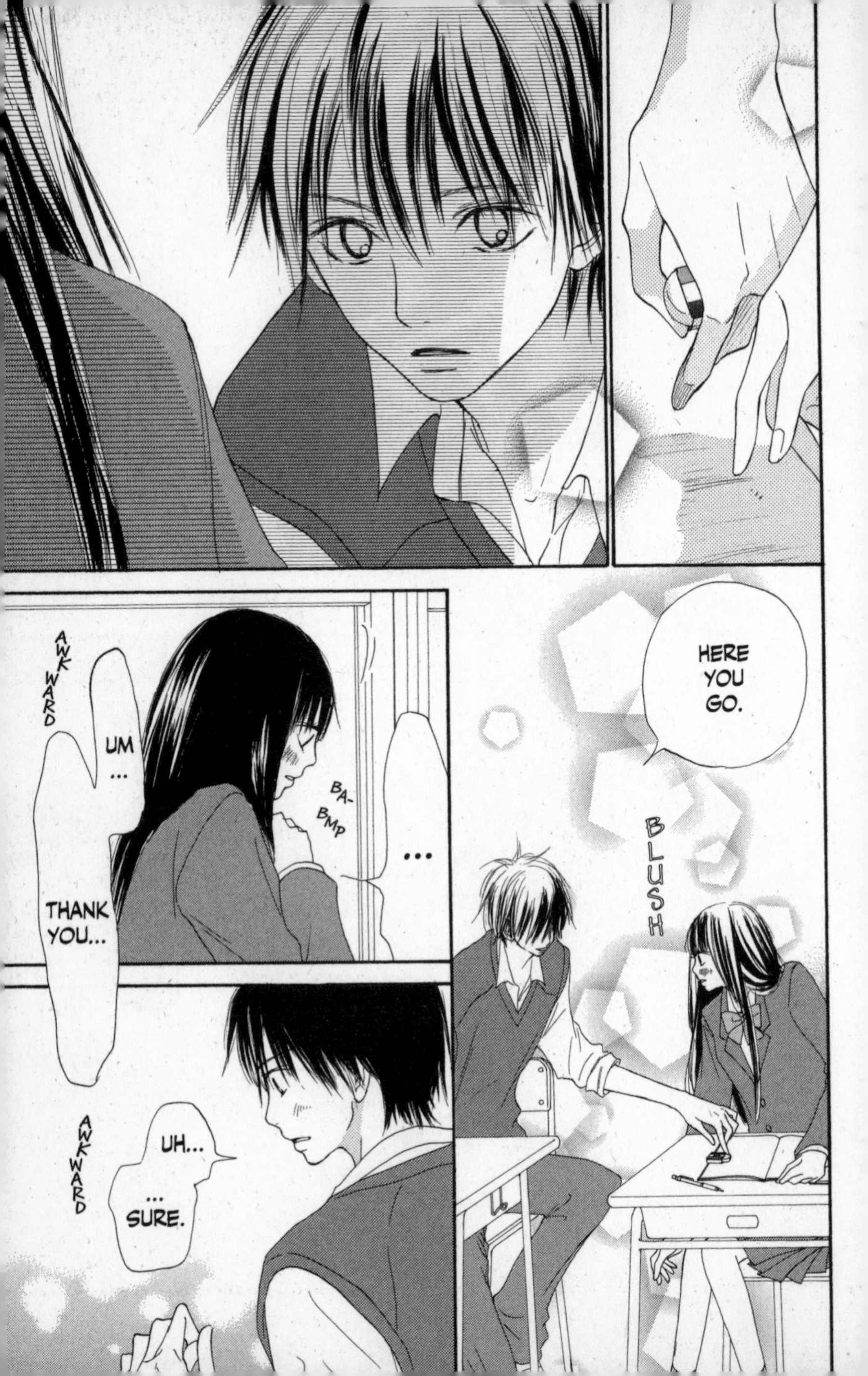
HERE YOU GO.
BLUSH
...
BA-BMP
AWKWARD
UM ... THANK YOU...
AWKWARD
UH... ... SURE.

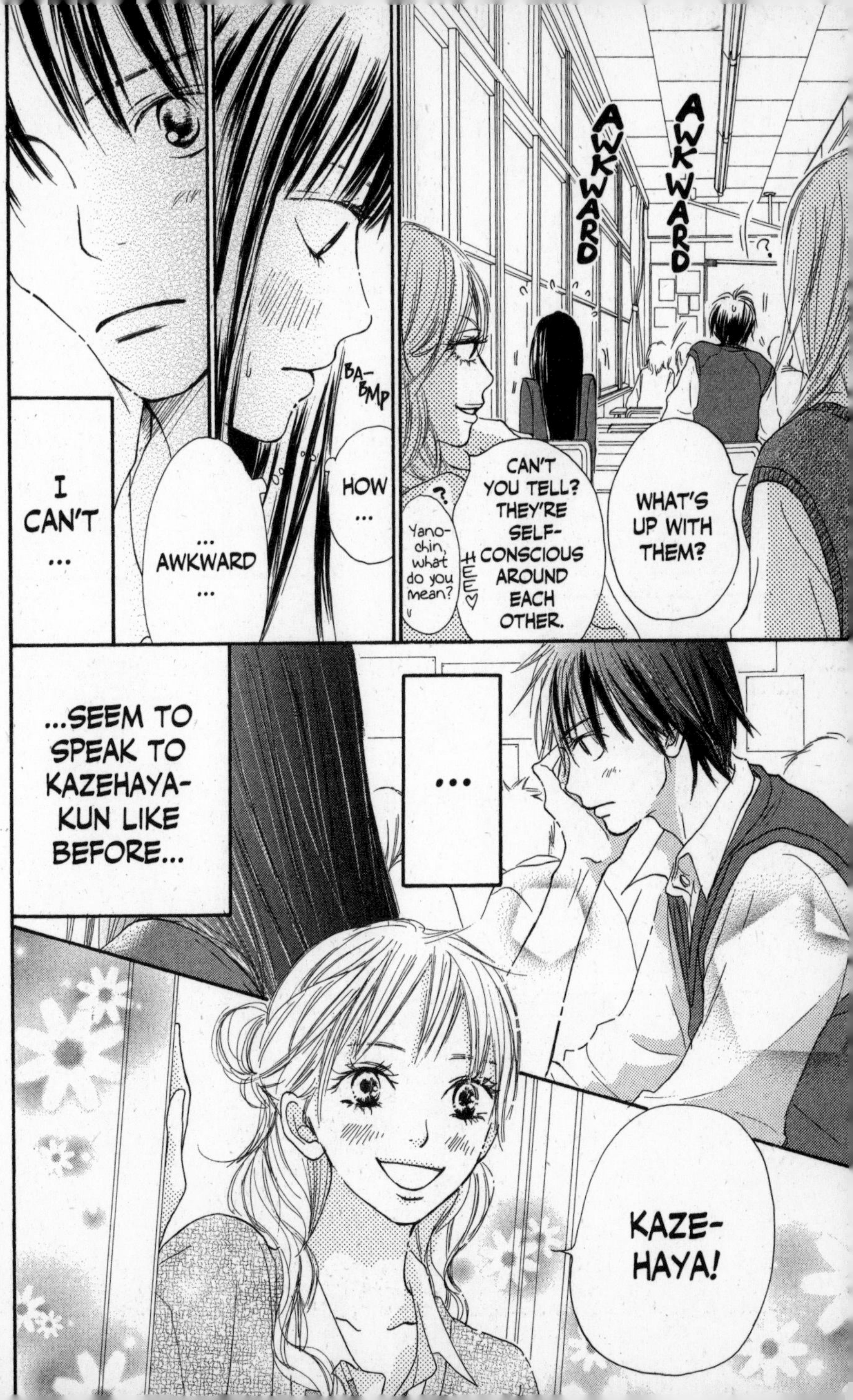
AWKWARD
AWKWARD
?
WHAT'S UP WITH THEM?
CAN'T YOU TELL? THEY'RE SELF-CONSCIOUS AROUND EACH OTHER.
HEE♥
?
Yano-chin, what do you mean?
BA-BMP
HOW ...
... AWKWARD ...
I CAN'T ...
...
...SEEM TO SPEAK TO KAZEHAYA-KUN LIKE BEFORE...
KAZE-HAYA!

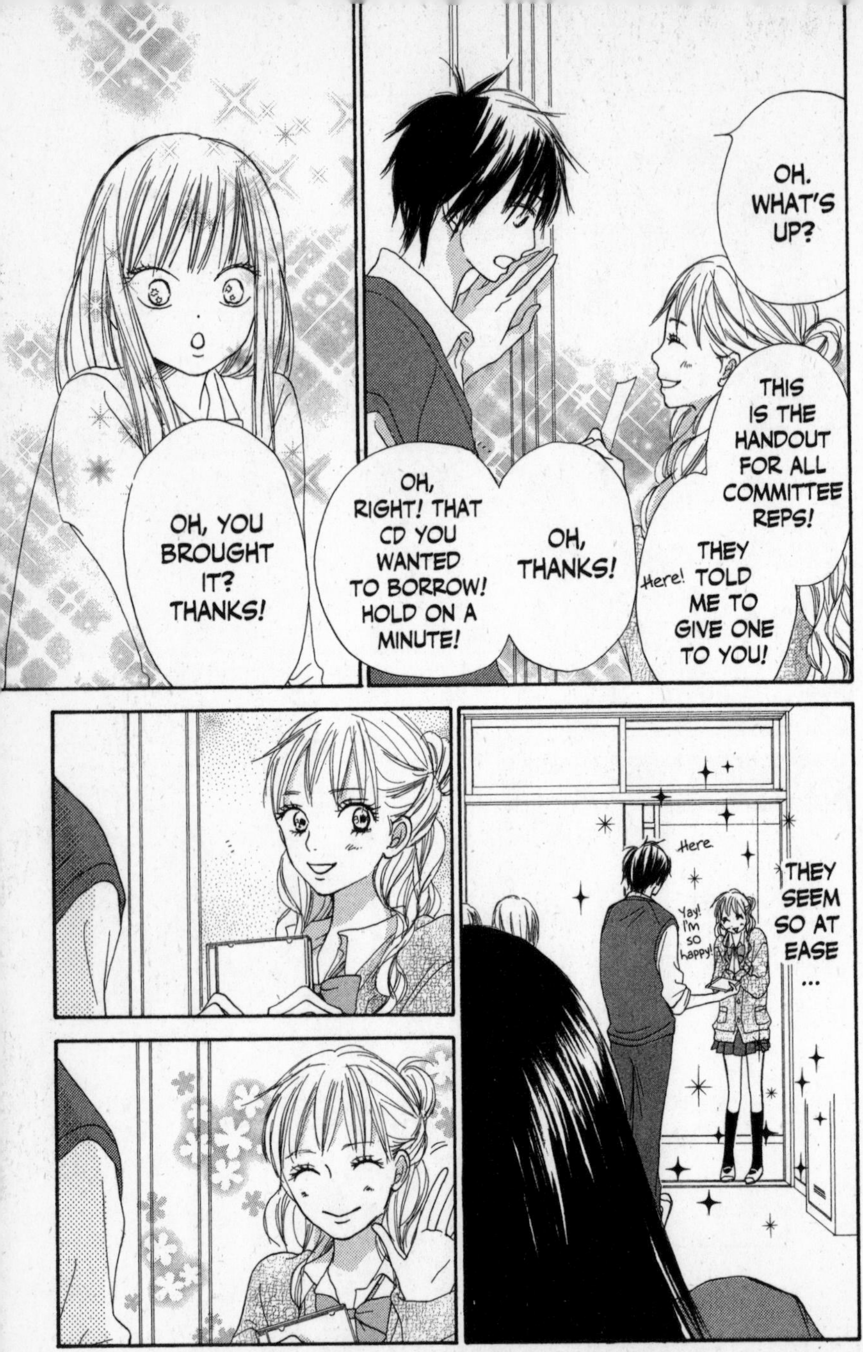
OH. WHAT'S UP?
THIS IS THE HANDOUT FOR ALL COMMITTEE REPS!
THEY TOLD ME TO GIVE ONE TO YOU!
Here!
OH, THANKS!
OH, RIGHT! THAT CD YOU WANTED TO BORROW! HOLD ON A MINUTE!
OH, YOU BROUGHT IT? THANKS!
THEY SEEM SO AT EASE ...
Here.
Yay! I'm so happy!

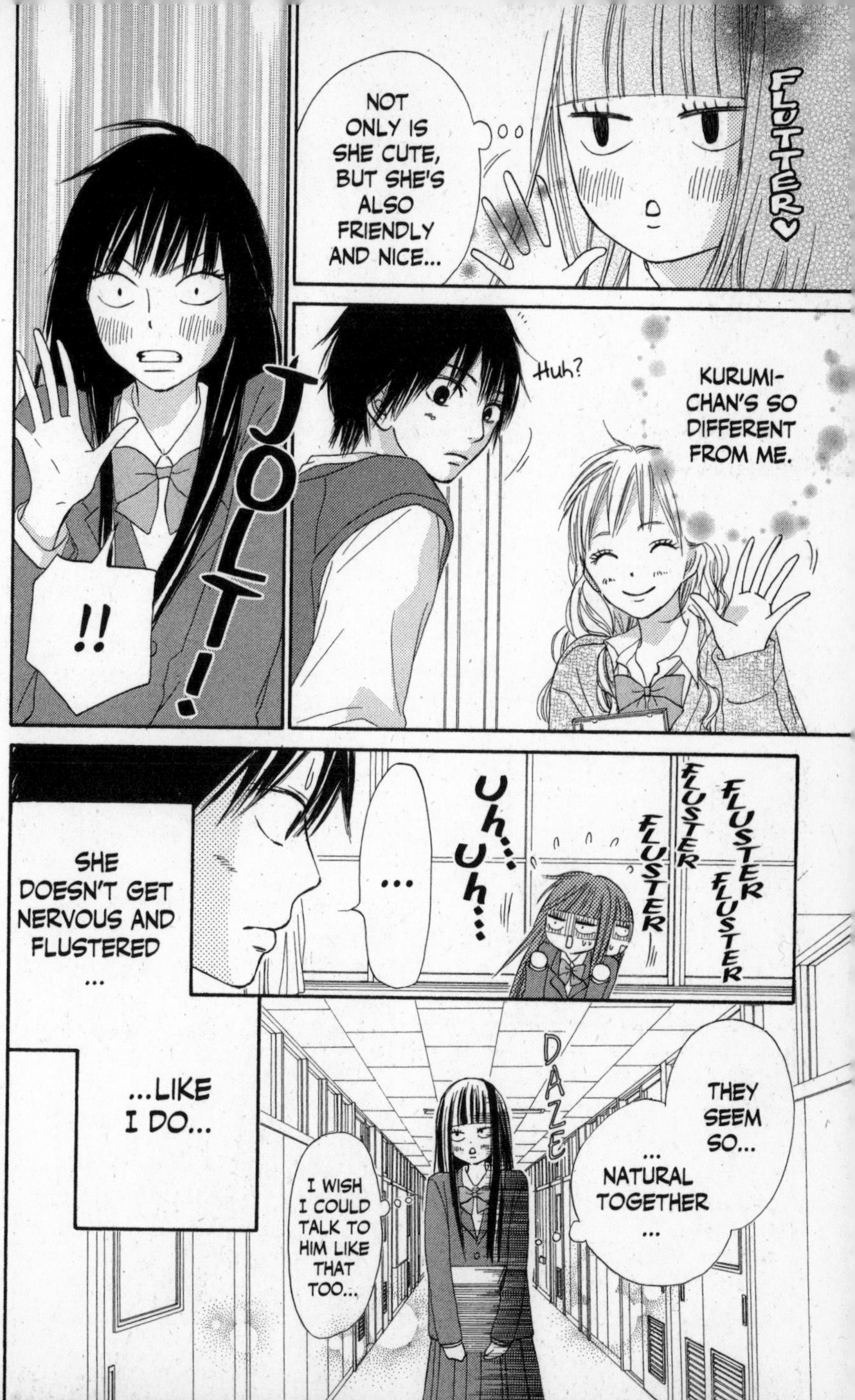
FLUTTER♥
NOT ONLY IS SHE CUTE, BUT SHE'S ALSO FRIENDLY AND NICE...
KURUMI-CHAN'S SO DIFFERENT FROM ME.
Huh?
JOLT!
!!
FLUSTER
FLUSTER
FLUSTER
FLUSTER
Uh... Uh...
...
SHE DOESN'T GET NERVOUS AND FLUSTERED ...
DAZE
THEY SEEM SO... ...NATURAL TOGETHER ...
I WISH I COULD TALK TO HIM LIKE THAT TOO...
...LIKE I DO...

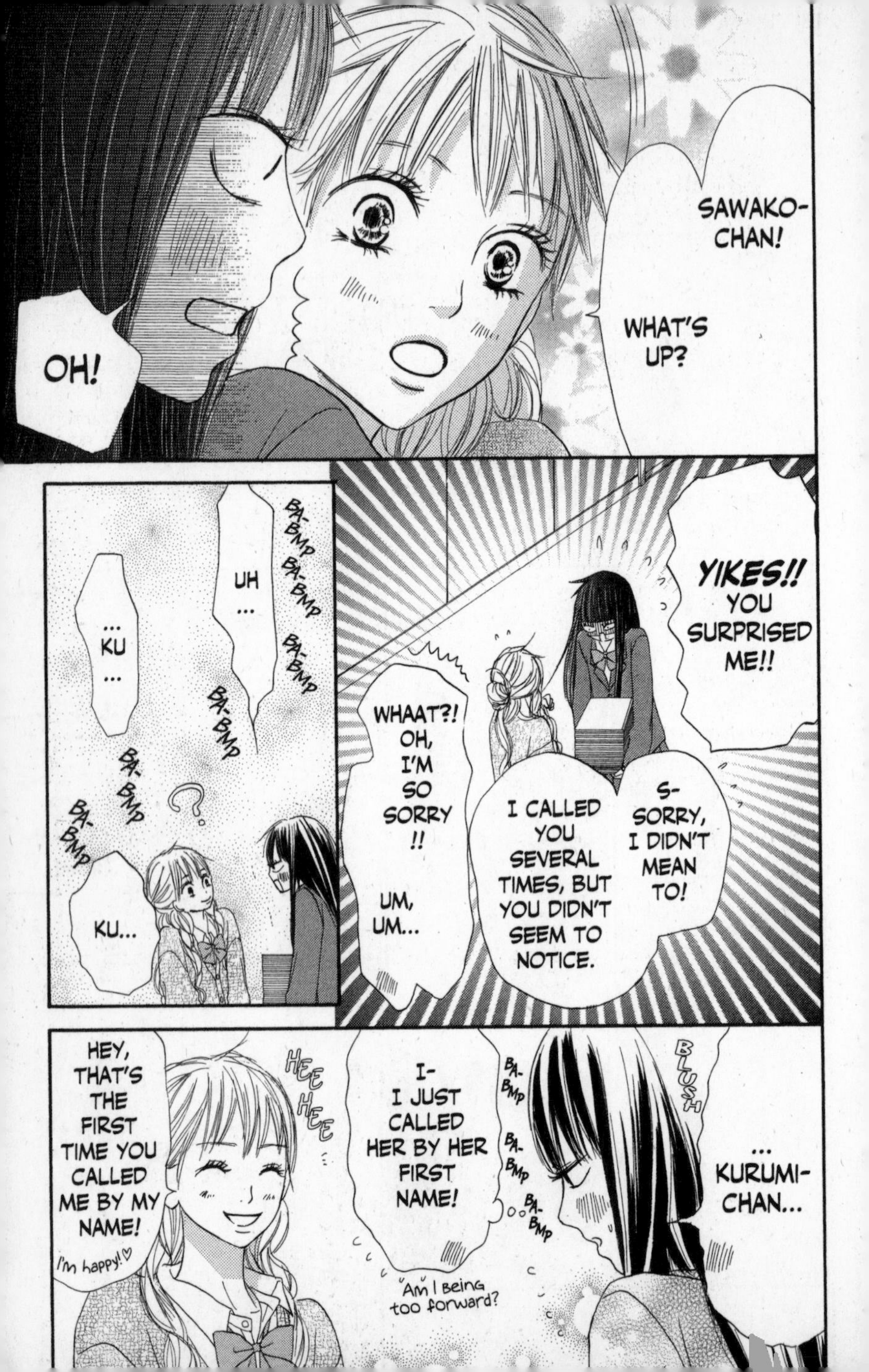
SAWAKO-CHAN!
WHAT'S UP?
OH!
YIKES!! YOU SURPRISED ME!!
S-SORRY, I DIDN'T MEAN TO!
I CALLED YOU SEVERAL TIMES, BUT YOU DIDN'T SEEM TO NOTICE.
WHAAT?! OH, I'M SO SORRY!!
UM, UM...
UH ...
BA-BMP BA-BMP
BA-BMP
BA-BMP
... KU ...
BA-BMP
BA-BMP
KU...
BLUSH
... KURUMI-CHAN...
BA-BMP
BA-BMP
BA-BMP
I- I JUST CALLED HER BY HER FIRST NAME!
Am I being too forward?
HEE HEE
HEY, THAT'S THE FIRST TIME YOU CALLED ME BY MY NAME!
I'm happy!♡

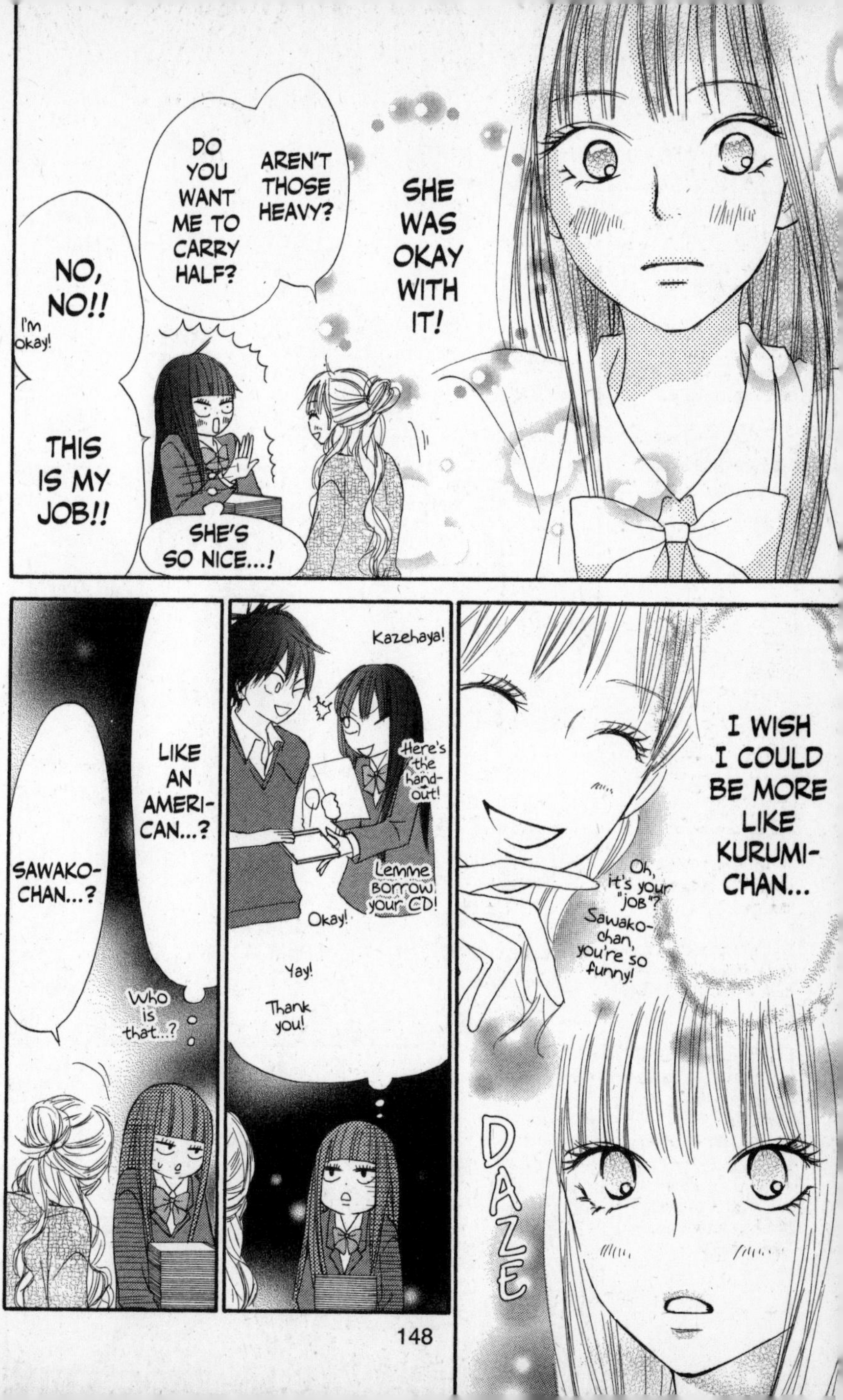
SHE WAS OKAY WITH IT!
AREN'T THOSE HEAVY?
DO YOU WANT ME TO CARRY HALF?
NO, NO!!
I'm okay!
THIS IS MY JOB!!
SHE'S SO NICE...!
I WISH I COULD BE MORE LIKE KURUMI-CHAN...
Oh, it's your "JOB"? Sawako-chan, you're so funny!
DAZE
Kazehaya!
Here's the hand-out!
Lemme borrow your CD!
Okay!
Yay!
Thank you!
LIKE AN AMERI-CAN...?
SAWAKO-CHAN...?
Who is that...?

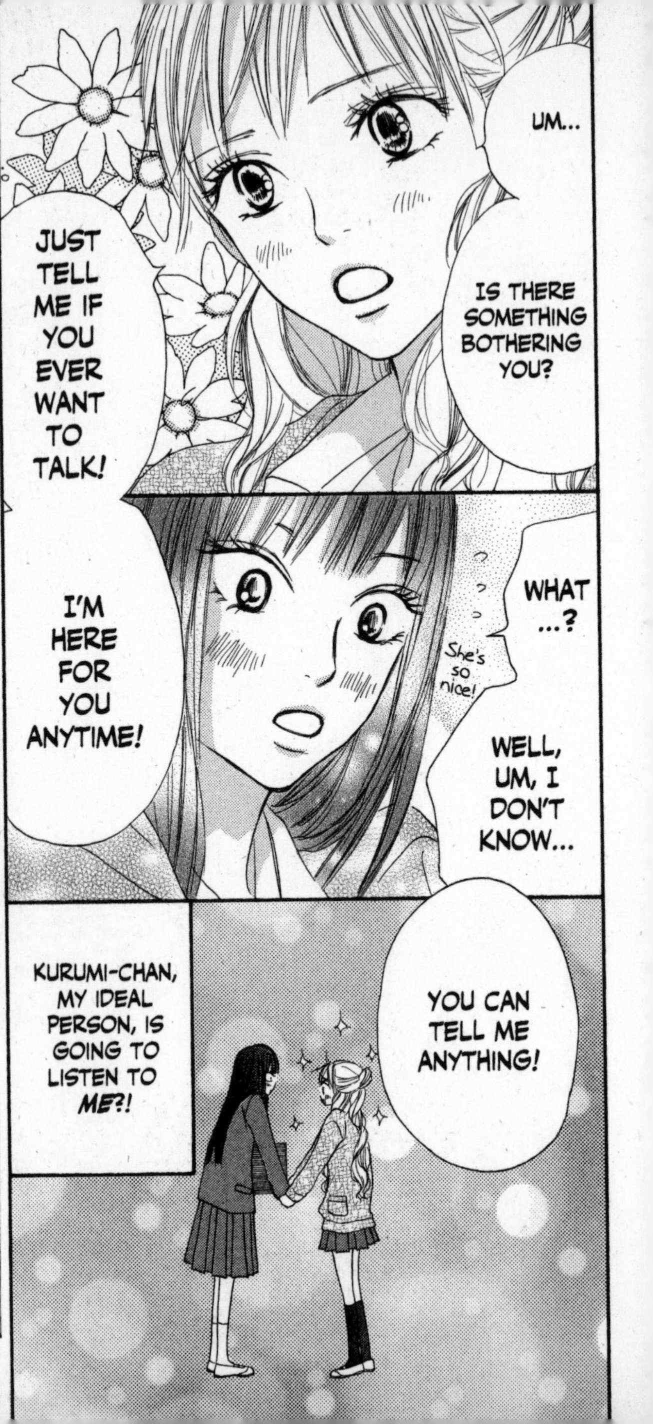
UM...
IS THERE SOMETHING BOTHERING YOU?
JUST TELL ME IF YOU EVER WANT TO TALK!
WHAT ...?
She's so nice!
I'M HERE FOR YOU ANYTIME!
WELL, UM, I DON'T KNOW...
YOU CAN TELL ME ANYTHING!
KURUMI-CHAN, MY IDEAL PERSON, IS GOING TO LISTEN TO *ME*?!

KARUPIN on JAPAN 4

Oh, this is the last blurb for this volume.

I had written about all the accidents that happened to me right before my deadlines back in volume 2...

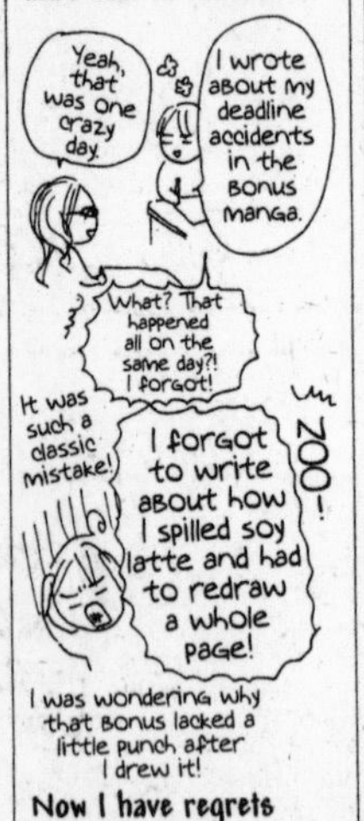
I wrote about my deadline accidents in the bonus manga.
Yeah, that was one crazy day.
What? That happened all on the same day?! I forgot!
It was such a classic mistake!
I forgot to write about how I spilled soy latte and had to redraw a whole page!
NOOO-!
I was wondering why that bonus lacked a little punch after I drew it!

Now I have regrets about that bonus manga...

Lately, my memory has been getting bad... Real bad. It's scary how bad it is...

I'm going to start forgetting my own weight as soon as I get off the scale.

A good thing

Anyway, I hope to see you again in volume 4! Huh? Volume 4 is next, right? Right?

Karuho Shiina

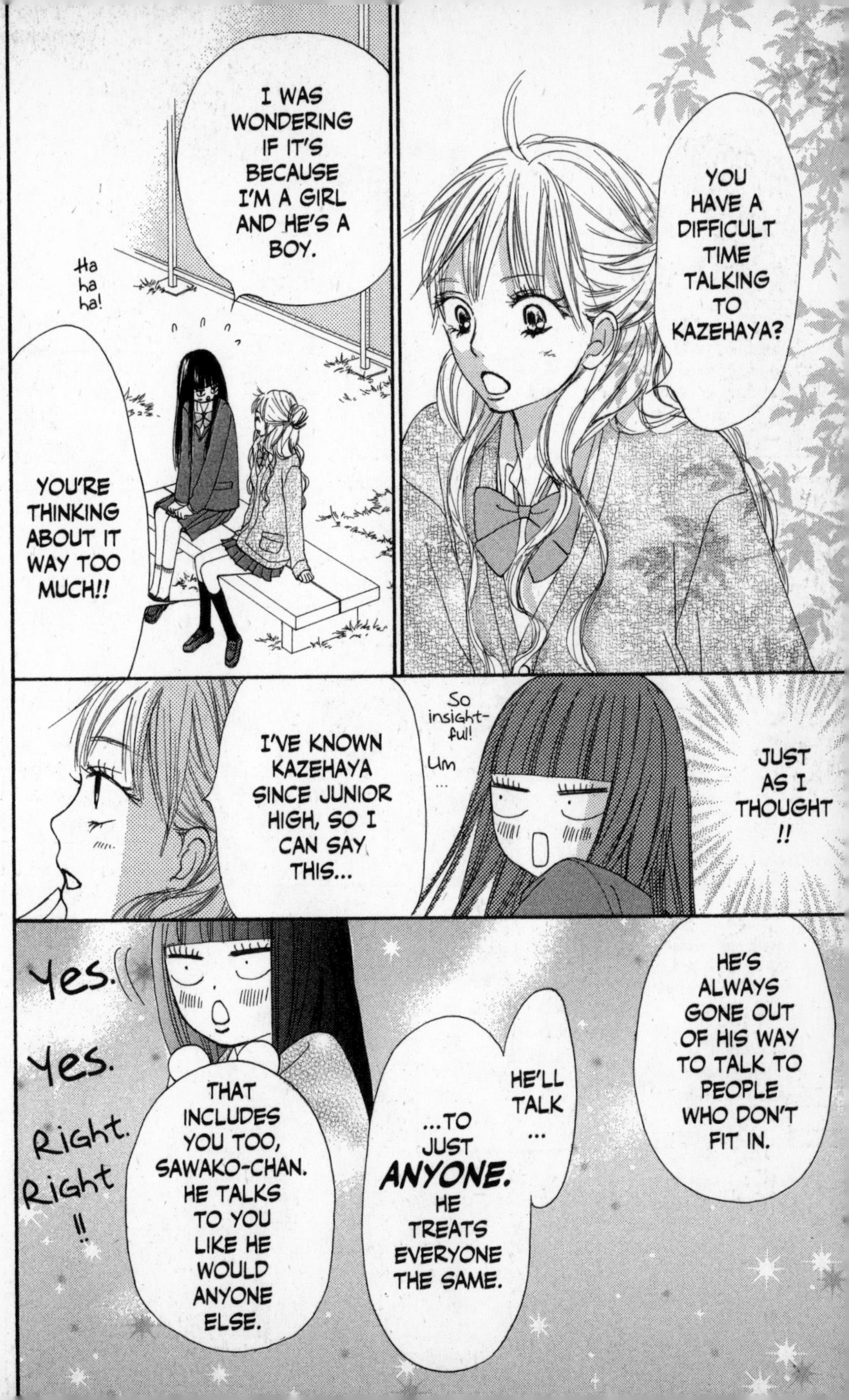
YOU HAVE A DIFFICULT TIME TALKING TO KAZEHAYA?
I WAS WONDERING IF IT'S BECAUSE I'M A GIRL AND HE'S A BOY.
Ha ha ha!
YOU'RE THINKING ABOUT IT WAY TOO MUCH!!
JUST AS I THOUGHT!!
So insightful!
Um...
I'VE KNOWN KAZEHAYA SINCE JUNIOR HIGH, SO I CAN SAY THIS...
HE'S ALWAYS GONE OUT OF HIS WAY TO TALK TO PEOPLE WHO DON'T FIT IN.
HE'LL TALK...
...TO JUST ANYONE. HE TREATS EVERYONE THE SAME.
THAT INCLUDES YOU TOO, SAWAKO-CHAN. HE TALKS TO YOU LIKE HE WOULD ANYONE ELSE.
Yes.
Yes.
Right.
Right!!

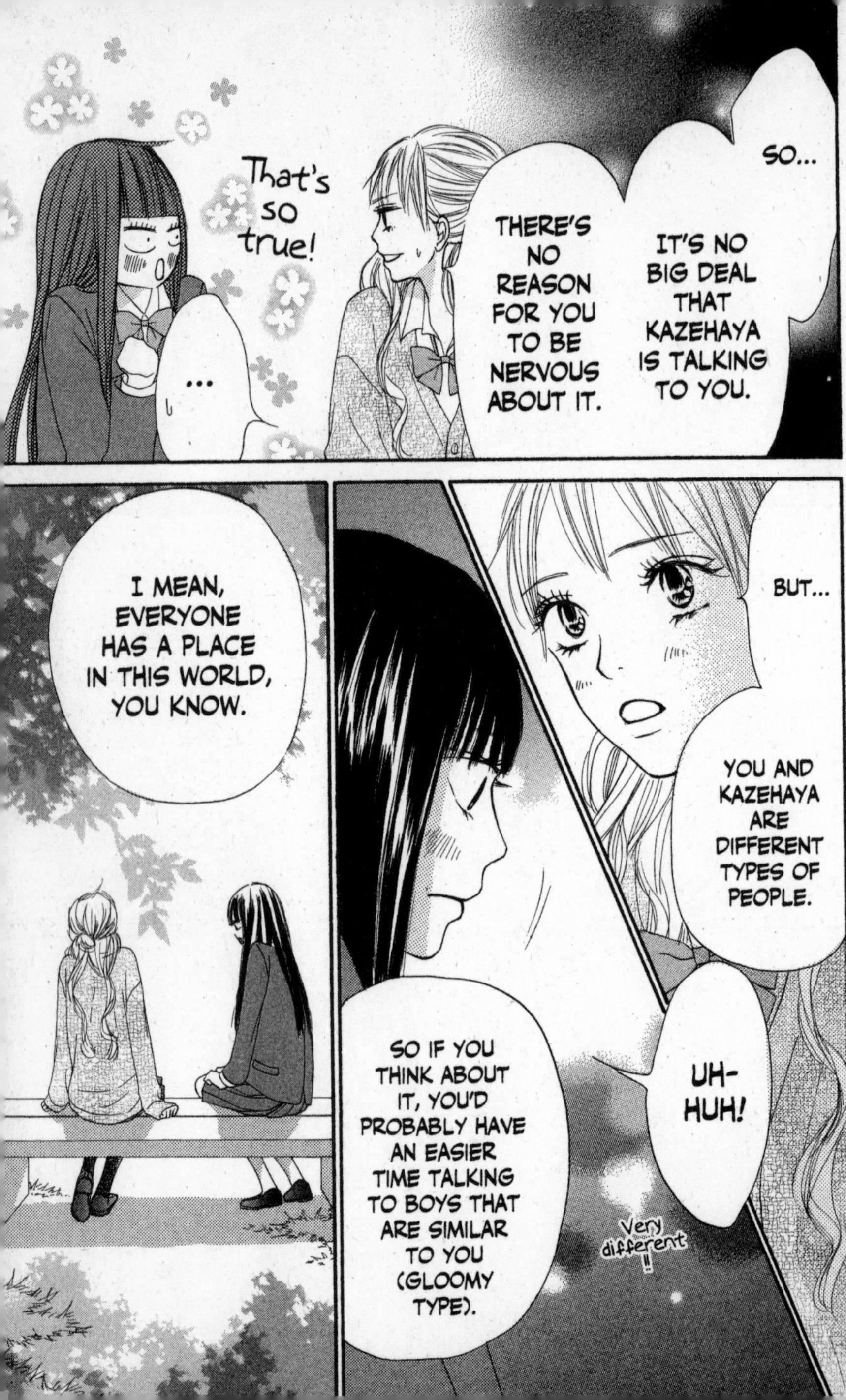
SO...
IT'S NO BIG DEAL THAT KAZEHAYA IS TALKING TO YOU.
THERE'S NO REASON FOR YOU TO BE NERVOUS ABOUT IT.
That's so true!
...
BUT...
YOU AND KAZEHAYA ARE DIFFERENT TYPES OF PEOPLE.
UH-HUH!
SO IF YOU THINK ABOUT IT, YOU'D PROBABLY HAVE AN EASIER TIME TALKING TO BOYS THAT ARE SIMILAR TO YOU (GLOOMY TYPE).
Very different!!
I MEAN, EVERYONE HAS A PLACE IN THIS WORLD, YOU KNOW.

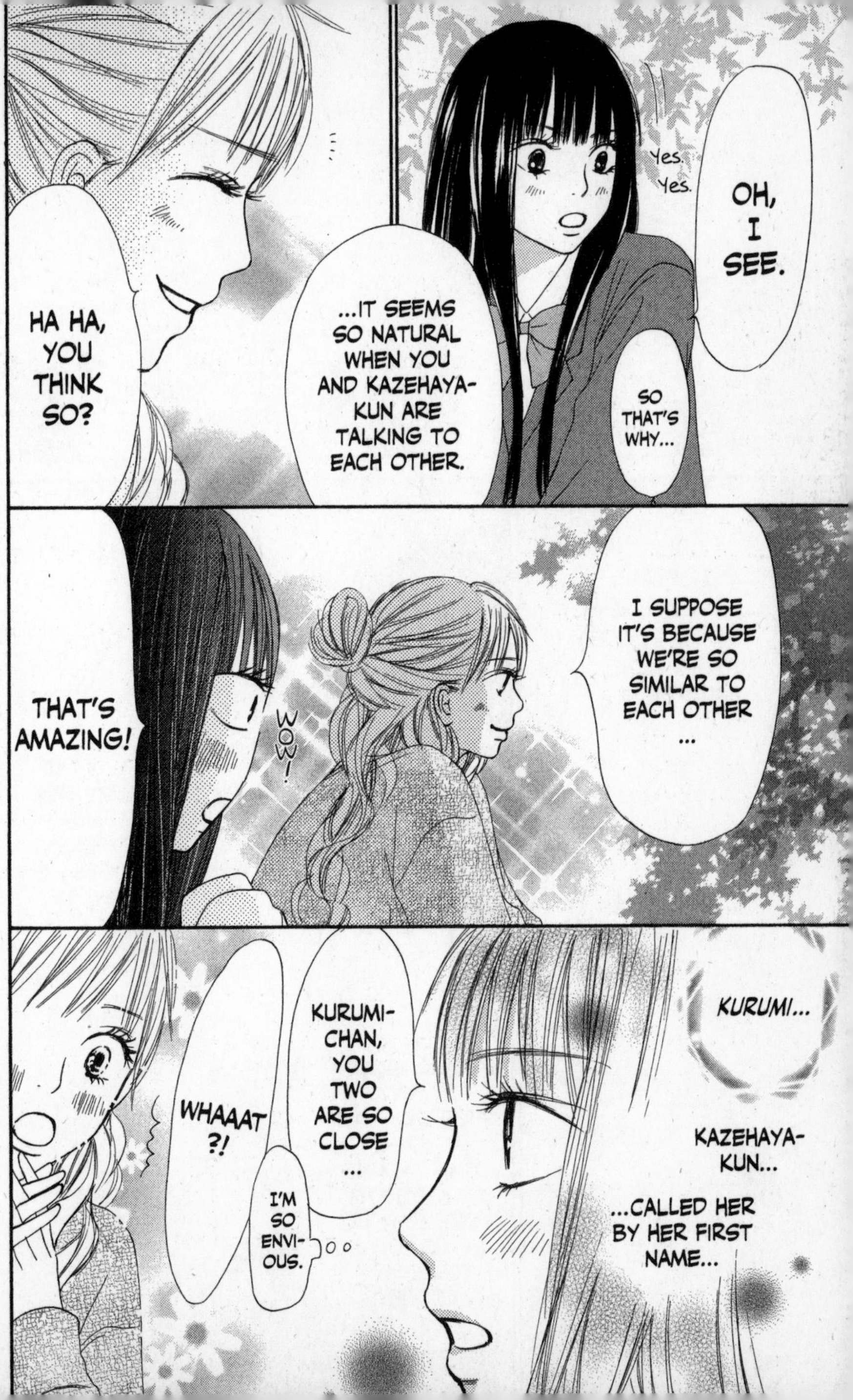
Yes. Yes.
OH, I SEE.
SO THAT'S WHY...
...IT SEEMS SO NATURAL WHEN YOU AND KAZEHAYA-KUN ARE TALKING TO EACH OTHER.
HA HA, YOU THINK SO?
I SUPPOSE IT'S BECAUSE WE'RE SO SIMILAR TO EACH OTHER ...
WOW!
THAT'S AMAZING!
KURUMI...
KAZEHAYA-KUN...
...CALLED HER BY HER FIRST NAME...
KURUMI-CHAN, YOU TWO ARE SO CLOSE ...
I'M SO ENVIOUS.
WHAAAT?!

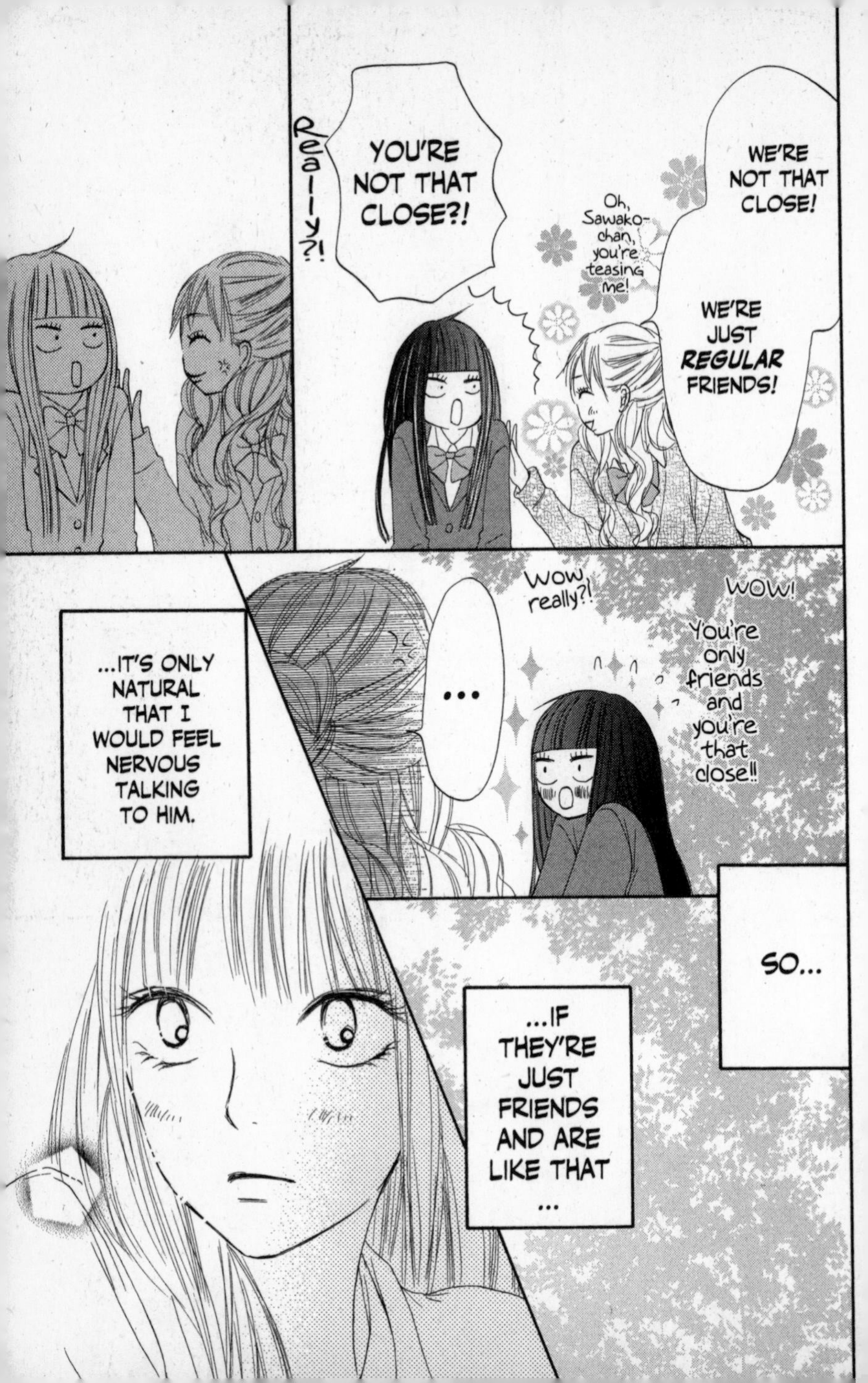

WE'RE NOT THAT CLOSE!
WE'RE JUST REGULAR FRIENDS!
Oh, Sawako-chan, you're teasing me!
YOU'RE NOT THAT CLOSE?!
Really?!
WOW! You're only friends and you're that close!!
Wow really?!
...
SO...
...IF THEY'RE JUST FRIENDS AND ARE LIKE THAT ...
...IT'S ONLY NATURAL THAT I WOULD FEEL NERVOUS TALKING TO HIM.

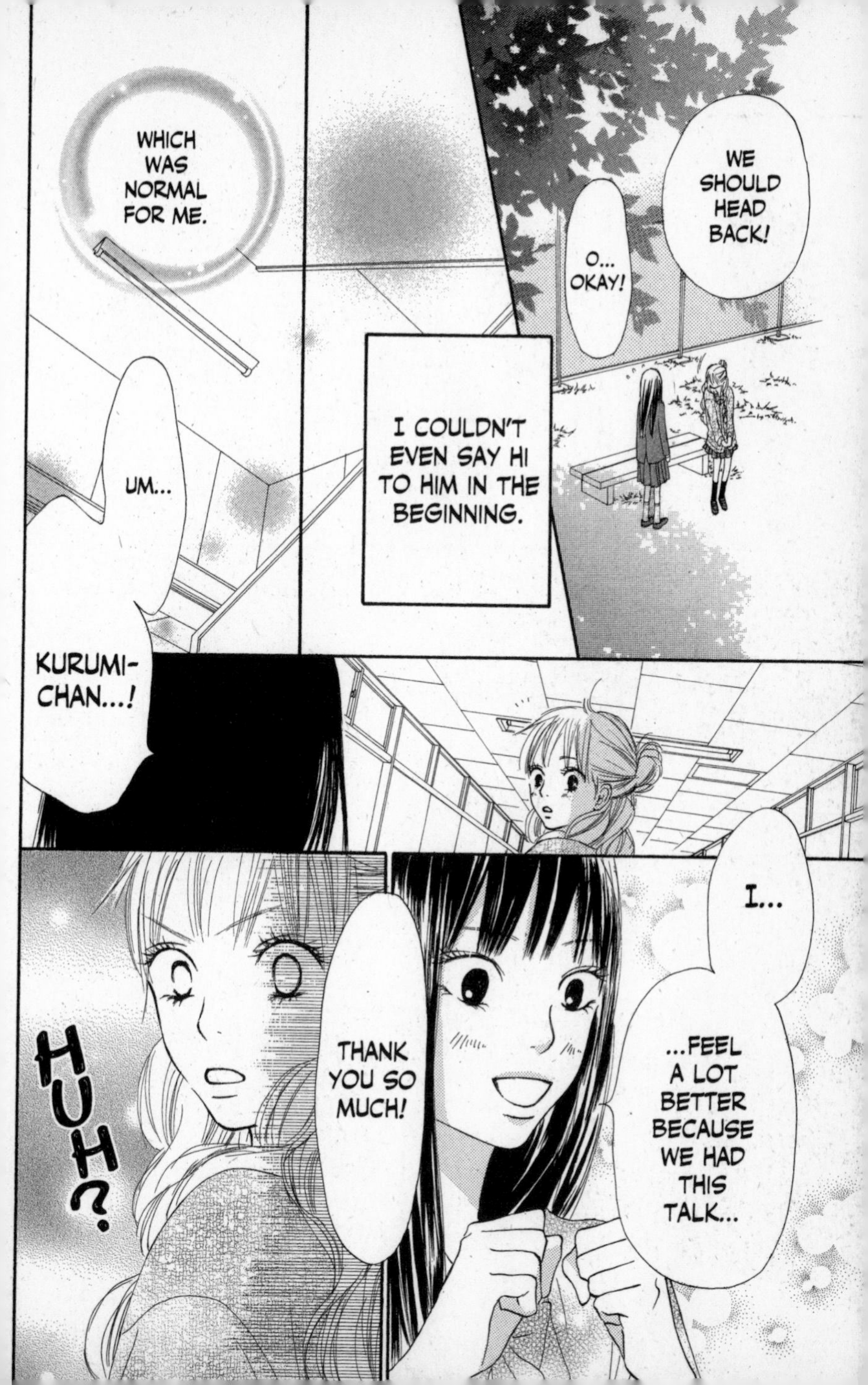
WE SHOULD HEAD BACK!
O... OKAY!
I COULDN'T EVEN SAY HI TO HIM IN THE BEGINNING.
WHICH WAS NORMAL FOR ME.
UM...
KURUMI-CHAN...!
I...
...FEEL A LOT BETTER BECAUSE WE HAD THIS TALK...
THANK YOU SO MUCH!
HUH?

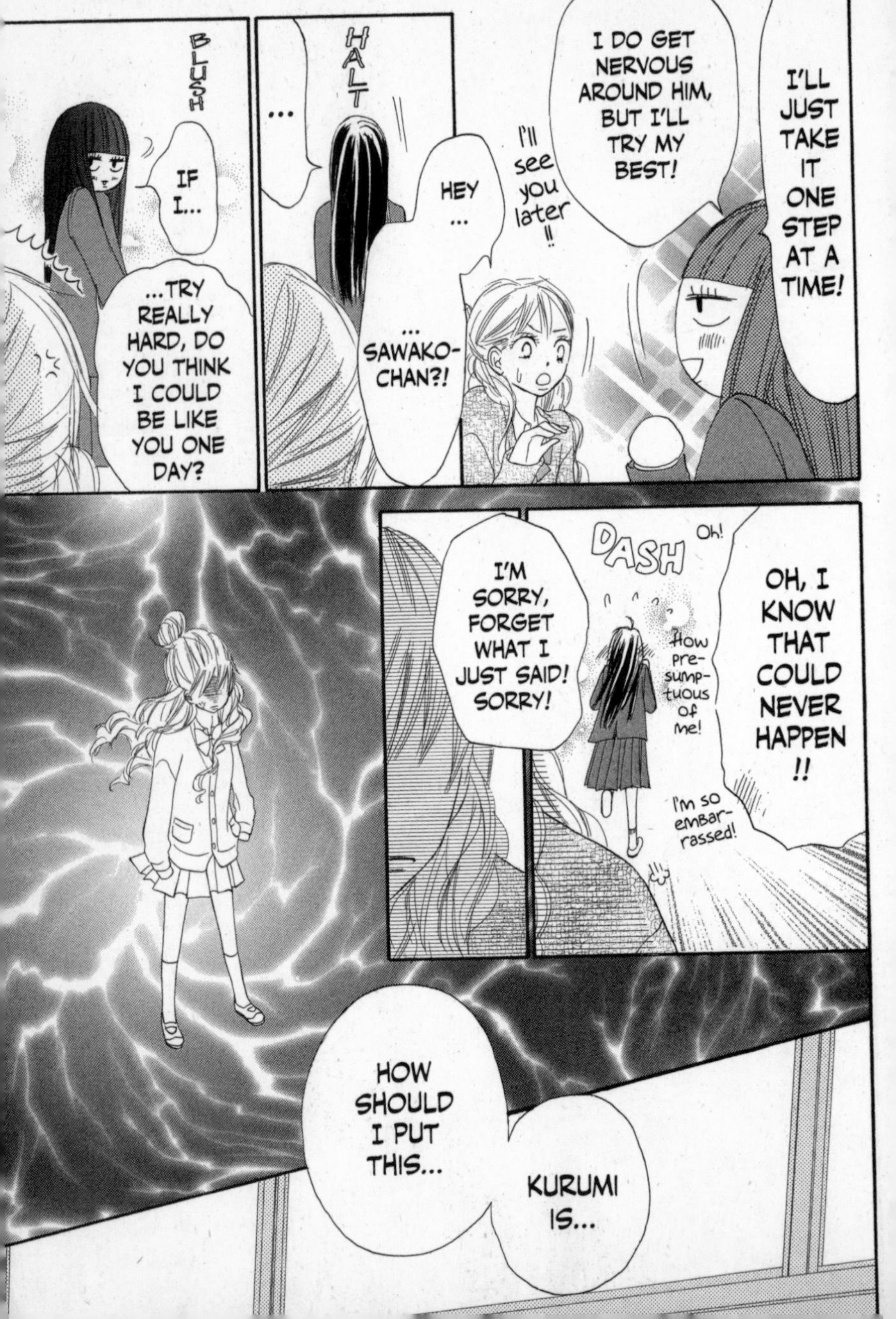
I'LL JUST TAKE IT ONE STEP AT A TIME!
I DO GET NERVOUS AROUND HIM, BUT I'LL TRY MY BEST!
I'll see you later!!
HALT
...
HEY ...
... SAWAKO-CHAN?!
BLUSH
IF I...
...TRY REALLY HARD, DO YOU THINK I COULD BE LIKE YOU ONE DAY?
OH, I KNOW THAT COULD NEVER HAPPEN!!
Oh!
DASH
I'M SORRY, FORGET WHAT I JUST SAID! SORRY!
How presumptuous of me!
I'm so embarrassed!
HOW SHOULD I PUT THIS...
KURUMI IS...

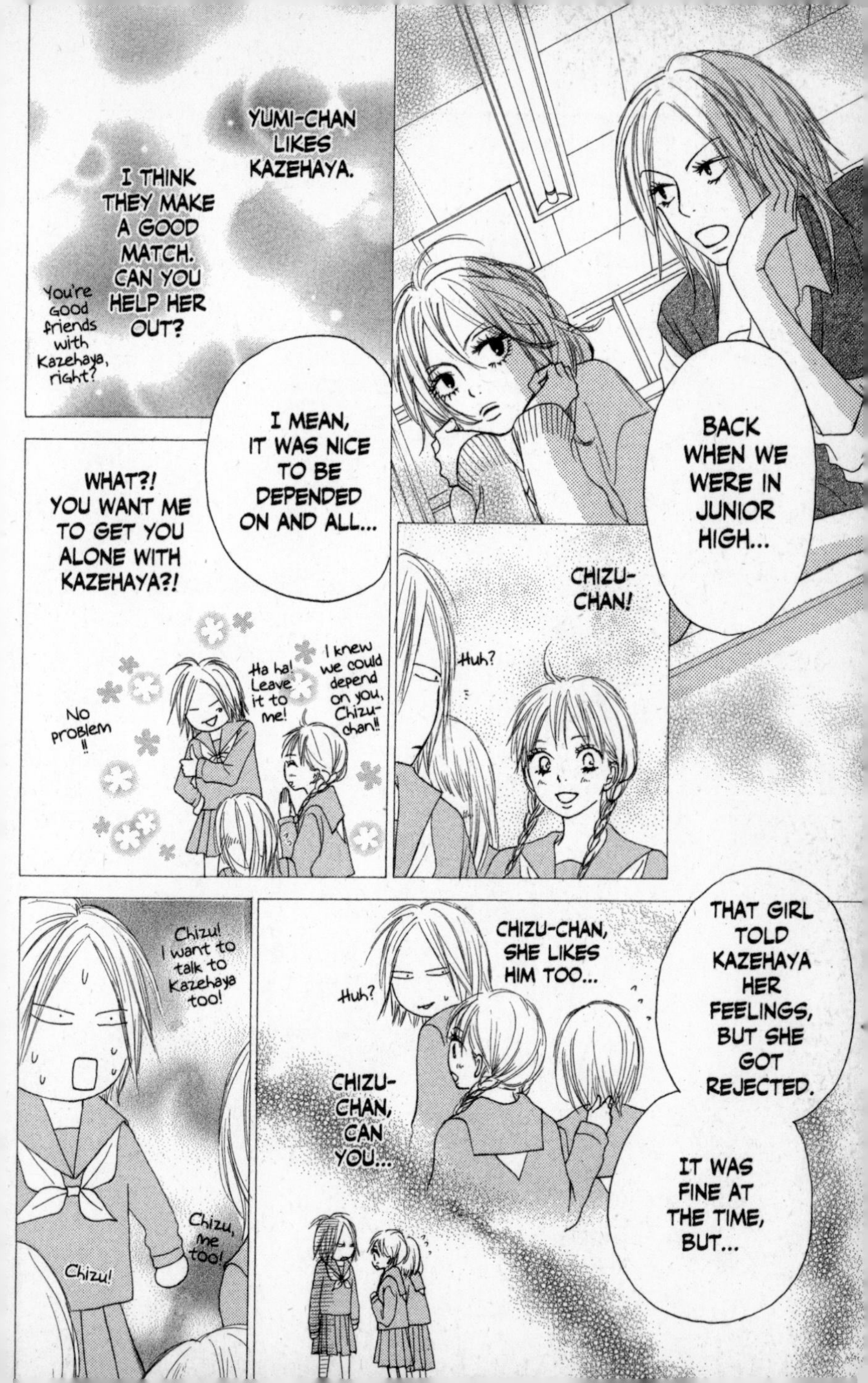
BACK WHEN WE WERE IN JUNIOR HIGH...
I MEAN, IT WAS NICE TO BE DEPENDED ON AND ALL...
YUMI-CHAN LIKES KAZEHAYA.
I THINK THEY MAKE A GOOD MATCH. CAN YOU HELP HER OUT?
You're good friends with Kazehaya, right?
CHIZU-CHAN!
Huh?
WHAT?! YOU WANT ME TO GET YOU ALONE WITH KAZEHAYA?!
I knew we could depend on you, Chizu-chan!!
Ha ha! Leave it to me!
No problem!!
THAT GIRL TOLD KAZEHAYA HER FEELINGS, BUT SHE GOT REJECTED.
IT WAS FINE AT THE TIME, BUT...
CHIZU-CHAN, SHE LIKES HIM TOO...
Huh?
CHIZU-CHAN, CAN YOU...
Chizu! I want to talk to Kazehaya too!
Chizu, me too!
Chizu!

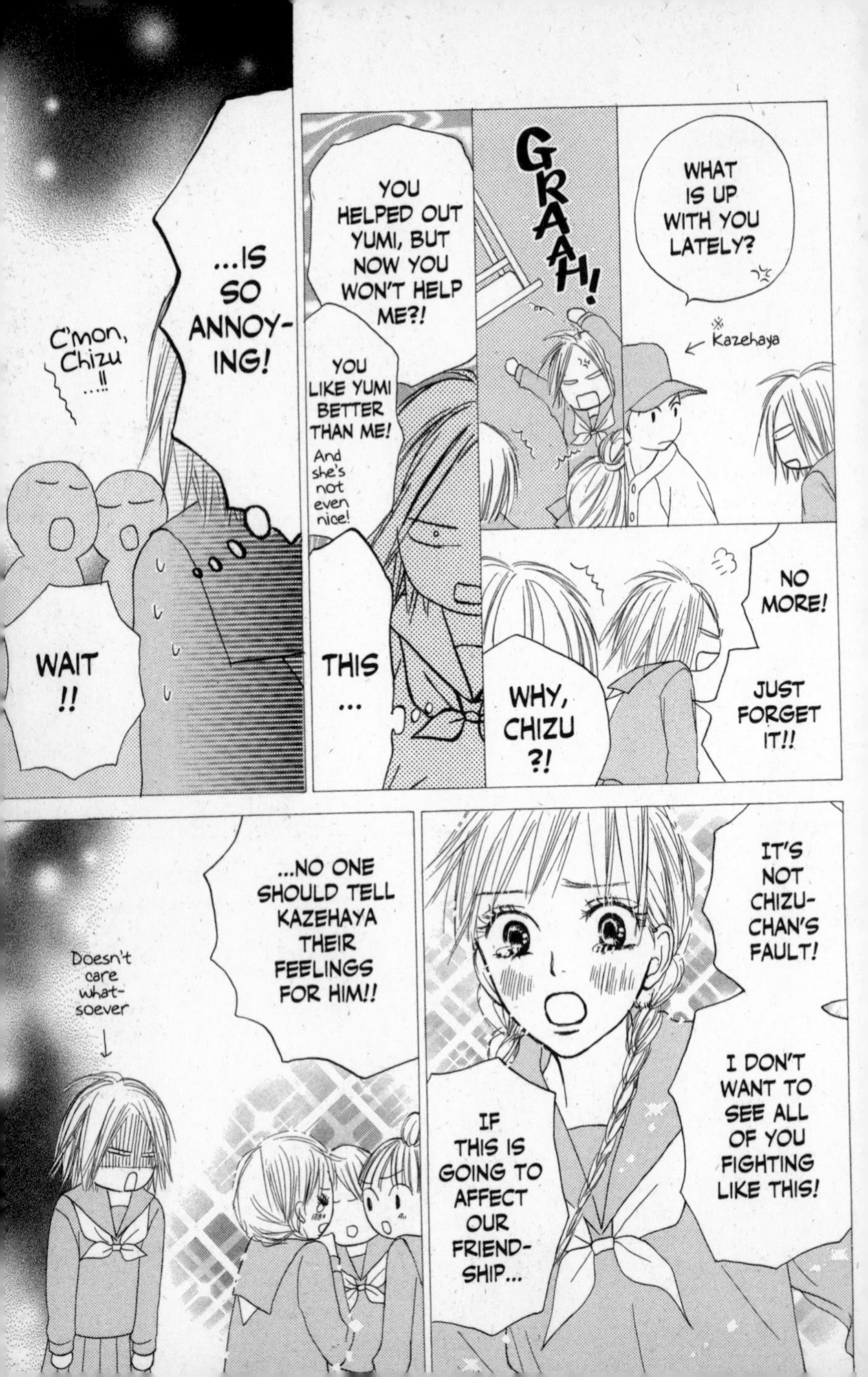
WHAT IS UP WITH YOU LATELY?
※ Kazehaya
GRAAH!
NO MORE!
JUST FORGET IT!!
WHY, CHIZU?!
YOU HELPED OUT YUMI, BUT NOW YOU WON'T HELP ME?!
YOU LIKE YUMI BETTER THAN ME!
And she's not even nice!
THIS...
...IS SO ANNOYING!
C'mon, Chizu...!!
WAIT!!
IT'S NOT CHIZU-CHAN'S FAULT!
I DON'T WANT TO SEE ALL OF YOU FIGHTING LIKE THIS!
IF THIS IS GOING TO AFFECT OUR FRIENDSHIP...
...NO ONE SHOULD TELL KAZEHAYA THEIR FEELINGS FOR HIM!!
Doesn't care whatsoever

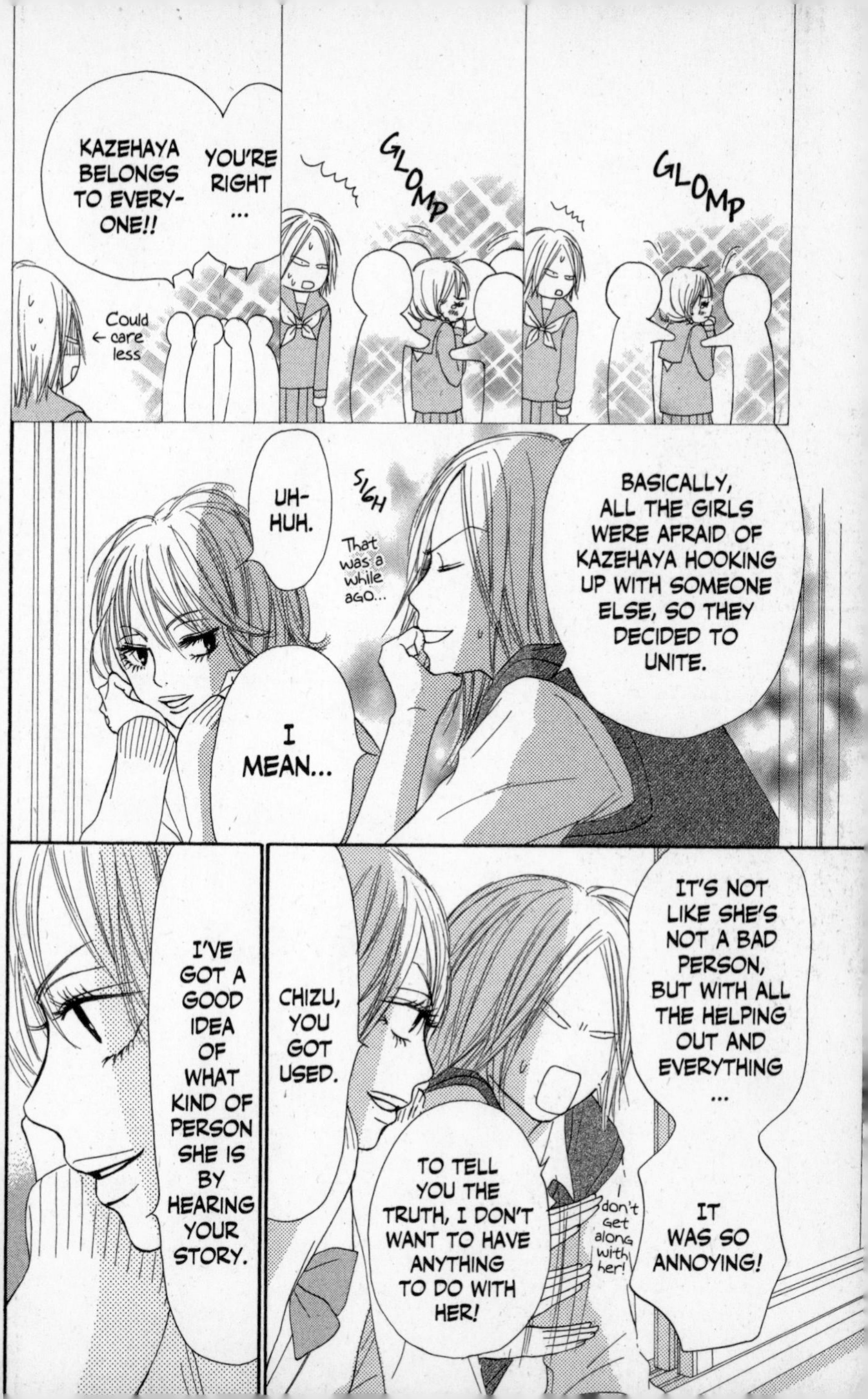
GLOMP
GLOMP
KAZEHAYA BELONGS TO EVERY-ONE!!
YOU'RE RIGHT ...
Could care less
BASICALLY, ALL THE GIRLS WERE AFRAID OF KAZEHAYA HOOKING UP WITH SOMEONE ELSE, SO THEY DECIDED TO UNITE.
SIGH
That was a while ago...
UH-HUH.
I MEAN...
IT'S NOT LIKE SHE'S NOT A BAD PERSON, BUT WITH ALL THE HELPING OUT AND EVERYTHING ...
IT WAS SO ANNOYING!
I don't get along with her!
TO TELL YOU THE TRUTH, I DON'T WANT TO HAVE ANYTHING TO DO WITH HER!
CHIZU, YOU GOT USED.
I'VE GOT A GOOD IDEA OF WHAT KIND OF PERSON SHE IS BY HEARING YOUR STORY.

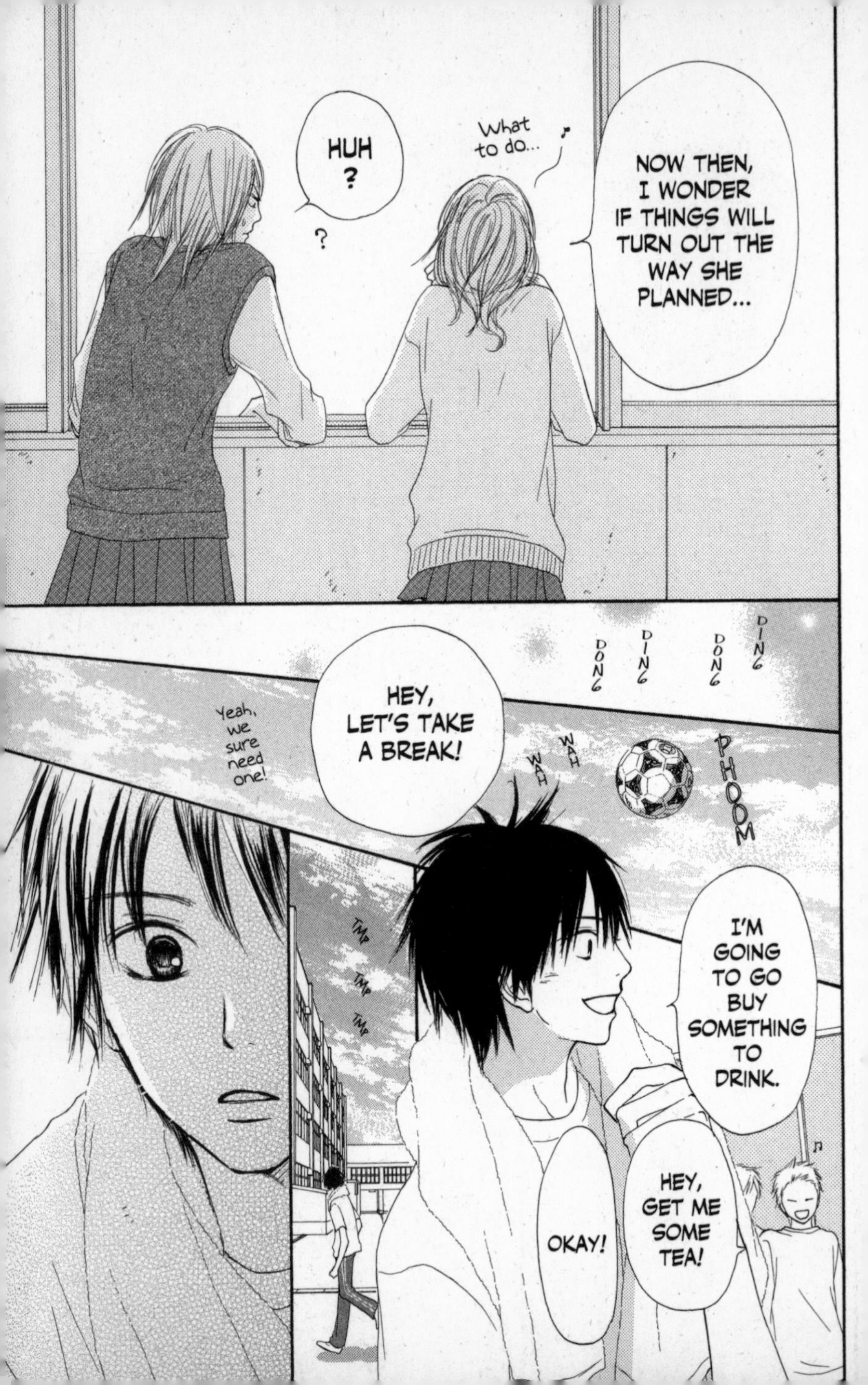
NOW THEN, I WONDER IF THINGS WILL TURN OUT THE WAY SHE PLANNED...
What to do...
HUH ?
?
DING
DONG
DING
DONG
HEY, LET'S TAKE A BREAK!
Yeah, we sure need one!
PHOOM
WAH
WAH
I'M GOING TO GO BUY SOMETHING TO DRINK.
HEY, GET ME SOME TEA!
OKAY!
TMP
TMP
TMP

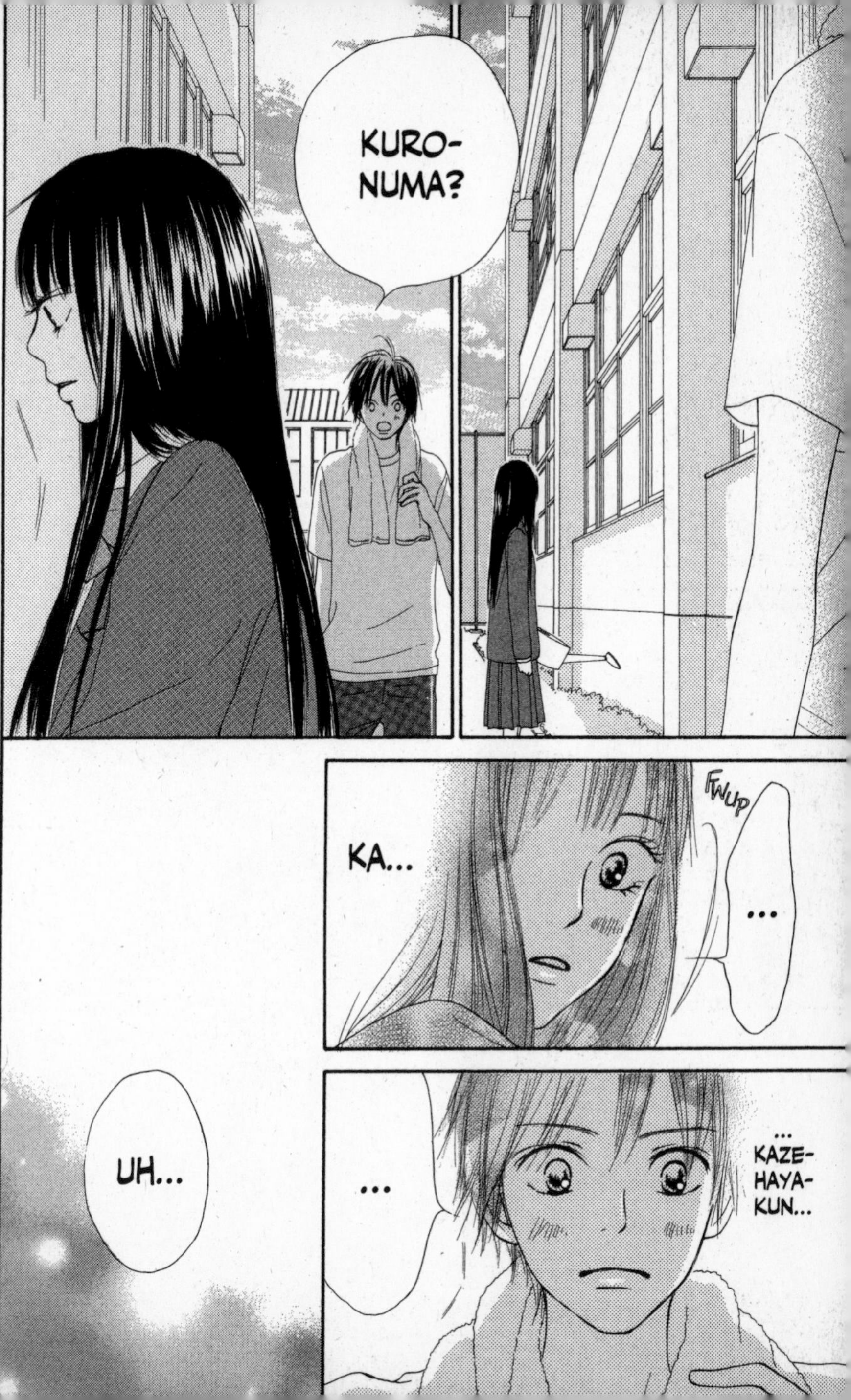
KURO-NUMA?
FWUP
...
KA...
... KAZE-HAYA-KUN...
...
UH...

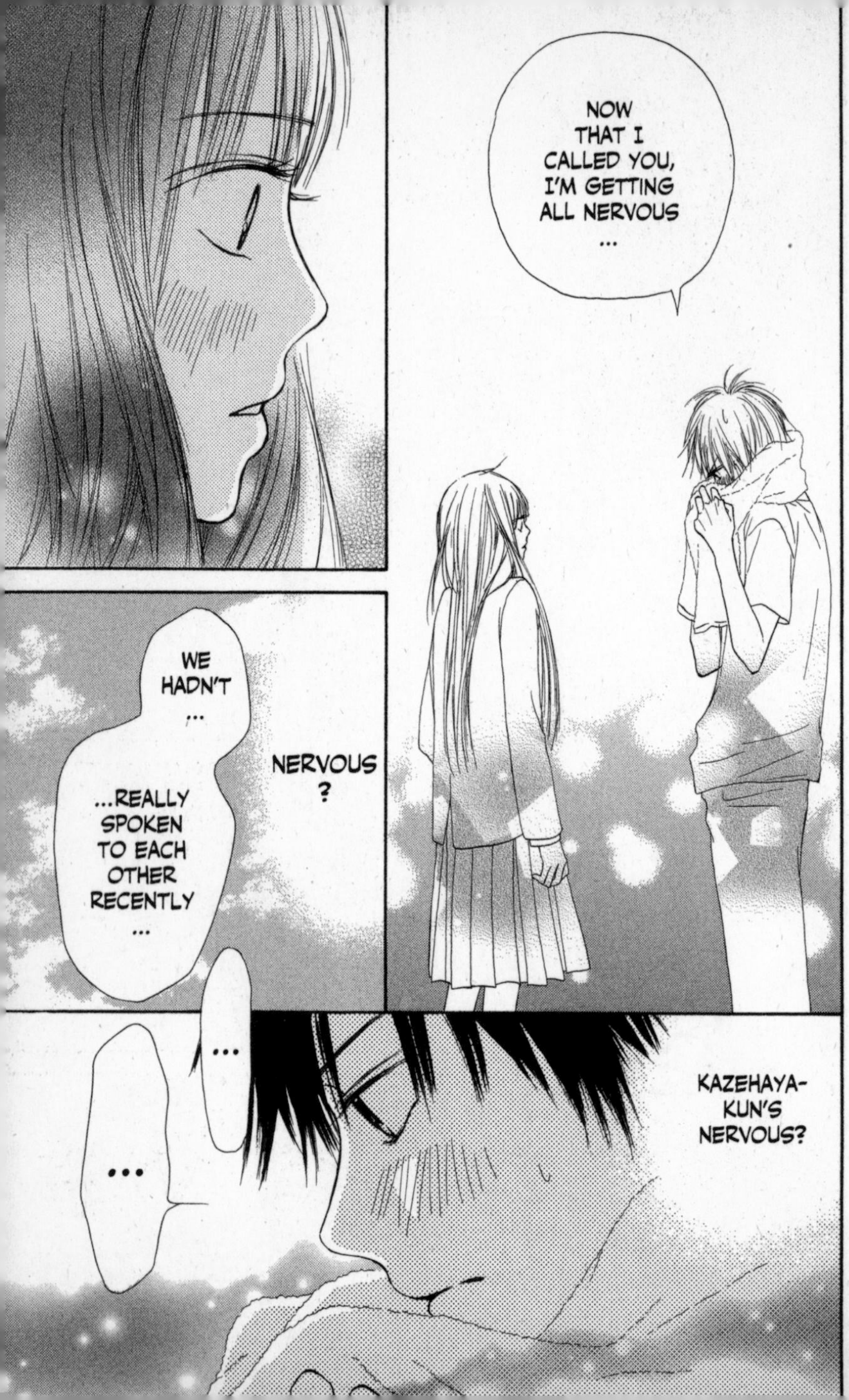
NOW THAT I CALLED YOU, I'M GETTING ALL NERVOUS ...
NERVOUS ?
WE HADN'T ...
...REALLY SPOKEN TO EACH OTHER RECENTLY ...
KAZEHAYA-KUN'S NERVOUS?
...
...

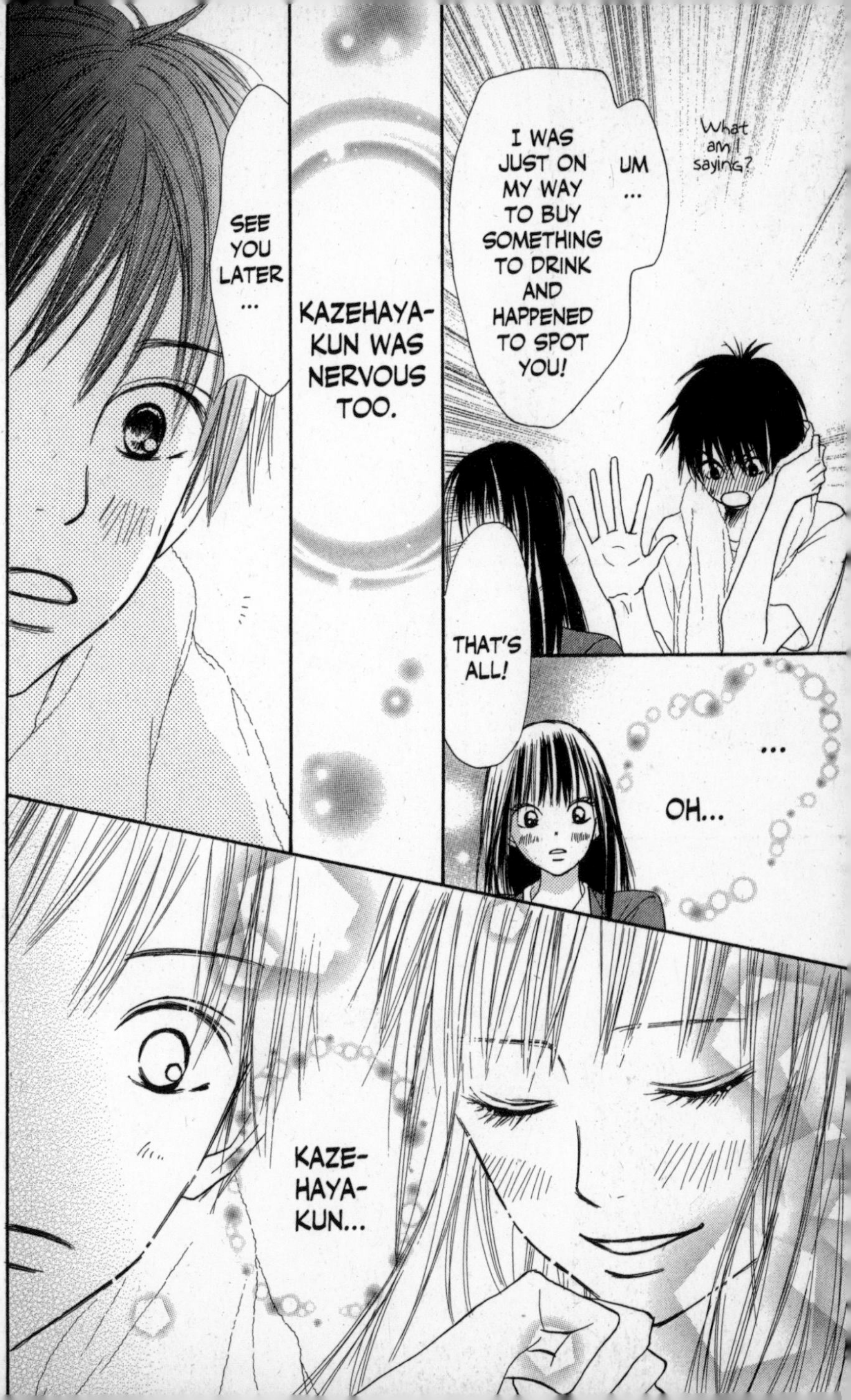
UM ...
I WAS JUST ON MY WAY TO BUY SOMETHING TO DRINK AND HAPPENED TO SPOT YOU!
What am I saying?
THAT'S ALL!
...
OH...
KAZEHAYA-KUN WAS NERVOUS TOO.
SEE YOU LATER ...
KAZE-HAYA-KUN...

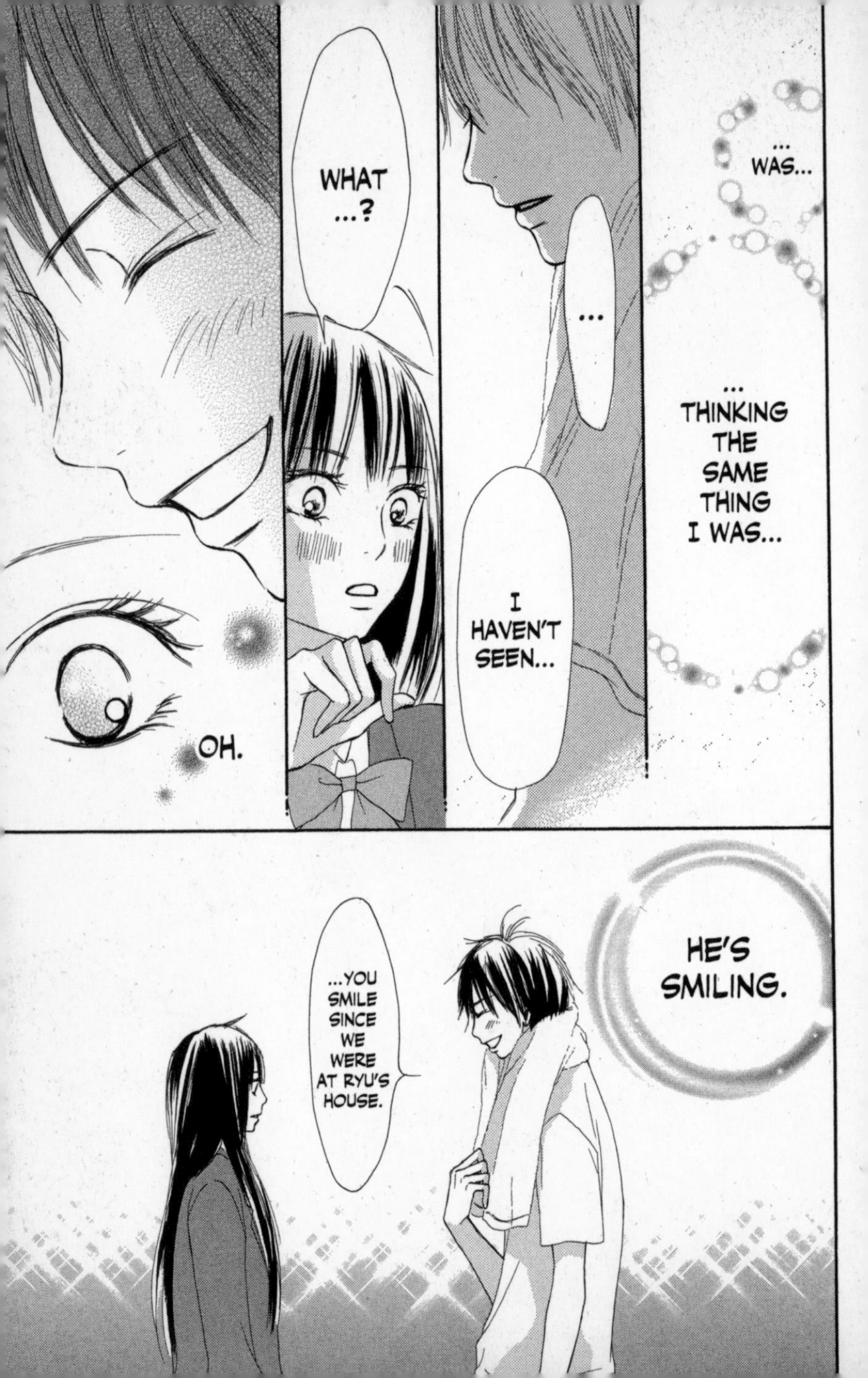
... WAS...
... THINKING THE SAME THING I WAS...
...
I HAVEN'T SEEN...
WHAT ...?
OH.
HE'S SMILING.
...YOU SMILE SINCE WE WERE AT RYU'S HOUSE.

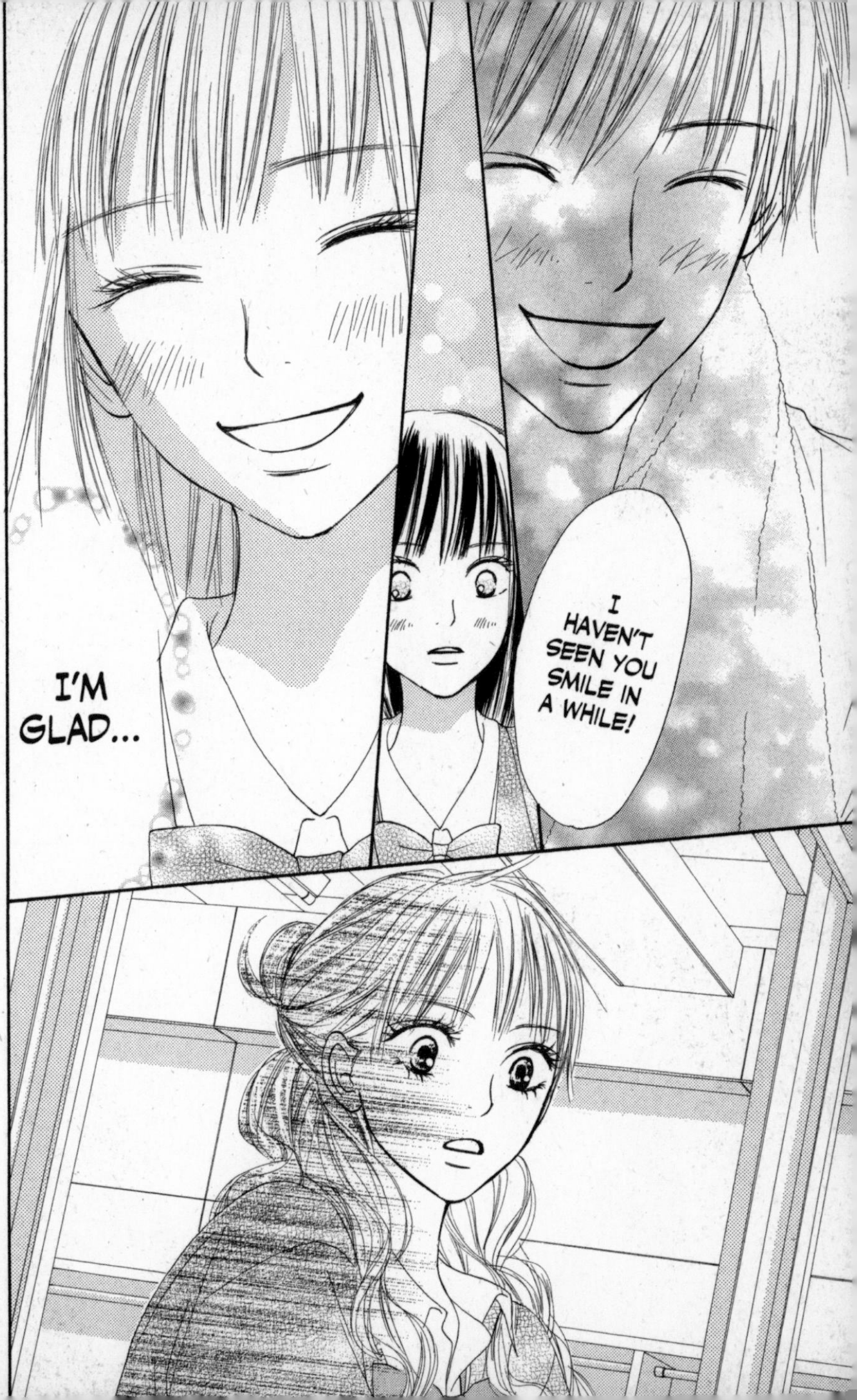
I HAVEN'T SEEN YOU SMILE IN A WHILE!
I'M GLAD...

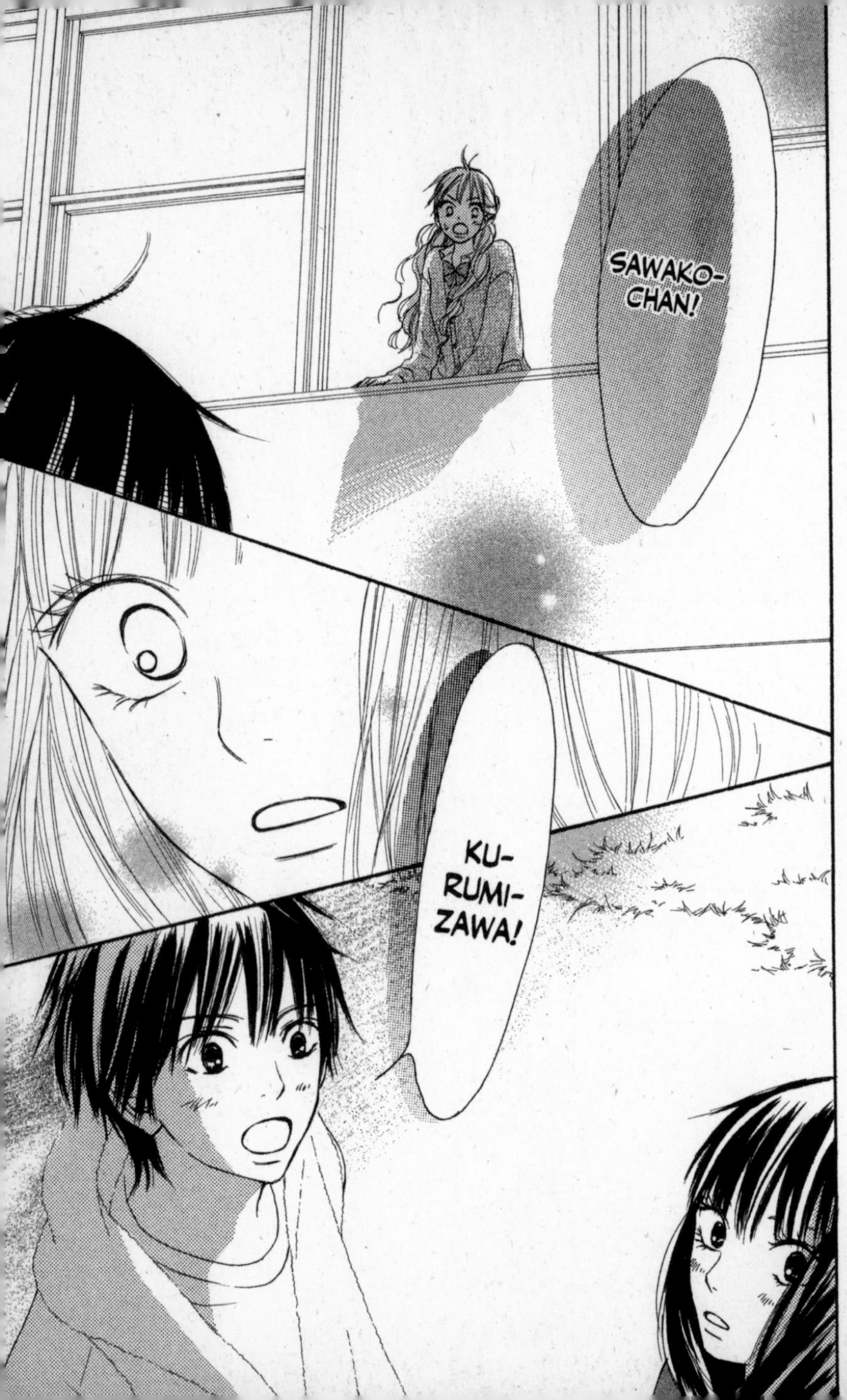
SAWAKO-CHAN!
KU-RUMI-ZAWA!

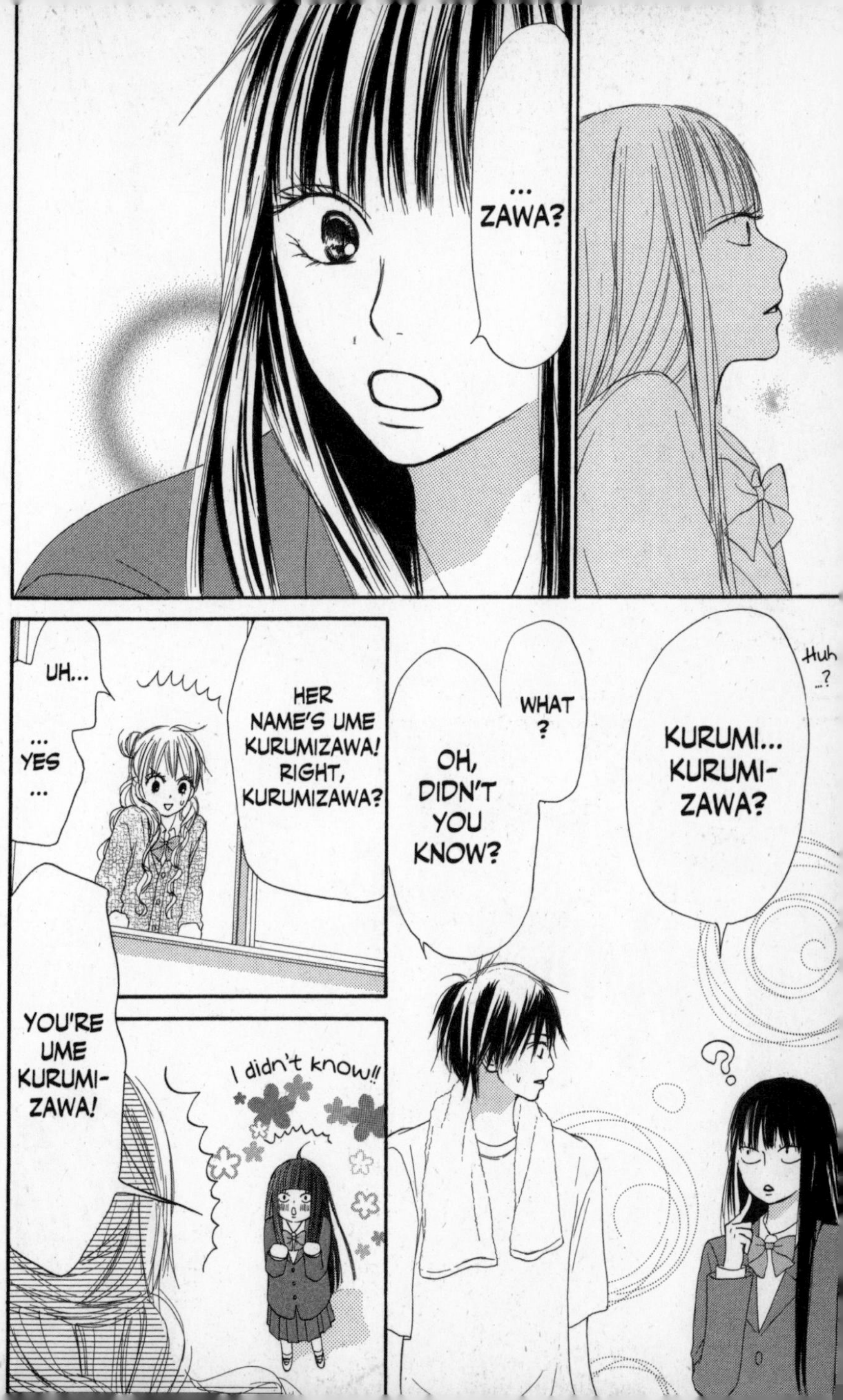
... ZAWA?
Huh ...?
KURUMI... KURUMI-ZAWA?
WHAT ?
OH, DIDN'T YOU KNOW?
HER NAME'S UME KURUMIZAWA! RIGHT, KURUMIZAWA?
UH...
... YES ...
I didn't know!!
YOU'RE UME KURUMI-ZAWA!

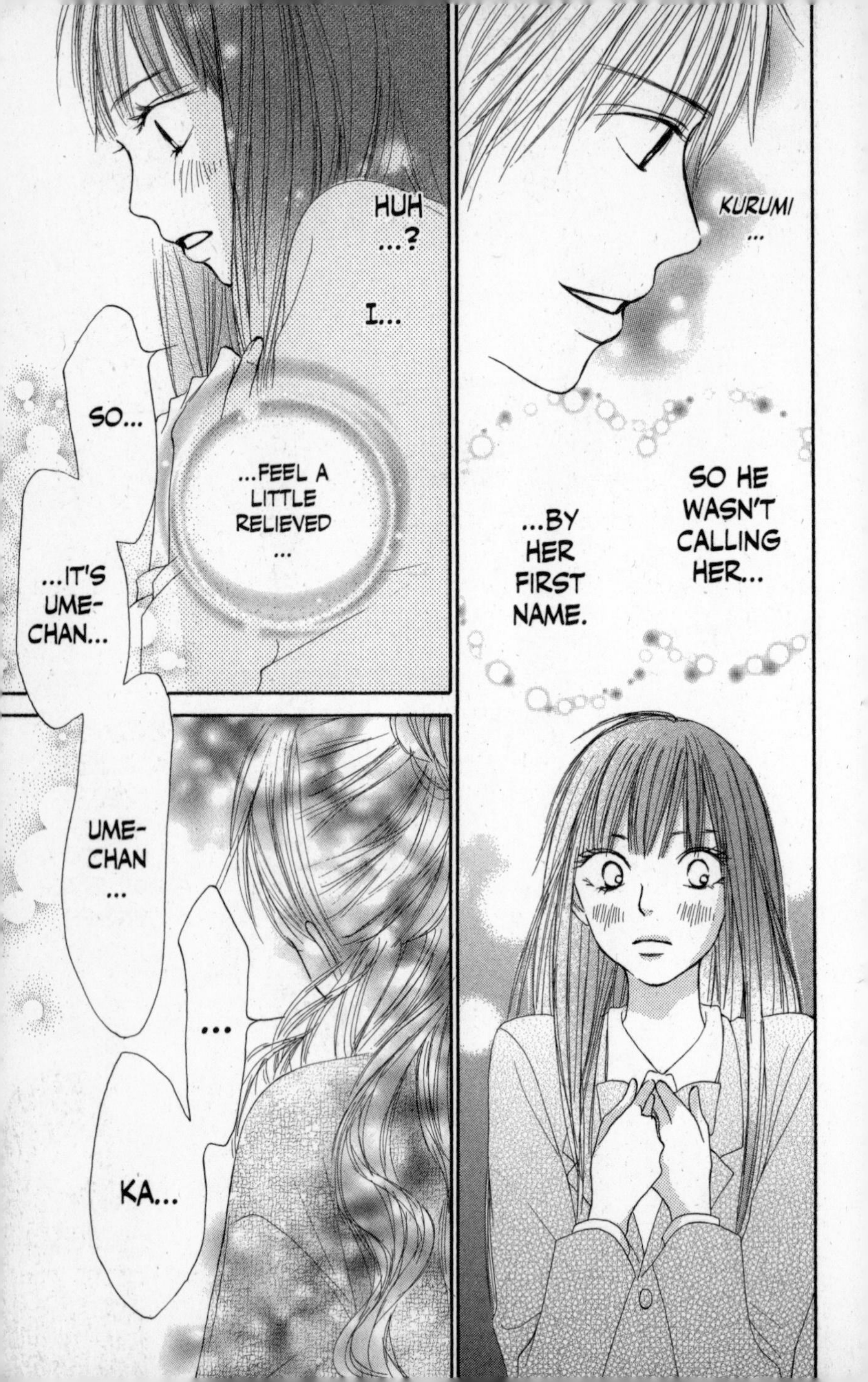
KURUMI ...
SO HE WASN'T CALLING HER...
...BY HER FIRST NAME.
HUH ...?
I...
...FEEL A LITTLE RELIEVED ...
SO...
...IT'S UME-CHAN...
UME-CHAN ...
...
KA...

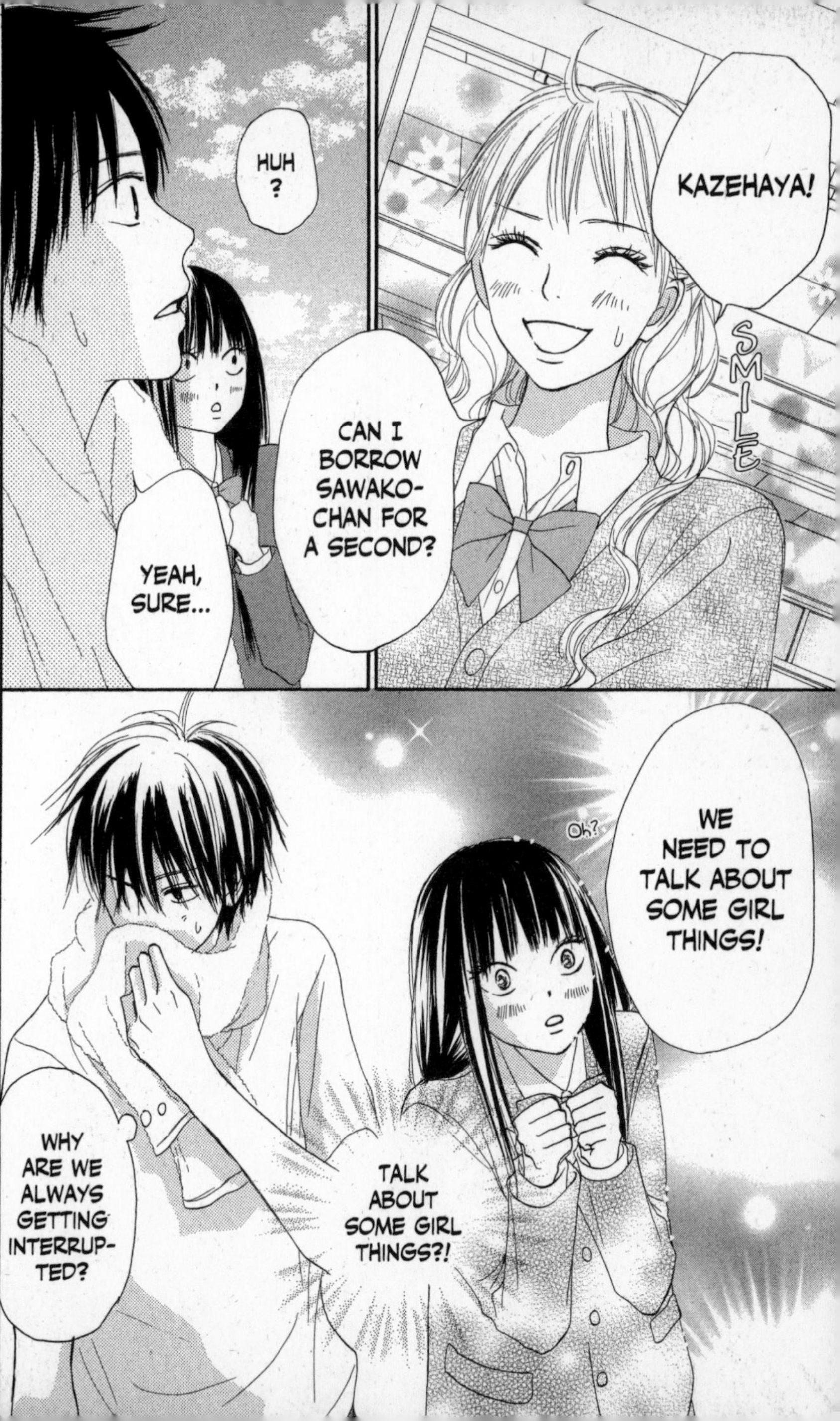
KAZEHAYA!
SMILE
CAN I BORROW SAWAKO-CHAN FOR A SECOND?
HUH?
YEAH, SURE...
WE NEED TO TALK ABOUT SOME GIRL THINGS!
Oh?
TALK ABOUT SOME GIRL THINGS?!
WHY ARE WE ALWAYS GETTING INTERRUPTED?

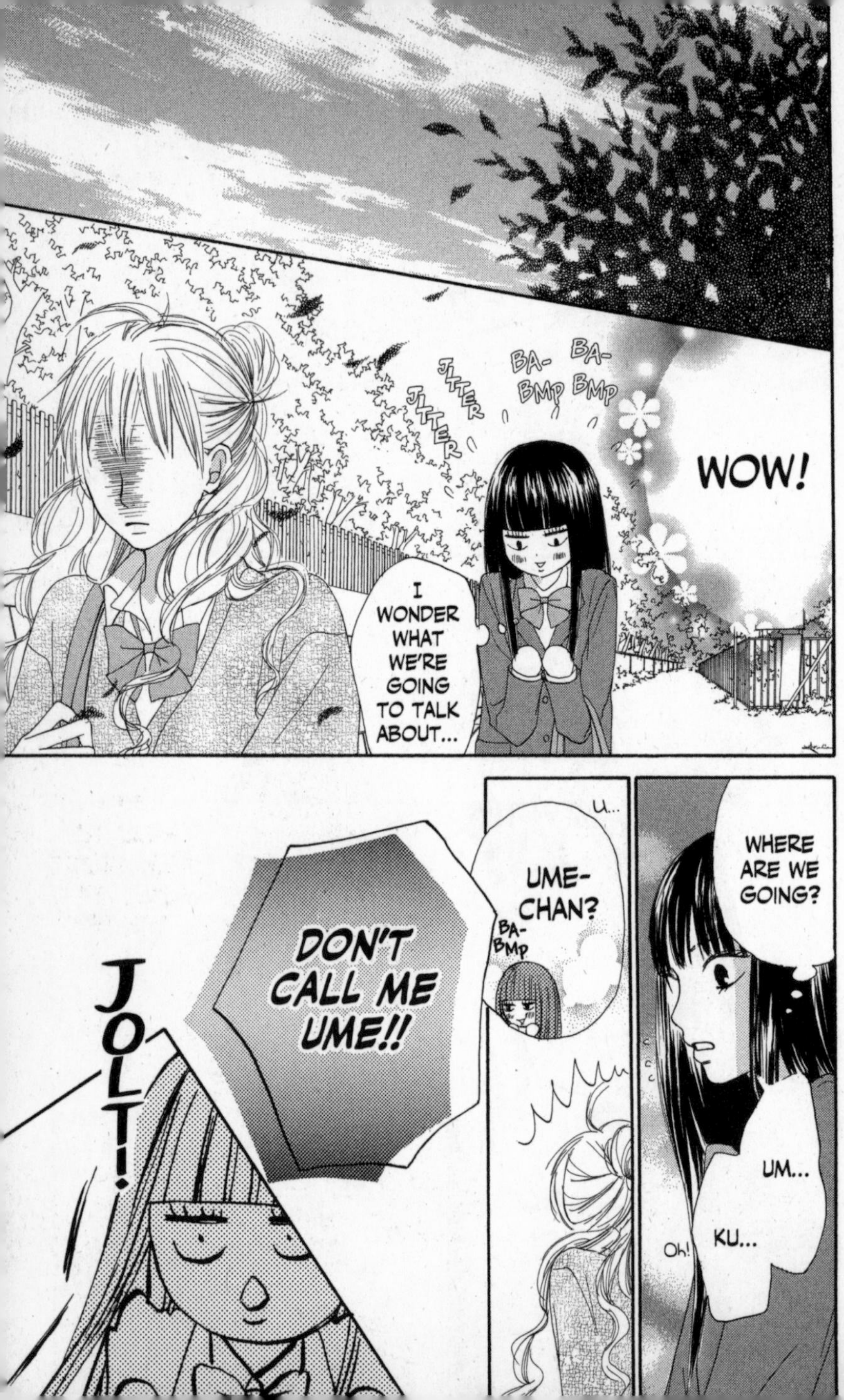
WOW!
BA-BMP BA-BMP
JITTER JITTER
I WONDER WHAT WE'RE GOING TO TALK ABOUT...
WHERE ARE WE GOING?
UM...
KU...
Oh!
U...
UME-CHAN?
BA-BMP
DON'T CALL ME UME!!
JOLT!

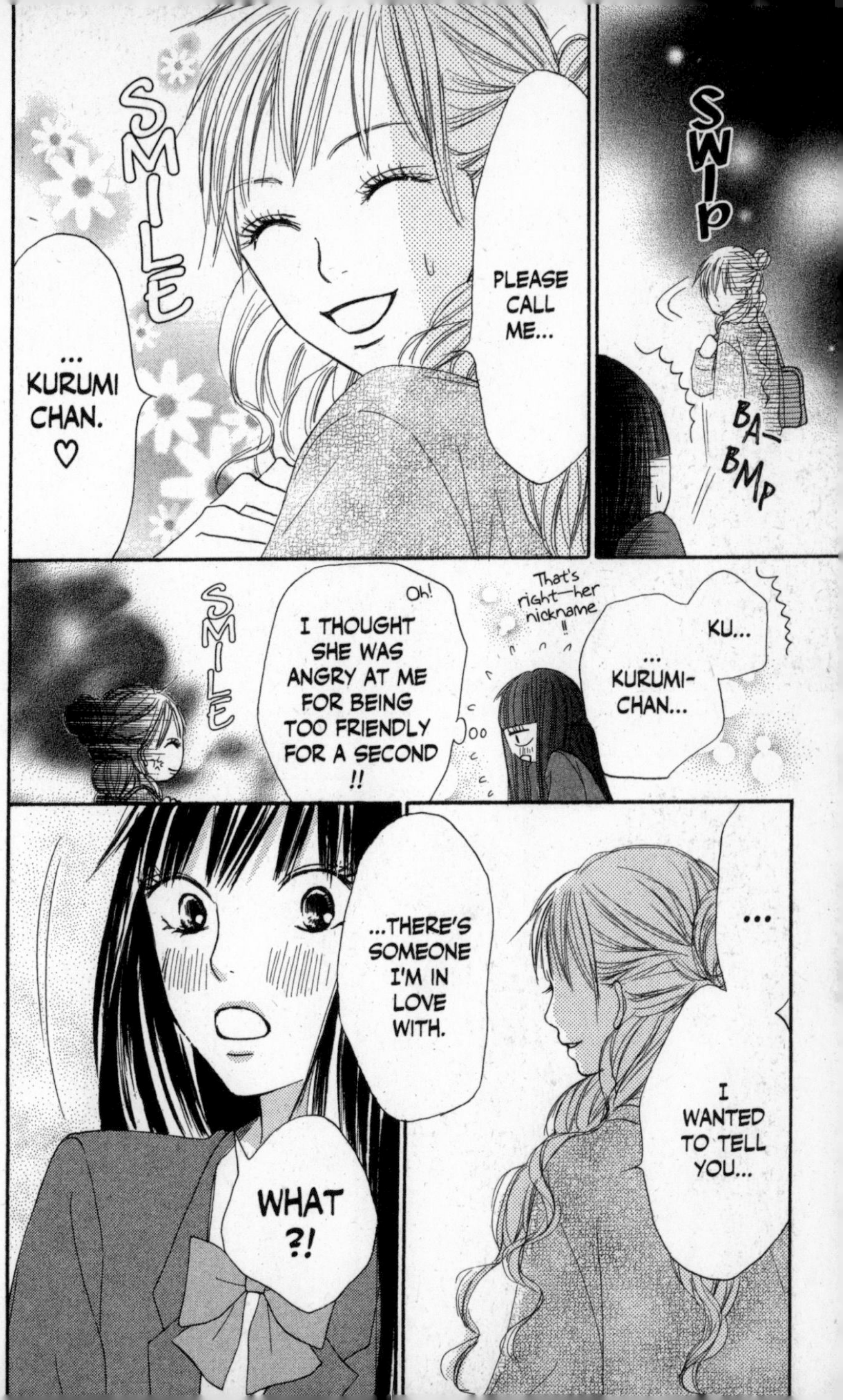
SWIP
BA-BMP
PLEASE CALL ME...
SMILE
... KURUMI CHAN. ♡
KU...
... KURUMI-CHAN...
That's right—her nickname !!
Oh!
I THOUGHT SHE WAS ANGRY AT ME FOR BEING TOO FRIENDLY FOR A SECOND !!
SMILE
...
I WANTED TO TELL YOU...
...THERE'S SOMEONE I'M IN LOVE WITH.
WHAT ?!

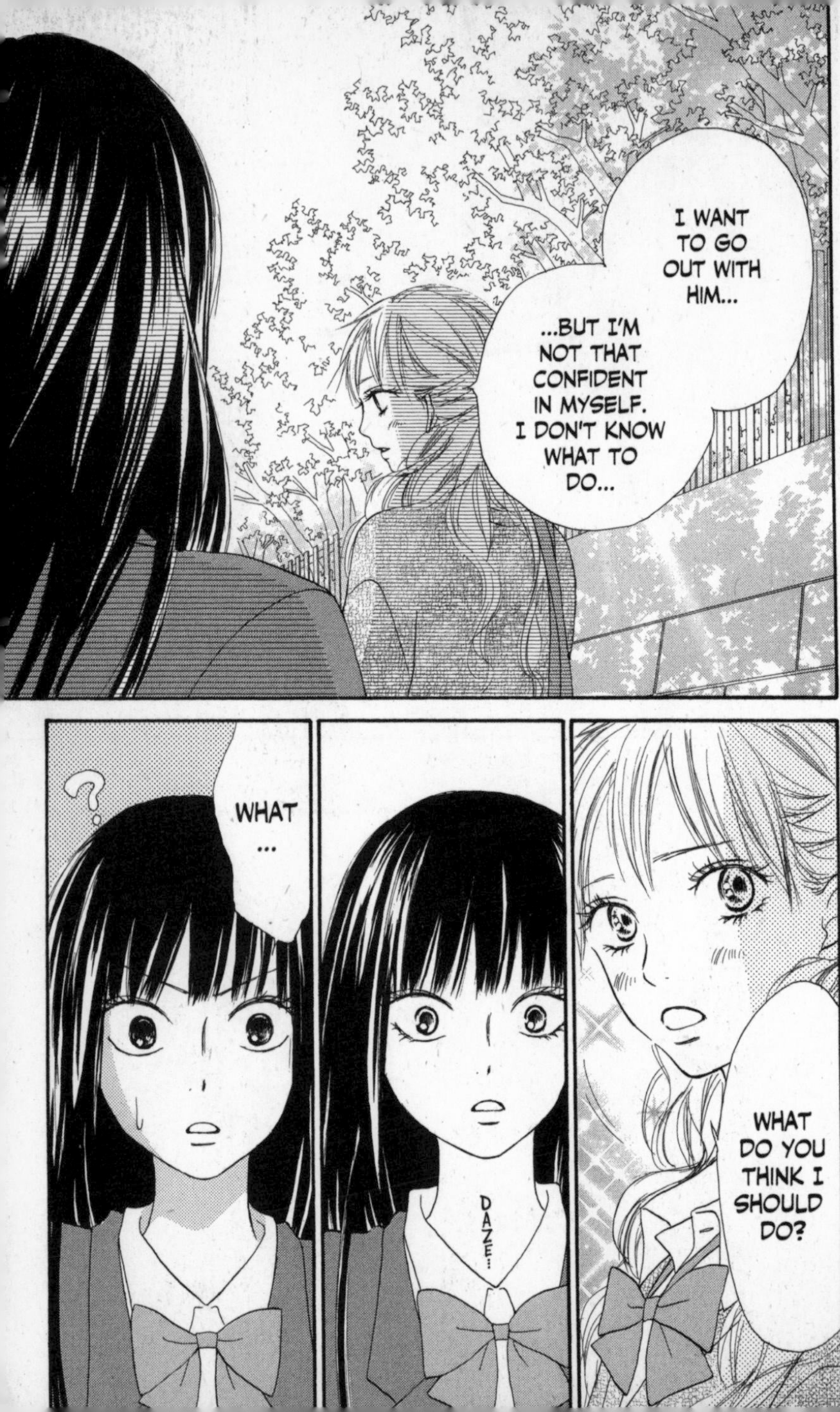
I WANT TO GO OUT WITH HIM...
...BUT I'M NOT THAT CONFIDENT IN MYSELF. I DON'T KNOW WHAT TO DO...
WHAT DO YOU THINK I SHOULD DO?
DAZE...
WHAT ...

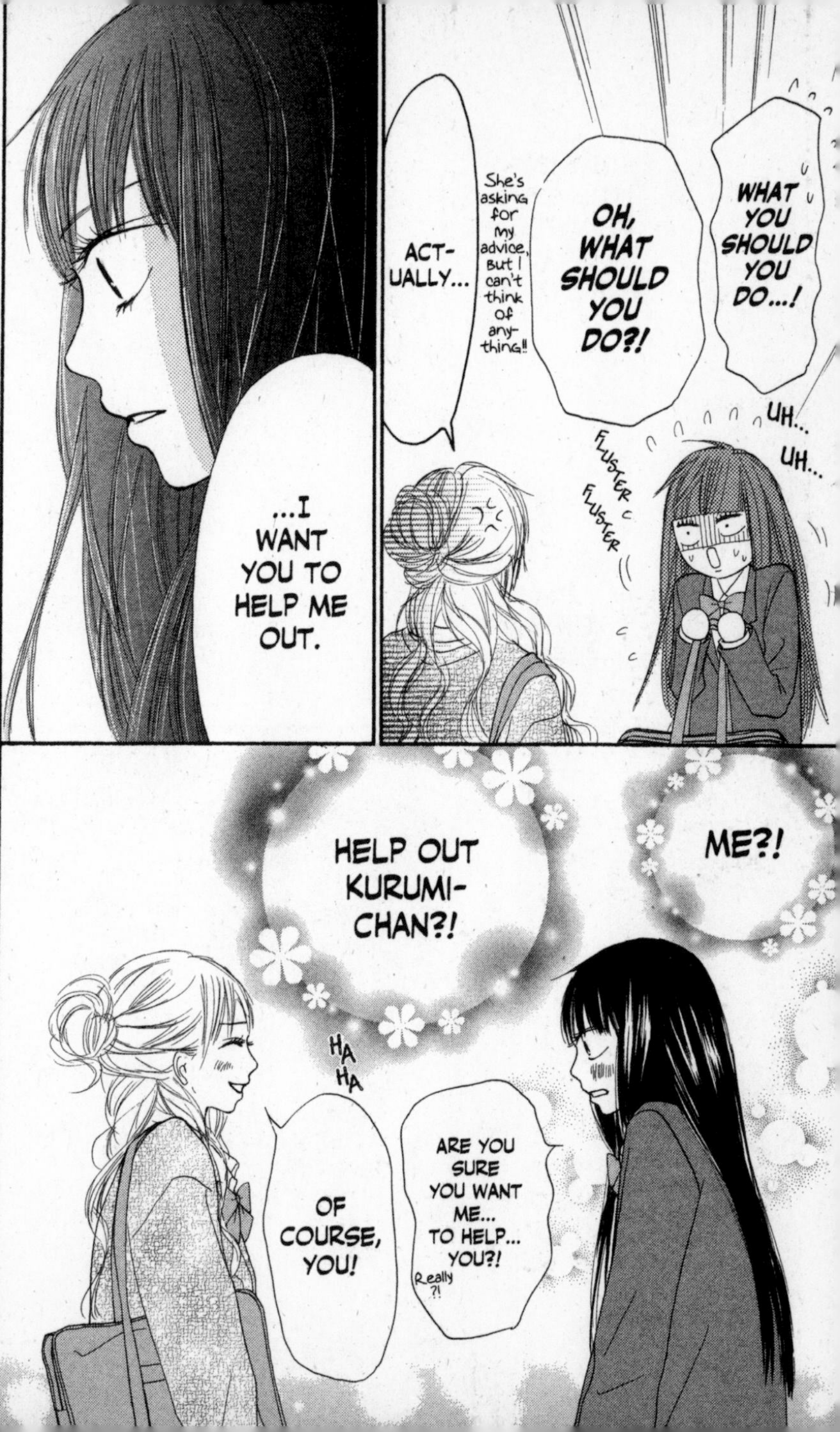
WHAT YOU SHOULD YOU DO...!
OH, WHAT SHOULD YOU DO?!
She's asking for my advice, but I can't think of anything!!
ACT-UALLY...
UH... UH...
FLUSTER FLUSTER
...I WANT YOU TO HELP ME OUT.
ME?!
HELP OUT KURUMI-CHAN?!
ARE YOU SURE YOU WANT ME... TO HELP... YOU?!
Really?!
HA HA
OF COURSE, YOU!

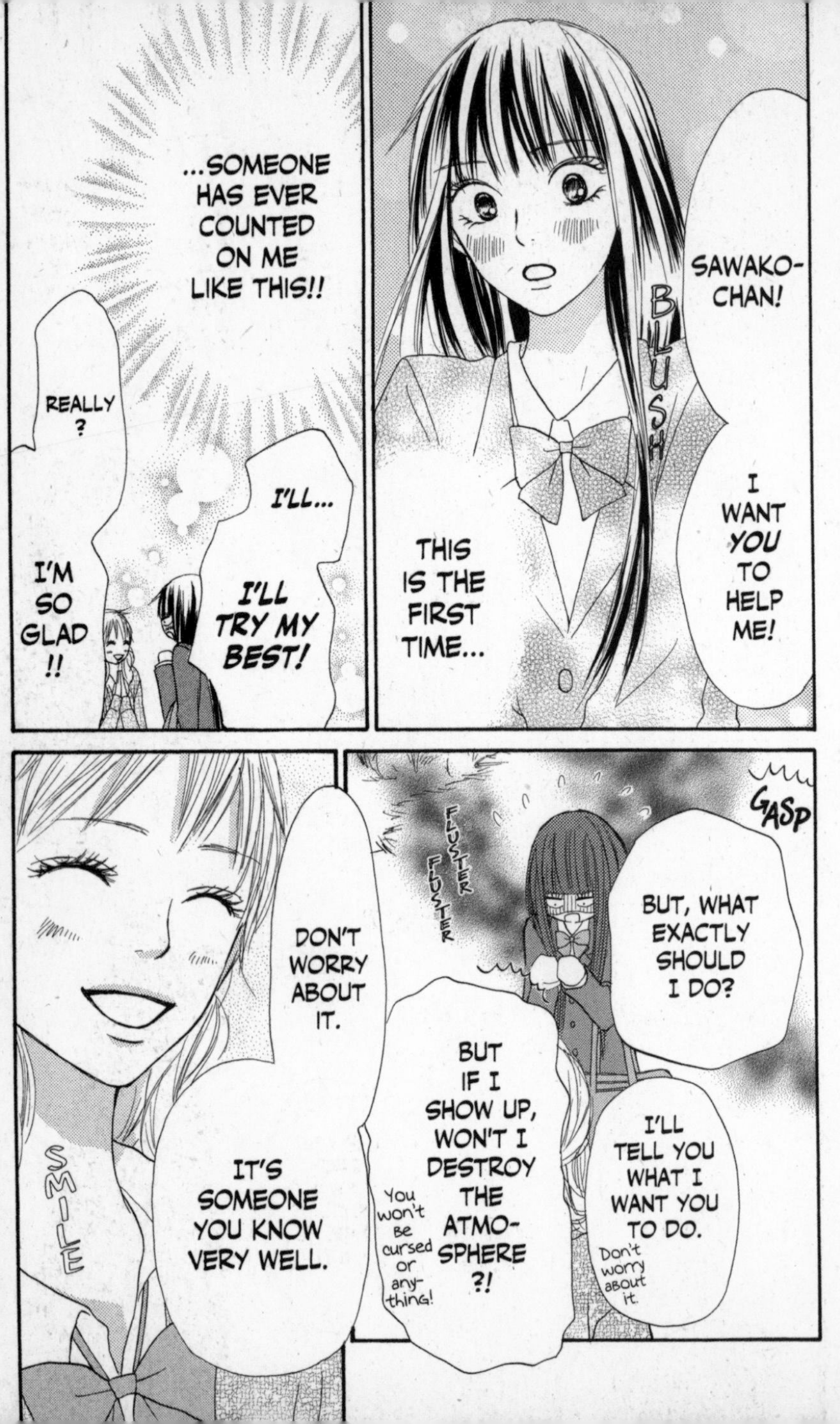
SAWAKO-CHAN!
BLUSH
I WANT *YOU* TO HELP ME!
THIS IS THE FIRST TIME...
...SOMEONE HAS EVER COUNTED ON ME LIKE THIS!!
I'LL...
I'LL TRY MY BEST!
REALLY?
I'M SO GLAD!!
GASP
BUT, WHAT EXACTLY SHOULD I DO?
FLUSTER FLUSTER
I'LL TELL YOU WHAT I WANT YOU TO DO.
Don't worry about it.
BUT IF I SHOW UP, WON'T I DESTROY THE ATMOSPHERE?!
You won't be cursed or anything!
DON'T WORRY ABOUT IT.
IT'S SOMEONE YOU KNOW VERY WELL.
SMILE

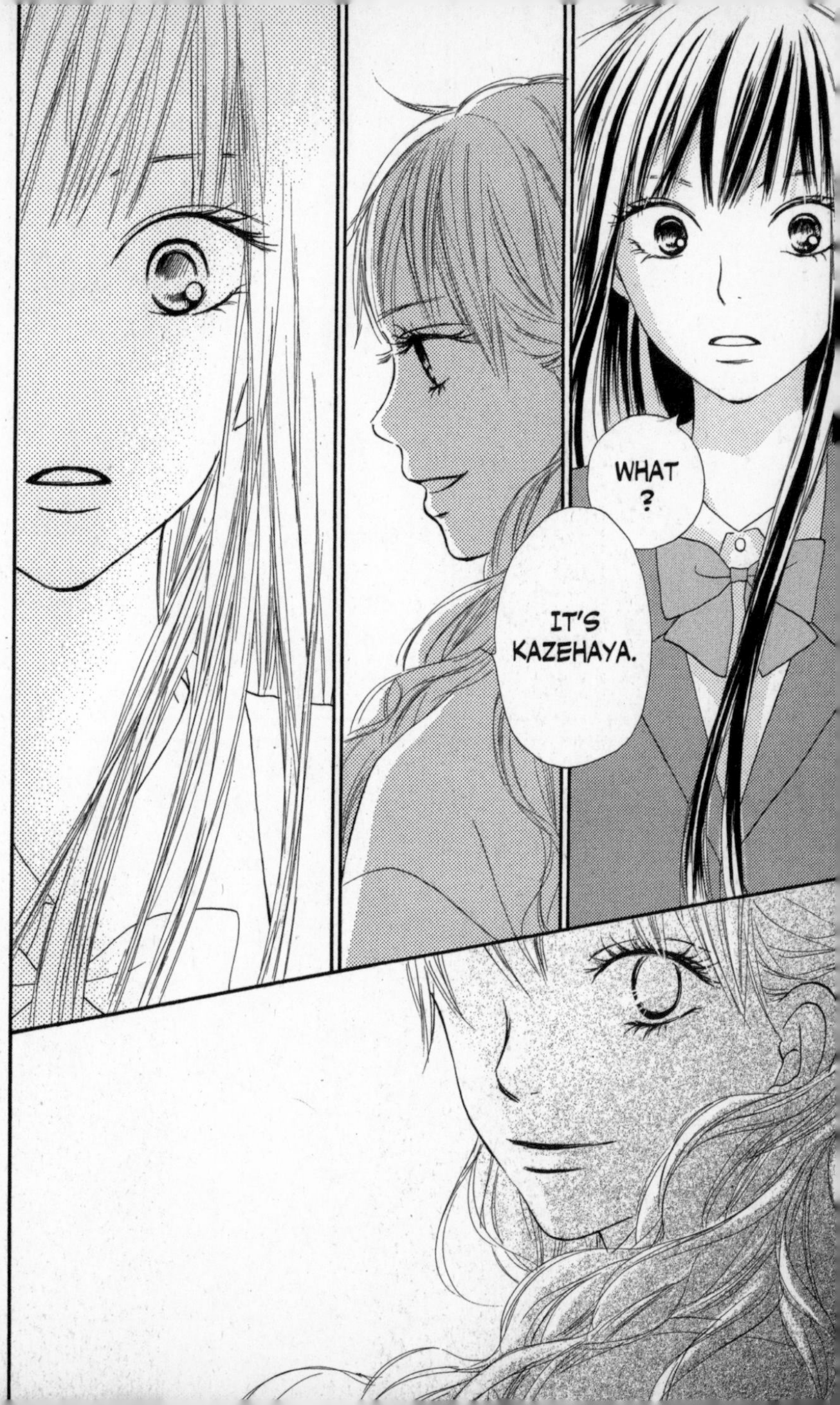
WHAT?
IT'S KAZEHAYA.

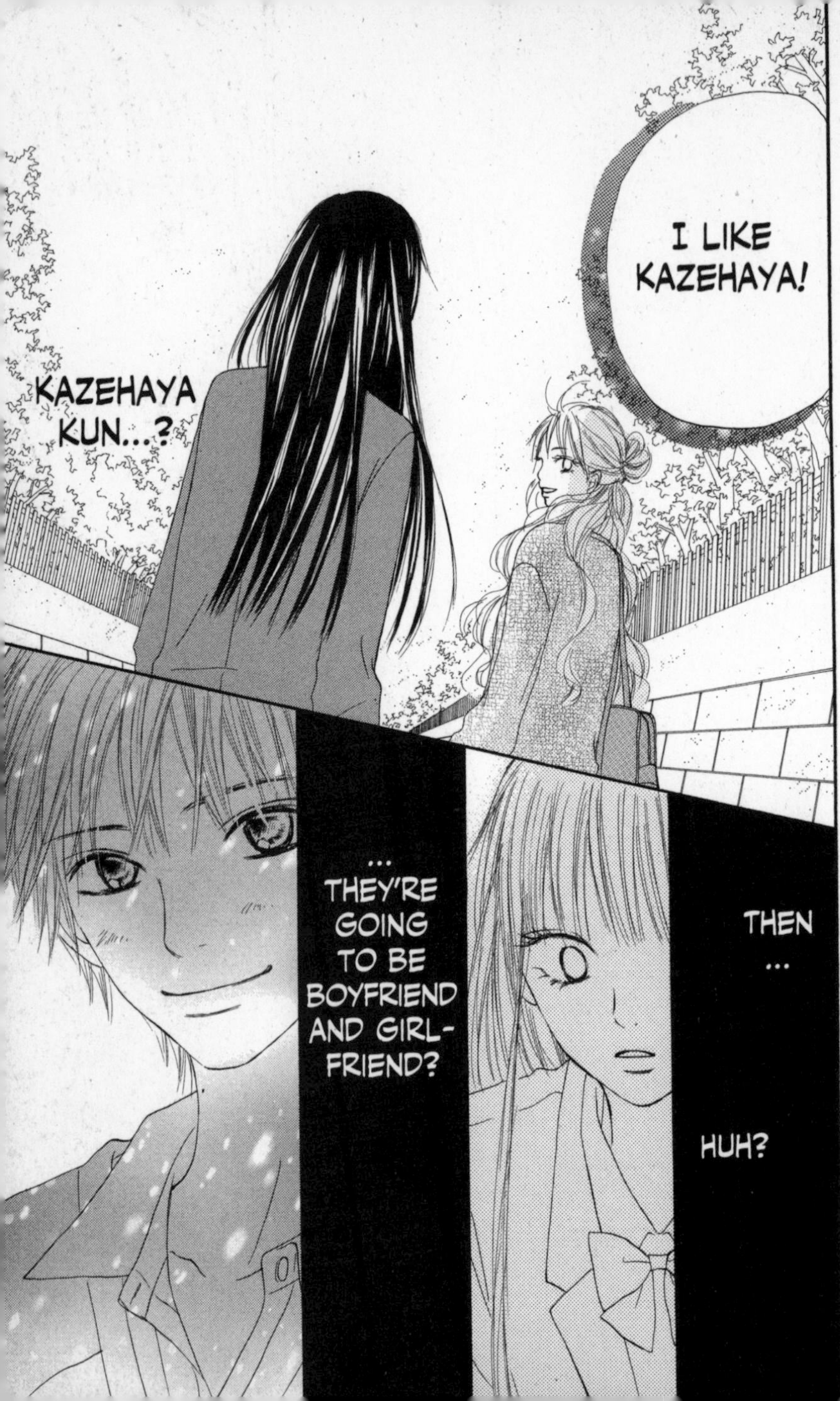
I LIKE KAZEHAYA!
KAZEHAYA KUN...?
THEN ...
HUH?
... THEY'RE GOING TO BE BOYFRIEND AND GIRL-FRIEND?

KAZEHAYA-KUN...
...WILL HAVE A GIRL-FRIEND?
AND I'M...
...GOING TO HELP MAKE THAT HAPPEN?

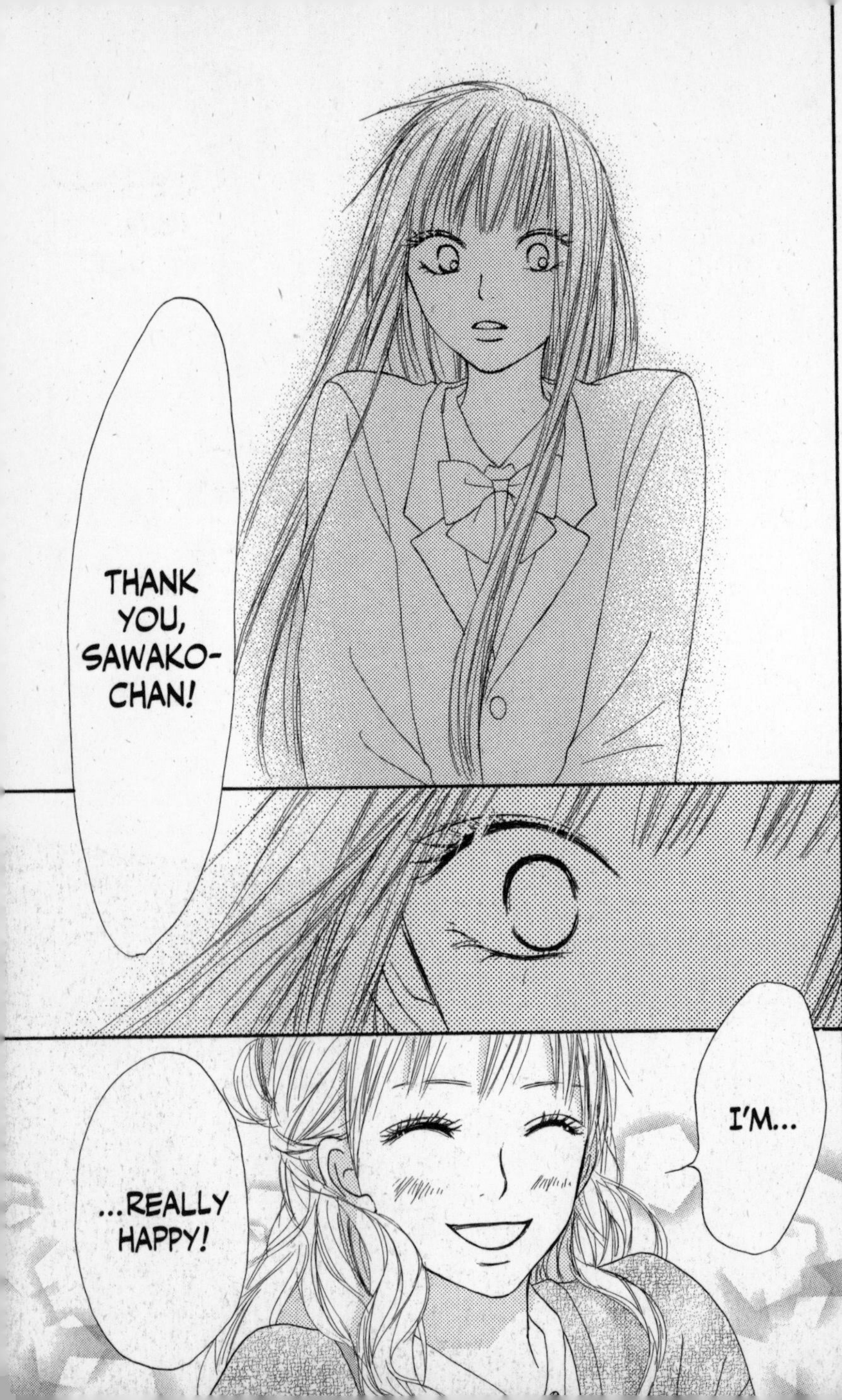
THANK YOU, SAWAKO-CHAN!
I'M...
...REALLY HAPPY!

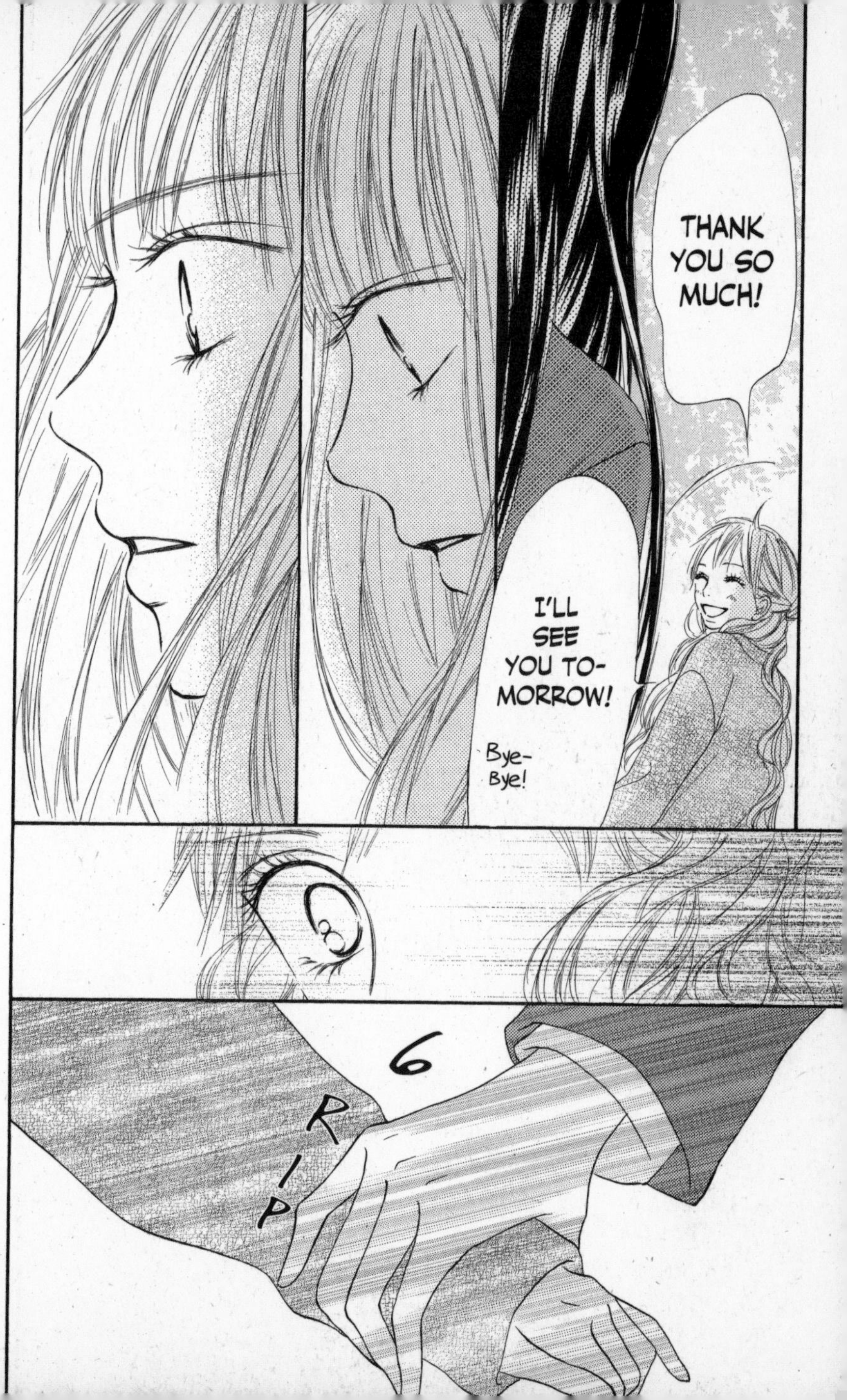
THANK YOU SO MUCH!
I'LL SEE YOU TO-MORROW!
Bye-Bye!
RIP

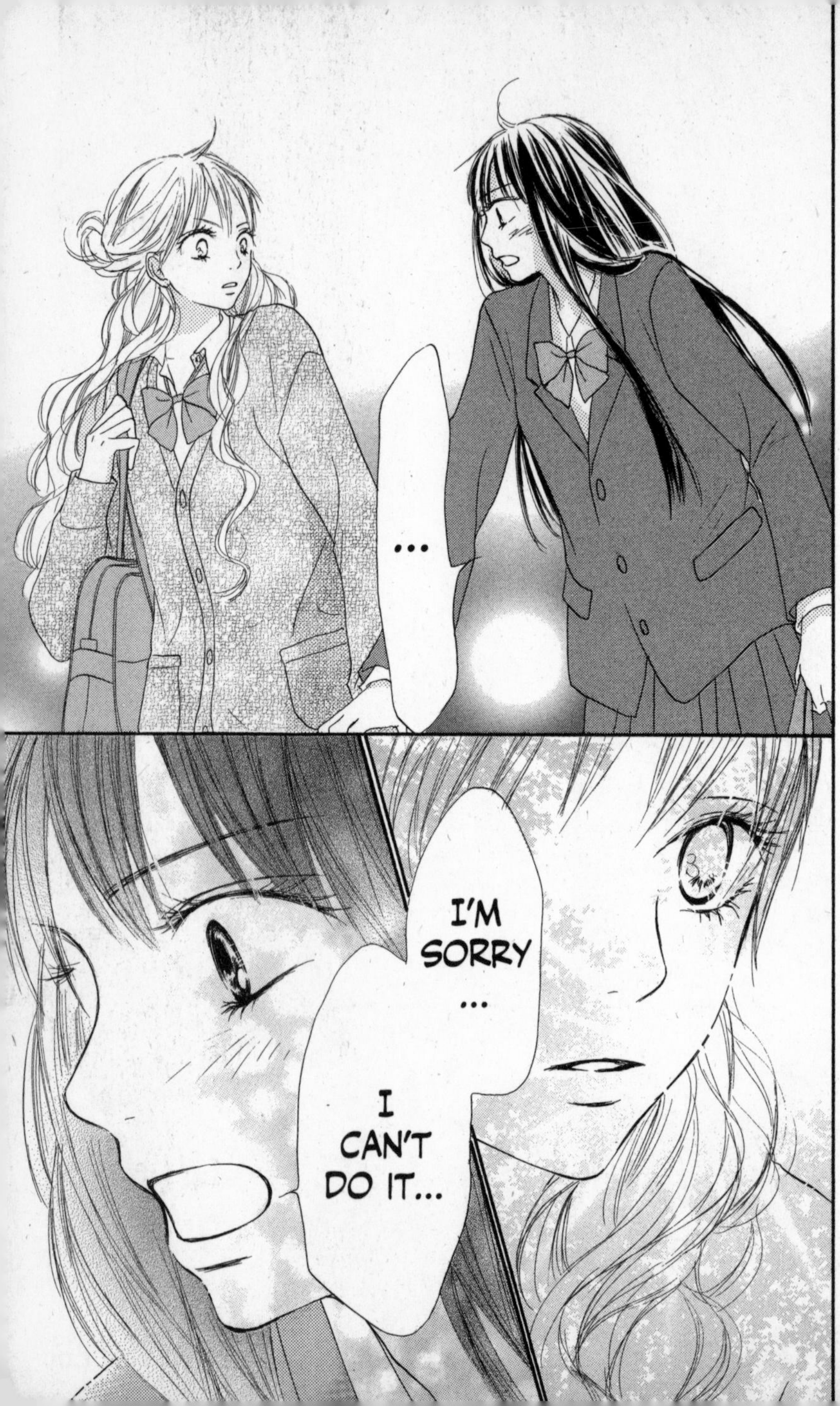
...
I'M SORRY ...
I CAN'T DO IT...

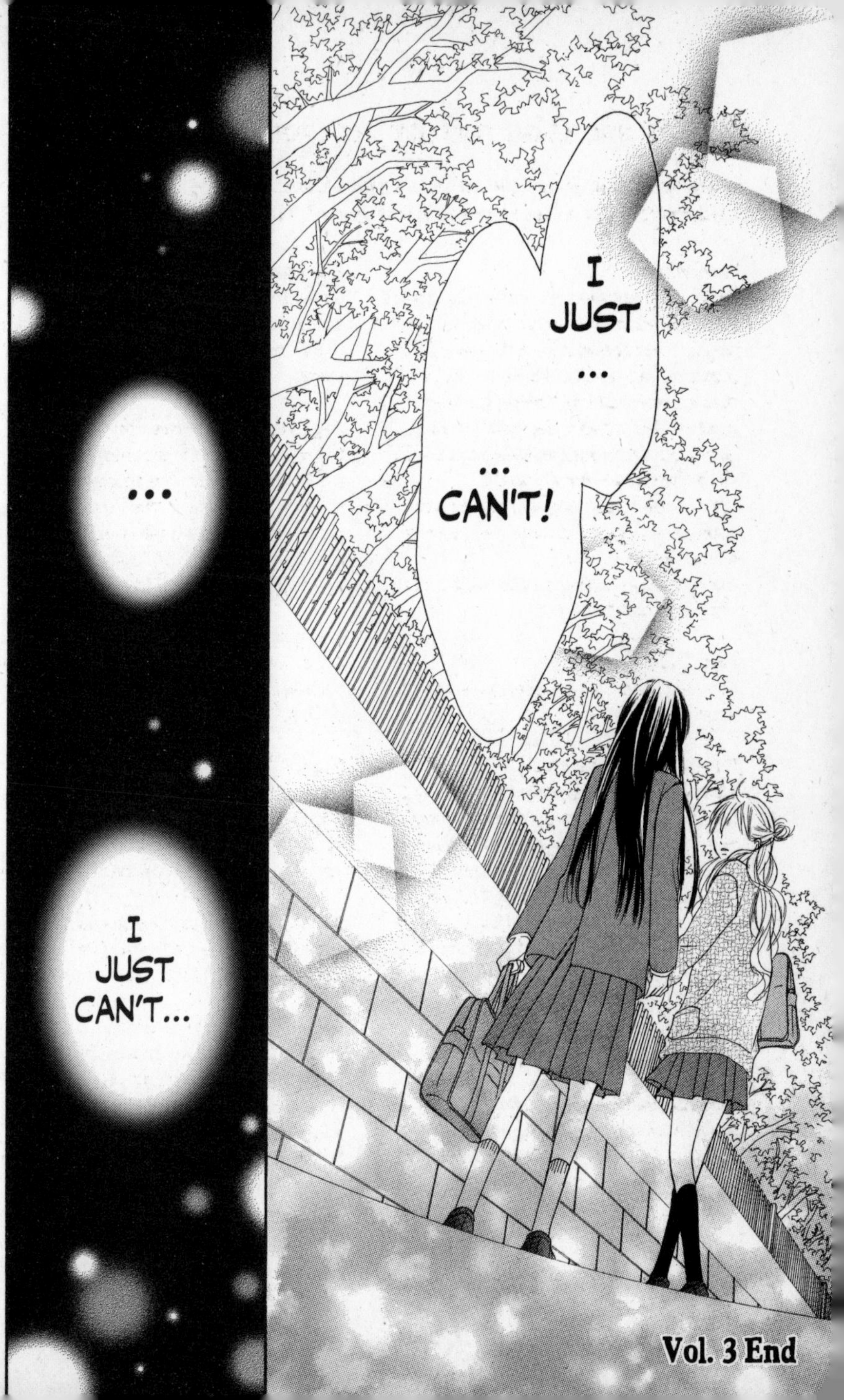
I JUST ... ... CAN'T!
...
I JUST CAN'T...
Vol. 3 End

From me (the editor) to you (the reader).

Here are some Japanese culture explanations that will help you better understand the references in the *Kimi ni Todoke* world.

Honorifics:
When saying someone's name in Japanese, a suffix is often attached to indicate how familiar the speaker is with the person. Some are more polite and respectful, while others are endearing. Calling someone by just their first name is the most informal.
-kun is used for young men or boys, usually someone you are familiar with.
-chan is used for young women, girls or young children and can be used as a term of endearment.
-san is used for someone you respect or are not close to, or to be polite.

Page 21, buzz cuts:
Members of school baseball teams often sport buzz cuts.

Page 22, Sports Festivals:
Sports Festivals are usually held in the fall. Specific events vary according to schools, but classes compete against each other in track races or team events. Students will practice for the events during their regular P.E. classes leading up to the big day.

There are also other school festivals where each class participates by putting on an event—a play or other stage performance, creating an art display, turning their class into a café, etc.

Page 27, fast-growing hair:
In Japan there's a saying that those with naughty thoughts have fast-growing hair.

Page 34, sleep paralysis:
Called *kanashibari* in Japanese, when one wakes up in the middle of the night and is unable to move, some think that a spirit is literally binding the person.

Page 78, New Year's money:
Called *otoshidama* in Japanese, children receive money from their parents and other relatives every year on New Year's Day. The money is put into a small envelope, and the amount can vary according to the child's age and their relationship to the giver.

Page 103, a living doll:
A spooky tale of a girl's soul that enters her favorite doll when she dies. It's said that the doll's hair keeps growing.

Page 119, cleaning duties:
Students in Japan are assigned cleaning duties at school. While some sweep the floors or throw out the trash, others may actually have to clean the bathrooms!

Page 148, the American stereotype:
Americans are stereotypically thought of as more outgoing than the Japanese.

Page 182, unlucky year:
There is a superstition in Japan that slates three years as unlucky in a person's lifetime. For women, it is the year they become 19, 33 or 37 years old. For men, it's when they become 25, 42 or 61. Many people become very cautious around that time since the bad luck can spill into the year before and after too.

This is the third volume. There are four episodes in every volume, so that means that it's been a year since I started writing this series! Wow! That went by quick! I mean, slow. Wait, did it go by quick or slow...? Uh, maybe slow?

Ha ha ha! Either way, it's a good thing! Also, I'm glad that this volume is being released in January*! It's supposed to be an unlucky year for me, but it's okay! It's all good!!

--Karuho Shiina

*This volume was originally published in Japan in January 2007.

Karuho Shiina was born and raised in Hokkaido, Japan. Though *Kimi ni Todoke* is only her second series following many one-shot stories, it has already racked up accolades from various "Best Manga of the Year" lists. Winner of the 2008 Kodansha Manga Award for the shojo category, *Kimi ni Todoke* also placed fifth in the first-ever Manga Taisho (Cartoon Grand Prize) contest in 2008. An animated TV series debuted in October 2009 in Japan.

Kimi ni Todoke
VOL. 3

Shojo Beat Manga Edition

STORY AND ART BY
KARUHO SHIINA

Translation/Koichiro Kensho Nishimura, HC Language Solutions, Inc.
Touch-up Art & Lettering/Vanessa Satone & Annaliese Christman
Design/Yukiko Whitley
Editor/Yuki Murashige

VP, Production/Alvin Lu
VP, Sales & Product Marketing/Gonzalo Ferreyra
VP, Creative/Linda Espinosa
Publisher/Hyoe Narita

KIMI NI TODOKE © 2005 by Karuho Shiina
All rights reserved. First published in Japan in 2005 by SHUEISHA Inc.,
Tokyo. English translation rights arranged by SHUEISHA Inc.

Printed in the U.S.A.

Published by VIZ Media, LLC
P.O. Box 77010
San Francisco, CA 94107

10 9 8 7 6 5 4 3 2 1
First printing, February 2010

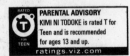
www.viz.com

www.shojobeat.com

Tell us what you think about Shojo Beat Manga!

Our survey is now available online. Go to:

shojobeat.com/mangasurvey

Help us make our product offerings better!

THE REAL DRAMA BEGINS IN...

JAN 2010